Complaints to the Authorities in Russia

This book considers the process of legal modernization in Russia from the development of the mechanism of complaints addressed to the authorities from the pre-revolutionary period to today. It analyzes wide-ranging data and sources, collected over 17 years, such as legislation, in-depth interviews, archival materials, original texts, and examples of different methods of complaints in Soviet and contemporary Russia.

Being marginal to the legal system and almost invisible for researchers of legal development, the complaint mechanism has functioned as an extremely important way of restoring justice, available to the majority of people in Russia for centuries. It has survived several historical gaps and, in a sense, acts as a thread that stitches together different eras, coexisting with the establishment and modernization of legal institutions, compensating, accompanying, and sometimes substituting for them. The research covers a period of over 100 years, and shows how and why at major historical crossroads, Russia chooses between full-fledged legal modernization and saving the authoritarian social contract between the state and society.

This book will be especially useful to scholars researching Soviet society and Post-Soviet transformations, socio-legal studies, and liberal legal reforms, but will also appeal to those working in the broader fields of Russian politics, the history of Soviet society and justice issues more generally.

Elena Bogdanova is a Research Fellow at the Centre for Independent Social Research, and Associate Professor at the European University at Saint Petersburg, and at the Russian Presidential Academy of National Economy and Public Administration.

Studies in Contemporary Russia

Series Editor: Markku Kivinen

Studies in Contemporary Russia is a series of cutting-edge, contemporary studies. These monographs, joint publications and edited volumes branch out into various disciplines, innovatively combining research methods and theories to approach the core questions of Russian modernisation; how do the dynamics of resources and rules affect the Russian economy and what are the prospects and needs of diversification? What is the impact of the changing state-society relationship? How does the emerging welfare regime work? What is the role of Russia in contemporary international relations? How should we understand the present Russian political system? What is the philosophical background of modernisation as a whole and its Russian version in particular?

The variety of opinions on these issues is vast. Some see increasingly less difference between contemporary Russia and the Soviet Union while, at the other extreme, prominent experts regard Russia as a 'more or less' normal European state. At the same time new variants of modernisation are espoused as a result of Russian membership of the global BRIC powers. Combining aspects of Western and Soviet modernisation with some anti-modern or traditional tendencies the Russian case is ideal for probing deeper into the evolving nature of modernisation. Which of the available courses Russia will follow remains an open question, but these trajectories provide the alternatives available for discussion in this ground-breaking and authoritative series.

The editor and the editorial board of the series represent the Finnish Centre of Excellence in Russian Studies: Choices of Russian Modernisation.

Social Distinctions in Contemporary Russia
Waiting for the Middle-Class Society?
Edited by Jouko Nikula and Mikhail Chernysh

Russia as Civilization
Ideological Discourses in Politics, Media, and Academia
Edited by Kåre Johan Mjør and Sanna Turoma

Russian Modernisation
A New Paradigm
Edited by Markku Kivinen and Brendan Humphreys

Complaints to the Authorities in Russia
A Trap Between Tradition and Legal Modernization
Elena Bogdanova

For more information about this series, please visit: www.routledge.com/series/ASHSER-1421

Complaints to the Authorities in Russia

A Trap Between Tradition and Legal Modernization

Elena Bogdanova

Routledge
Taylor & Francis Group
LONDON AND NEW YORK

First published 2021
by Routledge
2 Park Square, Milton Park, Abingdon, Oxon OX14 4RN

and by Routledge
605 Third Avenue, New York, NY 10158

Routledge is an imprint of the Taylor & Francis Group, an informa business

British Library Cataloguing-in-Publication Data
A catalogue record for this book is available from the British Library

Library of Congress Cataloging-in-Publication Data
Names: Bogdanova, Elena, 1978- author.
Title: Complaints to the authorities in Russia: a trap between tradition and legal modernization/Elena Bogdanova.
Description: Milton Park, Abingdon, Oxon; New York, NY: Routledge, 2021. | Series: Studies in contemporary Russia | Includes bibliographical references and index.
Identifiers: LCCN 2020055897 (print) | LCCN 2020055898 (ebook) | ISBN 9781138308725 (hardback) | ISBN 9781315143088 (ebook)
Subjects: LCSH: Petition, Right of–Soviet Union. | Petition, Right of–Russia (Federation)
Classification: LCC KLA2485 .B64 2021 (print) | LCC KLA2485 (ebook) | DDC 342.4708/54–dc23
LC record available at https://lccn.loc.gov/2020055897
LC ebook record available at https://lccn.loc.gov/2020055898

ISBN: 978-1-138-30872-5 (hbk)
ISBN: 978-1-032-00307-8 (pbk)
ISBN: 978-1-315-14308-8 (ebk)

Typeset in Times New Roman
by Deanta Global Publishing Services, Chennai, India

Contents

Illustrations

Acknowledgments

I owe this book to the help and support of many individuals, communities, and institutions.

This project started as a *kandidatskaia* dissertation in the Department of Political Science and Sociology at the European University at Saint Petersburg—in many ways a unique department for post-Soviet Russia. The study was devoted to the late-Soviet bureaucracy of complaints with a particular focus on the sphere of consumption. Once I got close to defending my *kandidatskaia* dissertation, I came to realize that there was a lot more I could do with the topic if only I could get more training. Moreover, in 2006, exactly when I defended my *kandidatskaia*, Law No. 59 "On the Order of Consideration of Citizens' Applications in the Russian Federation" was adopted, which launched a post-Soviet version of the complaint mechanism. At that point I made the decision to continue collecting data and to conduct more research on the topic. In the beginning of the 2010s I was lucky to meet Professor Soili Nystén-Haarala, who suggested to me to enter the doctoral program at the University of Eastern Finland, and to continue the work on the topic.

The period of my studies in the Department of Social Science and Business Studies was extremely fruitful and valuable for me. Seven years of my work on this book were full of new and exciting experiences. I collected a rich corpus of empirical data. Thanks to the support of the department I was able to present preliminary results of my research at major international conferences like a congress of the Law and Society Association or a convention of the Association for Slavic, East European, and Eurasian Studies.

I would hardly be able to complete this book without the support of my teachers, colleagues, and friends. I would like to thank my supervisors, professors Soili Nystén-Haarala and Anssi Keinänen. At different stages of my work I discussed parts of my book with Professor of the UCL Alena Ledeneva, Professor Emeritus at the University of Toronto Peter Solomon Jr., Professor at the School for Advanced Studies in the Social Sciences in Paris Laurent Thévenot, independent researcher Elizabeth Teague, Professor at Aarhus University Jeremy Morris, Professor at the University of South Florida Golfo Alexopoulos, professors at Princeton University Serguei Oushakine and Ekaterina Pravilova, Professor at the University of New Hampshire Cathy Frierson, Director of the

Centre for Socio-Legal Studies at Oxford Marina Kurkchiyan, Lecturer at the University of Helsinki and Aleksanteri Institute Anna-Liisa Heusala, Professor at the University of Helsinki Marianna Muravyeva, Professor at the Saint Petersburg State University Olga Makarova, Professor at King's College London Gulnaz Sharafutdinova, and Professor Emeritus at the University of Helsinki Risto Alapuro. Thanks to the interest and expert comments from all these scholars my ideas developed and gained shape.

During my work on this book I tried to use any opportunity to share my findings with the professional community. Group discussions during the international seminar "Complaints: Cultures of Grievance in Eastern Europe and Eurasia," organized by Serguei Oushakine at Princeton University, as well as my open lectures at King's College London, Washington University in St. Louis, and the Elliott School of International Affairs at the George Washington University tremendously helped me make my analytical work focused and ordered. The discussion of my paper at the international workshop "Law-Making and Law-Interpreting: Russia, 17th to 21st Centuries," held at the Wissenschaftszentrum Berlin für Sozialforschung/Wissenschaftskolleg zu Berlin, gave a major impetus to publish my doctoral thesis as the monograph. I would like to extend special thanks to Professor Emeritus at New York University Jane Burbank, Professor at the Higher School of Economics in Saint Petersburg Tatiana Borisova, and Professor at Princeton University Ekaterina Pravilova. Many thanks also to the Fulbright Program in Russia and the British Council Researcher Links program for financial support of my scholarships in the Elliott School of International Affairs at the George Washington University, and the Centre for Socio-Legal Studies at Oxford.

Critical comments on the final version of the book from Professor Emeritus at the University of Helsinki and former director of the Aleksanteri Institute Markku Kivinen, Professor Emeritus at Toronto University Peter Solomon Jr., and Professor Emeritus at the University of Vaasa Juha Tolonen allowed me to conclude my work and to gain confidence in its findings.

I am grateful to the supervisors of my first thesis—*kandidatskaia* dissertation—professors at the European University at Saint Petersburg Alexander Etkind and Boris Firsov for believing in me. I also want to thank my friends and colleagues from the Centre for Independent Social Research, European University at Saint Petersburg, and the Russian Presidential Academy of National Economy and Public Administration, and **especially my family** for their support and patience during more than seven years of my deep immersion in the work on this book.

Saint Petersburg, November 25, 2020
Elena Bogdanova

Abbreviations

BCS	Book of complaints and suggestions
GARF	*Gosudarstvennyi arkhiv Rossiiskoi Federatsii*—The State Archive of the Russian Federation
Goskontrol'	*Komitet gosudarstvennogo kontrolia*—The Committee of State Control
Ispolkom (raispolkom, gorispolkom, oblispolkom)	Executive committee (district executive committee, city executive committee, regional executive committee)
KPGK	*Komitet partiino-gosudastvennogo kontrolia*—Committee of Party-State Control
KPK	*Komissiia partiinogo kontrolia*—Commission of Party Control
KSK	*Komissiia sovetskogo kontrolia*—Commission of Soviet Control
LDPR	*Liberal'no-demokraticheskaia partiia Rossii*—Liberal Democratic Party of Russia
LOGAV	*Leningradskii oblastnoi gosudarstvennyi arkhiv v Vyborge*—Leningrad Regional State Archive in Vyborg
Narkompros	*Narodnyi komissariat prosveshcheniia*—People's Commissariat of Education
NK	*Narodnyi Komissariat (Narkomat)*—People's Commissariat
NKGK	*Narodnyi komissariat gosudarstvennogo kontrolia*—People's Commissariat of State Control
NK RKI (Rabkrin)	*Narodnyi komissariat Raboche-krest'ianskoi inspektsii*—People's Commissariat of Working-Peasant Inspection
NKVD	*Narodnyi komissariat vnutrennikh del*—People's Commissariat of Internal Affairs
Raikom, gorkom, obkom	District Party Committee, City Party Committee, Regional Party Committee

RGAE	*Rossiiskii gosudarstvennyi arkhiv ekonomiki*—the Russian State Archive of the Economy
RIK	*Raionnyi ispolnitel'nyi komitet*—District Executive Committee
RKP(b)	*Rossiiskaia kommunisticheskaia partiia (bol'shevikov)*—Russian Communist Party (of Bolsheviks)
Roszdravnadzor	Federal Service for Supervision in Healthcare
Rosprirodnadzor	Federal Service for Supervision of Natural Resource Usage
Rospotrebnadzor	Federal Service for Supervision of Consumption
RSFSR	*Rossiiskaia Sovetskaia Federativnaia Sotsialisticheskaia Respublika*—Russian Soviet Federative Socialist Republic
SM SSSR	*Sovet Ministrov SSSR*—Council of Ministers of the USSR
SNK RSFSR	*Sovet Narodnykh Komissarov RSFSR*—Council of People's Commissars of the RSFSR
TsGA SPb	*Tsentral'nyi gosudarstvennyi arkhiv Sankt-Peterburga*—Central State Archive of Saint Petersburg
TsIk	*Tsentral'nyi ispolnitel'nyi komitet*—Central Executive Committee
TsK KPSS	*Tsentral'nyi komitet Kommunisticheskoi partii Sovetskogo Soiuza*—Central Committee of Communist Party of Soviet Union (CC CPSU)
TsKK VKP (b)	*Tsentral'naia kontrol'naia komissiia Vserossiiskoi Kommunisticheskoi Partii (bol'shevikov)*—Central Control Commission of All-Russian Communist Party (of Bolsheviks)
VTsIK	*Vserossiiskii tsentral'nyi ispolnitel'nyi komitet*—All-Russian Central Executive Committee
Zhilkomservis	*Zhilishchno-kommunal'nyi servis*—Housing and Public Utility Service of local level, subordinated to a district administration

1 Introduction

At the beginning of 2016, news about Vladimir Ponomariov went viral in Russia. A resident of Saratov, Vladimir walked over 850 kilometers from his native city to Moscow—all in order to deliver a complaint letter to the president of the Russian Federation. According to Vladimir, the letter contained "a description of injustice concerning all progressive people in Russia: medicine, social care, housing and communal services."[1] Vladimir is a Russian amateur athlete, known for his loyalty to Putin's regime and long-distance walking. Vladimir did not expect a personal audience with the president. The goal of his journey was just to deliver the letter to Vladimir Putin. Ponomariov made it to Moscow, but the president refused a private meeting.

By performing this action, Vladimir Ponomariov was making use of a method of request for justice deeply rooted in the history of Russian society. Complaints were as common an attribute of relations between the Soviet people and authorities as *chelobitnaias* were in the period of the Grand Principality of Moscow and as solicitations (*prosheniia*) were to the Emperor in the Russian Empire. At the dawn of the Soviet era, "the walkers" (*hodoki*ˆ traversed thousands of kilometers to deliver their complaints to the Bolshevik government and to Vladimir Lenin personally.

The goal of the post-socialist modernizing legal reforms in Russia, which were initiated at the beginning of the 1990s, was to develop a legal system based on the rule of law, to develop legal institutions, and to implant law as a measure of justice in society. Multiple reform efforts were made to move towards independence of the judiciary, to establish a horizontal adversarial model of justice, and to consolidate the role of the courts as the sole agent of justice. In the present day, after decades of post-socialist legal reforms, and after being almost completely destroyed, direct complaints to the authorities have once again become a popular means for seeking justice.

The new life of the complaint mechanism coincided with particular changes in the political life of Russia. A consistent strengthening of vertical power, which intensified after Vladimir Putin's arrival on the political scene, has made the domination of the executive (presidential) power and the formation of a dominant party regime into the main institutional arrangements of Russia's authoritarian model in the 2000s. Among other measures, in 2006 the Duma adopted Law

No. 59 "On the Order of Consideration of Citizens' Applications in the Russian Federation." The Law established direct complaints to the authorities as an official way of solving problems, an alternative to the judiciary. Between 2006 and 2010 the bureaucracy receiving and processing complaints was reconstructed at all levels of the executive branch.

The mechanism of direct complaint is not unique to Russian society. The first complainant was Adam who, after he and Eve disobeyed, complained to God that "the woman you put here with me—she gave me some fruit from the tree, and I ate it" (Genesis 3:12). The practice of complaint appears to be found in all regimes, both democratic and authoritarian (Henry 2012:243). Some form of interaction between society and the authorities is necessary to maintain the stability of any socio-political system. Inequality and asymmetric access to resources of power generates the need to seek help from someone of higher authority (shaman, pastor, feudal lord, prince, monarch, congressman). The universal functions of the complaint mechanisms are multiple:

1. It delivers actual information about the functioning of the system from below. This type of information may be used by different levels of authorities with different aims. Local governmental bodies may correct their measures and programs taking into account feedback from citizens. Higher levels of governance may use citizens' applications to evaluate the probability of protest and dissent. In non-democratic systems with severe restrictions on the freedom of the press, central leaders themselves often lack information about local developments (Minzner 2006:117).
2. In comparison with all the other forms of interaction between citizens and society (non-governmental organizations, public protest, public petitions), the mechanism of complaints is the most predictable and convenient channel for state-society interactions for the authorities. The mechanism of complaints itself is accessible for control from the side of the state, because it is established by the state.
3. Whatever system it exists within, the complaint mechanism may be used to justify unpopular political decisions. Even in truly democratized systems, which make special efforts to turn the mechanism into a special tool providing transparency and accountability of governance, they are never entirely transparent. Information about the number of complaints and types of applications may be manipulated by the state. We never know the entire story of a complaint, shown as independent and sincere.
4. Complaint is a universal tool which can compensate for the most vulnerable features of regimes. Channels of direct communication with the authorities bring elements of flexibility and softness to democratic systems, which are often criticized for excessive legalism and formalism. Similarly, the usually low responsiveness of authoritarian systems can be compensated for by complaint mechanisms (Dimitrov et al. 2007). Therefore, "citizen complaints functioned as a fundamental mechanism of vertical accountability in communist regimes" (Dimitrov 2013:277).

5. Complaint mechanisms relieve social tension. In any type of society, complaint works as a safety valve (Almbjär 2019:1013). Complaint mechanisms help to address violations of citizens' rights, and at a minimum provide hope of protection. This function is important anywhere, and especially valuable if all other channels are unavailable.
6. Being addressed to the authorities, complaints reproduce trust and faith in their potency, supporting the legitimacy of power in general.

The existence of a complaint mechanism does not say anything in and of itself about a society (Henry 2012:243). While similar in form, applications to the authorities can perform dramatically different functions in different socio-political contexts, and their role in legal modernization may also be diverse. Socio-political conditions, legal and democratic traditions, models of citizens-to-authority communication—all these things are formed over the course of history. The degree and frequency of use of the complaint mechanism, as well as the issues to which it is applied and how formality and informality are delimited, may play a crucial role for the rule of law, and also for the reputation of the political regime.

The peculiar thing about the complaint mechanism today is that, for the first time in Russia's history, it coexists with legal institutions that have undergone a major modernization towards the Western model. For the first time in history, the complaint mechanism exists under conditions of the proclaimed separation of powers and the rule of law. Outwardly, the contemporary Russian legal system and the complaint mechanism exist as simultaneous but seemingly contradictory trends, which should generate a serious conflict affecting the process of legal modernization.

In this book I answer the following questions: is development of the Russian complaint mechanism consistent with legal modernization—if the mechanism itself is being modernized—or does it interfere with legal modernization in contemporary Russia?

Pre-modern features of the complaint mechanism

The mechanism of complaints is habitually discussed in relation to modernization. Formerly, complaints were considered a pre-modern channel of interaction with the authorities. Indeed, this was the first form of reporting to the authorities about discontent, the first available channel for petitioning for justice. This pre-modern form of complaint has several prominent features. *First*, it combines two functions, one of which concerns the optimization of governance, and the second with the restoration of justice. Legal modernization is usually associated with the separation of these two functions. This is a process that has occurred in different times and in different ways for different societies.

Democratic Western modernization is associated with efforts to overcome this double function of complaint mechanisms and any other contradictions that might violate principles of democratic governance and separation of powers. In the USA, the separation of administrative and judicial functions is associated with the

First Amendment to the Constitution. The question of how to share responsibility for consideration of various types of appeals between executive, legislative, and judicial authorities provoked changes in the First Amendment several times between 1789 and 1791 (Spanbauer 1993:17–18, 40).

Pre-modern complaint mechanisms are usually understood, in Russia specifically, as underdeveloped "tool[s] deeply rooted in imperial and Communist practices" (Minzner 2006:108). They usually combine the functions of governance and justice into one subject of power, who is also the main addressee of applications. In authoritarian regimes like the Soviet Union, China, and Vietnam, the maintenance of complaint mechanisms is usually justified in terms of their ability to ensure political stability by addressing public dissatisfaction and monitoring implementation of policies at lower levels of government (Henry 2012:243–244). The *xinfang* system that exists today in China is a mechanism, originally established to resolve political problems of governance, that has "gradually evolved into a system of assistance serving as a replacement for the judicial system" (Minzner 2006:106). The number of complaints addressed to petitioning bureaus in China is almost double the total number of appeals to the courts (Ibid:105). This familiar and free mechanism performs the function of justice for the poor.

The second pre-modern feature of the mechanism of complaints is its semi-informality, which contrasts especially against the formalized judiciary. Established by the state, the mechanism of complaints usually does have formal frames, although in practice it can accommodate derogations from the formal rules, ignorance of them, or their replacement by informal versions. Drawing on research on socialist type complaint mechanisms in the GDR, Inga Markovits argues that:

> [i]nstead of formal and neutral rules of procedure, we find informal self-review; instead of due process, office hours; instead of the vindication of individual claims, collective involvement; instead of an emphasis on providing administrative decisions with reasons so the citizen can fight back, an emphasis on reasons which will persuade and coopt a citizen into compliance and cooperation; instead of precise legal language, imprecise, human language; instead of confrontation, the illusion of family ties.
>
> (Markovits 1986:742)

The third feature by which one can assess the modernization of the complaint mechanism itself is the social contract that it serves. State-society interactions are at the heart of the complaint mechanism (Minzner 2006:107). In Russia, both during the imperial times and the Soviet period, the social contract ensured the sustainability of society. Evidence suggests that "the social contract plays a central role in the maintenance of single-party communist regimes, regardless of the economic model they adopt" (Cook and Dimitrov 2017:8). Historically the force that supported stability of society was an authoritarian social contract, in which the law played a weak role, if any. From the point of view of legal modernization, it is important to understand if the post-socialist legal changes had a chance to transform the social contract, to change its dominant role in maintaining stability, or to increase the role of law in regulation and restriction of this contract.

Each country has produced its own version of the complaint mechanism. While some take steps to reform or eliminate pre-modern features, others may try to preserve them. In essence, the complaint mechanism reflects processes of legal modernization insofar as legal modernization involves the principle of separation of powers, the value of an independent judiciary, and the principle of the rule of law. The success of the modernization of the complaint mechanism itself can be measured by how well its pre-modern features are overcome and how well it can be coordinated with adherence to general principles of democracy (Henry 2012:243–244).

Legal modernization in Russia: Expanding the concept

How to talk about legal modernization in Russia? Examining processes occurring with law in Russia through the prism of theories of legal modernization leaves no chance for in-depth and meaningful analysis. The reason is simple: theories of legal modernization are ultimately focused on disseminating Western liberal legalism. According to the theories of legal modernization, the state exercises its control over the individual through law, the law defines and determines the behavior of people, the courts have the principal responsibility for defining the effects of legal rules, and the behavior of social actors tends to conform to the legal rules (Burg 1977). David Trubek and Marc Galanter, who were probably the foremost scholars in the field of legal modernization theory, believed that liberal legalism is an instrument of modernization and the measure of the legal modernization is equivalent to its exportation (Trubek and Galanter 1974). From this point of view, the case of Russia is of little interest. The maxims of legal modernization, mentioned above, can hardly be found in their pure form in Russia today, or ever in the past. Most attempts to evaluate the transformation of Russian society from this point of view inevitably come to the conclusion that Soviet and post-Soviet modernization has been a series of fiascos. Historian Richard Pipes (1977) cast the entirety of Russian history as a tradition of "anti-modernism."

Researchers usually identify two main obstacles that distinguish Russia from successfully modernized countries. These are an intermittent development path, which always leads away from a consistent trajectory, and the importance of informal relationships and informality in all areas of society (Rose 1998: 2–3; Rose 2001). Meanwhile, exclusion of Russia from the debate on legal modernization is a mistake. Since at least the second half of the eighteenth century, Russia's development has been oscillating between attempts to modernize the legal system and backsliding to the old ways. With all the instability of development and the perpetual need to catch up, the attempts of legal modernization in Russia have always been oriented towards the Western model of law. The Western legal system has always been viewed as an ideal model or a desired goal of Russian legal modernization.

A broader sociologized, critical view of the development of law, legal relations, and legal culture is needed for the case of Russia and other societies that do not fit the Western legal model in their basic characteristics. The sociological ideas about modernization are usually derived from Max Weber's and Talcott Parsons's theories (Wagner 2008). Similarly to proponents of legal modernization theories, Parsons argues that modern society came to its full fruition only in the USA after the Second World War and all other parts of the world follow this model (Parsons 1971). However, Parsons considers legal modernization in conjunction with other changes reflecting the development of society towards sustainability and self-sufficiency. He suggests paying attention to changes in the economy, society, and politics, emphasizing the significance of the development of law and arguing that the establishment of impersonal legal norms indicates successful modernization (Parsons 1964). Such an expanded gaze on modernization allows, firstly, to dissect more critically the processes taking place with the law and, secondly, to get away from evaluating legal modernization ultimately by the development of official legal institutions.

This approach allows us to see different ways of conflict resolution, which exist stably not only in, but also outside, of the legal system, or only partially intersect with it. The law moves from the position of an indisputable benchmark into a series of multiple instruments for restoring justice that are connected by relations of mutual dependence and mutual influence. Thus, the processes of legal modernization include not only transformation of legal institutions, but also alternative ways of dispute resolution. It seems that this approach makes sense not only for Russia and post-socialist societies but generally for any society. It allows us to look beyond the limits of liberal legalism. There is always something there.

Parsons characterized the Soviet state as an authoritarian state, where the executive power dominated the judicial power. He believed in the ability of the Soviet system to modernize (Parsons 1971). However, Russia's historical path complicates the situation. Parsons emphasized the importance of continuous, consistent development for successful legal modernization. In case of Russia, the historical way of modernization is full of gaps. Long periods of stagnation were followed by periods of powerful breakthroughs, during which significant advances of the rule of law happened.

Furthermore, research on law in Russia is as uneven as the path of its development. Among scholarship on Soviet society, there is a dominant trend towards the study of official ideology, to the detriment of a substantive study of how Soviet institutions operated. The relationship between political ideologies and actual social processes in Russian studies has been over-simplified, as if social institutions were merely manifestations of ideological constructs. According to Markku Kivinen, the existing literature on the Soviet period is insufficient, due to the peculiarity of research methodology and the relative inaccessibility of the socialist system for direct research during the period of its existence. Now that information is more accessible, researchers have the opportunity to conduct more in-depth and comprehensive studies (Kivinen 2013:19). On the contrary, processes of legal modernization in post-Soviet Russia are customarily considered and evaluated at the level of institutions (Hendley 1997). This is not surprising, since changes to the Russian legal system during the first post-socialist decades were made primarily at the institutional level (Solomon 1995).

Concentration of the Soviet research around the ideology also has some consequences for understanding Russian modernization. Comparison of the socialist and Western systems was carried out at the level of ideologies. Confrontation between capitalist and socialist ideologies reinforced the idea that the vectors of legal development were also opposed. Contemporary research shows that these relations are much more complicated. In comparison with the Western models of modernization, Russia is neither exactly the same, nor totally opposite. It has different trends and priorities in its development, some of which coincide with those in the West and some others do not.

Investigation of ideology should not be separated from investigation of institutions. It is especially dangerous when we know that institutions can develop independently on ideology, or even completely contradict it. Understanding of Russian modernization processes cannot progress without further analysis of the complicated and contradictory relationship between the different levels of rhetoric and reality prevalent in Russian discourses (Kivinen 2013:19). It cannot be full and sufficient also without equivalent consideration of official judiciary and alternative ways of dispute resolution, common in society.

Authors, acknowledging the existence of multiple paths of modernization, tend to consider the communist period as a special type of modernization (Arnason 2002:61; Kivinen 2013:17). According to them, interruption between the past and the future caused by socialist revolutions should be considered as a modernizing transition rather than a rejection of modernization. Contrary to the Parsonian view, the transition to a modern society was not perceived as a gradual development towards the expansion of market orientation and professionalism, functional differentiation, and universal value patterns. Meanwhile, this revolutionary interruption was important for modernization rejection of the monarchy model. One of the main strategic goals of communist regimes was accelerated industrialization, even if it was carried out on the basis of outdated models of industrial development. Some spheres of life, such as private property relations, were completely excluded from modernization processes, while others, such as education, got a powerful modernization impetus under Socialism.

The place of law in the Soviet project, and its role in the modernization process, has been least studied. The reason for this probably lies in the fact that law as a regulatory force came into conflict with Soviet ideology. According to Marxist-Leninist theory, the law should eventually disappear and give way to socialist morality. In reality, on the contrary, the state has vastly increased its power in virtually all Marxist (-Leninist/Stalinist) systems; at the same time, the structures, roles, and functions of law have become progressively more complex, rather than simpler (Baum 1986:72).

The broken line of Russian modernization is still a line. Despite intermittent development, Russia's past helps to explain its present and vice versa. To understand contemporary processes of modernization in Russia we need creative approaches that take into account the interruptions, institutional patchworks, stable foundations of society, and the entire complexity of the Soviet and pre-Soviet past, with its natural and undesirable consequences (Giddens 1984; Kivinen 2006, 2009, 2013:24).

The role of the complaint mechanism in this long and complicated path of Russian modernization is really intriguing. Being marginal to the legal system and almost invisible for researchers of legal development, it functioned as an extremely important way of restoration of justice, available to the majority of people through centuries. It has survived several historical gaps and, in a sense, acts as the thread, stitching different eras. Research of mechanisms like this can explicate the general trends of social development and modernization, smoothing the wrinkles left by Russia's socio-political cataclysms of the twentieth century and the imposed revival of the institutions of the past.

The approach towards comprehension of legal modernization of Russia should be extended even wider. It is necessary to call into question another principle, firmly enshrined in research on modernization. This is a principle that strongly links legal modernization, and modernization in general, with the strengthening of formal legal institutions and bureaucratic mechanisms. Max Weber suggests understanding modernization as a formalization of the informal, when functions of informal relations and networks are neglected. What makes a modern society distinctive is the predominance, in both the market and the state sectors, of social capital in the form of large, impersonal bureaucratic organizations operating according to the rule of law (Weber 1968).

New studies offer much more flexible approaches to understanding modernization in general and legal modernization of post-Soviet Russia in particular. Within this approach, modernization is understood as a complex and not always unidirectional process. An important advantage of this approach is the fact that it pays attention not only to the formal side of transformations, but also includes informality as an important component of the processes of modernization. To study the modernization processes taking place in Russia, this is fundamentally important, since over the centuries informal rules and practices have often been at least as important to understanding the workings of power and commerce as formal constitutions and laws (Ledeneva 2012:18). Their capabilities and functionality changed over time. Alena Ledeneva (1997, 2008) shows how, in Soviet society, informal practices were monetized and provided the oil that lubricated a whole society, but were framed firmly within a teleology of modernization.

Informality is present everywhere, albeit in different forms and, though it can be limited in some areas, cannot be liquidated as it is an integral aspect of state-citizen interactions (Polese, Morris, and Kovács 2016). What we observe as part of a formal justice procedure is the tip of the iceberg. Hours of informal negotiations remain hidden from the sight of the researcher. Meanwhile, they are of great importance, sometimes determining the outcome of a trial. As Douglass North assures:

> Yet formal rules in even the most developed country make up a small (although very important) part of the sum of constraints that shape choices. In

> our daily interactions with others, whether within the family, in eternal social relations or in business activities, the governing structure is overwhelmingly defined by codes of conduct, norms of behavior, and conventions.
>
> (North 1990:36)

A turn to informality, both in the sphere of justice and in the sphere of government, has taken place in a wide variety of countries (Christiansen and Christine 2012). Any system, in the course of its development, goes through stages of strengthening and softening of legalism, solves problems by balancing between formality and informality, and chooses between formalization and efficiency. For instance, in modernized countries like the UK or the USA, accessing the system of justice is getting more and more expensive, and researchers recognize the impossibility of ensuring the equal access of all social groups to justice (Rhode 2003:372). In the late twentieth century, emerging markets and the wave of liberalization and privatization of public services that occurred in the Western world led to the introduction of alternatives to the state judicial system (Mistelis 2006).

It is not uncommon when legal issues, to be addressed in court, are easily resolved through informal or semi-informal ways of dispute resolution. A good example here is the institution of mediation, or pre-trial conflict resolution, formed on the crossroads of law and psychology. This is a structured, interactive process, which is arranged in accordance with formal rules. Simultaneously, it relies on specialized communication techniques and mutual empathy, which hardly can be completely formalized (Spencer and Brogan 2006).

A similar turn has been noted in the sphere of governance. Many new European strategies of governance are based on the conviction that not all relations "need to be governed by law but can be left to etiquette, social discourse, and informal commitments" (Shelton 2000:12). Transformations are carried out at both the institutional and normative levels. As a rule, new institutional bodies providing "soft" methods of dispute resolution, such as consumer dispute resolution systems, community methods, Ombudsmen, bureaus of complaints, and others, do not use national legislation as a normative base for the resolution of disputes, replacing them with regulation instruments such as international memoranda, directives, or treaties (Creutzfeldt-Banda 2013:228; De Bruijn and Hufen 1998). For instance, in the UK in 1973 the Office of Fair Trading was given the duty to encourage trade associations to develop codes of conduct (Fair Trading Act, s 124). Consumer Ombudsmen have the authority to develop agreements with trade organizations about interpretations of general fair trading provisions in various sectors (European Consumer Law Group 2001). Institutional providers of soft regulation are usually formed within a national system of governance, claiming to update the entire concept of management (Jacobsson 2001). However, the institutional role of new regulative bodies is not always evident. The European Ombudsman is a relatively new kind of "agent" whose status and role remain unclear. On the one hand, it is formally a parliamentary body designed to strengthen the control of EU institutions and administrations. On the other hand, the profile and role of this organ is close to that of a court (Magnette 2003).

The problem of unification of the normative base remains unsolved, as well as the problem of legitimacy of those. For comparison, legal regulation gets its legitimacy from the democratic process. Laws are made by governments, which are subject to elections and which are presumed to legislate for the public good. Although monitoring for breaches of the law may be inadequate because of lack of resources for enforcing bodies, both criminal and civil laws almost always carry sanctions for breaches. Soft law, where it is a substitute for, or supplement to, traditional regulation has to receive its legitimacy elsewhere (European Consumer Law Group 2001).

All these examples are taken from the model modernized societies. They show that the concept of legal modernization is not equivalent to the concept of formalization. Authors including Jeremy Morris, Abel Polese, Colin C. Williams, Ioana A. Horodnic, and Predrag Bejaković suggest a revised comprehension of the role played by informality in the organization and modernization of any society. They argue that understandings of informality as "socialist debris" or a "byproduct of transition," as a "pernicious phenomenon, which hinders the 'proper' development of the region" is both ideologically flawed and empirically unsubstantiated (Morris and Polese 2014:1). Contaminated by Western centrism, it reproduces the hierarchical ordering of societies from most to least modern and contributes to the othering of the post-socialist world (Ibid:7). At the same time, it fails to explain the pervasiveness of informal practices in former socialist countries dissimilar in economic development and political trajectory. Some authors take the argument one step further, considering that present-day informality is by and large a byproduct of the same neoliberal reforms seeking to eradicate it (Knudsen 2014:42; Cieślewska 2014:131).

Thus, the study of informality can be seen within a wider context of "de-othering" the study of the post-socialist space. While more pervasive and significant to household reproduction and social and economic life generally, informality should be seen as contributing to the construction of post-Socialism as a variant of our current modernity.[2] As Morris and his coauthors argue, "this is a version of modernity that the West needs to take note of, as we stand on the cusp of centrifugal economic and social forces at the heart of the formalization project of the EU acquis" (Morris and Polese 2014:7).

In addition to ubiquity, informality is difficult to separate from formality. Researchers often contrast complaint mechanisms and the judiciary as, respectively, pre-modern and modernized ways of solving problems, as informality and formality. At the same time, they frequently make a clear opposition between these two logics of problem solving. By following this approach, a researcher knowingly ignores everything that happens outside of the courtroom; or, on the contrary, slips into the archaic romance of the practice of "writing to the authority" (*pisanie vo vlast'*). Meanwhile, in practice, anyone who wants to solve a problem may well use both possibilities, sequentially or simultaneously. At first glance, it becomes quite obvious that this boundary, determined analytically by adherents of a clear distinction between the formal and the informal, is conditional.

The complaint mechanism in Russia is regulated by laws or supreme decrees that established complaints as a formal element of the modern national legal system. Meanwhile, the bureaucracy that processes these complaints is based outside of the judiciary. There are rules for filing complaints, there are deadlines; however, they are less stringent than those in a court. The filing procedure, the justification requirements, the review process, the execution of the decision, the oversight procedures are all there, but regulated to a much lesser extent. In reality, complainants often know about the formal rules, but ignore these limits (Minzner 2006:114).

Clear formal boundaries of legal institutions frequently only have the *appearance* of certainty (especially in socialist systems). When we attribute formality as a defining characteristic of a judiciary, we close our eyes to informal networks, emotionality, and political conjuncture, all of which are a part of law enforcement practice. Informal rules, or occasional obstacles, can play a key role in the judgment of a particular issue. In this book, I consider modernization as an ongoing dialogue between the formal and the informal. The formal and informal act simultaneously. A complaint to the authorities exists in parallel with the possibility of going to court. The border that separates one from the other is flexible, changeable, and situational. Formal rules may be accompanied, supplemented, or substituted by informal ones. One cannot be comprehended without the other.

Legal modernization can be judged by how the line is drawn between the complaint to the authorities and the judicial way of solving problems: how flexible and permeable this boundary is, how much the state law is recognized as the universal basis of justice in a society. The boundary may be soft or tough, permeable or impenetrable, flexible or inflexible. All these characteristics are comparable with the main principles of legal modernization: independence of the judiciary, adherence to the principle of the rule of law, and the separation of powers.

It is often thought that complaint mechanisms occupy peripheral positions in legal modernization in the majority of jurisdictions. However, as Julie Spanbauer, considering the American context, argues, "[s]o much of the history of petitioning government is intertwined with the development of the judiciary" (Spanbauer 1993:17). Taking into account historical, cultural, political, and legal dimensions in Russia, complaints acquire a special significance. It has coexisted with the establishment and modernization of legal institutions, compensating, accompanying, and sometimes substituting for them. All significant attempts at legal modernization in Russian history involve manipulation of the mechanism of complaints. In this book, I want to show that any investigation of legal modernization of Russia is hardly reliable without consideration of the complaint mechanism and its transformation. Successfulness of legal institutions development is certainly an important indicator of legal modernization. Meanwhile, the fate of the complaint mechanism in the context of legal modernization is equally informative since it tells a lot about ability, willingness and, most importantly, about the desire of the authorities to succeed in legal modernization.

This new approach encourages a comprehensive consideration of a problem in its historical development. It appreciates investigation of both formal and informal sides of the phenomenon. It also invites to incorporate a focus of research simultaneously on institutions, rhetoric, and ideology. This approach greatly complicates the conventional understanding of modernization, removing it from a single template; however, this is inevitable, since regulatory systems themselves tend to become more complex and internationalized, and external contexts often determine the work of institutions. When something interferes with the monopoly of law and begins to lay claim to powers of regulation, it cannot help but influence the status of the law. At least this approach should prompt investigation of everything that transgresses the limits of an idealized legal modernization.

We have to admit that the reconstruction of a complaint mechanism in post-Soviet Russia cannot by itself measure the direction and degree of legal modernization. New *ad hoc* foundations are needed, extending the Parsonian approach, in order to understand the level of legal modernization of contemporary Russian society. It is necessary to consider how informality acts in the background of formal structures; how the problems of the compatibility of the complaint mechanism with judicial institutions are being solved now and how they were solved in the past; how far the institutional design and normative framework are consistent with principles of democracy and the principle of the rule of law; whether the request for justice is being modernized; how the model of relations of citizens with the government is changing; and, finally, why contemporary Russian authorities want the restoration of justice to depend on this model.

What are mechanisms outside the judicial system able to tell us about the legal modernization of post-Soviet Russia? It is important to note that most likely, reconstruction of the complaint mechanism was not part of the task of reformers (Bogdanova 2014). The mechanism was rediscovered in the mid-2000s, after two decades of forceful legal reforms, as a reaction to certain socio-political processes. We are dealing with the glitches, undesirable consequences, and artificial reconstructions described by Kivinen, investigation of which promises the most heuristic findings. Investigation of the complaint mechanism cannot show the modernization of the national legal system as a whole. However, this research can penetrate areas that are closed to many other approaches.

The Russian case is an ideal one, allowing deeper exploration of the evolving nature of modernization, given that it captures some aspects of westernization while rejecting others (Kivinen 2013:18). The existence of a complaint mechanism in contemporary Russia is, I argue, an illuminating case showing how the contradictions of modernization arise and are resolved. It is also a case that can be viewed as a metaphor for the background of global crises of public administration, justice, mutual understanding, and trust between society and the authorities.

Methods, sampling, and periodization

Primary questions about the ability of the complaint mechanism to modernize and about its compatibility with processes of legal modernization arose from observations of the contemporary modification of the mechanism. My data covers the period of Putin's presidency, from 2001 to the present (about 20 years). Acknowledging the importance of historical background and seeing multiple instances of continuity between Soviet and contemporary forms of application to the authorities, I compare the institutional aspects of the Soviet version of the complaint mechanism to those of the contemporary period. Additionally, I analyzed the practice of complaint in the late Soviet period, when under Khrushchev's reforms the rules of complaining to the authorities were stabilized and universalized. To extend a space for historical comparison I also provide a brief overview of the pre-Soviet imperial modification of the complaint mechanism on the basis of scientific historical issues. Overall, the research covers about a century of the complaint mechanism's existence in Russia, in three manifestations: imperial, Soviet, and post-socialist.

Empirically, I consider the complaint mechanism and its connection to the judiciary on the levels of institutions, rhetoric, and ideology. An overview of the institutional (normative) frame of the Soviet and contemporary modifications of the complaint mechanism is of great importance. By design, the mechanism had in Soviet times, and has today, multiple connections with executive departmental authorities, supervisory bodies (especially procuracy), and the judiciary. A retrospective overview of the extended and very complicated normative frame was necessary to show the formal side of the complaint mechanism, its place in the system of the state governance and judiciary, and the changes to its role over time.

An attentive overview of the normative and ideological documents provides a basic understanding of the institutional arrangement of the mechanism. To answer the question of how institutional opportunities were applied by complainants, or how the mechanism actually worked, I analyzed data about usage of the mechanism. I draw on archival documents, ideological documents, correspondence between complainants and addressees, and statistical reports. In this part of the research, I applied the method of qualitative analysis of documents (Flick 2010:255–262; Bowen 2009:27–40). I analyzed all the legal and normative documents, regulating the process of complaints making, since the beginning of the Soviet epoch in 1917 till nowadays. Making a selection of ideological documents for analysis, I used the method of targeted thematic sampling. There were analyzed ideological documents, discussing the main principles of state-and-society relations and justice. Ideological documents related thematically to problems of complaints and processes of complaining were also selected for analysis.

It was important to obtain reflexive opinions from people having their own experience of participation in the process of complaining. There were conducted traditional semi-structured interviews with people involved in work with complaints or who made complaints themselves in the late Soviet and contemporary periods and the texts of complaints published in the newspapers. There was developed a questionnaire in accordance with the main purpose of the research. The interviews were conducted in the form of open conversation, when informants were asked to answer the questions in a free manner. This data allowed me to enrich my analysis of the normative formal dimension of the complaint mechanism with informal rules and strategies of complaining, which played an outstandingly important role in the functioning of the mechanism in all periods. Analysis of formal and informal rules of complaint showed the general set of addressees and identified the most influential ones. The interviews were analyzed in accordance with the method of thematic coding (Flick 2010:318–323). Simultaneous consideration of formal and informal sides of complaining helped me to evaluate the efficiency and functionality of the mechanism in its late Soviet and contemporary manifestations. It also showed how the boundary between the complaint mechanism and the system of state governance and judiciary manifests itself in practice.

I paid special attention to the rhetoric of complaints. I considered texts as an important aspect of the practice of complaining, when an author herself, or with assistance, selected a set of arguments that would have weight in her eyes and in the eyes of the addressee. This part of the research showed the transformation of a social contract and a request for justice, and role of law in these parts, from the late Soviet period until the present. Analysis of the texts of complaints revealed connections between the judiciary and complaint mechanism at the level of language. A method of qualitative analysis of documents was complemented by a critical approach applied to the study of the argumentation and justifications (see details in Chapter 2).

The empirical data of the book consists of:

- More than one hundred normative documents from the first days of the Soviet power up to the present day, regulating the mechanism of complaints: decrees, provisions, amendments, laws, open and internal orders, and sectoral regulations.
- About two hundred original archival documents of the late Soviet period from the State Archive of the Russian Federation (GARF), Leningrad Regional State Archive in Vyborg (LOGAV), the Russian State Archive of the Economy (RGAE), and Central State Archive of Saint Petersburg (TsGA SPb). The archival documents include complaints addressed to different addressees, responses, and cover letters.
- Sampling of local newspapers *Leningradskaia Pravda* and *Vechernii Leningrad*, published during the period 1960–1988. Altogether I analyzed 85 texts of complaints and responses published in the newspapers.
- Two hundred and fifty texts of complaints representing the contemporary modification of the complaint mechanism. These complaints were collected from 2006 until the present from the administration of one of the districts of Saint Petersburg, from public reception offices of the chairman of the party United Russia, and from websites. A number of websites contain collections of complaints addressed to different levels of authorities. Some of them are civil initiatives, inviting people to bring their complaints to the public space (for example http://medvedevu.ru, http://presidentu.ru or https://open-letter.livejournal.com). Some others are initiated by the authorities themselves to

provide the citizens with proper samples of complaints. All the official websites of governmental and executive bodies have the option for feedback, providing forms and samples of the complaints. The strategy of collecting complaints is also used by lawyers looking for potential clients (for example: http://письмапрезиденту.рф, https://владимиру-путину.рф, https://napisat-pismo-putinu.ru/, https://pravo.media/otkrytye-pisma/, etc.). Knowing about the popularity of complaining to different authorities, especially to the president, law companies set up websites that promise direct connection with the authorities, invite people to submit complaints, and recruit promising clients. These websites contain not only forms for submissions, but collections of original complaints (by tens of thousands), samples of complaints and responses, and recommendations on how and where to apply. In spite of the tricky nature of the websites, many people use these channels, believing in the opportunity to apply directly to the representatives of top-level authorities, or just trying to make their complaints public and visible. Websites with large numbers of visitors also attract the attention of the authorities. In my research I used texts of complaints and responses publicly available on the following websites: https://письмапрезиденту.рф, http://medvedevu.ru and https://pravo.media/otkrytye-pisma. Furthermore, between 2006 and 2018 I used the mechanism of complaints to solve problems of communal servicing of the house where I live. My personal archive of "a complaint-related correspondence" consists of 32 documents.

- Statistical reports presenting results of work with complaints on local, city, and presidential levels. These reports are available on the official sites of a district administration, the city administration of Saint Petersburg, and the website of the Administrative Office of the President of the Russian Federation on Work with Applications of Citizens and Organizations (http://www.letters.kremlin.ru).
- Seventeen semi-structured interviews with officials belonging to the Soviet and post-Soviet bureaucracies dealing with complaints and with people who had the experience of complaining.

Research was performed primarily in Saint Petersburg (known as Leningrad until September 6, 1991). Some data from the Central Russian archives were also used. Interviews with heads of the Public Reception Offices of the chairman of the party United Russia were conducted in three different cities, since only one Reception Office was available per city.

Investigating complaints over 17 years, I have collected an extended corpus of data related to both the Soviet and post-Soviet periods. In thinking about the design of the book I faced the challenge of selection. First, I had too many materials to discuss in a single book. The very process of selecting texts for analysis influenced the content of the book. As I dealt with the data, I thought about the specificity of the genre of complaint and realized the need to explain in detail what it is, and why, out of the whole variety of genres of appeals to the authorities, the complaint so directly reveals problems of legal modernization.

Secondly, the materials representing different epochs, which were available to me, turned out to be quite diverse and fragmented. It could not have been otherwise. The transition from the Soviet to the post-Soviet era influenced essentially the functions and role of the complaint mechanism. My idea of tracking the transformation of the complaint mechanism in the post-Soviet context demanded serious work to "balance" the data and carefully think through common grounds of analysis, without which the comparison of the post-Soviet mechanism with its earlier modifications became meaningless. The popularity of solving problems through complaints was defined as the common ground for the selection of the complaints for analysis. Thematic continuity of complaints was maintained only partially. If in the late Soviet years consumer complaints lead in popularity, in the post-Soviet period consumer issues moved almost entirely to the courts. Therefore, consumer issues are richly represented among the Soviet examples, but much less among contemporary ones. Meanwhile, complaints about housing, public services, and social welfare, common in the late Soviet years, remain popular today.

Structure of the book

In Chapter 2 I formulate the definition of a complaint and clarify the phenomenon of complaint to the authorities from historical, socio-political, and normative perspectives. The main mission of this chapter is to define what 'a complaint' is in the Russian context, how it can be analyzed, and what its heuristic potential is. I discuss how the complaint differs from other genres of appeal to the authorities and how it compares to a lawsuit. I take a critical capacity approach to the analysis of complaints addressed to the authorities. Before beginning my analysis, I clarify what we can definitively learn by investigating complaints, what we might be able to infer, and of what we can never be sure.

In Chapter 3 I present the configuration of the complaint mechanism and a set of bureaucratic rules that specify strategies and scenarios of complaints in the Soviet and particularly late Soviet epochs. Beginning with the moment of its establishment in 1918, I provide an overview of the development and transformation of the mechanism up to the end of the Soviet era. I show the spontaneous formation of rules at the beginning of the Soviet period, structural preconditions for the appearance of denunciations, and the bureaucratization of the rules of complaint-making in the late Soviet period. In this chapter I also characterize the structural links between the complaint mechanism and legal institutions in Soviet times as weak and unobvious. I argue that in the context of a socialist project the legitimacy of solving problems through complaints was quite high in comparison with legal ways. The complaint mechanism of the Soviet period performed a rather unique function, fulfilling citizens' requests for justice and transforming into a para-judicial institution. In the final part of the chapter I consider the destruction of the Soviet complaint mechanism and the institutional anomie of the 1990s. I use as empirical data regulations (laws, decrees, instructions) and archival materials.

In Chapter 4 I move on to the practical level of complaining, focusing on the late Soviet period. Analyses of complaints submitted to executive and Communist Party committees and the editorial offices of newspapers show paradoxical signs of modernization of the complaint mechanism. Due to Soviet neglect of the principles of separation of powers and rule of law, the complaint mechanism had no contradictions with the strict legal frame. The boundary between formality and informality was not problematized, nor was the boundary between the complaint mechanism and judiciary. Norms of Soviet morality were common arguments that provided mutual understanding between complainants and the authorities. All the addressees were representatives of the Soviet state, the author of the ideological doctrine. Being separated from the judiciary at the level of institutional arrangement, and at the level of language, the mechanism had a chance to develop into a para-judicial instrument. What was actually problematized in the late Soviet mechanism were its efficiency and formalization. I show the late Soviet mechanism of complaints as a functional modernizing project. In this chapter I use such empirical data as regulations (laws, decrees, instructions), interviews, archival materials, statistical reports, and newspaper publications.

In Chapter 5 I describe the formation of the contemporary complaint mechanism. Against the background of rather effective legal reforms, the recovery of the complaint mechanism in its archaic form does not appear functionally grounded. I consider the transformation of the judiciary, the complaint mechanism, and other bodies involved in work with complaints, like the procuracy and Ombudsman. Comparing the institutional dimension of the Soviet and post-Soviet complaint mechanisms, I discover similarities in general design embedded in the executive branch. The mechanism now emphasizes the opportunity for direct complaint to the representatives of top-level state authority. In particular, the president is identified as the main addressee of complaints, reproducing features of the pre-Soviet monarchical form of the complaint mechanism. In this chapter my empirical data includes regulations (laws, decrees, instructions), interviews, and archival materials.

Chapter 6 is devoted to the analysis of contemporary complaints. It appears as an artificial project reflecting features of the Soviet and pre-Soviet modifications of the complaint mechanism. The contemporary complaint mechanism is a political project created primarily to solve political problems of governance. It allows for the strengthening of authoritarianism and reinforces patterns of patriarchic monarchical power. The space in which it can demonstrate its effectiveness are issues that cannot be resolved by legal means. To strengthen the position of the complaint mechanism, the government is forced to expand the scope of informality. It turns informality into a space of state expertise and control. The influence of the complaint mechanism on legal modernization is negative, but rather derivative from political effects. In this chapter my empirical data includes regulations (laws, decrees, instructions), interviews, statistical reports, and the texts of complaints from different sources.

In the Conclusion I summarize the book's findings, focusing on the role of the complaint mechanism in the legal modernization of Russia.

Notes

1 Iz Saratova cherez Penzu. Peshii pokhod k prezidentu Rossii. 2016. *Argumenty i fakty*, 26, June 29. Retrieved on July 15, 2019 (www.penza.aif.ru/society/iz_saratova_cherez_penzu_peshiy_pohod_k_prezidentu_rossii).
2 See Thelen (2011) for this argument applied to the study of socialist societies.

References

Almbjär, Martin. 2019. "The Problem with Early-Modern Petitions: Safety Valve or Powder Keg?" *European Review of History: Revue Européenne D'histoire* 26(6):1013–1039.

Arnason, Johann. 2002. "Communism and Modernity." Pp. 61–90 in Shnuel Eisenstadt (ed.) *Multiple Modernities*. London: Transaction Publishing.

Baum, Richard. 1986. "Modernization and Legal Reform in Post-Mao China: The Rebirth of Socialist Legality." *Studies in Comparative Communism* 19(2):69–103.

Bogdanova, Elena. 2014. "Religious Justifications of Complaints, Addressed to the President in Contemporary Russia." *Laboratorium: Russian Review of Social Research* 3:55–79.

Bowen, Glenn. 2009. "Document Analysis as a Qualitative Research Method." *Qualitative Research Journal* 9(2):27–40.

Burg, Elliot. 1977. "Law and Development: A Review of the Literature and Critique of 'Scholars in Self- Estrangement'." *American Journal of Comparative Law* 25:492–530.

Christiansen, Thomas and Christine Neuhold. 2012. *International Handbook on Informal Governance*. Cheltenham Glos: Edward Elgar.

Cieślewska, Anna. 2014. "From Shuttle Trade to Businesswomen: The Informal Bazaar Economy in Kyrgyzstan." Pp. 120–134 in Jeremy Morris and Abel Polese (eds.) *The Informal Post-Socialist Economy. Embedded Practices and Livelihoods*. London: Routledge.

Cook, Linda, and Martin Dimitrov. 2017. "The Social Contract Revisited: Evidence from Communist and State Capitalist Economies." *Europe-Asia Studies* 69(1):8–26.

Creutzfeldt-Banda, Naomi. 2013. "The Origins and Evolution of Consumer Dispute Resolution Systems in Europe." Pp 228–252 in Christopher Hodges and Astrid Stadler (eds.) *Resolving Mass Disputes*. Northampton: Edward Elgar.

De Bruijn, Hans and Hans Hufen. 1998. "The Traditional Approach to Policy Instruments." Pp. 11–33 in Guy Peters and Frans van Nispen (eds.) *Public Policy Instruments: Evaluating the Tools of Public Administration.* Cheltemham: Edward Elgar.

Dimitrov, Martin. 2013. "Vertical Accountability in Communist Regimes: The Role of Citizens Complaints in Bulgaria and China." Pp. 276–303 in Martin Dimitrov (ed.) *Why Communism Did Not Collapse: Understanding Authoritarian Regime Resilience in Asia and Europe*. Cambridge: Cambridge University Press.

Dimitrov, Martin, Gandhi, Jennifer and Adam Przeworski. 2007. "Authoritarian Institutions and the Survival of Autocrats." *Comparative Political Studies* 40(11):1279–1301.

European Consumer Law Group. 2001. *Soft Law and the Consumer Interest*. ECLG/071/2001 – March. Retrieved on September 20, 2013 (http://ec.europa.eu/consumers/policy/eclg/rep03_en.pdf).

Fair Trading Act. 1986. *Consumer New Zealand*. Retrieved on September 19, 2019 (https://www.consumer.org.nz/articles/fair-trading-act).

Flick, Uwe. 2010. *An Introduction to Qualitative Research*. London: SAGE.

Giddens, Anthony. 1984. *The Constitution of Society. Outline of the Theory of Structuration.* Cambridge: Camgridge University Press.

Hendley, Kathryn. 1997. "Legal Development in Post-Soviet Russia." *Post-Soviet Affairs* 13(3):228–251.

Henry, Laura. 2012. "Complaint-Making as Political Participation in Contemporary Russia." *Communist and Post-Communist Studies* 3–4(45):243–254.

Iz Saratova cherez Penzu. Peshii pokhod k prezidentu Rossii. 2016. *Argumenty i Fakty*, 26, June 29. Retrieved on July 15, 2019 (http://www.penza.aif.ru/society/iz_saratova_cherez_penzu_peshiy_pohod_k_prezidentu_rossii).

Jacobsson, Kerstin. 2001. "Employment and Social Policy Coordination. A New System of EU Governance." Paper for the Scancor workshop on *"Transnational regulation and the transformation of states."* June 22–23. Stanford.

Jacobsson, Kerstin. 2002. *Soft Regulation and the Subtle Transformation of States: The Case of EU Employment Policy.* Retrieved on July 19, 2019 (https://www.score.su.se/polopoly_fs/1.26588.1320939800!/20024.pdfhttp://www.score.su.se/polopoly_fs/1.26588.1320939800!/20024.pdf).

Kivinen, Markku. 2006. "Classes in the Making? Russian Social Structure in Transition." Pp. 247–294 in Goran Therborn (ed.) *Inequalities of the World. New Theoretical Frameworks, Multiple Empirical Approaches.* London: Verso.

Kivinen, Markku. 2009. "Russian Societal Development: Challenges Open." Pp. 112–144 in Hiski Haukkala and Sari Sinikukka (eds.) *Russia, Lost or Found.* Helsinki: Edita: Ministry of Foreign Affairs in Finland.

Kivinen, Markku. 2013. "Interdisciplinary Approach to Russian Modernization." *Zhurnal sotsiologii i sotsial'noi antropologii* 4:12–28.

Knudsen, Ida Harboe. 2014. "The Story of Šarūnas: An Invisible Citizen of Lithuania." Pp. 35–51 in Jeremy Morris and Abel Polese (eds.) *The Informal Post-Socialist Economy. Embedded Practices and Livelihoods.* London: Routledge.

Ledeneva, Alena. 1997. "Lichnye sviazi i neformal'nye soobshchestva: Transformatsiia blata v postsovetskom obshchestve." *Mir Rossii* 2:89–106.

Ledeneva, Alena. 2008. "Telephone Justice in Russia." *Post-Soviet Affairs* 24(4):324–350.

Ledeneva, Alena. 2012. "*Sistema*—Russia's Informal System of Power." Pp. 17–27 in Katynka Barysch (ed.) *Three Views on Modernization and the Rule of Law in Russia.* Published by Centre for European Reform. Retrieved on July 19, 2019 (http://www.cer.org.uk/sites/default/files/publications/attachments/pdf/2012/e_3views_russia_23jan12-4553.pdf).

Magnette, Paul. 2003. "Between Parliamentary Control and the Rule of Law: The Political Role of the Ombudsman in the European Union." *Journal of European Public Policy* 5(10):677–694.

Markovits, Inga. 1986. "Pursuing One's Rights under Socialism." *Stanford Law Review* 38(3):689–761.

Minzner, Carl. 2006. "Xinfang: An Alternative to Formal Chinese Legal Institutions." *Stanford Journal of International Law* 42:103–180.

Mistelis, Loukas. 2006. "ADR in England and Wales: A Successful Case of Public Private Partnership." Pp. 139–180 in Nadja Alexander (ed.) *Global Trends in Mediation* (2nd edition). Alphen aan den Rijn: Kluwer Law International.

Morris, Jeremy, and Abel Polese. 2014. "Introduction: Informality—Enduring Practices, Entwined Livelihood." Pp. 1–18 in Jeremy Morris and Abel Polese (eds.) *The Informal Post-Socialist Economy. Embedded Practices and Livelihoods.* London: Routledge.

North, Douglass. 1990. *Institutions, Institutional Change and Economic Performance*. New York: Cambridge University Press.

Parsons, Talcott. 1964. "Evolutionary Universals in Society." *American Sociological Review* 29(3):339–357.

Parsons, Talcott. 1971. *The System of Modern Societies*. Englewood Cliffs: Prentice-Hall.

Pipes, Richard. 1977. *Russia under the Old Regime*. Harmondsworth: Penguin.

Polese, Abel, Morris, Jeremy and Borbála Kovács. 2016. "'State' of Informality in Post-Socialist Europe (and beyond)." *Journal of Contemporary Central and Eastern Europe* 24(3):181–190.

Rhode, Deborah. 2003. "Access to Justice: Connecting Principles and Justice." *Georgetown Journal of Legal Ethics* 17:372–373.

Rose, Richard. 1998. "Getting Things Done in an Anti-Modern Society: Social Capital Networks in Russia." Social Capital Initiative Working Paper No. 6. World Bank. Retrieved on December 12, 2019 ("http://siteresources.worldbank.org/INTSOCIALCAPITAL/Resources/Social-Capital-Initiative-Working-Paper-Series/SCI-WPS-06.pdf").

Rose, Richard. 2001. "Living in Anti-Modern Society." Pp. 293–303 in Archie Brown (ed.), *Contemporary Russian Politics: A Reader*. Oxford: Oxford University Press.

Shelton, Dinah. 2000. *Commitment and Compliance. The Role of Non-binding Norms in the International Legal System*. Introduction. Oxford: Oxford University Press.

Solomon, Peter. 1995. "The Limits of Legal Order in Post-Soviet Russia." *Post-Soviet Affairs* 11(2):89–114.

Spanbauer, Julie. 1993. "The First Amendment Right to Petition Government for a Redress of Grievances: Cut from a Different Cloth." *Hastings Constitutional Law Quarterly* 21:15–69.

Spencer, David and Michael Brogan. 2006. *Mediation Law and Practice*. Cambridge: Cambridge University Press.

Thelen, Tatjana. 2011. "Shortage, Fuzzy Property and other Dead Ends in the Anthropological Analysis of (Post)socialism." *Critique of Anthropology* 31(1):43–61.

Trubek, David and Marc Galanter. 1974. "Scholars in Self-Estrangement: Some Reflections on the Crises in Law and Development Studies." *Wisconsin Law Review* 1:1061–1101.

Wagner, Peter. 2008. *Modernity as Experience and Interpretation*. Cambridge: Polity.

Weber, Max. 1968. *Economy and Society*. Berkeley: University of California Press.

2 A complaint to the authorities

What it is, and what it can tell us

The phenomenon of complaint, with its mighty cultural and emotional components, goes way beyond the limits of an official address to the authorities. Considered from this angle, complaint emerges as a complicated discursive genre. As Katherine Lebow notes, "the idea of complaint is hard to disengage from its rich, sometimes contradictory associations in colloquial usage, which are always historically and culturally contingent" (Lebow 2014:15).

Until now, cultural, political, and historical views have dominated the study of complaints. Many researchers explored complaints in studies relating to the nature of denunciation and the Soviet/Russian self (Orlova 2004; Fitzpatrick 1996a; Nérard 2004), epistolary habits and Soviet personhood (Utekhin 2004), the political potential of complainants (Friedgut 1979; Gitelman and DiFrancesco 1984; Henry 2012; Fitzpatrick 1996b; Merl 2012), or as a cultural code of the whole society (Ries 1997).

Complaint as a tool for the restoration of justice has also been explored. Fitzpatrick argues that complaints in Soviet society executed the function of substitution of rights protection (Fitzpatrick 1996a:863–864). French historian François-Xavier Nérard (2004) likewise declares that the main stimulus for letter writing for citizens was the necessity to prove their rights. According to research carried out by Inga Markovits and Martin Dimitrov in Eastern Germany and in Bulgaria, complaint mechanisms performed a similar function. The mechanism of complaints performs analogous functions in different socialist systems, occupies a certain niche in the sphere of rights protection, and bespeaks the peculiarities of socialist legal systems in general. Natalia Pecherskaya problematizes the Soviet complaint as a request for justice in a philosophical manner and shows the penetration of the language of official Soviet ideology into the texts of complaints (Pecherskaya 2012).

Meanwhile, the boundary separating the ubiquitous practice of complaining to the authorities that has always flourished in Russian society from the other types of appeals has never been clearly defined. Analysis of the place of complaint among the whole field of genres of appeals has not been exhausted. Different researchers suggest different classifications of the applications to the authorities. Galina Orlova (2004) makes an attempt to create a comprehensive classification, including all types of applications, addressed to the Soviet authorities, and identifies such genres:

"complaint" (*zhaloba*), "solicitation" (*proshenie*), "letter" (*pis'mo*), "statement" (*zaiavlenie*), and "denunciation" (*donos*). Andrei Markevich unites all appeals to the authorities under the concept of "letters to the authorities" (*pis'ma vo vlast'*), which may be classified in accordance with purposes such as "letters-complaints," "letters-solicitations," "letters-requests," etc. (Markevich 2002:5). Sheila Fitzpatrick (1996a) identifies such types of applications as a "complaint" (*zhaloba*), "denunciation" (*donos*), and "pleading" (*khodataistvo*). Historical period, available empirical data, and particular purposes of research determine the view of a researcher. Each of the above researchers contributed to the understanding of the phenomenon of a complaint, although they all try to find the place of a complaint among the other applications to the authorities, avoiding matching it with an institutional framework. It does not allow to develop the universal classification. It does not give reliable definitions of a complaint either. It rather contributes to the comprehension of a complaint as a specific, and even exotic phenomenon of Russian society.

At the same time, there has been considerable chaos around definitions, especially in the English-language debate. The habit of labeling all the applications to the authorities as "petitions" adapts the phenomenon for Western audiences, but sacrifices an important cultural nuance. The opposite practice of borrowing idiomatic terms from the Russian language without translation—*kliauza*, *telega*, *navet*, *sutiazhnichestvo*—captures the spirit of the phenomenon, cultural and linguistic context, and even the historical period, but muddles efforts to grasp the origins and versatility of the phenomenon.

In my research I pay attention to the institutional framework and align the definition of a complaint with the function, prescribed by the normative documents. Namely, I define a complaint as an application to the authority with the purpose of restoration of justice, and I consider it not only among the other types of applications to the authorities, but among different ways of justice restoration, including applications to the courts or to the procuracy. A gaze on the complaint as an official tool for the restoration of justice does not negate other meanings of complaining. The administrative complaint and existential or even religious complaints have merged under a single label and a single object of research, and this is no coincidence. All these incarnations of complaint exist in a society simultaneously and even perform similar functions. There is a deep historical meaning behind this unity that makes one think about the nature of justice in Russian society. However, I see the point of singling out administrative complaints among the general practice of complaining—even if the boundary may be somewhat artificial. I also see the point in separating the complaint from all other forms and genres of appeals to the authorities, since the complaint is included under processes of legal modernization.

In this chapter I define the complaint addressed to the authorities as an object of the research and discuss its heuristic potential and limits.

What is a "complaint" in Russia: Origins of the concept

Complaint is the nearest English equivalent to the Russian word *zhaloba*. Contemporary dictionaries define it as a "statement that a situation is unsatisfactory or unacceptable, an expression of dissatisfaction" (*Oxford Dictionary*).[1] This translation conveys the meaning of the contemporary practice quite accurately, but further linguistic and socio-historical analysis of the Russian word *zhaloba* helps to much better explain the phenomenon and to show the limits of the translation.

Zhaloba is a pan-Slavonic word introduced into use in the thirteenth century (Semionov 2003). Originally the word meant a cry, sorrow, or grief. Medieval notions of the Slavonic word are similar to the Old French *complainte* (twelfth century) (*Online Etymology Dictionary*),[2] which has an almost identical meaning as *zhaloba*. More detailed analyses of the origins and development of the notion give some thought-provoking results.

The first systematic commentary on the origin, meanings, and use of the term is contained in the dictionary of Vladimir Dal' (1863–1866), according to which the word *zhaloba* comes from the Slavic verb *zhalet'* (to pity). The word *zhalet'* in Russian has a meaning akin to that of the verb "to sympathize" *(sostradat')* (Dal' 1996[1863]:525). A characteristic feature of this word is the variety of transmitted meanings, and the wide range of relationships, to which it may be applied. According to Dal' the verb *zhalet'* has a set of modifications (*zhalit'*, *zhalkovat'*) which define an emotional state, or compassion, that can be experienced in relation to another human, but not only a human. The practice of use suggests that most likely the words originally defined relationships and phenomena of private life, emphasizing their object-subject character. This is also indicated by the use of the adjective *zhalkii* (pitiful), which is allowed in two senses: "valuable, worthy of compassion," and the opposite: "worthless, contemptuous, bad" (Dal' 1996[1863]:525).

In both cases, the characteristics are dependent on the subject, i.e. the object acquires the corresponding qualities only in the presence of a subject who is capable of having feelings towards him or her. This interpretation is supported by another lexeme derived from the word *zhalet'*: *zhalobit'*, *razzhalobit'* (to inspire pity), which reproduces similar subject-object interdependence. This lexeme also opens up another group of meanings: to beg, to moan, to whine *(klianchit'*, *kaniuchit'*, *plakat'sia)* (Ibid:525), meaning emotional manipulation in order to get something that belongs to someone else. At the same time, the main instrument and basis of the request is to stimulate a feeling of pity in the person who owns it. The lexeme *zhalovat'* (to favor) is also akin to the word "to complain." This is an old Russian word, meaning literally "to give something out of love without a legal reason" (Vasmer 1967). Max Vasmer, the author of the dictionary, suggests semantic relatedness between the terms "a complaint" and "alms." The latter refers to the Christian practice of voluntary giving.

The meaning of the complaint as an official appeal can already be found in the 1863 dictionary by Dal', which comments on the complaint as an instrument of expression of displeasure (Dal' 1996[1863]:526). Interestingly, among the options of interpretation offered by Dal', there is also the verb *iskat'* (to seek), obviously akin to the contemporary Russian legal notion of *isk* (a lawsuit), which nowadays means an official claim in a judicial (civil, arbitral) proceeding (Sukharev 2007).

Analysis of the different meanings of complaint that predominantly existed in the nineteenth century manifests an implicit scheme of subject-object relations, which is applicable to the sphere of private life and to the public, official sphere. Relations arising between the subject and the object of a complaint imply an asymmetry of statuses in favor of the subject. The pattern of subject-object relations arising through a complaint shows the deep connection of this form of restoration of justice to the context of the hierarchical, estate patriarchal society that existed in imperial Russia. A complaint as an official appeal for help arises in the context of dependence and power, as a tool of compensation of a status of a complainant, wherein official legal grounds for compensation does not play a decisive role. The scale and the form of assistance depend on the subjective decision of the addressee. This, however, does not mean that grounds regulating the relevant relations of pleading are totally absent.

According to historical documents, the official complaint was by the fourteenth century regulated by a hard protocol. The bureaucratic form of the complaint in Russia was called *chelobitnaia*. This word comes from the old Russian *chelobit'e*, which is composed of two roots: *chelo* (a forehead) and *bit'* (to beat). The phrase "to beat with the forehead" refers to the low bow one makes to the addressee of the application. The word itself evokes once again the inequality between the addressee and the author of the application. Until the beginning of the eighteenth century the term *chelobitnaia* was used as a collective label for all types of official applications to the authorities: requests, complaints, and denunciations.

Chelobitnaia suggested a certain scheme for the compilation of a text and a procedure for filing to the appropriate authority. During the sixteenth century, the *chelobitnaia* acquired a three-part structure, including an introduction (or a title), main part, and conclusion. Overwhelmingly, illiterate people had to turn to scribes, who were able to put their *chelobitnaias* into writing. The structure and content of the text were directly dependent on the competence of the mediator. The introductory part of the text and its conclusion are, as a rule, clichéd. The rest of the text looks like a voluntary retelling of events, which acquires a plot, and is illustrated with colorful characteristics of the persons in the story. A standard introduction to the *chelobitnaia* is usually the following: "A serf beats with his forehead to his Tsar and Grand Duke of All Russia Ivan Vasilyevich." The conclusions of the *chelobitnaias* are also standardized: "Sovereign, have mercy, give your favor," or "Tsar, the Sovereign, have mercy" (Volkov 1974:26–27).

In imperial Russia, *chelobitnaias* were used as a tool for protection of interests by representatives of different groups of society, both the oppressed and the dominant. Specification of addressees and reasons for complaint were approximate and often ignored. Sviatoslav Volkov, author of the book *Vocabulary of Russian Chelobitnaia of the Seventeenth Century*, emphasizes that the range of problems presented in *chelobitnaias* was extremely wide. For example, appeals could contain requests for admission to service, for exemption from service due to old age or mutilation, for official relocation, for transfer of an estate to a son or another relative, for assistance, for subsidizing of money for a funeral, etc.

Contrary to popular opinion, *chelobitnaias* could be submitted not only to the Tsar, but also to central and local governmental institutions, landowners, church hierarchs, and others. Even if the Tsar was not an immediate addressee of the *chelobitnaia*, the standardized phrases were still inserted into the text. Applications could be filed by individuals or by groups of people. A statement of claim to a court was also called a *chelobitnaia* (Sukharev 2007).

Linguistic-epistemological analysis of the concept of the complaint allows us to make several important conclusions.

1. Multiple ways of understanding and using the notion of "complaint" have been preserved from the pre-revolutionary period. Among these are complaint as a form of expression of everyday discontent, complaint as an official appeal to the authorities, and complaint as a form of appeal to court. Despite the change of epochs, the concept retains a plurality of meanings.
2. Complaint as an official appeal to the authorities is traditional in Russian society, rooted in history, and appeared long before the judiciary as a legitimate form of request for justice. For many centuries, it has been performing the function of a legitimate form of solving diverse problems, operating out of judiciary.
3. The practice of complaint sets a pattern of subject-object relations between author and addressee, and reflects the dominant model of power and status relations in Russian society. This pattern contains a set of rules for addressing the authorities that is reflected in the structure and language of the complaint.
4. Like any form of direct communication, a complaint contains a strong emotional component.

How to recognize a complaint among other genres of applications?

In the Soviet period the practice of writing to the authorities was extremely popular. The authorities stimulated the flow of information from below. For their part, citizens felt the need to make regular appeals to the authorities. It was one of only a few channels (and on some issues, the only one) for reporting problems in the functioning of the system. Besides, the various effects of a totalitarian-authoritarian society in different periods of the Soviet era gave rise to a need for communication with the authorities among citizens, resulting in streams of private letters to the leaders, greetings, thanks, and so on. People wrote a lot and for a variety of reasons, and therefore the desire of researchers to classify the arrays of appeals, highlight genres, and limit areas of interest, makes perfect sense. Meanwhile no attempt at classification has achieved clarity and unambiguity in separating one genre of appeal from the others.

In fact, researchers are not the first to try to classify applications by genre. Initial attempts at classification have been the work of officials, who developed bureaucratic mechanisms for the effective handling of appeals. Each of the versions of laws dealing with complaints and appeals—from the very beginning of the Soviet period to 2006—necessarily contains a classification. The decree of 1919 which established the Central Bureau (Decree of NKGK 1919) introduced two main types of applications: complaints and statements. A Decree of

1968 established a triple classification of applications: suggestions, statements, and complaints, and a unifying term "applications" covering all three (Decree of Presidium of the Supreme Soviet of the USSR 1968). The same classification was reproduced in Law No. 59, in effect presently (Law No. 59 2006). Between these two laws, the classifications changed, and sometimes "complaint" was completely excluded from the category of appeals to the authorities (see Chapter 3).

According to legislation, each type of appeal is linked to its tasks, functions, and scenarios of bureaucratic processing. In practice, this ideal classification serves more as an approximate guideline for sorting of applications, but it has never been ignored entirely. The next stage of classification of applications is done by the employees of the apparatus receiving the applications. The work always starts from the review of recently received appeals, since the first task to solve is defining the problem and relating it to the competence of the addressee. This review establishes the genre and the further route of the application. There were and are no clear requirements for addressing appeals or general stylistic guidelines differentiating the applications by genre. This stage of classification depends on the particular employee tasked with evaluating incoming correspondence.

Sometimes, the authors of appeals themselves define the genres by titling their appeals. This is an important classifying argument; however, it cannot be trusted completely. If we believe that the author is likely unaware of the intricacies of bureaucracy, then we cannot be sure how consistent her views will be with the genres of official classification. On the other hand, if we believe that the author is aware, then we cannot exclude the possibility of manipulation. In other words, if bureaucracy processes complaints more efficiently than all other genres of appeal, then why would an author label her message any other way?

An application may be reclassified several times during processing. Finally, they are placed in archives, where they have to be classified once again in accordance with the logic of archival storage. At this stage applications may be resorted on new criteria. As a result, the researcher deals with an array of applications which are very different and which she must reclassify again from the perspective of her own research. When selecting texts for my research, I was guided by one simple rule: if the text contained a direct or indirect request for fairness, then it could be considered a complaint. It turned out to be the most difficult to specify a complaint among the types of appeals having semantic, functional, and institutional intersections: a petition, a denunciation, and an administrative lawsuit. The following subsections explain my classification methods.

Complaint versus petition

Translation of the term *zhaloba* as "petition" is normalized in academic discourse. It is explainable in terms of the practice of translation. "Petition" is really a rather close equivalent of *zhaloba*, especially in the context of Western legally modernized countries, from which most English scholarship on the subject comes.

The word "petition" was created in the eighteenth century from the Latin root "petō," which means "I assault, I attack, I demand." In English the meaning of the term "petition" is very close to the universal notion of application, which may mean both addressing the authorities or the courts.[3] With this versatility and variability of meanings, the noun "petition" is very similar to *zhaloba*. Both *zhaloba* and petition constitute a peaceful alternative for conflict resolution. Hence, petition is a notion and phenomenon belonging to Western political culture, formed primarily in Western Europe and North America. A petition is a forceful demand, while *zhaloba* is a humble request. Petition does not imply the political loyalty or weak position of an applicant, while *zhaloba* does. *Zhaloba* normally works as an individual emotional application, prompted by an individual problem, but the petition is typically understood as a formal written demand, signed by many people,[4] aimed at protecting a common good. Furthermore, a petition is usually comprehended as an initial act that can galvanize and mobilize people to further political action (Almbjär 2019:1), while the mechanism of complaints was traditionally used in Russia to extinguish public discontent and prevent protests.

In the context of contemporary Russian and, especially, Soviet reality, *petition* acquired specific meanings. Petition as a genre of application to the authorities was delegitimized in the Soviet period and was in some decades illegal. Collective applications have never been prohibited officially. Plenty of complaints signed by many people are available in the archives, although they are never labeled petitions. The concept of "petition" could be used to designate a collective complaint as an illegitimate or seditious form of appealing to the authorities. Nérard gives an illuminating example of the use of the word: "At the meeting of the Bureau of the Soviet Control Commission in December 1936, N. Antipov takes the floor in order to criticize the collective letter, sent to the Commission" (Nérard 2004:78). The letter is a complaint by nature, but before sending it, the authors "collected" the signatures. Thus, they sent a "petition," which, according to Antipov, the addressee cannot allow. The "petition" thus acquired a negative connotation, increasing the risks for its authors. Thus, a collective letter could easily be labeled a petition, which in minor cases could lead addressees to ignore it, and in serious ones could bring reprisals on authors' heads—especially during the early years of the Soviet period. In the late Soviet period the official attitude towards collective letters was noticeably softened, but the genre of petitions, in the Western sense, was never welcomed by the regime.

In the second part of the Soviet period hostility to petitions manifested itself overtly. The development of the petition movement took place between 1965 and 1968 on a wave of increasing dissident sentiments. Aleksander Sungurov connects the emergence of this social phenomenon with the resignation of Khrushchev and the relative easing of the regime that lasted until the entry of Soviet troops in Czechoslovakia (Sungurov 1998:32). Late-Soviet petitions were open letters to the party-state elite, expressing some collective opinion on policy issues, compiled by prominent figures of science and culture in the USSR. The themes of these letters were warnings against the possible rehabilitation of Stalinism and protests against the beginning of political trials. During this period the concept of a petition acquired the notion of a democratic means of fighting for rights, transplanted from democratically developed countries.

The development of the movement led to the banning of petitions and increasing repressions against petitioners. In March 1966, three petitions signed by famous figures in Soviet cultural and scientific life warned the Politburo that its actions were not approved. The signatories (including Sakharov and Solzhenitsyn) were labeled parasites, yet their petitions reached the West, aroused criticism, and injured the Soviet image abroad. In September 1966 the XXIII Congress denounced the protestors and introduced articles 190-1 and 190-3 (slander) into the Criminal Code. These articles were frequently used at the closed trials of petitioners and demonstrators (Lozansky 1989:7–8). Thus, under the conditions of Soviet society, the petition was excluded from the set of legitimate forms of appeal to the authorities. The concept itself was highly marginalized and endowed with negative connotations alongside collective action and open protest, which were severely suppressed by the state.

In contemporary Russia, especially in recent years, the Western type of petition has increased in strength. The contemporary Russian petition retains the meaning of a collective appeal to the authorities pursuing protection of collective goods. Petitions are now legitimate and quite effective. Through international websites like change.org and avaaz.com Russian petitions are attached to a global practice of petitioning. It is important to understand that in the Russian context a petition is not the same as a complaint. This is a fundamentally unique form with its own formal and informal regulations, possibilities of influence, and limits of effectiveness. Petitions are excluded from the category of appeals to the authorities regulated by Law No. 59. So these "new" petitions are not directly related to the complaint mechanism in Russia and developed separately.

Complaint versus denunciation

The genre of denunciations is the most studied in the entire Soviet and post-Soviet history of appeals to the authorities. This is not surprising, since the phenomenon of denunciation affected such a large number of spheres of human existence and opens up so many questions concerning both the motives of the authorities and human nature itself. The phenomenon of denunciation during the reign of Stalin presents an outstanding case of how the authorities could use the mechanism of appeals for their own purposes, subordinating everything to control, including the internal motives and moral choices of people. In this section, I compare the denunciation and the complaint in order to identify points of contact, traces of mutual influence, and also to feel the fundamental differences between these two forms of appeals to the authorities.

Due to the brightness and complexity of the phenomenon, the concept of denunciation sometimes seems to fit the general definition of appeals to the authorities—at least during the Soviet period. A review of Soviet legislation and historical research proves that denunciation is actually a modified form of complaint that arose in specific socio-political conditions for a rather short period, which was limited to the late 1920s to early 1940s.

The format of the denunciation is derived from the complaint simply because the regulatory framework governing work with complaints, as well as the institutional infrastructure serving this work, arose before the first flowering of denunciation. Work with denunciations was carried out partly by the Soviet bureaucracy of complaints, which had already been established by the end of the 1920s. The Bureau of Complaints, which was founded in 1920 and after the reform of 1923 became part of the administrative system, was an important body participating in the consideration of denunciations (Nérard 2004). In the process of increasing denunciations, however, the circle of addressees was expanded and specified.

Nérard in his book consistently shows that the prevalence of appeals to the authorities in the form of denunciations was the result of a deliberate policy of the Soviet government. Since the mid-1920s a number of measures were taken by the authorities in support of this genre. The first thing was the removal of the word "denunciation," which bore the stamp of an immoral act, from the official discourse. This was because the term had negative associations with the practice of informing on or betraying someone to the authorities. According to Nérard, until 1938, the concept was completely absent from official texts. The term "signal" was introduced into active use instead of "denunciation." Soviet official discourse created norms that justified the act of transmitting information and released it from feelings of shame and betrayal. "Signaling" to the authorities was not meant to be synonymous with "denunciation to the authorities."

In 1927, the state began to develop legislative and ideological support for whistleblowing. The efforts of the authorities were reinforced by the generally deplorable situation in a country suffering from mass poverty and hunger, experiencing mass migrations from villages to the cities. Simultaneously, researchers note a sharp increase in literacy precisely in this period. In generalized indicators, ignoring regional diversity, in comparison to the levels of 1913 the percentage of literate people in the USSR had almost doubled by 1930, from 33% to 63% (Sokolov 1999).

The following year, in 1928, a campaign of self-criticism was launched (*kampaniia samokritiki*). Self-criticism was explained by socialist propaganda as a necessary response to the evil resulting from excessive bureaucratization (*biurokratizm*), the increasing pressure of capitalism, and the resistance of hostile social groups (for example, *kulaks*). In February 1937 the authorities started a vigilance campaign (*kampaniia bditel'nosti*). It called on people to suspect everyone of sabotage and spying, to be attentive to the behavior and conversations of everyone around.

Initially, the People's Commissariat of Working-Peasant Inspection (RKI) was the main addressee receiving and processing denunciations, and after 1934 the People's Commissariat of Internal Affairs (NKVD) was added. The production of denunciations was intensified by a cohort of professional informers (*stukachi*) among workers (*rabkory*) and peasants (*sel'kory*). As a result denunciation acquired specific features. Firstly, the disclosure of certain phenomena, processes, or actions was to be the main motive for application. Secondly, denunciations used a specialized vocabulary, determined by the class approach, normative ideas about the behavior of a Soviet person and popular clichés from the emerging language of the Soviet ideology. Thirdly, denunciations had a particular circle of addressees. Finally, applications were to be signed. Anonymous letters were generally prohibited, except for cases when a public official was denounced:

> It is necessary to specify your last name and address correctly, because sometimes additional information is required … . If the complainant, for some reason—especially when exposing saboteurs and malicious bureaucrats—prefers not to disclose his or her last name, he or she may make such a statement.
>
> (*Zhaloby passazhirov* 1934)

In fact, real denunciations were often anonymous.

Meanwhile, classification of denunciations experiences the same problems as classification of any other genre of applications. Despite a clear definition of the addressees, it was possible to send "signals" everywhere. If the addressee recognized the characteristics of a denunciation, the application could be forwarded to RKI or NKVD. Similarly, the RKI and NKVD received a lot of different sorts of appeals, not just denunciations. As a result of sorting and forwarding, archives were built which are available today for study.

Nérard, who worked in the archives, says that the selection of denunciations from the total mass of letters is the result of analytical assessment, the criteria for which are not as straightforward as it may seem. Most of the appeals stored there are ordinary complaints, containing requests for help and assistance in solving private problems. At some point the regime created the conditions under which a revelatory letter became the primary code in communication between citizens and the authorities. Regardless of whether citizens believed in the existence of "enemies of the people," "alien elements," or "saboteurs," these categories temporarily became significant elements of the political language and, therefore, filtered into letters of complaints, as a complaint has to be composed in the language of its recipient:

> Documents that we find in accessible and open archives do not meet expectations. There are no or almost no letters of denunciations, as they are represented in films or works of art. No or almost no anonymous short, sharp notes. You can usually find extensive, reasoned and signed statements. Charges, typical for denunciations, are often included in long letters of complaints. If we have a letter addressed to the highest authorities with a complaint about someone's unfair decision (for example, unlawful dismissal), the author of the decision is named by name, disclosed in flaws or punishable actions, is it necessary to talk about a denunciation?
>
> (Nérard 2004:4)[5]

Of course, there were denunciations that were written purposefully as a powerful tool of political repression. These "real" denunciations are dissolved in a huge ocean of ordinary letters, complaints, and statements. Furthermore, an application compiled in accordance with the rules of denunciation could pursue the same purpose as a regular complaint. As much as the standard complaint, a denunciation could be used as a tool to protect private interests and restore justice. In a certain period of time, the feedback channel which citizens habitually used for solving their particular problems acquired dangerous features.

It is well known that denouncing was associated with a large number of risks and threats from the side of Soviet government, or from the side of "the people's" avengers, who punished informers in their own way. It is also known, meanwhile, that decisions on denunciations could be made very effectively. The code of disclosure together with the accusatory lexica became for a time common and popular, and took the place of important arguments in the texts of the appeals. The period of denunciation influenced the formation of the language of the Soviet complaint. In the following chapters, I show that characteristics of the denunciation were not completely developed until the end of the Soviet period, and the vocabulary of ordinary complaints retains their traces.

Complaint versus administrative appeal

In legal and socio-political sources, the complaint mechanism is usually called the "administrative way of solving problems." The appeal itself is called "an administrative complaint." The administrative way is usually distinguished from the judicial one, which is triggered by a court complaint, a lawsuit, or criminal statement, carried out under the conditions of the judiciary, and makes decisions under the norms of legislation. Work with a complaint addressed to the authorities occurs within the state administrative apparatus. In this sense, the hero of this book is the administrative (for the addressee) complaint and the bureaucratic apparatus that ensures its circulation.

A distinction between judicial and administrative complaints was commonly accepted until recently. However, if we label any complaint addressed to the authorities as an administrative complaint, we risk facing new intersections—this time due to historical features of the existence of administrative justice in Russia. The discourse of administrative justice which has been formed in recent years insists on the need to introduce specific terms denoting the law and specifying features of procedural relations in administrative cases: administrative case, administrative lawsuit, administrative complaint, administrative claimant (applicant), administrative defendant, etc. (Salishcheva 2003). In this sense, the concept of "administrative complaint" (substantively) means addressing violations and abuses stipulated by the administrative code. In contemporary Russia, a complaint with such content can be resolved both in court and by the administrative apparatus. Administrative (in content) complaints are considered as objects of my research only in cases where one was submitted to the authorities.

Research shows that these intersections go much deeper than the coincidence of definitions. Neither Soviet nor Tsarist Russia created a fully-fledged legal institution of administrative justice designed to resist the violation of the rights and interests of individuals, local communities, and public organizations by state and local governments. For many centuries, a complaint addressed to the authorities compensated for this gap in the judicial system (see Chapter 3).

In Tsarist Russia, attempts to introduce elements of administrative justice are usually associated with Alexander I (1801–1825), who extended the right to apply with "supplications to His Majesty" to all residents. The Commission for the Acceptance of Supplications to His Majesty, or the Chancellery of Supplications, was separated from the office of the General Master of Requests (*Reketmeister*) in the Senate in January 1810 and became a full-fledged state institution in January 1835. The legislation prohibited denunciations, but allowed "supplications or complaints, containing indication of abuse" (Nérard 2004). Illustrating the number of such requests, Margareta Mommsen writes that about 20,000 applications were filed annually in the late 1880s (Mommsen 1987:95).[6]

The only attempt to establish the administrative justice system was made when the Provisional Government came to power, in the period between March and October 1917. However, the idea did not take root and did not gain traction (Pravilova 2000:135). Having come to power, the Bolsheviks abolished the existing judicial system, including administrative courts. However, immediately after the Revolution, there emerged an acute need to deal with massive abuses of office. In 1918 the Committee of State Control prepared a proposal of the Committee for consideration of complaints on wrongdoing of officials and authorities. The proposal was considered at a special meeting, which found the establishment of administrative courts untimely and too complicated, and replaced it with the Bureau of Complaints (Zagriatskov 1924:34–35; Chechot 1973:62).

A new wave of interest in administrative justice arose during the years of New Economic Policy (NEP). Lawyers Matvei Zagriatskov, Vladimir Kobalevsky, and Arkadii Elistratov tried to find the origins of administrative justice in Soviet law. They attributed the complaints bureaus, the procuracy, insurance councils, land, housing, and other commissions as bodies implementing a form of administrative justice. Extrajudicial bodies, including the complaint mechanism, handled the bulk of such cases (Zagriatskov 1924).

In 1960–1970 the functions of administrative justice shifted to the judiciary. In 1970 the so-called functional theory of administrative justice became dominant. According to supporters of this approach, the absence of administrative courts did not mean the absence of administrative justice itself (Pravilova 2000:147). They gave a definition of administrative justice as the judicial procedure for resolving administrative disputes in jurisdictional bodies rather than a chain of administrative courts and concluded that administrative justice exists in the Soviet Union. In their opinion, it was presented in the form of a function implemented by the general courts and some para-judicial bodies.

Legislation of the late 1950s–1970s significantly expanded the competence of general courts in the field of administrative justice, giving citizens the right to appeal various categories of administrative violations in court. The Constitution of 1977 secured this right. However, only the 1989 law "On the procedure for appealing to court unlawful actions of state bodies and officials infringing the rights of citizens" and the 1993 law "On appealing to court actions and decisions violating the rights and freedoms of citizens" enforced guarantees on the protection of subjective public rights.

In recent years, interest in the issue of administrative justice has been increasing again. The main trend is related to the strengthening of judicial tools of administrative justice. In particular, the decision of the Constitutional Court of the Russian Federation confirmed the priority of the judiciary over the complaint mechanism in resolving administrative issues:

> the legislation on administrative offenses provides that the courts (judges) in the framework of administrative proceedings are vested both with the authority to hear cases of administrative offenses and bringing to administrative responsibility, and with the authority to monitor the legality and validity of decisions imposing administrative penalties, made by others authorized bodies (officials).
>
> (Constitutional Court of the RF 1999)

In 2015 the Administrative Code, which defined the procedures for administrative proceedings within the existing judicial system, was adopted. This strengthened the judicial apparatus, which implements the function of administrative justice. This also clarified the terminology, and the judicial system received another official confirmation of its dominance. However, the administrative court as an independent institution of the judicial system again was not created.

Today, despite support for the judicial method of resolving administrative issues, other ways are also available. The complaint mechanism, which has been realizing this function for decades and even centuries, remains an important addressee of appeals regarding violations by officials, authorities, and local self-government (Code of Administrative Court Proceedings 2015, Art. 6.1). The complaint to the authorities partly duplicates the function of opposing the actions or omissions of the authorities and local self-government with administrative justice to this day (see Chapter 5).

The confusion in terminology reveals the uncertainty that exists also in the institutional arrangement. The range of issues resolved through judicial and para-judicial administrative complaints is not delimited. The administrative complaint and judicial mechanisms are not isolated from each other. It is possible to appeal the results of an administrative complaint to a court (Code of Administrative Court Proceedings 2015, Art. 5, Clause 4), but it is not prohibited also to appeal the outcome of a trial through the mechanism of complaints. To this day, for some issues the administrative and judicial bodies receive equal numbers of complaints (see Chapter 6).

Multiple intersections in terminology, in functions, and in institutional structure characterize the sphere of administrative justice. For centuries, it was pushed out of the judiciary to para-judicial bodies and remained outside of the main processes of legal modernization. The history of the development of administrative justice allows us to trace multiple genealogical links between the complaint mechanism and the judiciary.

The context of complaint in Soviet society

The form of restoration of justice adopted by a society is deeply connected to patterns of social relations and social inequality, to its political system, and to features of the economy. Moreover, the form of restoration of justice not only depends on that context and reflects its features, but in a certain sense reproduces it and contributes to its assertion. To understand the meaning, role, and function of a complaint in Russian society, it is necessary to comment on all these statements.

Despite the fact that the reputation of the law as a regulatory system of society suffered greatly under the influence of Marxist-Leninist doctrine, the judiciary was not abolished entirely in any of the socialist countries. Already in the first years of Soviet power, a Soviet court system was established, and legislation was codified. The quality of the laws and the courts is arguable, but it is important that throughout the Soviet period, citizens had the opportunity to appeal to the courts, and judicial statistics show that they did.

On a number of issues, citizens could equally appeal to the court or to the authorities with their complaints. Certain types of civil cases (family law, labor law, housing law disputes, and non-claim cases) constituted about 70% of all civil cases in the early 1960s (Van den Berg 1985:158). The same set of issues—labor disputes, problems of housing and utility services, and consumer problems—are also brightly presented among the array of complaints addressed to the authorities.

Research data show that in authoritarian systems complaint mechanisms are more popular than the courts. For example, available Chinese statistics suggest that citizen use of complaining practices and *xinfang* bureaus far exceeds that of formal legal channels. According to the director of the national *xinfang* bureau, the number of applications totaled 8,640,040 during just the first nine months of 2002, corresponding with an annual rate of 11.5 million per year (Minzner 2006:105). By comparison, the entire Chinese judiciary handles six million legal cases annually. *Xinfang* channels rarely yield results for individual petitioners. According to a recent Chinese study, less than 0.2% of petitioners surveyed succeeded in having their complaints addressed (Ibid:106). Nevertheless, the mechanism is far more popular than legal institutions.

Inga Markovits, who had the unique opportunity to compare practices of dispute resolution in Eastern and Western Germany, also argues that in similar cases citizens of Western Germany applied to the courts much more frequently. “Despite a widely distributed, easily accessible system of lay tribunals, despite low court costs, uncrowded dockets, easily available legal advice, and official encouragement to make use of socialist courts, East German citizens do so only quite rarely” (Markovits 1986:744). Citizens had knowledge of the law, but did not apply to the courts. “It may be that some of them use their new knowledge to give added weight to informal petitions and complaints” (Ibid:745).

Markovits explains this phenomenon by three reasons. The first one is the dependence of every citizen on collectivity, personal relations, and inclusion in informal networks (Ledeneva 1998):

> The comparison suggests what socialist citizens seem to perceive themselves: That the socialist legal system does not treat them as isolated autonomous human beings, but (as in a family setting) as members of a collective, in need of support and guidance. The complaint, with its mixture of informality, collectivity, criticism, and concern seems best to reflect the legal philosophy of a state which refuses to accept the opposition of personal and societal interests and upon which the citizen knows himself to be dependent.
>
> (Markovits 1986:743)

People sue when they are socially unconnected with their opponent, when relationships are disrupted beyond repair, or when—as in the case of divorce—a suit is needed to sever a legal tie which in real life has already withered (Markovits 1986:746; Blankenburg, Schönholz, and Rogowski 1979; Blankenburg 1980:33; Galanter 1983). People who want to remain in continuous relationships, and for whom the relationships themselves are more valuable than compensation for individual grievances—e.g. business partners or colleagues—will not use the courts to settle their differences. People are more likely to sue, furthermore, if their claims involve money or are easily translatable into money. Socialist citizens cannot easily distance themselves from their state or their fellow citizen. Instead, many ties hold citizens and society together. One of these ties is ideology. More important, however, than ideological bounds are factual ties between people.

Kathryn Hendley comes to a similar conclusion about the unwillingness of the Soviet people to solve conflicts in courts. Investigating relations between neighbors in multiapartment houses, she found out that Soviet people make efforts to avoid serious litigations, no matter how difficult the conflict is. Solving problems inside of the community of neighbors or neglecting problems allows to save personal relations much better (Hendley 2017:69–70).

The second reason is connected with the lack of private property and relatively low significance of money in socialist society:

> Hence the widespread use of barter in socialist societies: In the GDR, housing, which cannot freely be bought, is increasingly exchanged through contracts to swap apartments, for instance. In the Soviet Union, suggestions have been made to award litigation victories in kind, in addition to rubles … . Without the social disconnection between prospective plaintiffs and defendants and without the universal utility of money, law seems to lose its usefulness as a means of resolving conflicts and coordinating interests.
>
> (Markovits 1986:750)

The distinction between rights and needs has little meaning in socialist administrative reality. In civil law, many consumer rights are not asserted through litigation (that is, as rights) but through complaints to local government bodies (that is, as needs), submitted without any means of pressuring authorities on whose fairness and generosity the complainant will have to rely (Ross and Littlefield 1978). A very large number of complaints deal with problems that in a capitalist legal system would be handled by the market: excessive waiting times for laundry service, a shortage of taxicabs, no oranges in the stores (Markovits 1986:737). For the average consumer, the planning and distribution system created unfavorable conditions. The amount of goods produced in the country was insufficient to meet the needs of all Soviet citizens. The planning and distribution system regularly failed, as a result of which even those goods that were produced in large quantities were unevenly distributed between urban and rural areas (Bogdanova 2015). Simultaneously, citizens and consumers had no regular channels for the market system feedback to express discontent and protect their rights.

The third reason is the nature of socialist law and the model of governance itself.

> The main moral support for socialist law does not come from its users and addressees, who, on the contrary, neglect and evade it, but from its proponent, the state … . Socialist law is very much the law of the socialist state, not of its citizens.
>
> (Markovits 1986:760)

It serves public institutions, and when all institutions are public, a citizen challenging their actions has a very slim chance of winning.

Soviet citizens really had little reason to address private issues to the courts. The complaint mechanism was much more relevant to the ideological doctrine, to the arrangement of society, power, economy, and social relations. While access to the courts was cheap, access to the complaint mechanism was free. Internal navigation of the applications made the mechanism convenient to use. The applicants did not need to know either rules of jurisdictions, nor legislation. In the late Soviet period the mechanism of complaints had outgrown dangerous repressive risks. Besides, complaining allowed one to preserve valuable informal relationships in comparison with litigation. The Soviet man had no need to protect his property, and a lawsuit in a state court against a state institution was fraught with so many risks that it was not worth the trouble. In the conditions of the Soviet system there was no point in demanding. It was more profitable to solicit.

The language of complaint, and what it tells us

In contrast to a lawsuit, a complaint initially does not have sufficient normative code for universalizing justifications of problems. To substantiate the request, a complainant must find proof of injustice and explain why intervention by the authorities is necessary. The language of the complaint, its cause, structure, and formula depend on context. In the Soviet context, the principle of writing complaints (to authorities) in the language of power held true (Kozlova and Sandomirskaia 1996:24).

Simultaneously, and exactly for this reason, the language of a complaint tends to be routinized and coded (Drew and Holt 1988). In all contexts the language of complaint finds its clichés. The interaction of the complainant with the addressee is determined by certain rules, which are public and are sustainable for a certain period of time. Studies show that the texts of complaints are always formulaic within a certain period, and they tend to change under the influence of external discourses.

While studying complaints from different periods of Russian history, many researchers note the relationship between the commonly used clichés and political language. Stephen Kotkin's book *Magnetic Mountain: Stalinism as a Civilization* offers a suitable illustration. In the chapter "Speaking Bolshevik," the author shows how the official language and rules of communicating with authority were transformed under the influence of Bolshevik discourse. As the Bolshevik regime grew stronger, official rhetoric penetrated into everyday language as well as into people's everyday ways of speaking about themselves (Kotkin 1995:217). Even those who were not required to learn the state language in order to interact within Soviet society mastered it gradually.

The Russian complaint addressed to the authorities has its own pragmatics, predetermined by two main tasks. The first task is to make the author understood by the authorities. This means that the form of presentation, the methods, and the arguments are focused on the perceptions of the authorities, on the concepts and arguments that they also use. The language of a complaint seeks a common code recognizable by both sides of the communication. The second task is to make the author noticed and heard among hundreds of other appeals, to force the addressee to react to the particular problem under conditions of limited resources (which they always were).

To what extent have the authors internalized the values of the political clichés in which they write? Accordingly, how rationally do the authors inscribe their requests in the framework of the legitimate? It is extremely important to raise these questions when examining complaints. Meanwhile, these questions are doomed to remain not fully answered. On the one hand, the language of a complaint is determined by contemporary political discourse; those in power must be spoken to in their own language (Kotkin 1995; Fitzpatrick 1996a; Kozlova and Sandomirskaia 1996; Nérard 2004). On the other hand, a complaint is a proprietary document grounded in a certain (either clearly stated or merely implicit) narrative, legal, and civic viewpoint informing the text. Finally, we can never know for sure if the author compiled the text by herself, or hired a "professional complainant." Probably the best answer to these questions is the one given by Israeli historian Igal Halfin, discussing how political discourse and the author of a subjective text mutually influence each other: "A historical actor is capable of creating new linguistic forms by interpreting and modifying existing political language, but his 'I' inevitably changes through this activity, and it is not up to him to foresee the nature of these changes" (Halfin and Hellbeck 2002:245).

I tend to view the complaint as a *fait accompli*. Based on this position, the following points are important. A complaint reflects its author's notions of how the authorities might fix the situation. The act of complaining demonstrates the author's belief in the addressee's ability to help, confirming her authority and legitimacy. At the same time, by choosing to complain to the powers that be, the writer reveals not only his or her notions of authority but also the general view of the world in which the complainant wishes to be located.

Complaint is a special pragmatic model. The complaint is trapped in the legitimate political discourse. This predetermines a complaint both as an action and as a text. A complaint is a request for help, assistance. At that moment, when the complaint begins to protest against anything, it turns into a claim, petition, or protest action. As long as the complaint is harmonized with the rules established by the authorities, it remains loyal. This can tell us a lot about the socio-political context that supports communication between citizens and the authorities in the form of complaint. At the same time, this very feature of the complaint imposes significant restrictions on its heuristic potential. Investigating complaints addressed to the authorities, we cannot find out which grounds of justice exist in the society in which it was written. This is because the complaint is too much determined by the situation of communication with the authorities. In fact, all that we can learn from the text of a complaint is what values and bases of justice have political legitimacy at the moment of writing; or in other words, what values and grounds of justice the authorities agree to recognize as legitimate. This is applicable to the form of complaint that has developed in Russia under the conditions of the official complaint mechanism, which has existed over many centuries and which the authorities have repeatedly tried to reform, but from which it was never able to escape completely.

How do we tell a legal modernization from a complaint?

The reason for filing a complaint is a particular problem situation, an imperfection in social reality. Compilation of the text of the complaint is accompanied by the selection of certain critical arguments by a particular complainant. Luc Boltanski and Laurent Thévenot offer a universal methodological instrument for the analysis of critical argumentation. Both Soviet and contemporary complaints allow for free narration of the problem. No code or set of rules of complaint drafting has been established. An author compiles and argues her complaint on the basis of her own comprehension of what is important and what is unimportant. *How* the authors of complaints learn which arguments carry more weight with the authorities—this is one of the central questions in the conception of critical capacity.

On the most general level, complainants are guided by common sense. Here certain explanations are needed. Common sense in Soviet society was a phenomenon repeatedly questioned by Western scholars. According to Frank Ellis, common sense, as well as reason and decency, "are assaulted often enough … The barrier between truth and lies is effectively destroyed" (Ellis 1998). It is most likely that there was no universal common sense that would be meaningful in all fields and dimensions of Soviet society. However, the late Soviet complaint produced a fairly reliable system of commonly known codes, understood both by addressees and complainants, which facilitated communication and enabled mutual understanding. It is obvious that justifications and arguments formed a quite sustainable system guiding the communication between citizens and public officials in cases of injustice. This system had its own axioms, rules, and taboos.

Complaining to particular authorities is a specific situation that requires specific justifications. The concept of a situated sense of justice, developed by Boltanski and Thévenot in later works on the analysis of everyday disputes (Boltanski and Thévenot 2000; Boltanski 2011), seems largely appropriate for analyses of complaints addressed to the authorities. According to this conception, the range of relevant justifications is restricted by the situation in which persons are placed (Boltanski and Thévenot 2000:211). Argumentation that is valid in one situation may be not valid in another. Yet Boltanski and Thévenot relate the situated sense of justice to general moral values existing in a particular society.

The situational sense of justice allows us to assume that sets of norms, rules, and generalizations which are used in argumentation—and which we perceive as common sense—are also multiple. Investigating the argumentation of complaints addressed to the authorities, we will not be able to reveal a general common sense prevailing in society. We may find out, however, which norms, rules, and generalizations the author found appropriate to use in a situation of complaint in a particular socio-political context.

In his recent work *On Critique: A Sociology of Emancipation*, Boltanski links critique firmly to institutions, by which he means those elements that define or construct social reality. These are always necessary to deal with "uncertainty, which is at the heart of social life" (Boltanski 2011: 70). The semantic function of an institution (Ibid:75) helps one to navigate a situation of uncertainty. The task of articulating and confirming what matters falls to institutions. This operation assumes the establishment of types, which must be fixed and memorized in one way or another (in the memories of elders, written legal codes, narratives, tales, examples, images, rituals, etc.), and often stored in definitions, so as to be available when the need arises, to qualify, in a situation of uncertainty, states of affairs that are the object of ambiguous or contradictory usage and interpretations. In particular, institutions must sort out what is to be respected from what cannot be (Ibid). For the complainant, this requires the skill of knowing exactly which institutions would consider their appeal. An appropriate setting of the vocabulary shows which institutions are granted the highest hope and trust. The presence and absence of a direct continuity between the declared problem and the responsibility of the institution is also informative.

As elsewhere, there is no formalized vocabulary and argumentation assigned to a specific institution. Everything that occurs in "institutions" constructed in the sense, is therefore far from being of a special institutional order, with a number of situations even unfolding in the register that we might characterize as "practical" (Ibid:80). To a greater or lesser extent, any complainant can possess so-called institutional competence. In the understanding of Boltanski and Thévenot, this competence is not only cognitive, but is above all a moral and practical quality. This is the ability to express universal value judgments and to coordinate actions and interactions on the basis of generally accepted higher principles, appropriate to specific situations (Koveneva 2007:61–62) and oriented towards a particular institution.

The relationships between institutions and criticism are mutually directed. On the one hand, institutions determine the semantics and argumentation of an application. On the other hand, institutions are formed under the influence of constant criticism from outside. Criticism is what ritualizes an institution, and what questions its expediency, provoking changes. The more opportunities for criticism an institution allows, the more easily it is able to transform, and vice versa. The more closed and regulated the institution, the less space for criticism it leaves. The rules established by the institution are primary, and criticism is derivative.

As indicated by the example of "wooden language" (Vail' and Genis 1996; Kotkin 1995), be it of a state, a party, a church, this use of language is founded on a catalogue of prescriptions and prohibitions—that is, on the basis of semantic violence. Semantics, which is the domain par excellence of institutions, would then completely prevail over the pragmatics of influence on the institute (Boltanski 2011:92). "Wooden language" has a very weak ability to provoke changes in an institution. In the case of Soviet and post-Soviet complaints addressed to the authorities, we can only talk about how the authors of complaints find, through a specific institutional vocabulary, a capable person who has sufficient power to help them.

Thus, in studying the text of complaints, I try to find sustainable generalizations that are clichéd. I draw attention to the arguments and justifications used by complainants. Remembering the limits of outcomes, which we may extract from the study of the complaints, I expect that the situational sense of justice is determined in many respects by contemporary ideas about political legitimacy, the operation of bureaucracy, and the general model of state-society interactions. Transformation of the language of complaint informs us first about transformations to the institutions of power. Examining the vocabulary of complaints, I do not expect to see the transformation of the legal consciousness of the people. The language of complaints was, and remains, too dependent on external discourses. What may be reliably suggested is how far the addressees will allow discussion in terms of law or, in other words, recognize the law as a norm of justice. It also reflects the search of complainants for the most influential and powerful force capable of protecting justice outside of the judiciary. Finally, institutional markers of language show the separation of the complaint mechanism from the judiciary.

Notes

1 *Oxford Dictionary.* Complaint. Retrieved on June 30, 2019 (https://en.oxforddictionaries.com/definition/complaint).
2 *Online Etymology Dictionary.* Complaint. Retrieved on June 30, 2019 (www.etymonline.com/index.php?allowed_in_frame=0&search=complaint).
3 *Cambridge Dictionary.* Petition. Retrieved on June 30, 2019 (https://dictionary.cambridge.org/ru/словарь/английский/petition).
4 *Oxford Dictionary.* Petition. Retrieved on June 30, 2019 (https://en.oxforddictionaries.com/definition/petition).

5 All the direct quotations from Nérard (2004) were translated by Elena Bogdanova.

6 On the view of Nérard, the counts of some other authors are more sophisticated. For example, Remnev writes about 9,267 solicitations between 1895 and 1899 (see: Remnev 1997:26). Mironov (2003:250) gives larger figures (11,582 in 1825; 21,382 in 1893; 32,336 in 1899; and 65,357 in 1908).

References

Almbjär, Martin. 2019. "The Problem with Early-Modern Petitions: Safety Valve or Powder Keg?" *European Review of History* 26(6):1013–1039.

Blankenburg, Erhard. 1980. "Möbilisierung von Recht." *Zeitschrift für Rechtssoziologie* 1(1):33–64.

Blankenburg, Erhard, Schönholz, Siegfried and Ralf Rogowski. 1979. *Zur Soziologie des Arbeitsgerichtsverfahrens*. Darmstadt: Luchterhand.

Bogdanova, Elena. 2015. "The Soviet Consumer – More Than Just a Soviet Man." Pp. 113–138 in Timo Vihavainen and Elena Bogdanova (eds.) *Communism and Consumerism. The Soviet Alternative to the Affluent Society*. Leiden and Boston: Brill.

Boltanski, Luc. 2011. *On Critique: A Sociology of Emancipation*. Cambridge: Polity Press.

Boltanski, Luc and Laurent Thévenot. 2000. "The Reality of Moral Expectations: A Sociology of Situated Judgement." *Philosophical Explorations* 3:208–231.

Cambridge Dictionary. Petition. Retrieved on June 30, 2019 (https://dictionary.cambridge.org/ru/словарь/английский/petition).

Chechot, Dmitrii. 1973. *Administrativnaia Iustitsiia. Teoreticheskie problemy*. Leningrad: Izdatel'stvo Leningradskogo Universiteta.

Dal', Vladimir. 1996[1863]. *Tolkovyi slovar' zhivogo velikorusskogo iazyka v 4 tomakh.* Tom 1. Zhaloba. SPb: Diamant.

Drew, Paul and Elizabeth Holt. 1988. "Complainable Matters: The Use of Idiomatic Expressions in Making Complaints." *Social Problems* 35(4):398–417.

Ellis, Frank. 1998. "The Media as Social Engineer." Pp. 192-223 in Catriona Kelly and David Shepherd (eds.) *Russian Cultural Studies: An Introduction*. Oxford: Oxford University Press.

Fitzpatrick, Sheila. 1996a. "Signals from Below: Soviet Letters of Denunciation of the 1930s." *Journal of Modern History* 68(4):831–866.

Fitzpatrick, Sheila. 1996b. *Stalin's Peasants: Resistance and Survival in the Russian Village after Collectivization*. Oxford: Oxford University Press.

Friedgut, Theodor. 1979. *Political Participation in the USSR*. Princeton: Princeton University Press.

Galanter, Marc. 1983. "Reading the Landscape of Disputes: What We Know and Don't Know (And Think We Know) About Our Allegedly Contentious and Litigious Society." *UCLA Law Review* 31(4):5–72.

Gitelman, Zvi and Wayne DiFrancesco. 1984. "Soviet Political Culture and Covert Political Participation." *American Political Science Review* 78:603–621.

Halfin, Igal and Jochen Hellbeck. 2002. "Interview." *Ab Imperio* 3:217–260.

Hendley, Kathryn. 2017. *Everyday Law in Russia*. Ithaca: Cornell University Press.

Henry, Laura. 2012. "Complaint-Making as Political Participation in Contemporary Russia." *Communist and Post-Communist Studies* 3–4(45):243–254.

Kotkin, Stephen. 1995. *Magnetic Mountain: Stalinism as a Civilization*. Berkeley: University of California Press.

Koveneva, Olga. 2007. "Grani opyta v svete amerikanskogo pragmatizma." *Chelovek. Soobshchestvo. Upravlenie*. 4:39–63.

Kozlova, Natal'ia and Irina Sandomirskaia. 1996. *Ia tak khochu nazvat' kino: "Naivnoe pis'mo": Opyt lingvo-sotsiologicheskogo chteniia*. Moscow: Gnozis.

Lebow, Katherine. 2014. "Autobiography as Complaint: Polish Social Memoir between the World Wars." *Laboratorium: Russian Review of Social Research* 6(3):13–26.

Ledeneva, Alena. 1998. *Russia's Economy of Favours*. Cambridge: Cambridge University Press.

Lozansky, Tanya. 1989. "The Role of the Dissident in the Soviet Union Since 1953." *The Concord Review* 2/1:1-22.

Markevich, Andrei. 2002. *Soldatskie pis'ma v tsentral'nye sovety kak istochnik dlia izucheniia obshchestvennykh nastroenii v armii 1917 g*. Moscow: Avtoreferat na soiskanie stepeni kandidata istoricheskikh nauk.

Markovits, Inga. 1986. "Pursuing One's Rights under Socialism." *Stanford Law Review* 38(3): 689–761.

Merl, Stephan. 2012. *Politische Kommunikation in der Diktatur: Deutschland und die Sowjetunion im Vergleich*. Göttingen: Wallstein.

Minzner, Carl F. 2006. "Xinfang: An Alternative to Formal Chinese Legal Institutions." *Stanford Journal of International Law* 42:103–180.

Mironov, Boris. 2003. *Sotsial'naia istoriia Rossii perioda imperii (XVIII – nachalo XX v.): v 2-kh tomakh*. T.2. Saint Petersburg: Dmitrii Bulanin.

Mommsen, Margareta. 1987. *Hilf mir, mein Recht zu finden. Russische Bittschriften von Iwan dem Schrecklichen bis Gorbatschow*. Frankfurt am Main: Ullstein

Nérard, François-Xavier. 2004. *Cinq pour cent de vérité la dénonciation dans l'URSS de Staline (1928–1941)*. Paris: Editions Tallandier.

Online Etymology Dictionary. Complaint. Retrieved on June 30, 2019 (http://www.etymonline.com/index.php?allowed_in_frame=0&search=complaint).

Orlova, Galina. 2004. "Rossiiskii donos i ego metamorfozy: Zametki o poetike politicheskoi kommunikatsii." *Polis* 2:133–145.

Oxford Dictionary. Complaint. Retrieved on June 30, 2019 (https://en.oxforddictionaries.com/definition/complaint).

Oxford Dictionary. Petition. Retrieved on June 30, 2019 (https://en.oxforddictionaries.com/definition/petition).

Pecherskaya, Natalia. 2012. "Looking for Justice: The Everyday Meaning of Justice in Late Soviet Russia." *Anthropology of East Europe Review* 30(2):20–38.

Pravilova, Ekaterina. 2000. *Zakonnost' i prava lichnosti: Administrativnaia iustitsiia v Rossii (vtoraia polovina XIX v.- oktiabr' 1927 g.)* Saint Petersburg: Institut Rossiiskoi Istorii RAN.

Remnev, Anatolii. 1997. *Kantseliariia proshenii v samoderzhavnoi sisteme pravleniia kontsa XIX stoletiia. Istoricheskii ezhegodnik*. Omsk: Omskii Universitet.

Ries, Nancy. 1997. *Russian Talk: Culture and Conversation during Perestroika*. Ithaca, NY: Cornell University Press.

Ross, Laurence and Neil Littlefield. 1978. "Complaint as a Problem-Solving Mechanism." *Law and Society Review* 12(2):199–216.

Salishcheva, Nadezhda. 2003. "Administrativnoe sudoproizvodstvo trebuet kodifikatsii." *Ezh-Iurist* 12:1–2.

Semionov, Anton. 2003. *Etimologicheskii slovar' russkogo iazyka*. Moscow: "IUNVES. Retrieved on June 30, 2019 (http://evartist.narod.ru/text15/011.htm).

Sokolov, Andrei. 1999. *Kurs sovetskoi istorii 1917-1940*. Moscow.: Vysshaia shkola.

Sukharev, Alexander (ed.). 2007. *Bol'shoi iuridicheskii slovar'*. Isk. Moscow: INFRA-M
Sungurov, Aleksander. 1998. *Funktsii politicheskoi sistemy: ot zastoia k postperestroike.* Saint Petersburg: Strategiia.
Utekhin, Il'ia. 2004. "Iz nabliudenii za poetikoi zhaloby." Pp. 274–306 in Albert Baiburin (ed.) *Studia Ethnologica: Trudy fakul'teta etnologii.* Saint Petersburg: Izdatel'stvo Evropeiskogo universiteta v Sankt-Peterburge.
Vail' Peter and Alexander Genis. 1996. *60-e: Mir sovetskogo cheloveka.* Moscow: NLO.
Van den Berg, Gerard. 1985. *The Soviet System of Justice: Figures and Policy.* Dordrecht: Martinus Nijhoff Publishers.
Vasmer, Max. 1967. *Etimologicheskii slovar' russkogo iasyka.* T.2. Zhalovan'e. Moscow: Progress.
Volkov, Sviatoslav. 1974. *Leksika russkikh chelobitnykh XVII veka: Formuliar, traditsionnye etiketnye i stilevye sredstva.* Leningrad: Izdatel'stvo Leningradskogo universiteta.
Zagriatskov, Matvei. 1924. *Administrativnaia iustitsiia i parvo zhaloby.* Moscow: Kooperativnoe izdatel'stvo.
Zhaloby passazhirov na vagony-restorany. 1934. Moscow: Steklograf.

Normative documents

Code of Administrative Court Proceedings [Kodeks administrativnogo sudoproizvodstva Rossiiskoi Federatsii] from March 8, 2015 No. 21-FZ. *KonsultantPlus.* Retrieved on July 19, 2019 (http://www.consultant.ru/document/cons_doc_LAW_176147/).
Constitution of the USSR [Konstitutsiia (osnovnoi zakon) SSSR], 1977. *Garant.* Retrieved on July 19, 2019 (http://www.constitution.garant.ru/DOC_1449448.htm).
Constitutional court of the RF in the Decree "In the case of the constitutionality of the second part of Article 266 and paragraph 3 of the first part of Article 267 of the RSFSR Code of Administrative Offenses in connection with complaints of citizens" [Konstitutsionnyi Sud RF v Postanovlenii "Po delu o proverke konstitutsionnosti chasti vtoroi stat'i 266.3 i chasti pervoi stat'i 267 Kodeksa RSFSR ob administrativnykh pravonarusheniiakh v sviazi s zhalobami grazhdan"] from of May 28, 1999, No. 9-P. 1999. *SZ RF No. 23.* Art. 2890.
Decree of the NKGK "Guidelines for Local Branches of the Central Bureau for Complaints and Statements" [Postanovlenie NKGK "O mestnykh otdeleniiakh Tsentral'nogo Biuro Zhalob i Zaiavlenii" (Prilozhenie)] from 24 May 1919. 1943. *Sobranie uzakonenii i rasporiazhenii pravitel'stva za 1919 g.* Moscow: Upravlenie delami Sovnarkoma SSSR.
Decree of Presidium of the Supreme Soviet of the USSR "On the Order for Considering Citizens' Suggestions, Statements, and Complaints" [Ukaz Presidiuma Verkhovnogo Soveta SSSR "O poriadke rassmotreniia predlozhenii, zaiavlenii i zhalob grazhdan"] from 12 April 1968. No. 2534-VII. *KonsultantPlus.* Retrieved on July 19, 2019 (http://www.consultant.ru/document/cons_doc_LAW_1929/).
Federal Law "On Appealing to the Court Actions and Decisions Violating the Rights and Freedoms of Citizens" [Zakon of RF "Ob obzhalovanii v sud deistvii i reshenii, narushaiushchikh prava i svobody grazhdan"] from 27 April 1993 No. 4866-1. *KonsultantPlus.* Retrieved on July 19, 2019 (http://www.consultant.ru/document/cons_doc_LAW_1889/).

Federal Law "On the Order of Consideration of Citizens' Applications in the Russian Federation" [Federal'nyi zakon "O poriadke rassmotreniia obrashchenii grazhdan Rossiiskoi Federatsii"] from 2 May 2006 No. 59-FZ. *KonsultantPlus.* Retrieved on July 19, 2019 (http://www.consultant.ru/cons/cgi/online.cgi?req¼doc&ts¼5684507820200621051699 2326&caheid¼6341A834A0DF5BBDFF43BE44B12D34E5&mode¼splus&base¼LAW&n¼283578&rn¼E1CB8E44A90433FE7135F1A230170A07#09858153796272937).

Law of the USSR "On the Procedure for Appealing Unlawful Acts of Officials Infringing the Rights of Citizens" [Zakon, SSSR "O poriadke obzhalovaniia v sud nepravomernykh deistvii organov gosudarstvennogo upravleniia i dolzhnostnykh lits, ushchemliaiushchikh prava grazhdan"] from 1989. Vedomosti Verkhovnogo Soveta SSSR 22, st. 416.

3 Development of the Soviet mechanism of complaints

A request for justice in the context of the socialist project

The mechanism of complaints prior to the Revolution: What did the Bolsheviks reform?

Substantial attempts at reforming the judiciary as it existed under the monarchy took place in the nineteenth century. Significant transformations in Russia's judiciary occurred in the latter half of the nineteenth century, most importantly due to Alexander II's 1864 reform. Among other things, the reform greatly simplified the system previously based on the estates of the realm. Prior to the reform, every estate used to have its own court. Instead, a unified judicial system was created, comprised of two kinds of courts, general and local. The Justices of the Peace and *Volost' Courts*[1] operated at the local level. District Courts and Courts of Justice constituted general settlements. The Governing Senate, made up of two cassation departments—in civil and criminal cases—remained the highest authority. Most important political cases were dealt with by the Supreme Criminal Court, which would only take up cases at the emperor's extraordinary command (Solomon 1996:20–21).

The 1864 reform postulated the fundamental principles of the judiciary: that a court of justice was to be independent, judges could not be removed from office, and procedural transparency and competitiveness of justice were to be observed. Besides, the reform instituted the jury, attorneys-at-law, and prosecution.[2] Altogether, 105 district courts and 14 courts of justice operated in Russia by the early twentieth century.

A 15-volume Code of Laws of the Russian Empire prepared by Michael Speransky served as a regulatory framework. A special emperor's manifesto of January 1, 1835 signed this code into law. No other code was adopted in Tsarist Russia. Despite considerable efforts by many Russian scholars and jurists, by 1917 the Civil Code (*Grazhdanskoe Ulozhenie*) was not yet ready for adoption. A draft of the Criminal Code had been prepared in 1903, but it was also not adopted. The rule of law did not become a universal practice. At the lowest levels of the judiciary, custom still played a vital role in conflict resolution (Burbank 2004).

Thus, in the second half of the nineteenth century a universal and rather modern judicial system came to be in Russia. The courts' function was to resolve conflicts and restore justice. However, a court procedure was subject to the Tsar's control up to the very last days of the monarchy, and this control was always a one-way street. In the words of John Quigley, "Under the tsars, no representative institutions of any consequence were established, and the courts did not exercise any significant control over the monarchy" (Quigley 2007:224).

Besides, a court of justice was not the only institution to protect citizens' rights and interests. Popular notions of how due order was to be restored were firmly linked to a patriarchal tradition of appealing to the Tsar, to the ideas of truth and justice, the Tsar's omnipotence and mercy, and the monarch's charismatic resistance to abuses of power by bureaucrats and the aristocracy. A hierarchical mechanism of complaining, including a (restricted, but still available) option to address the monarch directly, continued to play an important role as a means of restoring justice, as well as a way to affirm an established relationship between society and the state.

Similar to the judiciary, by the late nineteenth century the mechanism of complaints also went through multiple transformations and acquired consistency. An authority closest to the Tsar was the Emperor's Applications Committee. Next in the system of bodies dealing with citizens' petitions was the Special Tribunal for the preliminary consideration of complaints about the Senate departments' resolutions. It was created simultaneously with the Committee and, in essence, was one of the agencies acting on the Committee's behalf. The Committee, the Special Tribunal, and the General Assembly of the Senate were among the authorities to review complaints about the highest officials of the Russian Empire (Kabashov 2010:84). These three government bodies discharged an important function of compensating for the administrative injustice, for which Tsarist Russia did not have an independent institution (Pravilova 2000).

At the top of the system of bodies receiving complaints about the actions and resolutions of officials at a lower—governorate (*gubernia*)[3]—level stood one of the Senate's departments. This body considered appeals against resolutions by *gubernia* authorities, as well as final determinations by *gubernia*-level land surveys and other cases appertaining to the jurisdiction of the second department. Ministries also received complaints about the actions and resolutions by *gubernia* and district officials. At the lowest level among the organs receiving citizens' complaints were local authorities. They looked into complaints by private individuals, associations, and institutions about the actions and resolutions of county-level (*zemstvo*)[4] institutions and municipal governments as stipulated in the Statutes for the Provincial and County Institutions (1864).

In the late nineteenth century the discrepancy between the mechanism of complaints and the newly forming judiciary was felt acutely. In a broader sense, one could speak of a conflict between the judicial and administrative powers. The judicial system evidently clashes with the mechanism of complaints both at the institutional level and as far as its function of restoring justice is concerned. The Senate, performing executive, lawmaking, and judicial functions all at once, controlled both the courts and administrative bodies responsible for receiving complaints. Besides, by the very logic of monarchic governance, the Emperor was the source of supreme power capable of influencing both the court and complaint resolution.

The norms and practices used when working with complaints also demonstrated an affinity to court procedures. For the Committee to consider a complaint about some department of the Governing Senate, the complainant had to indicate what laws they thought were violated and list all the evidence and proof in support of their argument (Kabashov 2010:89). Thus, to an extent the mechanism of complaints emulated judicial procedure in that it took into consideration and passed resolutions on breaches of the law.

An awareness of these contradictions had immediate consequences for the Emperor's Applications Committee. In 1879 the Special Tribunal raised the question of the Committee's right to exist. It was suddenly discovered that the Applications Committee as an ancient institution for dispensation of royal mercy stands in glaring contradiction to the new judicial regulations adopted in 1864. Sergei Kabashov writes: "Open debates regarding the future of the Committee took place in the State Council in April 1884. As a result of the ministers' pressure, on June 9, 1884, Tsar Alexander III issued a decree dissolving the Applications Committee" (2010:84).

This did not, however, stop the stream of complaints. They kept coming in large quantities and demanded consideration. Over centuries, the practice of complaining to the Tsar turned into an important symbol of autocratic power. As one of the archetypes of public conscience, the idea of a "fair ruler" capable of solving every problem had defined the rules of political game in Russian society throughout the fifteenth to nineteenth century. It was impossible to just give up on such a vital means of support for the royal authority. Consideration of complaints submitted to His Majesty was delegated to the Chancellery for applications within the Emperor's headquarters, in whose jurisdiction it remained until March 20, 1895. This transfer of responsibilities indicated a return to archaic models of royal mercy from the past reigns (Ibid:84).

In 1895 Nicholas II, the last Russian Tsar, restored an independent central administrative organ—His Majesty's Own Chancellery for Receiving Applications, submitted in His Majesty's name. The same year saw the adoption of the Rules on the Order of Accepting and Redirecting Applications and Complaints Submitted to His Majesty (The Rules 1906). The jurisdiction of the Imperial Chancellery for receiving applications was greatly restricted by the end of the nineteenth century as compared to that established at the time of Alexander I. Only those solicitations could be submitted directly to the Tsar that could be resolved by means of granting royal mercy. A substantial part of complaints was transferred into the jurisdiction of ministries and department heads. This is important insofar as it shows that the Emperor's role in addressing complaints ceased to be practical and became more of a symbol. In turn, the mechanism of complaints transformed into a functional tool affirming the Emperor's power and mercy. This approach generally agreed with the logic of transitioning from patrimonial governance to a bureaucratic system of administrative and judicial institutions authorized by law to pass independent judgments (Kabashov 2010:87–88).

Increasing tensions between the development of legal practices and the mechanism of complaints were tangible not only at the royal chancellery's level. The same issues arose at the lowest levels. For instance, the institution of *zemskie nachal'niki* (bailiffs) stood in radical contradiction to the principles of rational judicial organization resulting from the judicial and administrative reform of 1889. This counter-reform in the sphere of judicial administration was carried out in most provinces of the European part of Russia based on the County Heads Law from July 12, 1889 (County Heads Law 1889). The reform reduced to naught one of the most important principles of the 1864 reform of the judiciary—the separation of the lowest court from local administration. Instead of separate administrative organs (district offices of peasant affairs) and judicial organs (elected commissioners of the peace and their councils), an institution of bailiffs was introduced to carry out both judicial and administrative functions in relation to peasants (Shatkovskaia 2000:47). The law allowed referring to local customs, which led to a lack of procedural unity in similar cases and the judges' negligence and arbitrariness.

Prior to the Revolution, court procedure and the mechanism of complaints were still very similar both institutionally and as regards to their normative base. While the very existence of the mechanism of complaints supported custom as a source of norms and justice, the court lacked the resources to fully give up applying the same norms to practice. Both the court and the mechanism of complaints were dominated by the monarch. Attempts at legal modernization notwithstanding, royal mercy remained the mightiest of powers. The population's lack of literacy and strong traditions of Christianity further bolstered this situation. A strengthening of institutions, whether judicial or executive, leads to their differentiation. The late nineteenth-century confrontation between the judicial institutions and the mechanism of complaints proved to be vital for the understanding of tensions escalating within the systems of governance, justice, and society as a whole. It also demonstrated the readiness, the possibilities, as well as the problems related to modernizing the sphere of law and state administration.

Multiple attempts at reducing the efficiency of the mechanism of complaints, and just as many efforts to keep it up, manifested clearly that by the end of the nineteenth century it remained in demand. The practice of complaining was an integral part of society's everyday life and remained a relevant way of restoring justice, especially among the mostly illiterate masses. Making this mechanism less relevant would require political will and further modernization of judicial institutions.

Thus the mechanism of complaints presented itself as a powerful means of supporting autocracy and its respective model of relationship with society. Sergei Kabashov dubs the mechanism of complaints "a mechanism for creating an organic unity of the monarch with the people" (2010:85). The mechanism of complaints was perfectly justifiable as a tool of centralizing power. From the principle "the monarch is the father of the people," it followed that the Tsar as a God's anointer and as a fighter against the bureaucrats' lies can never remain indifferent to his subjects' suffering, even if a show of mercy contradicts the law. The monarch's sustained efforts at safeguarding the mechanism of complaints testify that he was, among other things, expected to serve as a constituent supporting the actual model of autocracy.

The very first attempts at reforming the legal system showed that the mechanism of complaints stands in conceptual contradiction to modernization of the court and the judiciary on the whole. A strengthening of the law inevitably resulted in the weakening of the monarch's significance and undermined his authority as the principal, supreme source of justice and a religious figure. Despite all attempts to involve the mechanism into a general process of modernization, it remained an institution rooted in an archaic, patriarchal societal structure. A weakening of the mechanism's role undermined the entire model of autocratic power and, simultaneously, the established contract between power and society. It was the decentralization of power, previously concentrated in the Tsar's hands, and the multiplication of power institutions capable and legally authorized to pass judgment on many administrative issues that led to the final demise of the sacred patrimonial principle. Attempts at safeguarding autocratic institutions revealed a tendency to oppose legal modernization, which would push society into a certain pathway that would be difficult to turn away from.

Ultimately, the pre-revolutionary experience made it clear that the mechanism of complaints functions as an instrument of support for an autocratic power only when there is an actual monarch at the end of the line and communication is effective. A mechanism of complaints that does not generate a response does the opposite; it weakens the legitimacy of the royal rule. All that reforms of the mechanism of complaints, intended to expand autocracy's social base, could do against the backdrop of the judiciary's growing power was create an illusion of influence and greatly complicate the system of state governance. The newly formalized institutions had limited access to actual administrative issues, whereas informal institutions enjoyed an unduly large range of powers. As a result, the mechanism of complaints lost much of its efficiency, with an immediate detrimental effect on autocracy's prestige.

Law and justice in Soviet society

The 1917 Revolution played a very special role in the development of Russian law and the judiciary. Institutionally, both the court system and administrative apparatus have undergone radical transformations during the 70 years of the socialist regime. A socialist society also produced a peculiar normative base, which determined how conflicts were resolved and justice restored. This applied to legislation, as well as the general principles and values regulating social interactions in socialist society. Scholarship has dubbed this type of legal system socialist, or social. This chapter mostly looks into how the mechanism of complaints was built into the general assortment of ways to restore justice available to citizens of the USSR, how it was organized, and how it served as an institutional structure channeling a request for justice.

The *first reason* for radical changes occurring after the 1917 Revolution in the sphere of law and the foundations of justice lay in the total rebuilding of everything related to the Tsars—one of the revolution's major political promises. Following through on this promise brought about dramatic consequences for the judiciary. A Decree "On Court" No. 1 adopted on November 22, 1917, dissolved all pre-existing judicial institutions. In the first draft of his article "The Immediate Tasks of the Soviet Government," Lenin wrote:

> the absolute duty of the proletarian revolution was not to reform the judicial institutions, but to destroy them completely, sweep away the entire old court and its apparatus. This necessary task was accomplished successfully by the October Revolution.
>
> (1969a[1918]:162–163)

By 1922, a new court reform had been prepared. The Statute on the Judiciary of the Russian Soviet Federative Socialist Republic (RSFSR), adopted on November 11, 1922, set up a three-level system of general courts. The lowest level was represented by People's Courts (*narodnye sudy* or *narsudy*). These courts differed from their predecessors—Justices of the Peace—in their jurisdiction. The level of local courts, which included the Justice of the Peace and the Volost' Courts, and were closest to the people, were abolished. In the case of an unsatisfactory decision of the People's Court, the appeal could be submitted to a governorate (*gubernia*) level, but no further (Solomon 1996:21–22). The Supreme Court was established as the highest level of the judiciary and a supervisory body for all types of courts, however, under the Soviet system it was never completely independent. Judges of the Supreme Court were appointed by the Presidium of the Supreme Council of the USSR and later elected by the Supreme Court of the RSFSR.[5] The higher the court, the more desirable it was for a judge to have professional legal training. However, this was not a requirement for any court, including the Supreme Court. Much more important was the candidate's compliance with such criteria as public and party work experience, loyalty to the ideas of Socialism (the so-called "revolutionary consciousness"), their working-class background, and later, party membership (Ibid:30–31).

The decree On Court No. 1 abolished the laws of the former regime as contradicting the ones newly adopted by the All-Russian Central Executive Committee (VTsIK) and the Council of People's Commissars (SNK). Over the first years of the Soviet government, a lot of effort was invested into creating a new regulatory base. In 1918–1922, the first wave of codifying the new legislation took place.[6] The haste with which the first Soviet legislation was adopted took a toll on its quality. A researcher of the language of the first Soviet laws remarks on their extremely broad statements and an abundance of unclear definitions (Feldman 2006). This is partly to do with the general principles of the Bolshevik, and later socialist judicature, which granted judges quite a lot of freedom to interpret offenses and correlate judgments with the norms of socialist morality. Lenin also insisted that Soviet law be simple and popular and above all avoid the bureaucratic deformations he had encountered during his short career as a lawyer under the Tsar. But the more functions Lenin attributed to the law, the more difficult it would prove to keep it simple (Solomon 1996:28).

The freshly minted regulatory base suffered from multiple gaps. In spite of the declared principle to ban the Tsarist legislation, some of the earlier laws were acceptable to use during the first decades of the Soviet regime. As Stalin said in a conversation with the British author Herbert Wells, " If [...] any of the laws of the old order can be utilized in the interests of the struggle for the new order, the old laws should be utilized."[7] Also, in the process of compiling the Criminal Code of 1922 recourse was made to the project of the Criminal Code developed in 1903, but never fully enacted (Ibid:29).

New Soviet legislation was not supposed to go against the main premises of the Marxist-Leninist doctrine. Thus, certain legal spheres were doomed to remain underdeveloped or to be pushed out from the judiciary and into paralegal structures. This was especially true of civil law as pertaining to the protection of individual rights, private property rights, labor law, housing law, and laws protecting an individual's honor and dignity. Rejected for ideological reasons was administrative law regulating public relations in the sphere of governmental bodies' managerial activities and public officials' actions in the process of performing executive functions on behalf of the state. This area of law was supposedly relevant exclusively to a bourgeois society where policing and tensions between those in power and the populace were believed to exist. In contrast, socialist society would build on the principle of close-knit partnership between the power and the citizens and on the immediate involvement of the latter in state governance.

The *second* reason for a radical transformation of legal sphere under the Soviet regime follows from the powerful influence of the Marxist doctrine proposing an idiosyncratic vision for how public relations are to be regulated. Law was understood primarily as a bourgeois society's regulatory system. All law was necessarily class law, cementing the power of the ruling class and repressing the others. Human rights were "nothing but the rights ... of egotistic man ... , who is separated from other men and from community" (Marx 1970[1875]:44). According to the Marxist-Leninist doctrine, Socialism—a formation Russia entered through the Revolution—is a transitional phase on the way to a classless society with no private property and no priority given to individual rights—in other words, any of the things that the law protects in a bourgeois society.

The role of law in a socialist society became the subject of a heated debate among legal scholars in the 1920s. During the years of the formation of the Soviet system, the opinion was widespread that law as a system of regulating society was destined to dissolve. In particular, Evgenii Pashukanis, a famous legal scholar and the Deputy People's Commissar of Justice in 1936–1937, recognized the specific nature of the "Soviet law." Pashukanis (and many other Marxists) compared this new "inauthentic" law and the state, established under the dictatorship of the proletariat, to authentic law and state. He believed that not being rooted in the authentic legal paradigm would lead to the disappearance of the "Soviet law" in the future.

Marxism therefore hoped for a society in which goods would be distributed not in exchange for their equivalent value measured in terms of money, labor, or honors but, as in a family, in response to each recipient's individual needs. Just like in a family, interactions would be governed not by formal rules, designed and applied by professionals, but by informal, *ad hoc*, fact-specific decisions among comrades (Pashukanis 1980[1924]).[8] To Pashukanis and his contemporaries, with the establishment of Socialism, the market (and thus law) in the Soviet Union would be driven out by the Economic Plan, formal rules would be replaced by technical specifications, due process required to resolve conflicts would be superseded by the "unity of purpose" among the comrades bent over a common task (Ibid:137).

Gordon Smith (1988:138) argues that Vladimir Lenin accepted the Marxist conception of law and the state as instruments of enforcement that belonged to the ruling class. He presumed the eventual transition to a communist society in which enforcement instruments of the state and law would no longer be necessary and would, indeed, wither away. The situation Lenin confronted in the lawless and chaotic days following the overthrow of the Provisional Government in November 1917, however, called for a legal system to provide law and order. He wrote:

> There is no doubt that we live in a sea of illegality and that local influences are one of the greatest, if not the greatest, obstacle to the establishment of legality and culture … . It is clear that in light of these conditions we have the firmest guarantee … that the Party create a small, centralized collegium capable of countering local influences, local and any bureaucratism and establish an actual, uniform conception of legality in the entire republic and the entire federation.
>
> (Lenin 1970[1922]:200–201)

Andrei Vyshinskii, the procurator of the USSR in 1935–1939, formulated the Marxist-Leninist version of the understanding of the role of law in socialist society. Vyshinskii denied the disappearance of law as a system and advocated the establishment of the so-called proletarian law. In his work "*Revoliutsionnaia zakonnost' i zadachi sovetskoi zashchity*," he affirmed the conception of law as a means of fighting for Socialism and of reprisals against the enemies of socialist society (Vyshinskii 1934:18–20).

As a result, the socialist judicial system acquired very distinctive features, such as:

- the law plays second fiddle to ideology and socialist morality (Lukach 2004:450);
- collective rights trump individual rights;
- the judicial process is not an adversarial system; public prosecution is considered to be a "provider of justice";
- the judiciary is subordinate to the Communist Party.

Throughout the Soviet period, the judiciary evolved and changed. This process, like many other socio-political processes taking place in Soviet society, was characterized by certain ambiguity. *On the one hand*, the entire judicial system was expected to constantly reaffirm its subordination and loyalty to Marxist-Leninist teachings to highlight the differences from the bourgeois judicial system. A 1956 Soviet legal dictionary defined the principle of the rule of law as an "unscientific concept depicting the bourgeois state as one in which there is supposedly no place for arbitrariness on part of the executive authority and where law and legality are supposed to reign supreme" (Kudriavtsev 1956). The concept, according to the dictionary, is used "in a demagogic way" by the bourgeoisie of many countries "in their class interests" in order "to inculcate harmful illusions in the masses, to mask the imperialist essence of the contemporary bourgeois state and its law" (Quigley 1990:206).

On the other hand, as the Soviet regime stabilized, the Soviet legal institutions also did, but not without undergoing some modernization along the way. Even during the blackest years under Stalin, the rule of law was occasionally restored, with higher standards of professional training demanded of specialists, the language of the laws made more precise and to the point, and the Constitution amended and adopted (1918, 1936, 1977). The degree to which these changes correlated with the principle of supremacy of the law is open to discussion, however, attempts to bolster an established regime through constitutional order are valuable in and of themselves. Additionally, historians usually distinguish two waves of law codification: one during the short period between 1922 and 1924, another beginning in the late 1950s and lasting until the demise of the Soviet system.[9]

Thus, despite its stark contradiction to Marxist-Leninist teachings, the judiciary system did not disappear under the Soviet regime. The Bolsheviks assumed the typical monarchic ambiguity in regard to restoring justice. In pre-revolutionary Russia, the law as the body of basic regulations competed with customary practices, whereas Socialism developing alongside the judiciary paved the way for para-judicial mechanisms based on a large extent on newly formed socialist morality. In Tsarist Russia, the law failed to become the one and only principle regulating public relations; the socialist conditions made this scenario simply impossible.

Just like the judiciary was not entirely separated from the executive, so also the general separation of power in the Soviet state was rather tentative. The branches of power were distinguished nominally, however, their functions and ranges of responsibilities were neither clearly defined nor always observed. Meanwhile, the revolutionary interruption and denial of monarchical inheritance also brought a number of modernizing steps. The Bolsheviks project brought the first experiences of the codification of legislation. Besides, its anti-monarchist foundations destroyed a pattern of the divine origins of justice, which served the basis of monarchical power.

The bureaucracy of complaints in early Soviet years

The Tsarist mechanism of complaints met the same fate as the judiciary. A Decree by the Council of People's Commissars of the Russian Federation (SNK) from December 6, 1917, entitled "On the Abolition of Chancellery for Receiving Applications under the Provisional Government" and signed by the chair of the

SNK Vladimir Lenin, finally disbanded the former Chancellery for Receiving Applications in His Majesty's Name and transferred all of its affairs under the jurisdiction of relevant Soviet institutions.

The decree stipulated that Soviet citizens were to address their complaints to the newly formed Soviet administrative and judiciary organs. This does not necessarily mean that those organs emerged right away or that they discharged their duties efficiently. It took a few decades for the administrative and judiciary structures to take shape. The early days do, however, offer a vivid picture of the tensions and twists and turns of the new incarnation of the mechanism of complaints in the context of a socialist state this time. In its new format the mechanism of complaints may well be considered among the most significant elements of the organization and management of the Soviet state that allows for a better understanding of the new perception of power, the rapport between citizens and the state, and the coexistence of this mechanism with the legal system of the early Soviet period.

The new interpretation of the Tsarist mechanism of complaints: Advantages and objectives of the Soviet version

Lenin's ideas within the framework of the Constitution of the RSFSR, ratified in July 1918, laid the foundations for an important normative document to legitimize Soviet citizens' right to complain—The Resolution of the Sixth Extraordinary All-Russian Congress of Soviets "On the Exact Observance of Laws " (1918) that legally obliged all public officials and institutions of the RSFSR to accept complaints from "any citizen of the Republic wishing to appeal against their actions, unnecessary delays, or hardships in their lawful claims." This marked a substantial innovation in how the mechanism of complaints operated in that protection of citizens' interests was now seen as the *duty* of powers that be. All pre-revolutionary attempts at modernization notwithstanding, resolving a complaint under the Tsars had always been up to the solicitation's recipient's mercy and, ultimately, up to the monarch.

The same resolution also affirmed the universal right to file complaints. This, too, distinguished the newly created mechanism from its pre-revolutionary counterpart. The major drawbacks of the mechanism of complaints under the Tsars consisted in its estate-based nature and the limited range of issues that could be appealed. In spite of the detailed regulation of the procedure, no legal norms existed that would direct the work of the office receiving a complaint. No wonder that the majority of complaints were forwarded exactly to those departments or institutions whose resolutions or actions were being contested. Additionally, the complex procedure of submitting an application to His Majesty required special knowledge that only one estate, namely the gentry, would have possessed (Lobacheva 1999:102).

Another important innovation in the understanding of complaints and their function was introduced by the Decree of SNK of the RSFSR from December 30, 1919, "On the Elimination of Red Tape," which set the guidelines for submitting complaints to any Soviet institution and prescribed the procedure for their consideration. This legal act was especially significant in that it declared the principle of *glasnost'* (publicity), according to which all citizens' complaints without exceptions were to be given equal consideration. This was the third radically novel feature of the new mechanism of complaints. The laws of the Russian Empire used to impose strict limitations on the kinds of complaints public authorities could consider based primarily on their contents (Kabashov 2010:116–117).

Applying each of these principles in practice had its own issues, at times rather serious. However, as compared to its predecessor, the Soviet edition of the mechanism of complaints had indeed become more accessible to various demographics. The literacy campaign launched by the Bolsheviks also made addressing the authorities easier. Thus by expanding the scope of opportunities to get in touch with powers that be, the Soviets definitely managed to give a convincing demonstration of advantages of the new regime.

Setting up the bureaucracy of the Soviet mechanism of complaints

Just like in Tsarist Russia and in most socialist systems, the Soviet mechanism of complaints was set up as a structure of regulatory bodies controlling authorities. According to the logic of Soviet state administration, regulatory bodies controlling authorities were part of an executive administration.

In July 1918 the Tsar's Central Control Collegium was transformed into the People's Commissariat of State Control (NKGK) within the Council of People's Commissars (SNK) of the RSFSR. Over the first seven to eight years, the mechanism of complaints developed to Lenin's plan. It was conceived as an efficient instrument of control from below that was capable of influencing the system of management, as well as a tool for developing a socialist model of democracy. To Lenin's mind, this was to be a centralized mechanism with its own hierarchy, independent from local public authorities and largely reliant on average citizens' active involvement and conscientiousness. However, the population's lack of involvement in public affairs as well as the shortage of necessary specialists left virtually no chances for these plans to come to fruition. The newly created apparatus faced a much more mundane task of managing the never-ending stream of complaints about all sorts of problems that required immediate attention (Kabashov 2010:114–115).

In April 1919, the VTsIK and the SNK of the RSFSR issued a Decree "On State Control" that charged the NKGK with ensuring that:

> all kinds of complaints and statements are being received and processed correctly in all institutions, as well as with forming a special office within the NKGK for receiving statements about the wrongdoings, abuses, and offenses by officials, for consideration of these statements by the State Control.
>
> (Decree of VTsIK and SNK 1919)

The Decree was, in fact, just an injunction, as it did not offer any guidelines for processing complaints. The spirit of resistance to Tsarist bureaucracy, the loyalty to revolutionary ideas, and the presence of regulatory bodies were to serve as the core regulator. For the next few decades, obedience to the party line and loyalty to revolutionary ideas became the major virtues expected from those running the mechanism of complaints (Nérard 2004). A Decree of the NKGK from May 4, 1919, created the Central Bureau for Complaints and Statements, whereas a Resolution from May 24, 1919, ratified the Guidelines for Local Branches of the Central Bureau for Complaints and Statements (signed by the People's Commissar of State Control Joseph Stalin). Local bureaus for complaints and applications were formed in almost every provincial town, district, and even some counties of the RSFSR. Originally, their job was to receive and sort complaints and forward them to the correct recipients. This led to the appearance of a universal network of specialized governmental bodies involved in processing citizens' complaints. Kabashov (2010:115) notes multiple similarities between this new structure and the old Tsarist bureaucracy and calls it the fifth attempt in the history of Russia to reconstruct the *Chelobitnyi Order* as a function of the state, albeit under new political conditions.

Over the summer of 1919, the NKGK also issued the guidelines for provincial bureaus for complaints and applications and the guidelines for bureaus within Soviet public institutions. According to these documents, a bureau had to include a legal adviser, auditors investigating a complaint, and one representative each from the Bolshevik party and the trade unions. A bureau had to have an office with a secretary. All incoming complaints were recorded and forwarded for preliminary consideration to the person in charge or their deputy. Unsubstantiated complaints were rejected and the complainant informed. Complaints and statements requiring an investigation were, at the request of the person in charge or their deputy, forwarded to a respective state authority, the audit department of the provincial branch of State Control, or to an employee of the bureau for a closer look (Buliulina 2010:100).

In the early years, the mechanism of complaints underwent a very intensive development. By the end of 1919, three independent auditing systems existed in the country: NKGK, institutional control boards, and workers' inspectorates. The volume of complaints to the People's Commissariat grew yearly: from 26,529 grievances in 1919 to 47,322 in 1920 (Kabashov 2010:116). In order to bring this mechanism closer to the people, on February 8, 1920, the NKGK was reorganized as the People's Commissariat of the Working-Peasant Inspection (NK RKI). Local-level bureaus actively engaged workers and peasants in processing complaints. In fact, the early development of the mechanism of complaints was true to Lenin's ideas in that it had a central headquarters (The Central Bureau for Complaints at NK RKI) as well as independent local bureaus relying on help from actively involved population.

During the first years of the Soviet regime, the bureaucracy of complaints was created outside of the judiciary, although closely connected to it. Already in his Draft Theses for the Resolution "On the Exact Observance of Laws" from November 2, 1918, Lenin defined the court as a regulatory body for abuses by the bureaucracy of complaints: "V. A clearly unfounded, grossly abusive protocol requirement is to be prosecuted in court" (Lenin 1969b[1918]:130). Somewhat later, on June 30, 1921, a Circular Directive of the VTsIK "On the Order of Submitting Complaints and Statements" recorded one more reason for the mechanism of complaints to liaise with courts: "in connection with investigating complaints and statements of malicious or obviously slanderous nature" (Circular Directive 1921, Art. 3). These, according to the Directive, are punishable by sentencing in a court of justice.

The early 1920s, when the New Economic Policy (NEP) was declared, brought about the need for stable political structures and relations. NEP breathed life into precisely those spheres of life that the courts refused to deal with: individual entrepreneurship, renewal of trade and market relations, and the revival of the national economy. Intensive development of a depressed economy naturally fostered conflicts between salespeople and consumers and between entrepreneurs, as well as workplace grievances, complaints about the system of distribution, etc. Three independent structures to vet complaints that had come to exist by the end of 1919—the NKGK, institutional control boards, and workers' inspectorates—were overwhelmed with the volume of complaints. The alarm system in the form of a network of various structures receiving complaints and applications was thus considerably reinforced. The Circular Directive "On the Order of Submitting Complaints and Statements" stated that, in addition to the Central Bureau for Complaints of the NK RKI, the Presidium had formed a special department that would "simultaneously and on the same basis" also be receiving complaints from citizens (Circular Directive 1921). Departments for processing workers' complaints were formed in every central and local public agency, enterprise, and institution.

It was approximately at this time that the mechanism of complaints, until then powered by the executive branch alone, was additionally propped up by the party. Based on the decision of the Tenth Congress of the Bolshevik party in March 1921, party auditing committees were set up in the center, regions, and provinces in order to receive complaints and statements. Party membership was irrelevant; anyone could lodge a complaint or make a statement (*Desiatyi s"ezd* 1963:311).

In the following years, executive and party branches became the core of the mechanism of complaints. From 1923 to 1934, there was a joint organ of party and administrative control (TsKK-RKI) that resulted from the amalgamation of the state government body NK RKI and the Central Control Commission (TsKK) of the All-Russian Communist Party. The People's Commissar of the RKI stood at the helm of this joint party-state agency.

Functions of the Soviet mechanism of complaints

In the context of a newly formed socialist system, the mechanism of complaints was supposed to do a lot more than settle private disputes. Administrative management required information about the state of things on the ground. Mass complaints have traditionally been used to keep the authorities abreast of the problems, discontent, and social tensions. Besides, in the early years of the Soviet regime, at the time of the deepest institutional crisis, the mechanism of complaints took over important coordinating functions. According to the Decree of NKGK from May 24,1919, local bureaus for complaints were to assist members of the public in navigating the mechanism by receiving complaints and forwarding them to relevant authorities. This was meant to help citizens flustered by their lack of understanding of how the new system of governance worked and to ensure communication efficiency. Apart from helping citizens find out where to address their complaints, complaints bureaus were also responsible for maintaining mutual understanding between a complainant and the accused (institution, agency, or official) by making them provide explanations and report to the Central Bureau for Complaints:

> For complaints that do not contain specific indications of abuse and improper actions, but express only general dissatisfaction with one or another side of the Soviet apparatus, the head of the Bureau demands that the institution that caused the dissatisfaction explain the reasons for the latter. Upon receiving explanations, the head of the Bureau briefly reports their contents to the complainant and sends the file itself, with all the materials, to the Central Complaints Bureau.
>
> (Decree of the NKGK 1919, Art. 3)

As a matter of fact, bureaus for complaints were tasked with "educating" both citizens and officials and teaching them new communication rules and ways to resolve disputes and protect their interests. Given an acute lack of normative base capable of regulating public relations, the regime relied on a customary and widely known practice that had for centuries safeguarded stable contact between society and the authorities. The establishment of the mechanism of complaints gave citizens an opportunity to restore justice, which was especially valuable at the peak of judiciary crisis. The mission set for the mechanism of complaints and the powers its structures were endowed with invite a conclusion that in the Soviet system, the mechanism of complaints was from the very outset seen as a substitute for judicial institutions in its own right and an integral element of the socialist legal system.

The first decrees positioned the mechanism of complaints as a tool for protecting revolutionary lawfulness. Its traditional job of releasing social tension got quietly complemented with a very specific mission to protect and popularize the very idea of the new regime. Lenin wrote about this in his Draft Theses for the Resolution "On the Exact Observance of Laws" (Lenin 1969b[1918]:129–131). In this context, protection of legitimacy did not at all imply the supremacy of the law or a call to strict abiding by the law. New legislation had not even been passed at the time. The Bolsheviks' early texts interpreted the law much like the order established by the newly formed state. Accordingly, protection of lawfulness meant loyalty to this order, obedience to the authorities' directions, and sympathy towards revolutionary and Marxist-Leninist ideas (development of revolutionary conscience). In fact, protection of lawfulness equaled protection of the new state. Perversity of the Bolshevik understanding of the law and lawfulness notwithstanding, it is nevertheless remarkable that attempts at legitimizing the newly created state built, even if only superficially, on the categories of law and order.

The procuracy

One more organ to play an important role in the functioning of the Soviet mechanism of complaints was created in 1922. The procuracy was restored five years after its abolition. One of the reasons why public prosecution was disbanded after the October Revolution was the belief that in the Soviet state, administrative authorities would be perfectly able to exercise supervisory functions. However, the first years of the Soviet state's existence made it abundantly clear that this was not happening.

The Soviet procuracy was created as an independent agency in between the judiciary and administrative branches of power. According to the 1922–1936 legislation, the procuracy did not depend on federal authorities, local organs of self-governance, and public unions. Meanwhile, Glenn Morgan's (1966) statement that "the Procuracy has always been the arm and the eye of the Party—not its overseer with respect to the Party itself" remained valid for the entirety of its Soviet existence. Leon Boim wrote:

> The Prokuratura is neither prepared nor designed—by law, Party decisions or by its own principles or structure of responsibility—to defend the citizen against the State and Government, even in case of clear violation of explicit laws or civil rights. As part of the state apparatus, it constitutes an instrument of the regime, not of justice.
>
> (1974:511)

The main purpose of the Soviet procuracy was to supervise and to ensure faithful observance of the laws in the name of the state. It was, therefore, a self-contained state institution exercising control over law enforcement—keeping in mind that during Stalin's rule "the observance of legality" was almost nil, while during Khrushchev's period the situation greatly improved (Boim 1978:viii).

According to Lenin's principles as articulated in a well-known letter "On the 'double' subordination and legality," the Prosecutor General only passed judgment regarding legality, made sure the law was observed, and checked for violations. Particularly, Lenin (1970[1922]:100–102) wrote:

> The prosecutor has the right and obligation to do only one thing: to watch over the establishment in reality of a uniform conception of legality in the entire republic, notwithstanding local differences and in spite of local influences.

Like many prosecutors and Ombudsmen elsewhere, the Russian procurator also received and investigated citizens' complaints and grievances under the procuracy's power of "general supervision" (Smith 2007:1). From the moment of its restoration in 1922, the procuracy engaged in working with complaints at different levels. The bulk of processing was, of course, done by administrative authorities, but a similar mission of protecting socialist legality obliged the prosecutor to act in tune with the mechanism of complaints. A Circular Decree of Presidium of the VTsIK No. 130 from April 20, 1930, "On measures for consideration of peasants' complaints," directed the procuracy to pay special attention to working with complaints from peasants and Red Army soldiers. Among methods of prosecutorial work were mentioned "visits to the countryside, special periodic acquaintances with the work of village councils and district executive committees (RIK) on peasant complaints, instructions received in the course of work, and links with kolkhoz and poor-middle peasant population of the village" (Circular Decree of VTsIK 1930).

As the citizens' right to complain was semi-informal and as they had no legal means to enforce an investigation of their complaint upon the procuracy, the system could hardly be regarded as an effective guardian of citizens' rights (Boim 1974:511). With respect to supervision over the section of the laws concerning the handling of citizens' statements and complaints, the main concern is with ensuring the interests of the regime and the party and strict implementation of their policies, as expressed in the legislation concerned. Still, the objective of these laws is to protect citizens' rights, and the supervision of the procuracy over their strict execution, disclosure of deficiencies, and actions taken against persons guilty of violating these important laws undoubtedly provide a real defense of such rights (Boim 1978:x). As a result, the procuracy reviews of citizen complaints helped ensure that officials operating the welfare state (labor protection, pensions, housing) observed legal norms (Smith 1978, 1996).

In fact, for the mechanism of complaints the restoration of procuracy meant a bureaucratic expansion, as it added one more addressee for citizens to direct their complaints, and also one more body monitoring the quality of processing these complaints. Besides, the prosecution's involvement in the mechanism of complaints brought it considerably closer to judicial institutions both structurally and functionally. Later on, a thorough analysis of complaints and statements became an important function as explicated in the USSR's Prosecutor General's order, "On the Procedure for Resolving Citizens' Complaints and Applications by Organs of Prosecution" from December 14, 1957, and in his letter "On Improving the Work of Considering Citizens' Letters, Complaints, and Statements" from October 29, 1958.

Thus, the mechanism of complaints was conceived as a multifunctional tool to provide a prompt response to citizens' concerns and to assist a wobbly newly formed system of governance. It was universal enough to perform in spite of the lack of separation of powers, but also flexible enough to operate without a stable normative base. Institutionally and functionally, the mechanism of complaints is related to the spheres of administrative management (it utilizes administrative power), restoration of justice and, through the Central Bureau for Complaints, it has a means of launching a lawmaking initiative. Due to its origin, the Soviet mechanism of complaints is closely intertwined with executive and party administrations and, thanks to a commonality of functions and their missions, with the judiciary, the militia, and public prosecution.

In early Soviet years, there emerges within the mechanism of complaints a self-contained centralized hierarchy, independent from the local authorities. The tasks and methods of the agencies processing complaints are in many instances similar to those of law enforcement and judicial organs. The mechanism of complaints has sufficiently wide discretionary powers that include conducting investigations and prosecuting violators. As much as it can, the mechanism of complaints compensates for the gaps and imperfections of early Soviet law enforcement and legal systems. Spontaneously, the mechanism of complaints assumes jurisdiction over the sphere of civil and administrative justice excluded from the ambit of the court. In some ways, the mechanism of complaints achieved certain continuity. In particular, bureaus for complaints, which whimsically combined functions of a regular administrative organ with a number of special jurisdictionary functions, were rightly seen by domestic administrativists of the time as predecessors of future administrative courts.

Stalin's innovations. The mechanism of complaints and its role in repressions

After Lenin's passing in 1924, a tendency towards decentralization of the system of state control started to emerge, including that over quality of work with citizens' complaints. Just like in the nineteenth century, the central apparatus could not possibly deal with the stream of complaints and was forced to modify the order established in the early 1920s by transferring the network of previously independent local bureaus for complaints under the jurisdiction of regional and local authorities. Every executive committee of regional and local Soviets now had its own bureau for complaints under the leadership of the committee chair that would review all grievances on the ground. As a result, the system ran into the same trap that the pre-revolutionary setup had suffered from: complaints were now handled by those very people they concerned.

Starting from the mid-1920s, Stalin began to steadily crank up the whistleblowing hysteria, and the mechanism of complaints played a vital role in it. Starting from 1927, the state creates a legal and ideological padding for whistleblowing. Soviet citizens are obligated by law to denounce certain crimes. Article 58 of the Criminal Code in its June 1927 redaction qualifies failure to inform as a criminal offense. The law mandates that all citizens of the USSR blow the whistle on "counterrevolutionary" crimes as defined in previous paragraphs of Article 58. These are actions aimed at:

> overthrowing, undermining, or weakening the power of workers' and peasants' councils and elected by them, on the basis of the Constitution of the USSR and constitution of the Union republics, workers' and peasant governments of the USSR, Union and autonomous republics, or undermining or weakening the external security of the Union SSR and the main economic, political and national achievements of the proletarian revolution.
>
> (Criminal Code of the RSFSR 1937, Art. 58.1)

Failure to report a crime as defined in paragraph 12 entails imprisonment for at least six months (Art. 58.12).

The next step, which encouraged denunciations and motivated citizens to inform the authorities, was the campaign of self-criticism (*kampaniia samokritiki*). It was launched by a statement of TsK VKP(b), published on June 3, 1928, in the newspaper *Pravda*. The statement contained a call for disclosure and elimination of ideological opponents. Consistent measures taken by the authorities increased the clout of the press, thereby making newspapers an ever more popular complaint recipient. On the basis of such popular 1920s phenomena as a bulletin-board newspaper and rural and worker correspondents, the campaign of self-criticism gave a powerful boost to the practice of public whistleblowing on shortcomings of any kind. This form of criticizing from the bottom upwards snowballed rapidly (Fitzpatrick 1996; Nérard 2004).

In 1934, along with a new portion of other modifications, the Criminal Code introduced a concept of "treason against the motherland," defined in Article 58, paragraphs 1a and 1g as follows:

> actions committed by citizens of the USSR to the detriment of the military power of the USSR, its state independence or the inviolability of its territory, such as: espionage, extradition of military or state secrets, going over to the side of the enemy, fleeing or flying abroad.
>
> (Criminal Code of the RSFSR 1937, Arts. 58.1a and 58.1g)

In the same year complaints bureaus were reorganized, and the responsibility for reviewing complaints was taken away from special organs and assigned instead to all and any bodies of power, that is, the party and administrative apparatus: "The duty to ensure prompt and correct processing [of grievances] is now carried out by the Soviets and executive committees" (Decree of VTsIK 1934, Preamble). As a matter of fact, the processing of complaints now became every public official's responsibility. This ultimately cemented the subjectivity of the process. The resolution prescribed fact checking for all reports to the press about any institutional failings or public officials' personal shortcomings. It also set specific processing times for complaints, from one month to seven days depending on where the violation took place (Kabashov 2010:123).

A 1934 resolution of the Seventeenth Congress of the Bolshevik party abolished the system of party-state control previously represented by TsKK-RKI (*Rezoliutsii 1934*). The apparatus of the People's Commissariat of Working-Peasant Inspection (NK RKI) was now part of the People's Control Commission, whereas the TsKK merged with the Committee of Party Control (KPK) under the TsKK VKP (b). This reform meant inscribing organs of control into the executive power vertical, that is to say, replacing an independent omnipotent organization with a strong support on the ground with a decentralized, powerless one, fully dependent on the state (Kabashov 2010:12–123). Reforms of the party-state apparatus of the time reflect the tendency to strengthen the power vertical of the state and to sever connections between the apparatus and the people (Solomon 1996).

To make the modified mechanism of complaints more orderly, a Resolution of the TsIK of the USSR, "On the Situation with the Consideration of Workers' Complaints," was passed on December 14, 1935. For the first time guidelines were offered for processing citizens' grievances; until then, every institution followed its own rules. According to Article 3 section b, all institutions now had to redress complainants within 20 days. Forwarding complaints to those institutions and officials about whom they were made was strictly prohibited. This procedure remained operational for 30 years and is often reproduced nowadays.

The last campaign to foster whistleblowing was the vigilance campaign (*kampaniia bditel'nosti*), launched in February 1937. Citizens were warned that Soviet society was rife with spies and called upon to denounce their superiors, colleagues, and anyone else suspected of sabotage. The vigilance campaign finalized preparations for mass political repressions, wherein denunciation played an outstanding role.

A call to report wrongdoings had a potent motivational and mobilizing undercurrent. By asking citizens for protection, the state thereby overturned for a while the customary authoritarian model, according to which a Soviet citizen could only be an object in relation to the state, including an object of protection. Exposure was only allowed if it aimed to protect the state. This rule determined the legitimacy of a report and remained in force throughout the entire Soviet period. Inversely, exposing the state would automatically place the informer in a group of risk and invited prosecution. This rule endowed denunciation with ambiguity. Depending on who reports whom and why, an act of denunciation could be interpreted by the state as either good or evil.

In Peter Solomon's opinion, Stalin made advance preparations for purges and repressions within the apparatus and consciously strove to avoid involving the judiciary in this process. The judiciary had a separate segment for political justice. The People's Commissariat for Internal Affairs (NKVD), created in 1934, also received a steady stream of complaints. One would contact NKVD with a complaint containing any compromising or "counter-revolutionary" information (Solomon 1996; Nérard 2004). There were plenty of letters of this kind. NKVD under Stalin had unprecedented powers. However, NKVD's popularity as a recipient of grievances was also due to the fact that political campaigns had changed the language of complaints (see Chapter 2).

The Criminal Code and the Code of Criminal Procedure in effect during the years of Stalin's rule generally gave a modest place to denunciation. Meanwhile, judges, investigators, prosecutors, and investigative bodies were obliged to accept all statements about crimes committed by anyone or about crimes being prepared—even if the case was outside of their authority and the sphere of law in general. In the latter case, their responsibility was limited by the task to transfer the case to the target addressees, nevertheless, they were included in the general scheme of circulation of denunciations.

Work with denunciations contributed to the rapprochement of the administrative structures of government with the party organs and with the law enforcement and court authorities. At the institutional level, state control bodies, which were originally responsible for working with citizens since 1923 have begun to closely cooperate with the party organs. The promotion of the flywheel denunciations provoked the spread of the practice of investigations carried out at various levels by various departments. A famous 1928 August plenum required making investigations of violations, mentioned in the people's letters, mandatory (Ingulov 1928). The apparatus, processing denunciations, made their investigations independently, but could also engage judicial mechanisms. Criminal proceedings could be initiated due to denunciations.

A whole range of Stalin's actions paved the way for purges and repressions. Firstly, Stalin forced the military situation onto the country. Secondly, laws were passed consistently fostering denunciations and criminalizing any statements or actions against the socialist state. The practice of addressing the authorities laid some of the grounds for the entire project of Stalin's repressions, or, rather, it became the nervous system transmitting "signals" from society to various levels of power.

Stalin's mechanism of complaints and the function of justice

The range of issues to be dealt with through the mechanism of complaints was rather vaguely defined throughout the Soviet period. To the Bolsheviks' mind, justice in general was a penal institution. For all intents and purposes, the court's mission was to consider complex cases and serious criminal offenses. Yoram Gorlizki (1998) argued that the preference was for minor criminal conflicts and, especially, cases of civil offenses to be handled out of court or by para-judicial structures. An audit of the NK RKI activities in 1927 showed that most of the criminal cases considered by the courts ended with acquittals. That was seen as a waste of time. As an immediate consequence of this audit, comrade courts were established[10] and in so doing also the range of issues to be handled by the courts.

A Resolution of the People's Control Commission, ratified by the SNK of the USSR in 1936, introduced an extremely general rule, according to which the mechanism of complaints was to handle civil affairs, but by no means criminal cases:

> It is especially intolerable to consider the facts of transferring to the judicial-prosecutorial bodies cases of official misconduct that do not contain any signs of a criminal offense, as well as inadmissible to use a disciplinary procedure to resolve cases of a clearly criminal nature (embezzlement, use of official position, etc.).
>
> (Resolution of the People's Control Commission 1936, p. 8)[11]

This division was never faithfully observed throughout the entire Soviet period. According to statistics, the courts always worked with civil cases; as for the cases resolved through the mechanism of complaints, some could easily be qualified as petty criminal offenses, minor bodily harm, or violation of priority in distributing housing.

In the absence of stable legislation and universal law enforcement, the question of how one or another offense is to be qualified often left room for interpretation both by citizens and law enforcers. In different periods, one and the same crime could be qualified differently. Notable examples of such inconsistencies are the criminalization of juvenile crimes in 1935, abortions in 1936, and breaches of workplace discipline in 1940 (Solomon 1996:190–194). Simultaneously, Soviet authorities passed resolutions that gradually increased the severity of punishments meted out by Soviet judges. This was especially true for such widespread offenses as disruptive behavior and theft. Incidentally, in the late 1950s this did not prevent the authorities from singling out petty crimes as a separate group of offenses that were almost completely decriminalized and transferred under the jurisdiction of comrade courts (Gorlizki 1998:414).

Against the backdrop of the increasing volume of incoming complaints and the growing complexity of issues they concerned, the need to bring in professional legal help started to be felt acutely. The mixing of issues to be decided by the judiciary with those within the competence of administrative apparatus started to seriously stump those responsible for processing complaints. Besides, civil cases within the purview of the mechanism of complaints were far from straightforward. Knowledge of the norm of socialist morality was not always sufficient to make a ruling on the matter.

In his book, François-Xavier Nérard quotes an example of the editor of the *Peasant Newspaper* (*Krestianskaia gazeta*) M. Mikhailov requesting extra personnel in 1929:

> We would consider it expedient that the Collegium of the People's Commissariat of the RKI take into account the enormous role of the "Peasant Newspaper" in working with the peasant letter and the newspaper's inability to cope with the huge flow of letters coming in from the countryside, and suggest that the *Narkompros* organize a brigade made up of students of respective specialization for working with the peasant letter and raise a question before the Board of Attorneys regarding the need for a full staffing of the "Peasant Newspaper's" legal department with legal contingent.[12]

Earlier, the mechanism of complaints had had at its disposal a certain range of powers sufficient to impose such penalties as "dismissal of the accused; bringing to trial; transferring the matter to the judicial authorities" (Resolution of NKGK 1919). In 1927 the powers of the RKI were significantly expanded, and its organs were authorized to resolve a whole range of matters to do with improving the apparatus, as well as take disciplinary actions, up to dismissal from office "for evident mismanagement, bureaucratism, and red tape" (Resolution of TsIK SSSR 1927, Art. 1).

Thus, under Stalin, the mechanism of complaints lost much of its independence by becoming a tool in the hands of powers that be. The significance of a letter from the ground grew exponentially. In addition to a question or a request, it could now contain revelatory information necessitating an investigation and penalties. Where in the early years of their existence, bureaus for complaints used to simply receive complaints and monitor their processing by relevant institutions (like a Master of Requests at the time of Peter the Great), starting from the mid-1920s they were tasked with carrying out independent inquiries (like under Nicholas I). Other recipients of complaints also saw their tasks and powers greatly expand during this period. The burden of undertaking an investigation and punishing wrongdoings falls also on ordinary editorial staff and employees of executive committees.

In the period of Stalin's terror, the standard language of complaint started to include definitions and transgressions that had a status of criminal or political offenses. This caused a number of changes in the functioning of the mechanism of complaints. To begin with, administrative organs of the mechanism of complaints entered a closer collaboration with the prosecution, NKVD, and the judiciary. Citizens' reaction to this multiplication of instances was to choose from among them the authority that would potentially be most efficient at solving their problem.

Metamorphosis, which for a time modified the complaint to the denunciation, says a lot about the mechanism as such, how it was conceived and implemented: centralized, controlled from above, and accumulating a very valuable function of solving problems. An important role in the fact that denunciation has developed into a mass phenomenon, no doubt, was played by the difficult social and economic situation of the Stalinist period and the rigidity of the political regime. In those conditions it manifested itself as an exceptionally flexible and dangerous tool in the hands of the authorities.

Late-Soviet mechanism of complaints: A drift towards a para-judicial institution

Symptoms of post-Stalin modernization

After the exposing of the personality cult of Stalin that took place at the secret meeting of the Twentieth Congress of the Communist Party of the Soviet Union on February 25, 1956, a shadow was cast on the entire system of state governance and control. Stalin's ways of using the mechanism of complaints made a lot of damage to its reputation. From an instrument intended to help citizens solve their problems, solidify their mutual relations and trust in powers that be, the mechanism of complaints transformed into a rigid, dangerous, divisive weapon.

In early 1957 at the February plenary meeting of the Central Committee of the Communist Party of the Soviet Union (TsK KPSS), significant changes were introduced which reconstructed the control apparatus (Pyzhikov 2001). In fact, this was a new stage of development for the mechanism of complaints as well as the rest of the country. After long decades of taking shape, stabilizing, and turning ever more bureaucratized, People's Control started looking for new forms of organization and methods of work, or, rather, for ways to renew mass engagement of citizens in exercising control. The Commission of Soviet Control (KSK) of the Council of Ministers of the USSR (SM SSSR) was created instead of the Ministry of State Control of the USSR (Decree of Presidium of the Supreme Council 1957). This was a return to the old organ of control from the mid-1930s. All work was supposed to be done in conjunction with local party and Soviet organs and public organizations so that the working masses would be actively engaged (Nikolaeva 1960:19).

Signs of legal modernization became tangible in the early 1960s. A significant reorganization of civil justice was accompanied by major legislative enactments, such as The Basic Principles of Civil Law of the USSR and Federal Republics (May 1, 1962), The Basic Principles of Civil Procedure of the USSR and Federal Republics (May 1, 1962), the Civil Code of the RSFSR (October 1, 1964), and the Code of Civil Procedure of the RSFSR (October 1, 1964). A number of documents regulating various aspects of civil relations—consumer-, labor-, and housing-related—were issued at the same time.

These documents undertake to reach several important goals. Firstly, they determine a range of civil cases to be handled by courts. Considering that virtually all regulations passed in the 1960s in one or another way touch upon this matter, the problem of separating civil litigation from the activities of administrative authorities and arbitrational and comrade courts was taken very seriously. However, the attempted solution to this problem was hardly a success. The wording in both The Basic Principles of Civil Law and the Civil Code is painfully vague:

> Courts have jurisdiction over disputes arising from civil, family, labor and collective farm legal relations if at least one of the parties to the dispute is a citizen, a collective farm, intercollective or state-collective enterprise, organization, or their association, except for cases when the resolution of such disputes is referred by law to the jurisdiction of administrative or other organs.
>
> (The Basic Principles of Civil Procedure 1962, Art. 4)

Likewise in the Civil Code: "In cases specified by law, protection of civil rights is carried out in an administrative procedure" (Civil Code 1964, Art. 6).

Resolutions regulating certain spheres of civil relations reiterated the distinction established already by the resolution of the People's Control Commission ratified by the SNK of the USSR back in 1936, which stipulated that cases with criminal intent were to be handled by courts and everything else by administrative authorities. For example, Resolutions of the Plenum of the Supreme Court of the RSFSR from

December 12, 1964, No. 24, "On Judicial Practices in Cases of Deceit of Consumers" and No. 43 "On Improving the Work of Courts of the RSFSR on Fighting against Deceit of Consumers" from December 11, 1968, with modifications introduced by the Plenum's resolution No. 53 from January 28, 1970, presupposed directing cases of theft of state property, collusion, and mass production of defective products to courts. These crimes had relevant articles in the Criminal Code (156, 157) describing certain degrees of criminal acts and specific penalties.

At the same time, a whole sphere of marketplace, service, and labor management relations had no clearly delineated criteria for violations and conventional penalties. Employees of the mechanism of complaints had at their disposal the Resolutions on Disciplinary Responsibility (1921, 1927, 1932). The 1921 resolution permitted penalties like: a) a reprimand, b) a punitive reprimand with publication in the press, c) detention for up to two weeks. The number of such statutes kept growing, and during the Second World War, and in the 1949–1950s they underwent a review, but finally the Resolution of TsIK and SNK RSFSR on Disciplinary Responsibility of 1932 was canceled only in January 13, 2020 (Resolution of Government 2020). By this time, detention was no longer used as a disciplinary measure. Mostly used were such measures as demotion, divestment of privileges or titles, or transfer to another position. Additionally, administrative organs relied on multiple resolutions and ordinances calling for improvement, conscientiousness, commitment to quality, etc., as well as on the norms of socialist morality, which by 1961 had finally been articulated in the Moral Code of the Builder of Communism.

1. Loyalty to Communism and love of the socialist Motherland and other socialist countries.
2. Conscientious work for the good of society: whoever doesn't work, doesn't get to eat.
3. Care for the preservation and augmentation of collective property.
4. Acute awareness of social responsibilities and intolerance of violations of social interests.
5. Collectivism and brotherhood: All for one and one for all.
6. Humane attitude and mutual respect between people: being one another's friend, comrade, and brother.
7. Honesty and truthfulness, moral purity, simplicity and modesty in private and in public.
8. Mutual respect in the family and care for the upbringing of the children.
9. Intolerance of injustice, social parasitism, lying, careerism, and greed.
10. Friendship and fraternity with all the peoples of the USSR, intolerance of all ethnic and racial discrimination.
11. Intolerance of the enemies of communism, peace, and freedom of the peoples of the world.
12. Brotherly solidarity with workers of all countries and all nations.

(*Moral'nyi kodeks* 1965).

The necessity to distinguish between the civil law issues falling within the ambit of courts and those to be handled by administrative organs was amply clear from the wording of The Basic Principles of Civil Law and the Civil Code by the mid-1960s. For a number of reasons drawing the line was extremely difficult in the context of existing legislation and, moreover, of the practice of law enforcement. *Firstly*, in order to transfer some of the civil cases under the jurisdiction of courts, the established concept of Soviet penal justice had to undergo significant changes. *Secondly*, Soviet law in its origins was not designed to protect individual rights, right of private property, honor, and dignity. *Thirdly*, a substantial reduction of the mechanism of complaints was not in the interests of powers that be. Just like under the Tsars, in Soviet Russia the mechanism of complaints assumed a function of highest importance—to serve as a conduit between the people and the authorities.

Starting from the mid-1960s, the mechanism of complaints started getting caught up in serious contradictions. It was getting clearer that complaint as a special genre of addressing the authorities was turning into a para-judicial institution that carried out the function of a court outside of the judiciary and its rules and procedures. The 1964 Civil Code was partially to blame for this development in that it endowed the issues handled by the mechanism of complaints with legal nature. E.g. Article 4 states that legal relations "may arise from administrative acts, including—for state, cooperative, and other public organizations—from planning acts." These violations of various instructions, issues of discipline, underperformance, negligence, individual shortcomings—all those most frequently dealt with through the mechanism of complaints—were equated with breaches of civil law.

In the latter part of the 1960s, the mechanism of complaints acquired substantial grounds for stabilization. An important document to standardize the work of the mechanism of complaints across the country was the Resolution of the TsK KPSS from August 29, 1967, "On Measures to Further Improve the Consideration of Letters and the Reception of Workers." This document highlighted the importance of citizens' letters for strengthening and expanding the Party's connection with the people and the population's participation in managing state affairs. Party guidelines served as a basis for the Decree (*Ukaz*) of the Presidium of the Supreme Council of the USSR from April 12, 1968, No. 2534-VII, "On the Order for Considering Citizens' Suggestions, Statements, and Complaints," which in redactions of Decrees of the Presidium of the Supreme Council of the USSR from March 4, 1980, and February 2, 1988, remained in effect up to 2006.[13] Even though the initial resolution was only a bylaw, the resolution of the Supreme Council of the USSR signed it into law of the Soviet Union. Fifty years past the establishment of the Soviet regime, this was the first attempt to regulate the procedure for working with citizens' complaints as a single mechanism operating uniformly across the country. The republican level was now correlated with the federal. A uniform complaint-processing period of one month was introduced for all levels of the mechanism (p. 9).

For the first time ever the resolution employed a broadly understood concept of an "application to the authorities," interpreted as "an important means of realizing and protecting the rights of individuals, strengthening ties between the state apparatus and the population, an essential source of information necessary for solving current and future issues of state, economic, and socio-cultural building" (Decree 1968, Preamble). Apart from the concept of complaint, the Decree also introduced such forms of addressing the authorities as statements and suggestions.[14] Such an approach testified to an expanding understanding of a citizen's role in relation to the state, as was the case under Alexander I and occurred again in the late 1960s.

The resolution detailed a procedure for addressing citizens' complaints and established legal guarantees for their timely consideration (including officials' responsibilities). State and public bodies, enterprises, institutions, and organizations, as well as their leaders and other officials, were obliged to accept and, in accordance with their level of competence, in a timely fashion consider citizens' suggestions, statements, and complaints, respond to them, and take necessary action.

The resolution described an order of subordination. Commonly accepted rules, carried over from one resolution to another, such as "not to complain to the guilty" and "to complain to the boss of the guilty," finally acquired formal definition. However, this resolution also fell short of the target as it did not set forth any legal accountability for violations of the prescribed procedure. As well, other important procedural moments were left unfinished, such as the way of "holding someone liable" or the criteria for "taking measures" (p. 4). The resolution did not explicitly state that the processing of a complaint is only completed after the decision made on its basis is actually carried out. The resolution also failed to state the maximum time span during which such a decision must be implemented, which may have led to unwarranted delays.

Point 16 stipulated that organs of People's Control and the procuracy "systematically oversee and watch that Soviet laws are carefully observed when suggestions, statements, and complaints of citizens are being addressed." The fact that the prosecution was mentioned alongside the People's Control made the task of supervision vague and legally ambiguous.

To boost quality control over complaint processing and resolution, the Presidium of the Supreme Council of the RSFSR passed a Resolution on July 15, 1968, "On Citizens' Suggestions, Statements, and Complaints Addressed to the Session of the Supreme Council." The Resolution named the Presidium of the Supreme Council of the RSFSR as the body monitoring the execution of decisions made by heads of state and public organs, enterprises, and institutions in response to complaints they had received. The resolution made the entire mechanism of complaints subject to the highest organ of state power outside of the judiciary.

Bureaucracy was still responsible for forwarding letters. In case of error, a complaint was to be resent to the relevant addressee. All top managers were made personally accountable for accepting and responding to suggestions, statements, and complaints. Quite novel was the recognition of a special kind of citizens' suggestions, statements, or complaints—those coming through letters to the editors of newspapers, journals, radio, TV, and other mass media, as well as public speeches and materials published in the press, as long as they had to do with suggestions, statements, and complaints (p. 11), which would previously not have been considered by the state authorities as "not delivered to them." This innovation made mass media hugely more influential. A grievance published in or forwarded by a mass media editor turned into a weapon helping to defeat all bureaucratic tricks invented over the period of existence of the Soviet bureaucracy of complaints. Such a complaint could not be lost, misplaced, considered superficially or ignored. A public complaint shone the searchlight not only on the guilty, but also on their immediate boss or a higher authority.

The bureaucratic apparatus to process complaints acquired a definite and stable shape. There was a network of organs of general competence, including the party-state power vertical (party committees, executive committees, deputies, incumbent council members, mass media of every level). In order to get the masses accustomed to working with complaints and also to get help with streams of incoming correspondence, the organs of general competence actively engaged members of the public (people's controllers, advanced workers, collective farm laborers, and factory workers). In addition to the apparatus inscribed into the organs of state and party power, departmental structures also processed complaints. Officials at every level were mandated to receive citizens' complaints and react to them in a timely fashion. Reports on complaint processing were to be delivered at people's deputies' sessions and meetings of regulatory and executive bodies.

The structure of the mechanism of complaints underwent transformations as well. Conceptually, one aimed to return to Lenin's model of the mechanism rooted in popular forces. Between 1962 and 1965, the second attempt was undertaken to bring executive and party powers together for working with the complaints. A Committee of Party-State Control (KPGK) under the TsK KPSS and the Council of Ministers of the USSR was created and chaired by Alexander Shelepin, the then chief of KGB and simultaneously deputy chairman of the Council of Ministers of the USSR.[15] The 1965 law "On the Organs of People's Control in the USSR" transformed the joint organ into the Committee for People's Control under the Council of Ministers of the USSR. The connection between the state control and the mechanism of complaints led to the creation of a special complaints department as part of the Committee. According to the Statute on the Organs of People's Control in the USSR ratified by a joint resolution of the TsK KPSS and the SM SSSR on December 19, 1968, they were tasked with watching that officials carefully observe Soviet laws when considering citizens' suggestions, complaints, or statements, monitoring how this work is done by ministries, state committees, departments, enterprises, institutions, organizations, as well as collective farms, cooperatives, and other public organizations.

The 1977 Constitution of the USSR: New contradictions and new contract between the state and society

By the mid-1960, a new idea of contract between the state and society began to emerge. While under the monarchy this relationship was governed by an idea of royal mercy, and under Stalin by an idea of defending the state from external and internal enemies (Vihavainen 2004), now in the Soviet state it was conceptualized as a close collaboration between the authorities and the people and the state's care for its citizens (Bogdanova 2006). Just like the monarch could not ignore the tribulations of his subjects, even if a show of mercy went against the law, so also the Soviet state could not help but care for its citizens. This fundamental formula for a relationship between citizens and powers was finalized in the 1977 Constitution, according to which "The main law of a socialist society is the care of all for the welfare of everyone and the care of everyone for the welfare of all."

Ratification of the 1977 Constitution further manifested the clash between the necessary legal modernization and the preservation of stability of the socialist system. Article 151 of the Constitution declared that "Justice in the USSR is carried out solely by the court." A similar statement was made in the 1936 Constitution, but in the late 1970s truth could not be bent as easily as in the 1930s. The mechanism of complaints as it were by the late 1970s stood in glaring contradiction to Article 151. *De facto* it played the role of the lowest-level court, whereas *de jure* it was not part of the judiciary. In the circles of professional lawyers, the debate about administrative justice, and the form it took under the Soviet conditions by the 1970s, has resumed. Dmitry Chechot in his book *Administrative Justice* examines a number of issues that testify to the awareness of deep contradictions that had formed between the judiciary and the complaint mechanism. In particular, it identifies such problems as the uncertainty of the jurisdiction of the issues contained in the complaints (in terms of their severity, some of them had a legal component and required a serious trial) and the scope and limits of administrative discretion—a principle used by most addressees, processing complaints in the absence of clear criteria for trial and punishment (Chechot 1973). Peter Solomon recalls that "in the 1970s Soviet legal scholars had already begun discussing the expansion of the scope of judicial review of administrative acts and in 1977 succeeded in securing an entry for this subject in the 1977 Constitution of the USSR" (2004:555).

The Constitution found a rather original solution to this conundrum; the term "complaint" was excluded from the range of customary forms of applications to the authorities. Article 49 legitimized addressing officials with statements and suggestions. Complaint as a form of application was mentioned in another article. In point of fact, complaint's function was equated with an administrative appeal:

> Citizens of the USSR have the right to appeal against the actions of officials, state and public bodies. […] The actions of officials committed in violation of the law, in excess of their powers, which infringe upon the rights of citizens, may be appealed in court in accordance with the procedure established by the law.
>
> (Constitution of the USSR 1977, Art. 59)

An attempt to take the function of restoring justice out of the mechanism of complaints was evidently purely nominal; in reality this would have been impossible. The longstanding habit of contacting the authorities generated a huge volume of letters. Classifying them by type was very difficult. Still harder was constructing a navigation system that would have filtered complaints reporting violations of the law out of the general stream of letters. Even figuring out whether a complaint had to do with a breach of the law was extremely tricky. The legislation failed to describe a number of violations specifically and unambiguously; besides, for several decades the authorities consciously separated the mechanism of complaints from the legal system; complaint was almost fully purged of the language of the law (see Chapter 4).

After the Constitution broke the previously integral mechanism into two both in terms of bureaucracy servicing it and its practical application, no other document was issued to help distinguish the procedure for processing statements and suggestions from that for responding to complaints. Nor was the current legislation abolished. In fact, little changed in the way administrative apparatus handled complaints, except that this terminological quirk produced situations in which one and the same letter addressed to a respective body was viewed by its recipient and the author as total opposites: a suggestion or a complaint. Sergei Kabashov argues that this resulted in heterogeneity and legal inconsistencies in the normative base that determined the procedure for handling complaints.

Further development of the mechanism of complaints can be defined as a balancing act. On one side were powers that be invested in preserving the system and thus also the mechanism of complaints which handled incoming letters and helped sustain the ideologeme of the socialist care of citizens. On the other side were tendencies for society's development towards the newly rehabilitated concept of law-based society and specific steps towards modernization of the legal system.

In 1979, one more law "On People's Control in the USSR" was passed which confirmed the return to engaging the populace in managing and processing complaints. This expanded the range of possible complaint recipients, now complemented by public organizations, but simultaneously weakened the state support of the mechanism.

In 1980, the 1968 Decree was modified to separate the functions and responsibilities of the People's Control and the procuracy. The People's Control retained the responsibility for monitoring the mechanism of complaints and fighting its nemeses—red tape and formalism (p. 16). The procuracy was made the top supervisory authority for complaint processing. According to the amendment, the Prosecutor General of the USSR and his subordinate prosecutors were to maintain oversight over the exact and uniform observance of the laws in addressing citizens' suggestions, statements, and complaints in all instances, "take measures to restore violated rights and protect the legitimate interests of citizens and organizations, bring legal cases against violators, and take other measures in accordance with the law … 'On the Procuracy in the USSR'" (1979). The Prosecutor General remained subordinate to the Supreme Soviet of the USSR, however, the emphasis in the supervision of the work of the mechanism of complaints has shifted towards the judiciary.

The late 1970s to early 1980s were marked by a series of attempts to separate the responsibilities of the judicial and para-judicial structure active at the time. This was especially tricky as far as petty crime, civil, and administrative offenses were concerned, which fell within the ambit simultaneously of the mechanism of complaints, comrade courts, and people's courts. A Decree of Presidium of the Supreme Council of the RSFSR, "On the Approval of Regulations on Comrade Courts and Regulations on Public Councils for the Work of Comrade Courts" was issued on March 11, 1977. Article 7 gave a detailed list of offenses to be handled by comrade courts. Other articles determined community sanctions, procedures for the application of labor legislation, fines and penalties, compulsory medical treatments, as well as the cases when comrade courts were obligated to involve judicial organs and the prosecution, such as repeat infractions or when legal instances passed cases to comrade courts.

No similar document was created to define the range of issues to be handled by the mechanism of complaints. Up until the end of the Soviet rule, there was no certainty as to the range of issues to be handled by the mechanism of complaints, nor in regard to its institutional design that overlapped both with administrative management and the judicial and legal system. Legislative changes that took place in the last decade of the Soviet regime prove that overcoming this tanglement was on the agenda and that most likely there was a plan to focus activities of the mechanism of complaints in the sphere of administrative offenses. Not an easily intelligible attempt to exclude civil cases from the competence of the mechanism of complaints was made in the Model Provision (*Polozhenie*) on Record Keeping as Regards Citizens' Suggestions, Statements, and Complaints, issued on November 30, 1981. The provision introduced special rules of recordkeeping for complaints, statements, and suggestions handled by the mechanism of complaints and excluded from among them:

> the suggestions, statements and complaints of citizens, the procedure for consideration of which is established by the criminal procedure, civil procedural legislation of the Union of the SSR and Union Republics, the Regulations on the procedure for resolving labor disputes, the Regulations on discoveries, inventions and rationalization proposals, the Charter of Communications and other legislation of the USSR and the Union Republics.
>
> (Model Provision 1981, p. 12)

The technique of limiting jurisdiction by means of specifying the recordkeeping procedure was not reliable enough to exert significant influence on the practice of working with complaints.

The next important event was the ratification on June 20, 1984, of the Code of the RSFSR for Administrative Offenses. This was the first attempt at codifying administrative offenses in the history of the Russian state. The Code introduced the concept of administrative offenses, their typology, and determined types of administrative sanctions. The handling of cases of administrative violations, sentencing, as well as prevention were the responsibility of local Soviets of people's deputies and their executive committees (*ispolkomy*) (Art. 6), that is to say, structures that by the last decade of the Soviet rule had become central to the general design of the mechanism of complaints. The Code made provisions for transferring administrative cases to comrade courts, public organizations, or workers' associations (Art. 21, 31, 32, 40), thereby giving definition to a complete structure of instances responsible for administrative offenses that was almost entirely outside the boundaries of the judicial system.

Apart from handling administrative wrongdoings and imposing administrative sanctions, the Code endowed the Soviets of people's deputies with an unprecedented right to independently "establish rules, for the violation of which administrative responsibility arises" under certain articles (85, 101, 144, 149) of this Code (Art. 6). Thus the role of the Soviets and their executive committees exceeded that of mere executors of the norms established by law and expanded to include the right of defining, correcting, and interpreting the norms of administrative offenses.

On the whole, the Administrative Code of the RSFSR introduced a long-awaited certainty into the division of responsibilities between the administrative and the judicial systems. Soviet administrative law made better distinctions between the basic forms of state activity, such as the government, state administration, the judiciary, and the prosecution. As a matter of fact, the jurisdiction of the mechanism of complaints was now limited to administrative offenses, finally given a comprehensive characterization thanks to the administrative code.

The contradiction between the mechanism of complaints and the legal system that infringed on the uniqueness of the court's function found no easy resolution. No document dealt with this issue explicitly. At the same time, legally the mechanism of complaints was getting as close as it possibly could to judicial institutions both structurally and functionally. Through continuity of functions, the mechanism of complaints was institutionally connected to comrade courts, which, in turn, were an acknowledged and legitimate part of the Soviet judicial system (See the 1981 law "On the Judicial System of the RSFSR" (Art. 26.8)). The cases handled by the mechanism of complaints were definitively given a legal status. Functionally, the instances of the mechanism of complaints were authorized not only to apply legal norms, but also to correct them. The problem was that changes in legislation did not, in fact, impact the real operation of the mechanism of complaints. The major problem was dealing with unceasing streams of letters reporting all sorts of issues in a language far removed from that of the law. The mechanism of complaints lacked resources for their prompt consideration and classification according to the jurisdiction under which the issues they reported fell, and forwarding to relevant authorities. In the eyes of the people, the mechanism of complaints remained a number of customary complaint recipients inscribed in the administrative hierarchy.

Transformations that took place in the mechanism of complaints in the 1980s occurred against the backdrop of the incipient Perestroika and noticeable legal modernization. The concept of the rule of law was publicly rehabilitated. Mikhail

Gorbachev introduced the rule-of-law theme into the public discourse in his address to the Nineteenth Party Conference in 1988. To achieve the "democratization of the life of the state and society," Gorbachev said that the USSR must "move along the path of creating a socialist state under the rule of law" (*sotsialisticheskoe pravovoe gosudarstvo*). To elaborate on his theme, Gorbachev focused primarily on the need to delineate functions among the executive, legislative, and judicial branches of government in order to strengthen the legislative and judicial branches.[16]

It is surprising, therefore, that Gorbachev and other contemporary Soviet jurists (Manov 1989) have embraced the concept of a state under the rule of law. Notably, however, Gorbachev called for a socialist state under the rule of law, an indication that the USSR was not abandoning the socialist aspects of the Soviet social order (Levitsky 1990:227–230). Simultaneously, the state apparatus was becoming less efficient and the demand for a faster transition to free market was growing. The existing formula of a contract between the citizens and powers that be, according to which the state promised to take care of the citizens in exchange for loyalty and obedience and which was upheld, among other things, by the mechanism of complaints, was clearly becoming obsolete. Starting from 1990, activities of People's Control, which used to permeate all spheres of society, revealed their utter inefficiency. On May 16, 1991, the fifth session of the Supreme Council of the USSR adopted the law "On the Control Chamber of the USSR," which did not oblige this organ to receive and respond to citizens' applications. For the first time in several centuries of Russian history, the institute of addressing the authorities lost the state support.

Thus, after the 1917 Revolution and the establishment of Soviet rule, the mechanism of complaints became an integral part of the system of administration. If such a mechanism did not exist in Russia prior to 1917, it would be necessary for the Bolsheviks to invent it. For them, it was in many ways indispensable. Firstly, by using a familiar mechanism of complaints, the Bolsheviks managed to demonstrate to the population advantages of the newly established regime. Secondly, the mechanism of complaints allowed for a happy compromise with the Bolshevik views on law and governance by providing an alternative to the judicial system. Thirdly, the mechanism of complaints proved to be functional in the context of post-revolutionary institutional void since it easily made do without a legal basis and the separation of powers and was operated manually.

The Soviet history of the mechanism of complaints allows us to describe it as a flexible, efficient and multifunctional instrument in the hands of the authorities, easily adjusted to the needs of those in power. In the absence of the separation of powers, the mechanism of complaints turns into a cumbersome, unwieldy, at times redundant network of recipients interconnected with a great diversity of power structures. This blurs the boundaries between the branches of power and allows using the mechanism of complaints as an additional means of exerting influence on each of them.

Over the course of the Soviet period, the mechanism of complaints undergoes a complex chain of transformations: from the multiplicity of functions to their narrowing and concretization, from simple bureaucracy to a complex one, from vague and muddled rules to the more precise and defined ones. Developmental dynamics lead to the necessity for a greater separation of powers as a rational and effective trajectory, which brings about contradictions. Dynamics of the Soviet mechanism of complaints generally shows a complex but ultimately inexorable movement from rejecting the law to increasing roles of regulations and formalization.

In the context of Soviet society, the mechanism of complaints developed as a para-judicial institution. From the outset of the Soviet period, the mechanism of complaints imitates legal institutions by carrying out investigations, emulating inquests, imposing certain sanctions on perpetrators. Gradually, the mechanism of complaints takes on handling a sufficiently well-defined range of civil and administrative matters, which determine its niche in the system of law enforcement and justice. It just so happened that the function of the mechanism of complaints in regard to a certain number of issues was unique. No other department dealt with consumers' problems, issues of communal living, breaches of ethics in interpersonal communications, etc.

It was exactly this type of para-judicial institute that allowed a Soviet model of justice to form, wherein the court is a penal instance in contrast to an alternative method of restoring justice that is considerably less formal, mild, open, and free. The methods utilized by the mechanism of complaints in working with complaints and the guilty were not supposed to be tough. In addition to restoring justice, the mechanism of complaints also had to embody the ideologeme of the authorities' close rapport with citizens, to instill socialist consciousness and to prevent wrongdoings. As for the organs of state power, they retain the function of the main recipient of complaints and supreme justice.

Based on such a complex history of the Soviet mechanism of complaints, it is imperative for it to be considered as one of the premises that exerted influence on the legal culture, the practice of solving legal problems, perception of justice, and ways to restore justice in the context of Soviet society.

Conclusion

Neither the pre-Soviet nor the Soviet modifications of the mechanism of complaints overcame their pre-modern features completely. Even a brief retrospective journey into the history of the mechanism of complaints clearly manifests certain patterns of its existence in Russian society and the state. Both before and after the Revolution, the mechanism of complaints had an important function of a communicational conduit between the state and society. It was in many ways through the mechanism of complaints—its design, mandate, strength of the apparatus, and efficiency—that the authorities articulated and conveyed to the population the main formula of a contract between the authorities and people that helped preserve balance in society and legitimize the government in place. Between the end of the nineteenth and the end of the twentieth centuries this formula underwent several transformations. Prior to the Revolution this was a monarchic idea rooted in the belief in the mercy and justice of the Tsar as the Lord's anointed, and resulted in a contract: protection in exchange for faith. In the context of the Soviet system, the contract between the state and society went through complex transformations, and as it stabilized and became more humane, it arrived at a formula of care in exchange for obedience.

Both the Tsar and the Soviet political elite used the mechanism of complaints simultaneously as a way to reinforce, legitimize, and retain power, and as a way of restoring justice. Due to inadequate development of the judicial system, difficulty for the wider population accessing judicial institutions, and low level of literacy, an extra opportunity to restore justice in the form of the mechanism of complaints was indispensable. A pre-revolutionary judicial and legal system had not developed to such a degree as to completely give up on the mechanism of complaints. Similarly, in Soviet society the mechanism of complaints had unique functions important for the justification of socialist ideology and the functioning of the top-down system, as well as compensating for the shortcomings of the Soviet judiciary and the whole legal system. The Soviet mechanism of complaints had become so integral to all the systems of Soviet society that its elimination or even significant reduction was fraught with serious institutional transformations. Finally in both cases the norms that the mechanism of complaints built on were not based ultimately on the law. In Tsarist Russia it was custom, in the Soviet Union—the Marxist-Leninist doctrine and Soviet ideology.

Meanwhile, the coexistence of the complaint mechanism with the institutions of justice in Tsarist and Soviet Russia were different. Overclocking legal modernization entered into an inevitable conflict with an absolutist form of ruling and devalued the monarchical contract of society with the government. The value of the Tsarist mechanism was precisely in its archaism. It was isolated from legal modernization and contrasted with it. The specificity of the Soviet mechanism of complaints was initially in its freedom from such a conflict simply because the Soviet system denied the main principles of the rule of law. Due to this, the Soviet mechanism pursued the task of maintaining the contract, but it had no task of preserving the archaic features. Paradoxically, the socialist context, free from the principles of the rule of law, allowed it to show signs of modernization.

The two stories, of the mechanism's demise at the last stages of the monarchy and at the end of the socialist state, demonstrate obvious similarities. In both cases the mechanism of complaints was weakened under the strengthening of legal institutions and increasing request for legal modernization, but till the last breath enjoyed the support of the ruling authorities. In both cases the authorities viewed it as a very powerful instrument to help sustain the prevailing contract with society and society's loyalty. The dissimilarity is in the fact that the monarchic mechanism of complaints was abolished by the Bolsheviks, whereas its Soviet counterpart lost the authorities' support due to the legal and market-oriented modernization of society. Most of the laws and other regulations controlling the functioning of the Soviet mechanism of complaints were not abolished. Rather, the contract between society and powers that be, which used to be supported through the mechanism of complaints, had lost its relevance. These two stories show that the mechanism of complaints is a fairly efficient instrument for maintaining (and constructing) a contract between the authorities and society—as long as this contract remains relevant.

Notes

1 Before the administrative reform of 1923–1929 *volost'* was a small rural area subordinated to the city. The union of several volosts (including the city or village as a center) formed an *uyezd.*

2 During Alexander III's reign there occurred something of a setback; local justices of the peace were replaced by zemstvo bailiffs elected from among the gentry. Some case categories were withdrawn from the ambit of the jury and political cases were made less transparent.

3 A governorate (*gubernia*) was a major and principal administrative subdivision of the Russian Empire and the early RSFSR. In 1917 there were 78 governorates.

4 *Zemstvo*–an institution of elected local government, established under the reform of 1861. After the October Revolution the *zemstvo* system was shut down by the Bolsheviks and replaced with a multilevel system of workers' and peasants' councils ("soviets").

5 The highest organ of state administration that had lawmaking and some executive and controlling power. Was established by the 1936 Constitution. Replaced the Congress of Soviets and the Central Executive Committee of the Soviet Union.

6 As early as 1919 Petr Stuchka suggested codifying the new law. Constitution was to have pride of place, followed by the "social law" comprised of family law and social welfare law. After that were supposed to be "property rights" or, rather, laws abolishing and limiting these rights (land and industry nationalization, as well as ""the acceptability of using the residual vestiges of private property rights during the period of transition." The collection was to be completed by codified labor regulations, "leftovers of contractual law," and international law. Thus the systematized norm would become "the basic law that is compulsory for everyone," while all subsequent legislations would be nothing but technical guidelines. This first attempt to tackle the issue of a legal system was determined by a practical necessity due to the formation of the Soviet legislative system. The 1920s were a period of intensive work on codification of the law. This was when the *Civil Code*, the *Criminal Code*, the *Land Code*, the *Code of Civil Procedure*, the *Code of Criminal Procedure*, and the *Labor Code* were adopted and became operative, and the projects for the *Commercial Code*, *Industrial Code*, *Co-Operative*, and *Administrative Code* developed.

7 Joseph Stalin's conversation with the British author Herbert Wells. July 23, 1934. www.magister.msk.ru/library/stalin/14-1.htm. Quoted from www.marxists.org/reference/archive/stalin/works/1934/07/23.htm.

8 Pashukanis, Evgenii. 1980[1924]. The general theory of law and Marxism, in: Beirne, P. and Sharlet, R. (eds.) *From Evgeny Pashukanis, Selected Writings on Marxism and Law*, London and New York. pp. 32–131. Cit by: (Markovits 2007).

9 As a result of the postwar large-scale codification, the *Basic Principles of Law*, the *Civil Code*, the *Code of Civil Procedure*, the *Criminal Code*, and the *Code of Criminal Procedure* were adopted in all Soviet republics. In total, 15 basic legislative documents were adopted between 1958 and 1977. In the 1970s–1980s, the *Labor Code of the RF* (1971), the *Housing Code of the RF* (1983), and the *Code of Administrative Offenses of the RF* (1984) were adopted. In 1993, the *Customs Code of the Russian Federation* was adopted. In 1994–1995, two parts of the new *Civil Code of the Russian Federation* were adopted. In post-socialist Russia, the new *Family Code*, *Water Code*, *Forest Code*, new *Criminal Code*, etc., were also adopted.

10 Then the controllers from the NK RKI suggested to convey minor conflicts such as illegal production of alcohol (*samogonovarenie*), disputes between peasants, and civil lawsuits—to the public courts (*obshchestvennye sudy*), or to create the so-called "comrade courts" (*tovarishcheskie sudy*) and "rural public courts" (*sel'skie obshchestvennye sudy*). Supporters of the idea of the establishment of these types of courts interpreted these steps as a movement ahead from the formal legal structures and institutions to more socialistic and revolutionary forms of dispute resolution. In March 1928 *Sovnarkom* affirmed the decision about the foundation of the public courts. So, the civil justice was in a large scale withdrawn from the sphere of professional legal proceeding.

11 Resolution of the People's Control Commission at SNK SSSR "On Consideration of Worker's Complaints" [Postanovlenie Komissii Sovetskogo Kontrolia pri SNK SSSR "O rassmotrenii zhalob trudiashchikhsia"] from May 30, 1936. 1946. *Sobranie zakonov i rasporiazhenii Raboche-Krest'ianskogo Pravitel'stva SSSR za 1936 g.* No. 31, Art. 276.

12 GARF. F. 374, Op. 28. D. 3288. L. 160 (f.v.) (Cit. by Nérard 2004).

13 Simultaneously, the Resolution of Presidium of the TsIK SSSR "On Considering Workers' Complaints and Taking Requisite Measures" from April 13, 1933, and the Resolution of the TsIK SSSR "On the Situation with the Consideration of Workers' Complaints" from December 14, 1935, with additions by the Presidium of TsIK SSSR from May 7, 1937, were considered obsolete.

14 These kinds of addresses were established back when Alexander I founded the Commission for the Acceptance of Supplications, in the form of various petitions and projects advocating changes in various spheres of state structure.

15 In fact, at every level, from the federal to the district, the KPGK duplicated both the party and the Soviet system, augmented also by the right to conduct investigations, impose penalties and fines, and bring matters into court and prosecution. http://kpss-ru.livejournal.com/3178.html.

16 O khode realizatsii reshenii XXVII s"ezda KPSS i zadachakh po uglubleniiu perestroiki: Doklad General'nogo sekretaria TsK KPSS M. S. Gorbachev na XIX Vsesoiuznoi konferentsii KPSS 28 iuniia 1988 goda [The Progress of Carrying Out the Decisions of the 27th Congress of the RKP(b) of the Soviet Union and the Tasks of Deepening the Restructuring: Report of the General Secretary of the TsK KPSS, M. S. Gorbachev, at the 19th All-Union Conference of the Communist Party of the Soviet Union of June 28, 1981. 1988. *Izvestiia*. June 29, at 2, col. 1 [hereinafter Gorbachev].

References

Bogdanova, Elena. 2006. "Traditziia pravovoi zashchity ili 'v ozhidanii zaboty'." *Zhurnal sotsiologii i sotsial'noi antropologii* 9(1):77–90.

Boim, Leon. 1974. "Ombudsmanship in the Soviet Union." *American Journal of Comparative Law* XXII:509–540.

Boim, Leon. 1978. "Introduction." Pp. vii–xvi in: Leon Boim and Glenn Morgan (eds.) *The Soviet Procuracy Protests, 1937–1973 : A Collection of Translations*. Leiden: Alphen aan den Rijn: Sijthoff & Noordhoff.

Buliulina, Elena. 2010. "'Zhalobshchiki' i 'udruchionnye': O rabote s zaiavleniiami grazhdan v raboche-krestianskoi inspektsii v 1919–1920-e gg." *Istoriia Rossii* 2:98–105.

Burbank, Jane. 2004. *Russian Peasants Go to Court: Legal Culture in the Countryside, 1905–1917.* Bloomington: Indiana University Press.

Chechot, Dmitrii. 1973. *Administrativnaia Iustitsiia. Teoreticheskie problemy.* Leningrad: Izdatel'stvo Leningradskogo Universiteta.

Fel'dman, David. 2006. *Terminologiia vlasti. Sovetskie politicheskie terminy v istoriko-kul'turnom kontekste*. Moscow: RGGU.
Fitzpatrick, Sheila. 1996. "Signals from Below: Soviet Letters of Denunciation of the 1930s." *Journal of Modern History* 68(4):831–866.
Gorlizki, Yoram. 1998. "Delegalization in Russia: Soviet Comrades' Courts in Retrospect." *The American Journal of Comparative Law* 46(3):403–425.
Ingulov, Sergei. 1928. *Samokritika i praktika eio provedeniia*. Moscow: Gosizdatel'stvo.
Izvestiia. 1988. June 29, p. 2, col. 1.
Kabashov, Sergei. 2010. *Organizatsiia raboty s obrashcheniiami grazhdan v istorii Rossii*. Moscow: Flinta.
Kudriavtsev, Petr (ed.). 1956. *Iuridicheskii slovar'*. T.2. Pravovoe gosudarstvo. Moskow: Gosiurizdat.
Lenin, Vladimir. 1969a[1918]. "Ocherednye zadachi sovetskoi vlasti." Pp. 127–166 in *Polnoe sobranie sochinenii*. T. 36. Moscow: Izdatel'stvo politicheskoi literatury.
Lenin, Vladimir. 1969b[1918]. "Nabrosok tezisov o tochnom sobliudenii zakonov ot 2 noiabria 1918." Pp. 129–131 in *Polnoe sobranie sochinenii*. T. 47. Moscow: Izdatel'stvo politicheskoi literatury.
Lenin, Vladimir. 1970[1922]. "O 'dvoinom' podchinenii i zakonnosti." Pp. 197–202 in *Polnoe sobranie sochinenii*. T. 45. Moscow: Izdatel'stvo politicheskoi literatury.
Levitsky, Serge. 1990. "The Restructuring of Perestroika: Pragmatism and Ideology (The Preamble to the Soviet Constitution of 1977 Revisited)." *Cornell International Law Journal* 23:227–230.
Lobacheva, Galina. 1999. *Samoderzhets i Rossiia: Obraz tsaria v massovom soznanii rossiian (konets XIX- nachalo XX vv.)*. Saratov: Saratovskii gosudarstvennyi technicheskii universitet.
Lukach, Georg. 2004. "Rol' morali v kommunisticheskom proizvodstve." Pp. 449–455 in *Moral' v politike. Khrestomatiia*. Moscow: Izdatel'stvo Moskovskogo Universiteta.
Manov, Grigorii. 1989. "Sotsialisticheskoe pravovoe gosudarstvo: Problemy i perspektivy." *Sovetskoe Gosudarstvo i parvo* 3:3–10.
Markovits, Inga. 2007. "The Death of Socialist Law?" *Annual Review of Law and Social Science* 3:463–511.
Marx, Karl. 1970[1875]. "Critique of the Goths Program." Pp. 13–30 in Marx Karl and Engels Friedrich. *Selected Works*, Vol. 3. Moscow: Progress Publishers.
Moral'nyi kodeks stroitelia kommunizma. Posobie dlia propagandistov i slushatelei sistemy politicheskogo prosveshcheniia. 1965. Moscow: Politizdat.
Morgan, Glenn. 1966. "The Protests and Representations Lodged by the Soviet Procuracy against the Legality of Governmental Enactments: 1937–1964." Pp. 103–289 in Leon Boim, Glenn Morgan, and Alexander Rudzinski (eds.) *Legal Control in the Soviet Union*. Alphen aan Den Rijn: Sijthoff and Noordhoff.
Nérard, François-Xavier. 2004. *Cinq pour cent de vérité: La dénonciation dans l'URSS de Staline (1928–1941)*. Paris: Editions Tallandier.
Nikolaeva, Liubov'. 1960. "Zadachi i metody deiatel'nosti Komissii sovetskogo kontrolia Soveta Ministrov SSSR." *Pravovedenie* 3:15–24.
Oda, Hiroshi. 1984. "Judicial Review of the Administration in the Countries of Eastern Europe." *Public Law* 29:112–134.
Pyzhikov, Aleksandr. 2001. "Vnutripartiinaia bor'ba i evoliutsiia sistemy vlasti (1953–1957)." *Vestnik Rossiiskoi Akademii Nauk* 71(3):246–251.
Quigley, John. 1990. "The Soviet Union as a State under the Rule of Law: An Overview." *Cornell International Law Journal* 23(2):205–225.

Quigley, John. 2007. *Soviet Legal Innovation and the Law of the Western World*. New York: Cambridge University Press.

Shabalina, Evgeniia. 2007. *Istoriko-pravovoe issledovanie mesta i roli organov prokuratury v mekhanizme Sovetskogo gosudarstva: 1920–1930 gg. XX veka. Dissertatsiia na soiskanie stepeni kandidata iuridicheskikh nauk* (unpublished). Elektronnaia biblioteka dissertatsii. Retrieved on July 15, 2019 (https://www.dissercat.com/content/istoriko-pravovoe-issledovanie-mesta-i-roli-organov-prokuratury-v-mekhanizme-sovetskogo-gosu).

Shatkovskaia, Tat'iana. 2000. "Zakon i obychai v pravovom bytu krest'ian vtoroi poloviny XIX veka." *Voprosy istorii* 11–12:47.

Smith, Gordon. 1978. *The Soviet Procuracy and the Supervision of Administration*. Alphen aan Den Rijn: Sijthoff and Noordhoff.

Smith, Gordon. 1988. *Soviet Politics*. London: Palgrave.

Solomon, Peter H. 1996. *Soviet Criminal Justice Under Stalin*. Cambridge: Cambridge University Press.

Solomon, Peter H.. 2004. "Judicial Power in Russia: Through the Prism of Administrative Justice." *Law and Society Review* 3(38):549–582.

Vihavainen, Timo. 2004. *Vnutrennii Vrag. Bor'ba s meshchanstvom kak moral'naia missiia russkoi intelligentsii*. Saint Petersburg: Izdatel'skii dom "Kolo".

Vyshinksii, Andrei. 1934. *Revoliutsionnaia zakonnost' i zadachi sovetskoi zashchity*. Moscow: Redaktsionno-izdatel'skii sector mosoblispolkoma.

Normative documents

Circular Decree of Presidium of the VTsIK "On measures for consideration of peasants' complaints" [Tsirkuliarnoe Postanovlenie Presidiuma VTsIK "O meropriiatiiakh po rassmotreniiu krest'ianskikh zhalob"] from April 20, 1930, No. 130. 1930. *Izvestiia TsIK* No. 118.

Circular Directive of the VTsIK "On the Order of Submitting Complaints and Statements" [Tsirkuliarnoe postanovlenie VTsIK "O poriadke podachi zhalob i zaiavlenii"] from June 30, 1921. 1944. *Sobranie uzakonenii i rasporiazhenii pravitel'stva za 1921 g*. No. 49, st. 254. Moscow.

Civil Code of the RSFSR [Grazhdanskii Kodeks RSFSR] from October 1, 1964. *KonsultantPlus*. Retrieved on July 29, 2019 (http://www.consultant.ru/document/cons_doc_LAW_1838/).

Code of Civil Procedure of the RSFSR [Grazhdanskii protsessual'nyi kodeks RSFSR] from October 1, 1964). *KonsultantPlus*. Retrieved on July 29, 2019 (http://www.consultant.ru/document/cons_doc_LAW_2237/).

Code of the RSFSR for Administrative Offenses [Kodeks RSFSR ob administrativnykh pravonarusheniiakh] form June 20, 1984. *KonsultantPlus*. Retrieved on July 29, 2019 (http://www.consultant.ru/document/cons_doc_LAW_2318/).

Constitution of the RSFSR [Konstitutsiia (osnovnoi zakon) RSFSR] from July 10, 1918. *KonsultantPlus*. Retrieved on July 15, 2019 (http://www.consultant.ru/cons/cgi/online.cgi?req=doc&base=ESU&n=2929#07830313927410344).

County Heads Law [Zakon o zemskikh nachal'nikakh] from July 12, 1889. 1891. *Polnoe sobranie zakonov Rossiiskoi Imperii (PSZ RI)*. Vol. IX, No. 6196.

Criminal Code of the RSFSR [Ugolovnyi kodeks RSFSR]. 1922. *KonsultantPlus*. Retrieved on July 15, 2019 (http://www.consultant.ru/cons/cgi/online.cgi?req¼doc&base¼ESU&n¼3006#02329189944766851).

Criminal Code of the RSFSR [Ugolovnyi kodeks RSFSR]. 1926. *KonsultantPlus*. Retrieved on July 15, 2019 (http://www.consultant.ru/cons/cgi/online.cgi?req¼doc&ts¼3932787057891283574675 77&cacheid¼DFCA20D6D70CF9C518315827B660D1C0&mode¼splus&base¼ESU&n¼44458&rnd¼0.7541976983375034#06237323093016762).

Criminal Code of the RSFSR [Ugolovnyi kodeks RSFSR] with corrections by July 1, 1937. 1937. Moscow: Iuridicheskoe izdatel'stvo NKIu SSSR.

Decree of Presidium of the Supreme Council "On the Approval of Regulations on Comrade Courts and Regulations on Public Councils for the Work of Comrade Courts" [Ukaz Prezidiuma Verkhovnogo Soveta "Ob utverzhdenii polozheniia o tovarishcheskikh sudakh i polozheniia ob obshchestvennykh sovetakh po rabote tovarishcheskikh sudov"] from March 11, 1977. *KonsultantPlus*. Retrieved on July 15, 2019 (http://www.consultant.ru/cons/cgi/online.cgi?req=doc&base=ESU&n=1788#04989597648942343).

Decree of Presidium of the Supreme Council of the USSR on Establishment of Commission of Soviet Control [Postanovelenie Prezidiuma Verkhovnogo Soveta SSSR ob organizarsii Komissii Sovetskogo kontrlia] from August 23, 1957. 1957. *Vedomosti Verkhovnogo Soveta SSSR* No. 18, Art. 474. Moscow: Verkhovnyi Sovet SSSR.

Decree of Presidium of the Supreme Soviet of the USSR "On the Order for Considering Citizens' Suggestions, Statements, and Complaints" [Ukaz Presidiuma Verkhovnogo Soveta SSSR "O poriadke rassmotreniia predlozhenii, zaiavlenii i zhalob grazhdan"] from April 12, 1968. No. 2534-VII. *KonsultantPlus*. Retrieved on July 19, 2019 (http://www.consultant.ru/document/cons_doc_LAW_1929/).

Decree of SNK RSFSR "On Courts" [Dekret SNK RSFSR "O sude"] from November 22, 1917. *KonsultantPlus*. Retrieved on June 30, 2019 (http://www.consultant.ru/cons/cgi/online.cgi?req=doc&base=ESU&n=4029#04957375764177958).

Decree of SNK RSFSR "On the Abolition of Chancellery for Receiving Applications under the Provisional Government" [Postanovlenie ob uprazdnenii "Kantseliarii dlia priniatiia proshenii pri Vremennom pravitel'stve"] from December 6, 1917. 1956. *Dekrety Sovetskoi vlasti*. Vol. 25. Moscow: Politizdat.

Decree of SNK RSFSR "On the Elimination of Red Tape" [Dekret SNK RSFSR "Ob ustranenii volokity "] from December 30, 1919. 1974. *Dekrety Sovetskoi vlasti*. Vol. VII, December 10, 1919–March 31, 1920. Moscow: Politizdat.

Decree of the NKGK "Guidelines for Local Branches of the Central Bureau for Complaints and Statement" [Postanovlenie NKGK "O mestnykh otdeleniiakh Tsentral'nogo Biuro Zhalob i Zaiavlenii" (Prilozhenie)] from May 24, 1919. 1943. *Sobranie uzakonenii i rasporiazhenii pravitel'stva za 1919 g.* Moscow: Upravlenie delami Sovnarkoma SSSR.

Decree of VTsIK and the SNK of the RSFSR "On State Control" [Dekret VtsIK i SNK "O gosudarstvennom kontrole"] from April 12, 1919. 1943. *Sobranie uzakonenii i rasporiazhenii pravitel'stva za 1919 g.* Moscow.

Decree of VTsIK "On Ordering of Consideration and Resolution of Complaints" [Postanovlenie VtsIK "Ob uporiadochenii dela rassmotreniia i razresheniia zhalob"] from July 1, 1934. *KonsultantPlus*. Retrieved on July 15, 2019 (http://www.consultant.ru/cons/cgi/online.cgi?req=doc&base=ESU&n=24417#09754120112081706).

Desiatyi s"ezd RKP(b). Stenographicheskii otchiot. Mart 1921g. 1963. Moscow.

Law "On the Control Chamber of the USSR" [Zakon "O kontrol'noi palate SSSR"] from May 16, 1991. *Garant*. Retrieved on July 19, 2019. (https://base.garant.ru/6335024/).

Law "On the Procuracy in the USSR" [Zakon "O prokurature SSSR"] from November 30, 1979 No. 1162-X. *KonsultantPlus*. Retrieved on July 15, 2019 (http://www.consultant.ru/cons/cgi/online.cgi?req=doc&base=ESU&n=44512#05763704096986295).

Law of the RSFSR "On the Judicial System of the RSFSR" [Zakon RSFSR "O sudoustroistve RSFSR"] from July 8, 1981. *KonsultantPlus*. Retrieved on July 19, 2019 (http://www.consultant.ru/document/cons_doc_LAW_913/b45d333b1ef0087c643cdd1c12ca68f3062f1dbb/).
Law of the USSR "On People's Control in the USSR" [Zakon "O narodnom kontrole v SSSR"] from November 30, 1979. No. 1159-H. *KonsultantPlus*. Retrieved on July 15, 2019 (http://www.consultant.ru/cons/cgi/online.cgi?req=doc&base=ESU&n=44514#000539016565 7626067).
Letter of the General Prosecutor "On Improving the Work of Considering Citizens' Letters, Complaints, and Statements" from October 29, 1958.
Model Provision (Polozhenie) on Record Keeping as Regards Citizens' Suggestions, Statements, and Complaints [Tipovoe polozhenie o vedenii deloproizvodstva po predlozheniiam, zaiavleniiam i zhalobam grazhdan v gosudarstvennykh organakh, na predrpiiatiiakh, v uchrezhdeniiakh i organizatsiiakh] from November 30, 1981. No/ 463/162/298. *Garant*. Retrieved on July 19, 2019 (https://base.garant.ru/70417292/#friends).
Order of the General Prosecutor "On the Procedure for Resolving Citizens' Complaints and Applications by Organs of Prosecution" from December14, 1957. *Rezoliutsii XVII s"ezda VKP(b)*. 1934. Moscow: Partizdat.
Resolution of Disciplinary Responsibility VTsIK "On Disciplinary Action for Violation of Official Discipline in Soviet Organizations" [Postanovlenie o distsiplinarnoi otvetstvennosti VTsIK "O distsiplinarnykh vzyskaniiakh za narushenie sluzhebnoi distsipliny v sovetskikh uchrezhdeniiakh"] from January 27, 1921. 1986. *Dekrety sovetskoi vlasti v 14 tomakh*, Vol. 12. Moscow: Politizdat, pp. 224–225.
Resolution of Government of the Russian Federation "On the recognition of certain acts and provisions of the RSFSR and the Russian Federation, as invalid" [Postanovlenie Pravitel'stva RF "O priznanii utrativshimi silu nekotorykh aktov RSFSR i Rossiiskoi Federatsii i ikh otdel'nykh polozhenii"] from January 13, 2020. *KonsultantPlus*. Retrieved on February 10, 2020 (http://www.consultant.ru/cons/cgi/online.cgi?rnd=5B32A9ADB43291D701C374D9FE92E11D&req=doc&base=LAW&n=342928&dst=100086&fld=134&stat=refcode%3D16876%3Bdstident%3D100086%3Bindex%3D0#b6gc5d300pk).
Resolution of NKGK "On Local Branches of the Central Bureau for Complaints and Statements" [Prilozhenie k § 13 Postanovleniia NKGK "O mestnykh otdeleniiakh Tsentral'nogo Biuro Zhalob i Zaiavlenii"] from May 24, 1919. 1943. Pp. 392–394 in *Sobranie uzakonenii i rasporiazhenii pravitel'stva za 1919 g*. Moscow: Upravlenie delami Sovnarkoma SSSR.
Resolution of Presidium of the Supreme Council of the RSFSR "On Citizens' Suggestions, Statements, and Complaints Addressed to the Session of the Supreme Council" [Postanovlenie Presidiuma Verkhovnogo Soveta RSFSR "O predlozheniiakh, zaiavleniiakh i zhalobakh grazhdan, postupaiushchikh v adres Verkhovnogo Soveta RSFSR"] from July 15, 1968. *Pravovaia Rossiia*. Retrieved on July 19, 2019 (https://www.lawru.info/dok/1968/07/15/n1190104.htm).
Resolution of Presidium of the TsIK SSSR "On Considering Workers' Complaints and Taking Required Measures" [O rassmotrenii zhalob trudiashchikhsia i priniatii po nim neobkhodimykh mer] from April 13, 1933. *Sobranie zakonov i rasporiazhenii Raboche-Krest'ianskogo Pravitel'stva SSSR za 1933 g*. No. 26. Retrieved on January 19, 2019 (http://istmat.info/node/36152).
Resolution of the People's Control Commission at SNK SSSR "On Consideration of Worker's Complaints" [Postanovlenie Komissii Sovetskogo Kontrolia pri SNK SSSR

"O rassmotrenii zhalob trudiashchikhsia"] from May 30, 1936. 1946. *Sobranie zakonov i rasporiazhenii Raboche-Krest'ianskogo Pravitel'stva SSSR za 1936 g.* No. 31, Art. 276.

Resolution of the Plenum of the Supreme Court of the RSFSR [Postanovlenie Plenuma Verkhovnogo Suda RSFSR] from January 28, 1970, No. 53. *Garant*. Retrieved on July 19, 2019 (https://www.garant.ru/products/ipo/prime/doc/1682130/).

Resolutions of the Plenum of the Supreme Court of the RSFSR "On Improving the Work of Courts of the RSFSR on Fighting against Deceit of Consumers" [Postanovlenie Plenuma Verkhovnogo Suda RSFSR "Ob uluchshenii raboty sudov RSFSR po bor'be s obmanom pokupatelei"] from December 11, 1968, No. 43. *Garant*. Retrieved on July 19, 2019 (https://base.garant.ru/10164481/).

Resolutions of the Plenum of the Supreme Court of the RSFSR "On Judicial Practices in Cases of Deceit of Consumers" [Postanovlenie Plenuma Verkhovnogo Suda RSFSR "O sudebnoi praktike po delam ob obmane pokupatelei"] from December 12, 1964, No. 24. 1965. *Biulleten' Verkhovnogo Suda RSFSR*. No. 2. Moscow.

Resolution of the Sixth Extraordinary All-Russian Congress of Soviets "On the Exact Observance of Laws" [Postanovlenie VI Vserossiiskogo Chrezvychainogo S"ezda Sovetov "O tochnom sobliudenii zakonov"] from 8 November 1918 g. 1935. *S"ezdy Sovetov Vserossiiskie i Soiuza SSR v postanovleniiakh i rezoliutsiiakh*. Moscow. pp. 103–104.

Resolution of TsIK, SNK RSFSR "On Discilinary Responsibility in Order of Subordination" [Postanovlenie TsIK i SNK RSFSR "O distsiplinarnoi otvetstvennosti v poriadke podchinionnosti"] from March 20, 1932. *SU RSFSR*. No. 32, Art. 152.

Resolution of TsIK SSSR, SNK SSSR "On Extension of Rights of Working-Peasant Inspection" [Postanovlenie TsIK SSSR, SNK SSSR "O raschirenii prav raboche-krest'ianskoi inspektsii"] from May 4, 1927. *Pravovaia Rossiia*. Retrieved on July 25, 2019 (https://www.lawru.info/dok/1927/05/04/n1202100.htm).

Resolution of the TsK KPSS "On Measures to Further Improve the Consideration of Letters and the Reception of Workers" [Ob uluchshenii raboty po rassmotreniiu pisem i organizatsii priioma trudiashchikhsia] from August 29, 1967. 1972. Osnovnye zakonodatel'nye akty po sovetskomu gosudarstvennomu stroitel'stvu i pravu. Vol. 1. Moscow: Mysl', pp. 71–74.

Resolution of the TsIK of SSSR "On the Situation with the Consideration of Workers' Complaints," [Postanovlenie TsIK SSSR "O polozhenii del s razborom zhalob trudiashchikhsia"] from December 14, 1935. 1942. *Spravochnik raionnogo prokurora*. Moscow: Iuridicheskoe izdatel'stvo NKIu SSSR.

Resolution of VTsIK and SNK RSFSR "On Approval of the Regulations on Disciplinary Responsibility in the Order of Subordination" [Postanovlenie VTsIK i SNK RSFSR "Ob utverzhdenii Polozheniia o distsiplinarnoi otvetstvennosti v poriadke podchinionnosti"] from July 4, 1927. *KonsultantPlus*. Retrieved on July 19, 2019 (http://www.consultant.ru/cons/cgi/online.cgi?base=ESU&n=20689&req=doc#0 021357828088688358).

Statutes for the Provincial and County Institutions [Polozhenie o gubernskikh i uezdnykh zemskikh uchrezhdeniiakh ot 1 ianvaria 1884 goda]. 1864. Pp. 1–10 in *Polnoe sobranie zakonov Rossiiskoi Imperii*. Part I, Vol. 39, No. 40457.

Statute on the Organs of People's Control in the USSR [Polozhenie ob organakh narodnogo kontrolia v SSSR] from December 19, 1968. *KonsultantPlus*. Retrived on February 12, 2020 (https://www.consultant.ru/cons/cgi/online.cgi?req=doc&base=ESU&n=17477 #04274782552555565).

The Basic Principles of Civil Law of the USSR and federal republics [Osnovy grazhdanskogo zakonodatel'stva SSSR i soiuznykh respublik] from May 1, 1962. *StudFiles*. Retrieved on July 29, 2019 (https://studfiles.net/preview/1956207/page:71/).

The Basic Principles of Civil Procedure of the USSR and federal republics [Osnovy grazhdanskogo sudoproizvodstva SSSR i soiuznykh respublik] from May 1, 1962. *StudFiles*. Retrieved on July 29, 2019 (https://studfiles.net/preview/1956207/page:87/).

The Rules on the Order of Accepting and Redirecting Applications and Complaints Submitted to His Majesty [Pravila o poriadke priniatiia i napravleniia proshenii i zhalob, na vysochaishee imia prinosimikh]. 1906. *Polnoe sobranie zakonov Rossiiskoi Imperii (PSZ RI)*. Vol. XXVI. No. 27808.

The Statute on the Judiciary of the RSFSR" [Polozhenie o sudoustroistve RSFSR] from November 11, 1922. *KonsultantPlus*. Retrieved on July 15, 2019 (http://www.consultant.ru/cons/CGI/online.cgi?req=doc&base=ESU&n=8322#09004516584234421).

4 Request for justice through the late Soviet mechanism of complaints

How and to whom?

The late Soviet bureaucracy of complaints: How to use it and make it solve problems effectively

The formal rules of the mechanism of complaints, established by the 1960s, obliged virtually every official to accept complaints and respond to them in accordance with official regulations. The centers of political power—the Soviet and party bodies—represented the main hierarchical axis of the mechanism and handled all complaints regardless of subject. Individuals sent their complaints to their local district government and party offices. This main axis was supplemented by numerous branches of internal structures, which provided additional opportunities to restore justice. For example, in addition to the Soviet and party bodies, Soviet consumers could appeal to the agencies within the bureaucratic structure of the trade sector.

Within any sector of the Soviet economy, complaint recipients were organized hierarchically. The sector of trade included (listed from bottom to top) store management (head of the department, store manager, store director, accountant); organizational department (torg);[1] department of foodstuffs/industrial merchandise; general department of trade of the region (oblast') or the city; Ministry of Trade of the union republic; and finally, Ministry of Trade of the USSR.

Within individual sectors of the economy, an application followed a trajectory similar to the one defined by the general rules of complaint to the Soviet and party bodies. In the event of a problem, the consumer's complaint (either oral or written in the book of complaints and suggestions) first found its way to the management of a trade or service enterprise. If the management refused to redress the consumer's request, the complaint could be forwarded to the torg, to the trade industry department, to the General Department of Trade of the region (oblast') and the city, and ultimately to the Ministry of Trade of the USSR. As the intra-sectoral structures communicated with the Soviet and party bodies, complaint could be easily forwarded between them in compliance with the corresponding principles of subordination.

The basic rules of the mechanism determined the procedure of filing a complaint, the rules and time limits for its consideration, the rules of routing the complaint through the bureaucratic structure, and the sanctions for certain violations. The standard term of consideration was one month from the date of receipt of the complaint, which meant that the responsible actor had to compose and send a reply within one month. If the facts stated in the complaint needed to be verified, it also had to be done within the allowed month. If the complaint was redirected from one body to another, a new, shorter period of proceedings was established. In this way, the complaint would come full circle within a month—reach the right addressee (even in case of forwarding), be considered at some level of authority, and return to the author with a reply.

Different addressees had different sets of powers and, correspondingly, different opportunities to influence the problem. Higher Soviet and party bodies—district and higher-level executive committees (*ispolkomy*)—had the largest directive (*rasporiaditel'nye*) opportunities, in other words, the power to make administrative decisions or apply sanctions against the violators. Directive powers were concentrated in the executive committees of different levels: district (*raiispolkomy*), city (*gorispolkomy*), and region (*oblispolkomy*); the Council of Ministers of the Russian Federation or the USSR; and, finally, the Supreme Soviet of the USSR at the top level of the Soviet system. Structural units of the Council of Ministers of the USSR/Russian Federation—various ministries and departments—were also considered directive bodies, albeit with a narrower focus. Besides, like the executive committees, party bodies of all the levels also had directive powers. In order for a complaint to yield results, it usually had to be considered by one of the above-mentioned "directive" bodies.

However, a circle of "directive" bodies can be defined only tentatively. No Soviet document clearly determined what addressee was responsible for what type of complaints. Therefore, understanding which agency would be more effective in solving a particular problem became important informal knowledge for the Soviet complainant. Behind that knowledge, there was a recognition of manifold covert mechanisms of the society, an idea about how power was really distributed within the society, and a notion of how influential an addressee was. For instance, the Soviet press handled a certain range of problems well, despite a lack of administrative powers, because it directed the flow of complaints and did follow-ups. I will now examine how the complaint mechanism functioned in the late Soviet society, how one could make the enormous bureaucratic mechanism work effectively, and what complaint effectiveness meant in the late Soviet society.

Complaints to the highest Soviet and party bodies

The results of the work of the complaint mechanism have never been considered systematically alongside judicial statistics, although episodic studies conducted in the late Soviet years indicated that the number of complaints was huge. The Communist Party's Central Committee was also a very popular and influential addressee of citizens' complaints (see Table 4.1). During the period between the 25th (1976) and 26th (1981) Party Congresses, according to the Central Committee statement, the Central Committee received nearly three million letters

Table 4.1 Complaints to the Communist Party's Central Committee in 1976–1980

	Number of complaints
1976	693,260
1977	657,360
1978	558,740
1979	570,880
1980	671,600

Source: Spravochnik partiinogo rabotnika 1981:503–504

and accepted nearly one million visitors. Meanwhile, local party organs received 15 million written and oral submissions.[2]

The formal procedure determined in the normative documents required that the top levels of administration should consider complex, large-scale problems, those that could not be solved at the lower levels. However, archival records indicate that this rule was not always followed. The Council of Ministers received appeals regarding all kinds of difficulties in the everyday lives of the citizens, and some of these appeals were indeed resolved by the Council. Let us look at an example. In March 1968, an envelope arrived to the Council, signed: "Moscow, Kremlin, To Chairman of Ministers Kosygin." Inside the envelope, there was a letter of complaint:

> To the Chairman of Ministers Kosygin from Belov Ivan Sergeevich[3] res[iding at] st[ation] Ashukino n[orthern] r[ailroad]. Complaint. Comrade Kosygin the whole Khitrov market[4] moved to the stores whichever grocery you go to fraud is everywhere. Here are the facts. On March 11 in Moscow, store No. 35 on Masha Poryvaeva street, I bought a kilo of sausage. They weighed [for me] 40 grams less of Liubitel'skaia [*sort of sausage—E.B.*]. This is 12 kopecks. They didn't give me my money back and they didn't give me the book of complaints. I asked the name of the manager, they said Lapina Tamara Fedorovna. Salesperson Mikhailova Ira. I wrote to the general department many times, but this did not change the situation. I get a small pension and a store is worse than the Khitrov market, and when you ask for the book they scold you—like you have nothing to do but demand your kopecks. The question is, what is the general department doing? Isn't it time to dekulakize them like the old merchants were dekulakized. Belov.[5]

There is evidence in the archives that this complaint was forwarded to the Ministry of Trade of the RSFSR. As a result, an inspection was carried out, and measures were taken, as the violation was confirmed:

> To: The General Affairs Department of the Council of Ministers of the USSR. Moscow. Kremlin. The Ministry of Trade of the RSFSR reports

> that, in connection with the letter by Mr. Belov, we audited the store No. 15 "Gastronom" with respect to trade rules violations. The facts set out in Mr. Belov letter were confirmed. Salesperson Mikhailova was punished by a store order for violation of trade rules. Mr. Belov was informed of the results of the audit and the measures taken in a letter dated April 9, 1968.[6]

When filing an appeal straight to the higher levels of power, such as the Council of Ministers, the Central Committee of the Communist Party, any ministry, or a city level executive committee, complainants risked wasting their time.[7] Their appeals could remain unanswered, as the problems at the heart of the complaint were formally inconsistent with the recipients' level of power. Still, by appealing to higher levels, complainants acquired a number of advantages. If the complaint was indeed considered and resulted in a satisfactory decision, that decision, in fact, was an order not to be challenged. If the higher authorities redirected such an appeal to a lower level, it officially took precedence over other appeals and was considered as a matter of priority. Besides, the fact that the appeal was forwarded by direct or indirect superiors had an additional disciplining effect on the subordinate body. As seen from the complaint above, the damage amounted to just 12 kopecks—the cost of a medium-size loaf of bread or of an empty beer bottle brought in for recycling. Despite the problem being relatively small and the fact that it could have been attended to by local authorities, the complaint was considered at a high level of power hierarchy.

According to Aleksandr Sungurov, decisions of the party bodies had the real power in the socialist society, while in the legal sense the Communist Party had no powers of authority (Sungurov 1998:32). One of the interviews clearly demonstrates that an appeal addressed to a party body was considered most effective. The interviewee repeatedly pointed out that party bodies had priority among other addressees:

> You could complain to your superiors, but the Soviet government had no such powers to restore justice as the party. Of course, the party was much more powerful and had more resources. Therefore, often ... actually, all the time—the secretary of the district party committee [*raikom—E.B.*] was more important than the chairman of the executive committee [*ispolkom—E.B.*]. As well as a major of a city was nothing compared to secretary of a local party committee [*partkom—E.B.*]. For example, everybody knew the secretary of the Leningrad party committee, but far from everybody knew who ruled the city.[8]

The practice of filing complaints to the higher levels of authority was widespread; however, actual consideration of a complaint by a high-level addressee was the exception rather than the rule. A letter to a high-level Soviet authority would usually be redirected to a lower level with a comment, but only if that letter did not contain evidence of previous refusals or unsatisfactory responses from lower-level bodies. The comment was usually an order to consider the complaint within a given time frame, reporting back to the sender and all the people in charge who have dealt with the appeal. Non-compliance with such an order was regarded as insubordination, which could entail unpleasant consequences.

Much more often the complaints arrived to the higher levels in the form of reports from the subordinate levels of power. The reports contained generalized information on the structure, quantity, and dynamics of the received complaints. The Russian State Archive of the Economy (RGAE) stores many folders of excerpts from articles published in local periodicals[9] that cover the appeals received by newspaper editors. An archive folder like this would include both complaint texts published in full and excerpts from the articles based on complaints received. All these materials would be presented to the State Committee of the Council of Ministers of the USSR so that the highest authorities would get acquainted with the "situation on the ground." Markings and notes on the pages of the folder indicate that measures were actually taken based on the information received from the complaints—orders were issued to conduct additional inspections and bring the culprits to justice.[10] Thus, the Soviet complaint mechanism functioned as an essential instrument of governance and bottom-up control.

The late Soviet complaint mechanism functioned according to formal rules, which declared that local Soviet and party power agencies should be the primary bodies to resolve complaints. However, the formal rules were full of inconsistencies and ambiguity, and, in fact, their application was accompanied by multiple violations. The practice of work with complaints in the late Soviet era developed stable informal rules of involving higher Soviet and party administration in the resolution of complaints. Knowledge of these informal rules became an important resource that ultimately strengthened argumentation of the complaints.

Local executive committees

Receipt and processing of complaints were one of the central functions of the district executive committees (*raiispolkomy*) (Kerimov 1956:28). In cases when a complaint was not considered at the district level for some reasons or in cases when the complainant was not satisfied with the result, they directed their next complaint to the city executive committee (*gorispolkom*). In general, most complaints were resolved at the level of *raiispolkomy* and *gorispolkomy*.

The administrative function of *ispolkomy* enabled these bodies to make administrative and disciplinary decisions following the consideration of a complaint.[11] As the opportunity to file complaints was formally unlimited, *ispolkomy* were flooded with letters. In 1978, Theodore Friedgut presented the results of a study concerning work with citizens' complaints in local Soviet executive committees. Friedgut discovered that the flow of complaints was so massive that the officials did not have enough time to process all incoming appeals. According to the study, one of the district executive committees in Moscow[12] received 11,803 complaints during the first four months of 1962 (Friedgut 1978:466). Such a deluge of letters made it necessary to involve all the committee staff in the consideration of complaints pro bono. Meanwhile, according to the 1918 Constitution of the RSFSR, the staff of a district *ispolkom* should not exceed 15 persons (Kulikov 2003:140). In the 1960s and 1970s, this rule was still in force. Due to fixed time limits for the consideration of appeals, volunteers were involved in their processing. As a result, committee staff was continuously expanded due to the involvement of people's deputies and activists (Friedgut 1979:53).

According to Friedgut, the chairman of Moscow's regional executive committee (*oblispolkom*) received 7,815 letters and 1,561 visitors during the year of 1960. About a third of newly received applications were redirected to lower-level authorities, while 3,707 of all received appeals were forwarded to the *oblispolkom* from higher bureaucratic levels and were considered as a matter of priority. However, even among these important applications, about two thirds remained unanswered (Ibid:225).

The most labor-intensive stage of complaint management was fact checking, as it required the involvement of a large number of people. The facts of a complaint were most frequently clarified by a telephone call to the head of the enterprise mentioned in the complaint—or a visit, if it was necessary. Based on fact checking, decisions were made whether to grant or not to grant the complainant's request, and orders were issued specifying measures and sanctions against the violators.

The results of fact checking are available in the archives. The next example (see below the text of the complaint) is a reply to a complaint readdressed from a newspaper desk to the Kirishi *ispolkom*[13] in May 1972, and it shows that fact checking could be very thorough:

> There is an enterprise here in Budogoshch.[14] For many years, there has been a "mass-market sewing manufactory." The owner of this so-called manufactory is the Kirishi household production plant [*bytpromkombinat—E.B.*]. About 50 women work in that manufactory, but there is only one maintenance employee for every four members of staff! What does the manufactory produce? Duvet covers and pillowcases … . What pretty penny is this production worth? After all, the manufactory uses prehistoric technical equipment! Do we need this manufactory? Of course not. In the town of Kirishi, there is a long-standing need for a manufactory where duvet covers, pillowcases, and other things are made. Let's furnish it with today's equipment! And relocate these 50 women there! That's where they belong! V. Udilov. Budogoshch, Leningrad region, Ispolkomskii 21.[15]

The reply states the results of fact checking and provides the reason for rejection:

> The Kirishi City Executive Committee has verified the facts and the validity of the questions raised in V. Udilov's letter to the editorial office of the newspaper Sovetskaia Rossiia. The verification found: 1. V. Udilov indicated in his letter that the Budogoshch mass-market sewing shop of the Kirishi consumer services manufactory employs 50 women, while there is only one maintenance employee for every four workers. This fact is unreliable. In reality, verification has shown that the manufactory employs 59

people, including 50 piecework workers and nine time-workers, among them a mechanic, two quality inspectors, two cleaners, two seasonal stokers, and one driver. The shop is managed by one supervisor with a salary of 80 rubles per month, who is simultaneously entrusted with the management of other consumer services enterprises (hairdressing salon, shoe repair shop, etc.) V. Udilov raised the question that this manufactory is not needed in the settlement of Budogoshch but it should be relocated to the town of Kirishi. This question is improper for the following reasons: a) The manufactory produces mass consumption merchandise amounting to 1,350 rubles per year. B) The organization of this workshop has solved the problem of employment of the able-bodied population, mainly women. C) The relocation of the shop to Kirishi is impossible, even if it was viable, due to the lack of production facilities and accommodation—no funds were allocated for the construction of these facilities [*the settlement of Budogoshch is 35 km away from the town of Kirishi—E.B.*.] D. Rubanov, Chairman of the Committee. June 1, 1972.[16]

If *ispolkoms* reacted to complaints, their reaction was usually problem-oriented and focused on solving a specific issue. Individual complaints or groups of recurring complaints could result in a new park walk, bus route,[17] or service unit:

> In response to numerous complaints from residents of 3th–9th Lines of Vasil'evsky Island about the lack of laundries in their area, S. Varlamov, deputy head of gorispolkom, has declared that it is planned to open a laundry on 4th Line of Vasil'evsky Island, 62, in the upcoming quarter.[18]

One of the complaints concerned the noise caused by the unloading of bread delivered to the nearby bakery in the nighttime. In effect, the store committed no violations and followed the general standards of night bread delivery which existed in Leningrad at that time.[19] However, archival documents suggest that the time of bread delivery to that particular store was changed after the complaint—while the general rules of night bread delivery remained in effect, probably bothering residents of other houses in close proximity to bakeries.

It was much more difficult to achieve general improvements in the functioning of the administrative-command system—that is, in the smoothly running processes of production, distribution, and services. However, archival data show that it was possible in rare cases when the number and frequency of appeals regarding the same issue was sufficiently high or when the issue affected a large number of people. The system reacted when a specific problem or a specific complainant began to turn up often, drawing attention to themselves in the pile of letters. In this case, the problem was more likely to be considered and resolved. For example, a critical number of complaints about the same issue could initiate changes in the production plans of an enterprise: "There were other unflattering reviews of Krasnyi Treugol'nik[20] products, which necessitated management's decision to discontinue the 118–SFD molded boots."[21]

Table 4.2 Number of complaints on social security issues, received by the Leningrad City executive committee (1963–1965)

Years	*Total considered*	*Including repeat complaints*	*Results*	
			Redressed	*Dismissed*
1963	2,913	557	63	2,850
1964	2,854	455	32	2,822
1965	3,363	369	3	3,360

Source: Chechot 1973:104

Massive flows of complaints were always beyond the capability of the addressees. The law prohibited the executive authorities to ignore appeals, and, therefore, various strategies were developed to reduce the amount of letters for consideration. Complaints were rejected on formal grounds, forwarded to lower levels, or "lost" at any opportunity. According to Friedgut, among the 15,000 complaints composed by citizens in 1973, 10,000 did not go further than the local level of bureaucracy due to "poorly articulated statement" (*nevniatnost' izlozheniia*) (Friedgut 1978:470).

The likelihood of a complaint being redressed at the high levels of executive authorities was very low. Chechot (1973) gives data on the number of complaints received and considered by the Leningrad City executive committee (social security issues) (Table 4.2) and the Leningrad branch of the Ministry of Social Welfare of the RSFRS in the 1960s (Table 4.3). As we see from the data, the percentage of redressed complaints by the bodies of the Ministry of Social Welfare does not exceed 0.5% and in some years falls to 0.1%. The bulk of the Ministry's results of consideration is made up of clarifications and readdressings.

The work of local executive committees in the late Soviet period was less than effective. However, it would be wrong to consider it completely ineffective. In order to be taken up for consideration, the complaint had to overcome multiple entry barriers, but when succeeded, it could bring about all kinds of outcomes. Usually, if a complaint underwent consideration, the specific problem identified in the complaint was resolved—but without any interference with the general rules of operation of the administrative-command system. In resolving individual problems, the mechanism could work ultra-effectively. In rare cases, broader administrative changes could also be achieved under the influence of complaints.

Press

As the Soviet press evolved, departments for processing readers' letters were created in the editorial offices of all printed publications under the State Television and Radio Broadcasting Committee. The Soviet and party bodies exercised full control over the media, which meant that the editorial offices were included in the general mechanism dealing with complaints to authorities. The 1968 Decree

Table 4.3 Outcomes of complaints to the Ministry of Social Welfare of the RSFSR

Year	*Total received*	*Outcomes*					
		Redressed	*Redressed as an exception*	*Dismissed*	*Readdressed to lower levels*	*Clarifying responses*	*Readdressed to the local level*
1964	100%	0.5%	1.1%	15.6%	2.2%	38.3%	42.3%
1965	100%	0.3%	1.1%	12.5%	1.8%	39.0%	45.3%
1966	100%	0.4%	1.2%	11.3%	9.0%	38.6%	39.5%

Source: Chechot 1973:104

granted the press special powers to control the processing of complaints (Decree 1968:11), which significantly increased the importance of newspaper editors and their popularity as complaint addressees. Any public mention of a complaint—direct publication, a mention in a complaint digest, or a lampoon based on the complaint—did not only expose the guilty party but made the entire chain of those responsible for the resolution of the issue a target for criticism. This launched the process of fact checking and reaction from authorities.

As a result, the complaint mechanism attained its highest level of use in the 1960s and 1970s (see Table 4.4). The famous Soviet researcher Boris Grushin estimated that in 1966–1967, the newspaper *Komsomol'skaia Pravda* received 900–1,000 letters daily, or 300,000 annually (Grushin 2003:178). Stephen White (1983:52) gave even more impressive figures, arguing that all the Soviet national newspapers together received 60 to 70 million letters a year. The biggest-circulation national dailies—*Pravda, Izvestiia,* and *Trud*—received about half a million letters of complaints annually. For comparison, the number of civil litigation cases was between 3.5 and 3.8 million in 1957–1961 and between 2.5 and 2.8 million in 1962–1974 annually (Van den Berg 1985:145).

All local newspapers, including those published in Leningrad, *Leningradskaia Pravda* and *Vechernii Leningrad,* had special sections dedicated to complaints. These sections, titled "Measures Taken" (*Mery priniaty*), "You Wrote Us" (*Vy nam pisali*), or "Follow-Up to Your Letters" (*Po sledam vashih pisem*), published complaints and their outcomes almost every day. Radio stations that also had broadcasts with similar content were based on the complaints received by their editorial offices.

Technically a supplementary element in the complaint mechanism, the press turned into an important dispatcher in the circulation of complaints after the 1968 Decree. It became capable of improving the effectiveness of complaints by influencing other addressees. The editorial offices forwarded incoming letters to the addressees who were in charge of solving relevant problems. If a complaint was originally sent to an editorial office, it was redirected to an agency just above the offender higher in the administrative hierarchy. However, if the complaint was accompanied by evidence that it had already been filed elsewhere, as prescribed by the rules, but then rejected or processed improperly, then it could be forwarded to higher-level authorities, such as a district or city executive committee. Like the Supreme Soviet and party bodies, newspaper editorial offices used their own letterheads, and appeals on these letterheads were considered as a matter of priority.

Table 4.4 Number of complaints to the national newspapers in 1974–1981

	Pravda	*Izvestiia*	*Trud*
1974	456,000		
1975		467,858	548,174
1977		520,000	
1981	514,000		415,417

Source: Various Soviet Publications. See White 1983:52

As we can see from archival documents, if an editorial office took on a complaint, the editorial staff could do fact checking before forwarding the complaint to the authorities. In this case, the complaint was annotated accordingly, which facilitated its further processing and increased its chances of being considered. The archives show that editorial staff often retyped on a typewriter complaints written in illegible handwriting. This greatly facilitated further work and increased the chances that the complaint would be considered at a higher level of power, as it was much more difficult to reject it due to the most common reason—"inarticulate statement." After forwarding the complaint, the editors regularly followed up on it. They sent requests to the responsible bodies checking up on the progress with the complaint, with a "CONTROL" stamp on their letters. A copy of the notice on the results of the complaint was always sent to the editorial office. Thus, media outlets additionally monitored compliance with the time limits for the consideration of appeals. One of the informants, a newspaper editor, claimed that there were very few violations of the time limits for the consideration of appeals during the 1960s–1980s:

> They should definitely reply within a month. If there was no reply within … well, actually, there wasn't a case when they didn't send us a reply. A reply was mandatory. And in ninety percent of the cases, these were replies corresponding to reality.[22]

Published complaints, in other words, complaints introduced into the public space, had significant weight:

> any publication that was negative … let's say, a statement of complaint in a newspaper or on television, yielded most effective results. We had the newspaper Leningradskaia Pravda, and no senior official wanted to appear on the pages of that newspaper. Ever. Because they would face consequences up to dismissal. A publication in the newspaper of the obkom—and we were an obkom newspaper … an obkom and gorkom one … . I won't mention that, for any district official, the publication could pretty much result in dismissal. Well, a reprimand at least.[23]

The interviewee cited measures written in the 1960s–1980s statutes of discipline and disciplinary liability. This means that the officials who considered and resolved complaints may have acted in accordance with the law. However, the application of legal norms was optional and the correlation between the punishment and the violation was not always obvious. Complaint replies found in the archives contain such general wordings as "the store director has been punished" or "the situation has been rectified," without any mention of specific sanctions applied to the offenders.

Apart from directing the circulation of complaints and monitoring their processing, the press had at least one more important function, namely conveying the ideal-typical model of communication between citizens and authorities. My interview with an editor of a mass-circulation Leningrad newspaper suggests that complaints' texts were revised before publication. Both facts and style were checked, and every complaint was edited and modified to varying degrees. Just as importantly, a complaint published in a newspaper would be almost always accompanied by a reply. The publication could take the form of a question-and-answer compilation, when the complaint and the reply were published sequentially on the same page in the same issue. In other cases, a delayed reply could be published sometime after the complaint, which gave the impression of a time-consuming, realistic complaint processing. This public presentation of complaints along with replies was a powerful tool to convey the effectiveness of the mechanism, the responsiveness of the authorities, and the compromise between the interests of the sender and the addressee. Ultimately, this instrument broadcast the dominant model of communication between the society and the government—the model with room for dialogue, however indirect, distorted, ineffective, or non-equitable this dialogue might be.

The book of complaints and suggestions

The Soviet standard for the book of complaints and suggestions (hereafter BCS) appeared in Soviet institutions immediately after the Revolution. By Lenin's personal order, "every Soviet institution should get a book so as to record, in the most concise form, the name of the applicant, the essence of their statement, and the direction of the case" (Lenin 1973:366–367). The BCS was a stitched booklet with numbered pages. It was required that the book had the seal of the enterprise and the start date indicated inside. There was also a certain order of maintaining the book: the appellant's entry had to be followed by a reply from the management about the measures taken.

The BCS became most popular in trade enterprises and consumer services. An entry in the BCS turned out to be a way to inform the managers of the trade and service enterprises about consumer problems, and this way could bring positive results. According to the interviews, entries in the BCS could lead to all kinds of disciplinary actions and even to legal investigations.[24]

The interviews demonstrate that complaints in the BCS were subject to a hierarchy. Entries were sorted by importance or "seriousness" during inspection by the organizational department (torg), trade department, or inspectors of the People's Control. One of my informants was a store director in the late Soviet years. When speaking about violations, their seriousness, and the sanctions imposed, she combines moral categories (such as "being rude") with specific articles of the 1960 Criminal Code, albeit without specific references: "Deceit of consumers" (Art. 156), "Concealment of goods from sale" (Art. 156.3). "Not so serious" complaints were resolved at the level of store management. A serious complaint in the BCS, however, triggered a scenario in which the message was transferred to the higher authorities or to the court.

Thus, citizens received an opportunity to leave comments in the BCS regarding the work of the employees in a retail or service enterprise, which may have had some disciplining effect on the employees. Here is an excerpt from a complaint published in a newspaper: "After a rude response from salesperson M. Budilova, I asked for the book of complaints and suggestions. An apology followed immediately."[25]

An entry in the BCS was extremely undesirable for a store employee.[26] Therefore, retail and service employees developed various ways to conceal the BCS from their customers (Figure 4.1).

Meanwhile, according to official rules, failure to provide the BCS was a violation. Complaints often mentioned failure to provide the book under various pretexts or even without any explanation: "When I asked for the book of complaints, I was told that the manager took the book for inspection,"[27] "the book of complaints was missing."[28] The inaccessibility of the book of complaints was a frequent motive of Soviet caricatures during the 1960s–1970s. Along with plain failure to give the book to the customer, various schemes were developed to "mitigate" complaints in the book. For example, the book pages could remain unnumbered so that any unwanted entry could be removed at any time. Besides, salespeople wrote notes of appreciation in the BCS alongside customers' complaints in order to compensate for the violations in the eyes of the inspectors.

Like the complaint mechanism in general, the BCS had a complicated combination of guidelines, both formal and informal. The rules of operation, the sanctions,

Figure 4.1 Concealing the BCS book from customers.

and the classification of violations formed a fusion of regulations that brought together the legal basis, the socialist morality, and the managerial approach adopted in a specific institution. The boundaries between the mentioned systems were blurred, which is confirmed by my informants, who during the Soviet years served as a merchandise specialist, a store director, and an editor of a newspaper. Complaints resolvable by means of disciplinary instruments were classified as less serious, while more serious complaints required intervention of the court. However, there were no clear criteria to determine the severity of violations, and employees devised many ways to avoid or mitigate punishment and escape the consequences.

"Popular forces" and "professional complainants"

Mediating forces played a crucial role in the bureaucracy processing the appeals of Soviet citizens. By involving a "high-status" person as a proxy, one could make their complaint effective. My interviewees gave the names of specific people with the reputation of a "good person" or a "helper." These were usually high-ranking officials, people's deputies, prominent scientists, or cultural figures. A person in trouble could involve a deputy at the stage of drafting the application and choosing the addressee (Friedgut 1978:463). As deputies were part of the power structures, they were vested with the role of "experts" on the norms and rules of solving various problems in the late Soviet society. According to the interviews, the intervention of status providers could contribute to solving a problem, even if there were no legal grounds for it. Our first example occurred in the late 1950s:

> The families that were evacuated … like, common population, had no right to return to Leningrad.[29] Here's what happened with my mom: her parents died during the blockade. Her middle sister was evacuated with her school in August 1941. And my mom with her little sister were evacuated in June or July 1942, after the death of their parents. Then my mom brought her little sister from Central Asia to … to the orphanage where the middle sister lived, and went to my father in Chimkent. And there she got mobilized in Tashkent and went to the army. When she came back from the army, she had nowhere to live. She couldn't live in Leningrad. She couldn't make it, even though she's a frontline soldier, a Leningrader, she's … . It was so weird for me. She's got … parents buried there, yes. But she had no right to live there. Her apartment was occupied [*by somebody else—E.B.*]. And Nina Vasil'evna Peitser (*real name—E.B.*) helped her. She was a ballerina in the Theater of Musical Comedy, who knew my mom before the war. Nina Vasil'evna took care of my mother, she helped her during the blockade. Like, she was bringing her milk and some other stuff. Well, she helped my mom and my little sister survive. And Nina Vasil'evna was a deputy. A people's deputy, that's what they were called. And Nina Vasil'evna helped to my mom to write a

proper complaint, and they got the approval for my mom, and my mom was given a room [*in a communal apartment in Leningrad—E.B.*].[30]

The informant believed that the keys to solving that problem were social reasons, such as the status of a participant in the Great Patriotic War and the fact that the appellant and her family resided in Leningrad before the war. Besides, a prominent cultural figure was involved as an additional resource to resolve the situation.

Another story dates back to the early 1970s. Here, the lack of formal law is offset by the modesty of the request, the acuteness of the family's problem, and the informant's extensive experience in communicating with large bureaucratic structures by means of complaints:

> At the time, I lived in a small room in a communal apartment with my wife and my child. Before I got registered there, I lived in a very large apartment, so I had no legal right to get on a waiting list for a cooperative apartment. I wasn't put on the waiting list. I started writing complaints to every agency, like the bureaucracy works. Getting replies, and so on. One of the highest agencies at that time was the Session of the Supreme Soviet. I wrote a small letter there, saying that it's more, like, for the sake of courage. It was clear that they would refuse. They didn't. After some time—a long time, actually—I got a response from the housing cooperative. So basically, I was put on the waiting list.[31]

The skill of "writing complaints" was elevated to a "profession" in the late Soviet society: "This was a large category of people—"professional complainants"—who knew how to write complaints, complained about everything, and actually achieved a lot in this way."[32] The need to involve "experts" in drafting complaints arose due to particularly complex rules of the bureaucratic mechanism. Meanwhile, formally, the rules of filing a complaint were extremely simple. The complainant did not have to pay any fees, know the legislation, or understand the jurisdiction of the problem, as the complaint was forwarded to the appropriate addressee within the bureaucratic hierarchy. However, there were multiple barriers at the entry, as the bureaucratic apparatus was chronically overloaded and used any pretext to minimize the number of complaints.

Despite the apparently simple rules, it was extremely difficult to compose an "effective," "productive" complaint, which would force the mechanism to work in favor of the complainant.[33] To attain this result, one needed to know all formal and informal rules of the mechanism, the order of subordination within the power hierarchy, the addressees' level of influence at the moment of filing the complaint, the personalities and capabilities of staff members, and so on. If the mechanism was used with shrewdness, a complaint could help solve practically any problem. The sophisticated complainants, deputies, and public figures who regularly used complaints to solve various problems, as well as the bureaucracy employees themselves, were the best assistants in the preparation of effective complaints.

Combination of the complaint mechanism with the judiciary

It was not forbidden to file complaints to the courts. However, over the years the courts gained the right to review a short list of specific complaints (Solomon 2004:555). The 1964 Civil Procedure Code of the RSFSR listed among others the following complaints: errors in electoral disputes, seizure of property to cover unpaid taxes, fines and license suspensions imposed by the police, the actions of judicial enforcers (implementing debt collection decisions), and certain complaints against housing officials (Treushnikov 1997). As of 1980, courts were hearing annually around 11,000 such cases, especially against tax collectors (90%) and the police (9%) (Barry 1978:249–250; Oda 1984:124–125). The Law of the USSR "On the Procedure for Appealing Unlawful Acts of Officials Infringing the Rights of Citizens" in the 1987 version required that the complainant exhaust all administrative remedies before turning to the courts (Barry 1989).

Before the 1987 law was adopted, division between the complaint mechanism and judiciary remained penetrable. The late Soviet complaint mechanism was almost entirely locked on the state executive apparatus. The mechanism rarely came into contact with judicial institutions, but such contacts were not improbable; some archival documents demonstrate that a complaint's trajectory could indeed involve the judiciary.

One example is Pavlova's complaint regarding improvement of living conditions for her extended family of 12 people, who lived in two rooms with a total area of 43 square meters. The complaint was composed in 1962. Surviving correspondence shows that the complaint's trajectory involved legal action.[34] The grievance was initially sent to the editors of the magazine *Rabotnitsa*. From there, the complaint was redirected to the city executive committee. The request for the housing improvement in its initial form was denied, since the standards of that time provided for three square meters of living floor space per person. That is, according to the law, the family was not in need of more living space but, as a matter of fact, occupied nine square meters more than "necessary." After the initial rejection, the family appealed, successfully, to the court so as to divide the housing shares between two rooms, registering nine people in one room and three in the other. As a result, one of the rooms formally became overpopulated. Then, another complaint to the city executive committee followed, presenting the new version of the problematic situation. The reply from the committee contained the following sentence:

> By dividing their housing shares in this way, they deliberately worsened their living conditions. Given that these families had been promised improved living conditions, the Committee decided to resettle part of the family from the room with an area of 22.5 square meters (where 9 persons are registered).[35]

This means that the city executive committee granted the request regarding the expansion of the living space. This example demonstrates the success of a highly elaborate operation where each addressee played its role. The family's initial goal was divided into stages, one involving the courts, and, based on law, the court made a ruling favorable to the complainants. In fact, the registration of nine people in a 22.5-square-meter room was a violation of the minimum living space norm. The final decision of the city executive committee made it clear that, although the complainants' plan and their efforts were transparent, the power holders decided in their favor after the court judgment.

This case suggests that the link between the courts and the state and party bureaucratic structures responsible for reviewing complaints was weak, and some citizens took advantage of this fact to increase their chances of success. Each of the addressees made independent decisions, and the decision by the *ispolkom* was based on law, as was the court's judgment. There is a reason to believe that it is the combination of successive applications to both structures that helped the complainant to achieve positive results. Note that the whole proceedings took 2.5 months—the initial letter to the editors of the magazine was sent on February 28, 1962, and the *ispolkom* made the final decision on May 16, 1962. During this period, the district *ispolkom* reported twice to the city *ispolkom* on the results of fact checking, and the city *ispolkom* twice sent notices to the magazine editors.

It was interesting to find in the archive a similar complaint from Glushko[36] regarding the renewal of her place on the waiting list for housing. According to a newly issued order, a new housing waiting list was formed, and Glushko's family went from the top to the bottom of the queue: "my current number in the queue is 20,377." In her complaint, Glushko asked to restore her previous place in the queue. The living conditions depicted in her complaint were no less severe than those in Pavlova's one. A family of six people, among them three children and one elderly woman, lived in a 10-square-meter room. The room was refurbished from the kitchen and part of the hallway area on the ground floor. The house had no sewerage, no gas supply, and no running water. The complaint was sent to the newspaper *Pravda*, from where it was forwarded to the city *ispolkom*. Although the living space standards (three square meters per person) were grossly violated in this case, the city *ispolkom* did not grant the request.

The examined archival materials provide very little information about the relations between the complaint mechanism and judicial institutions. However, we can argue that citizens did employ strategies involving legal recourse, which sometimes brought positive results. Court decisions were treated with attention, apparently being important arguments to reinforce the complainant's position.

Thus, expectations that the complaint mechanism would fully replace the lower level of the judiciary never came true. There was always a lack of financial support, human resources, formal criteria, and formal authority to handle complaints and enforce decisions. The complaint mechanism offered no other instruments to enforce the decision on a complaint than filing another round of complaints to a higher authority. The areas of law displaced to the mechanism acquired a special status—they were considered unimportant and not requiring strict regulation.

The obligation to accept complaints and work with them connects all potential addressees into a common network: from a salesperson of a regular store to the head of the government; from the editor of a regional newspaper to the party's general secretary. Traveling from table to table, from office to office, from level to level, complaints blur the boundaries between departments, levels, and branches of government. Communications about handling of complaints generate mutual control and, also, strengthen informal networks among officials and everyone involved in complaints handling. Parallel to the formal power hierarchy, there emerged informal centers of power which were capable of resolving complaint issues better than the formal structures.

During its development, the Soviet complaint mechanism became an instrument to solve certain civil and administrative issues, including issues related to administrative justice. If this instrument had any degree of effectiveness, it was only due to its informal dimension. Throughout the existence of the Soviet complaint mechanism, the jurisdiction of problems had never been clearly defined. As there was no universal classification of violations by gravity, there was no universal sanctioning system either. By using the complaint mechanism, both the addressees and the complainants practiced derogation of formal rules. Techniques were developed that worked in parallel with the formal rules or bypassed them altogether. In order to make their complaints more effective, citizens devised methods that allowed selecting the addressee and defining the trajectory of their complaints. For example, addressees were implicitly ranked according to their ability to influence problematic situations. The choice of the primary addressee could affect both the trajectory and the result of the complaint, and it is no coincidence that addressees from the party and state apparatus were at the top of the complainants' lists of addressees. Complainants could also draw on additional resources, such as experienced complainants, deputies, the press, representatives of the authorities, or other experts who knew the whole complex of formal and informal rules for the functioning of the mechanism. Without knowing informal rules for the circulation of complaints, the distribution of powers among the addressees, and the order of their subordination it was almost impossible to turn the complaint into an effective instrument.

The addressees—the government and party officials—had to balance between the actual capabilities of the mechanism, the norms of socialist morality, and the formal legal requirements defining the procedure and providing minimal universal criteria. Caught up in these conditions, the mechanism could not function in a stable manner. For citizens, the demand for justice was similar to a lottery, where effectiveness was unpredictable, akin to an accidental prize. This explains why the complaint mechanism, completely ineffective in most cases, became ultra-effective with some problems. However, it is important to note that the government tried to improve the effectiveness of the complaint mechanism throughout the entire Soviet period. With its development, the mechanism became increasingly standardized and formalized, which simplified interactions by means of the complaint mechanism both for citizens and public officials. As the formal rules of operation grew clearer, the informal norms also took a certain shape, becoming "common sense." This development gradually helped overcome uncertainty and increased the predictability of results. Over time, a field of mutual understanding formed between citizens and addressees.

Late Soviet justifications: How to write a proper complaint?

In order to utilize the complaint mechanism effectively, one needed to know not only where and to whom to complain but also how to compose the complaint. Indeed, there were certain formal rules regarding the text of complaints. However, just as in the case of choosing the right addressee, these formal rules were only the tip of the iceberg of knowledge. The complainant had to know how to draft a complaint understandable to the addressee, one that would attract their attention and arouse sympathy.

Formal requirements for letters of complaint in the late Soviet period

A late Soviet complaint had a rather stable structure, and this was a result of a long process. The early 1930s saw the beginning of mass-distributed manuals and guides explaining the rules, procedures, and compilation of complaints (*Zhaloby passazhirov* 1934). But these manuals gave the least amount of guidance regarding the text and format of complaints. In particular, they indicated that "a complaint does not need to have any specific form. It is most important to express the matter as clearly and simply as possible" (Ibid:26).

The format of the complaint's text was shaped by various events and processes. On the one hand, the rules governing the complaint mechanism were formulated. On the other hand, the general principles of Soviet justice also had influence. Violations committed by officials were specially emphasized among legitimate reasons for a complaint: "incorrect decisions, formalism and red tape, ideological backsliding, distortion of the class line, rude and dismissive attitude, nepotism, suppression of self-criticism and prosecution for exposure, mismanagement, and other official misconduct." Anonymous letters were generally prohibited. A complaint should be signed to allow a response from the complaint's addressee. According to the same rules, collective complaints were undesirable (especially in the early Soviet years). Simultaneously, a collective problem was more important than a personal one: the statement of the problem had to contain a justification of its public importance (Grekov 1931). Finally, just as in the Soviet judicial procedure (Solomon 1996:21), class approach was key in the work with complaints. An explanatory text indicates that the complainant's status determined the significance of the problem:

> It is advisable to indicate your social origin in the complaint. This is necessary because we have a class approach to complaints. It is one thing if a farm worker complains that he was maliciously deprived of his electoral rights, and another thing if a former merchant complains about the same problem.
>
> (Grekov 1931:27)

Style requirements were also class-oriented:

> The Soviet regime takes note of the appeal content, and the less literate the complainant is, the more attention they get in the handling of their case [...] .

> There will not be any trouble if the text is written poorly or clumsily. If anything is unclear, it's possible to ask the complainant about it later."
>
> (Ibid)

The described components, formed in the 1930s, became the foundation of general requirements for complaint letters.

Later on, the rules of using the complaint mechanism underwent specification and refinement. In the mid-1940s, the Russian language curriculum for the fifth and sixth school grades included lessons dedicated to the rules of composing letters of complaint.[37] In the late 1950s, special manuals were published on composing complaints. A letter template was provided to help state the problem. The manuals also included recommendations regarding positioning of text elements on the page. General requirements for the structure of the text were also provided: "It is preferred that any written statement contains the following elements, besides the content (text) itself: name of the addressee, last name, first name, patronymic, address of the applicant, and a list of appendices, date of application, and signature" (Kozlov 1959:56).

Due to Nikita Khrushchev's reforms (see details in Chapter 3), the early 1960s saw a dramatic increase in the number of appeals to the authorities (Friedgut 1979:7–8). In order to optimize the handling of complaints, their text had to become even more standardized. Therefore, complaints manuals prescribed the following: "Write very honestly. Point out anything you do not know exactly, so that the editorial office has less work to do" (Zhidkov 1979:53).

The government tasked the mechanism with increasing the effectiveness of complaint handling. In order for this to actually happen, it was important to standardize the procedures of consideration and decision making. Hence, as the mechanism developed, requirements for the clarity of complaints' content increased accordingly, and it became mandatory for complainants to provide their contact information for feedback. By the beginning of the 1960s, complaints began to conform to the structure recommended in the complaints manuals. In a typical late Soviet complaint we can usually distinguish four elements: a salutation to a recipient, an outline of the problem, a description of the guilty party, and a description of the author of the complaint (Kozlov 1959:56). Herewith, throughout the Soviet period, the complaint maintained a free narrative form. At first glance, this may have offered the complainant complete freedom to choose arguments when demanding justice. However, this freedom was constricted by spontaneously developed particular rules and guidelines, and if a complaint did not conform to these rules, it could hardly be effective.

Hierarchy as a justification

The value of hierarchy manifested itself in complaints in several ways. First, there was a hierarchy of social statuses: the mechanism of the Soviet complaint (as well as of its predecessors) was based on demonstrating the difference in status between the addressee and the complainant. However, Soviet complainants faced a difficult task of emphasizing the hierarchy of relations when hierarchy itself was rejected by the norms of socialist morality. Essentially, the appellants used techniques that involved elevation of the addressee's capabilities and demonstration of their own powerlessness in the face of the problem: "You can do anything," "You are our last hope," "It is within your power to solve my problem." At the same time, a certain intimacy was typical of the relations between the complainant and the public official. The official salutations featured such epithets and linguistic constructions as *dorogoi* (dear, darling), *liubimyi* (beloved), and so forth. The paternalistic model of relations between the citizen and the government gained a friendly and kindred tone within the text of complaint (Utekhin 2004:283). This model of interaction implied that power holders were expected to help citizens, as if the power holders were older family members. Thus, complainants could use such addresses as *otets* (father), *brat* (brother), *synok* (sonny), phrasings like "You're like a member of the family to us," and so on. In the Russian/Soviet context, this type of address demonstrated respect, reduced distance, and personalization of the relationship. Meeting in person was presented as a pleasant opportunity. One complainant regretted that he failed to meet with the addressee: "When I was in Kirishi, I came by your office. You were away on a business trip. Therefore, I had to appeal in writing."[38]

The use of such techniques in Soviet complaints was far from accidental. First, they helped correlate the very act of complaining with the norms of socialist morality, which proclaimed humanism in social relations: "Man is a friend, comrade, and brother to his fellow man" (*Moral'nyi kodeks*, p. 6). Besides, the metaphor of comradeship and family facilitated the acknowledgment and support of hierarchical relations at a time when inequality, dependency, or problems could not be called by their proper names. Note that complainants attempted to establish a relationship of trust with their addressees by means of written text. This suggests that the outcome depended critically on the particular official who handled the case and on that official's personal attitude to the problem.

Public good as a justification

Complainants frequently used various generalizations to legitimize their complaint and reinforce their argument. An individual problem—a purchase of a defective bicycle or rotten vegetables, or a poor performance of public utility services—is presented as a large-scale issue affecting entire groups of citizens—or even the interests of the whole country.

L. Boiko, facing the problem of poor service at one of the dry cleaners, justified her complaint as follows:

> The service—the household service [*sluzhba byta—E.B.*]—is a big deal. It does not tolerate the indifferent. Today, when one of the main tasks of the Communist Party is to provide quality service to Soviet citizens, there is no place for indifference in the household service.[39]

> Another example is a complaint by M. Panova, who was unsatisfied with the cologne she had purchased: "Fighting for product quality is a matter of great national importance and a matter of honor for every enterprise collective."[40]

Here is a quote from a complaint by A. Karmanov, who purchased a faulty measuring instrument:

> Fighting for the honor of the factory brand, for good quality manufacturing, for the reliability and durability of machines, instruments, and devices is one of the conditions for successfully creating the material and technical base of Communism and improving every Soviet person's well-being.[41]

Generalizations concerned not only the scope of the problem but the number of people affected. The number of people filing a complaint, or the number of "victims," could attract attention of the addressees. An appeal signed by a single sender could be submitted on behalf of a group or community, like in the following example: "Photo albums priced 2 rubles 80 kopecks used to be in great demand among customers. Now these albums are no longer available. It turns out that the Svetoch factory discontinued their production. It's a pity. B. Tatarov, amateur photographer."[42]

Here is another example:

> Sports enthusiasts are pleased to note that Leningrad shops offer quite a wide selection of skis nowadays. I didn't have much trouble buying excellent downhill skis for my son. I bought the shoes, too, but both [*the skis and the shoes—E.B.*] lie idly in the hall closet. The problem is that it is impossible to buy slalom ski bindings in the whole city. They are unavailable now, and they were unavailable last year, too. No Leningrad enterprise, including the experimental plant "Sport," would come to the aid of ski lovers?[43]

To elevate the importance of the problem, an appeal could be signed by a whole collective of people concerned. The exact number of signatures was usually indicated in collective appeals:

> We, drivers of the 2nd Leningrad Taxi Fleet, are compelled to appeal to the newspaper. Until recently, we used to have lunch breaks in the canteen of the taxi company. The menu always left a lot to be desired, and there was always enough space for one shift only. There were often waiting lines, and one had to wait for a seat. The administration fed us with promises to attend to the nutrition of the employees next year. Guess what? Now our canteen is closed for good (107 signatures).[44]

The ideological principles proclaimed the priority of collective problems over personal ones, but they were hostile to collective action. Technically the complaint mechanism in the late Soviet society was based on the principle of signal accumulation. In order to draw attention to the problem, complaints had to repeat and pile up. The complainants aligned their messages with this rule, keeping in line with the norms of socialist morality encouraging everyone to fight for the public good, but avoid provoking collective activity.

Efforts of the state as a justification

A complaint filed with the authorities usually contained criticism of the living environment. However, the ideology did not envisage the existence of citizens dissatisfied with the organization of the Soviet society, the Soviet economic regime, or the quality of domestic merchandise and services. According to Soviet ideology, safeguarding the rights of the citizens was a permanent concern of the Soviet state, while "legal norms were easily implemented due to the conscious behavior of Soviet citizens" (Kerimov 1956:16). The ideological framework also maintained that Soviet society had perfect legal order, with only "rare and exceptional" cases of violation. The fact of complaining itself required explanation. As a result, justification of the complainant's position was often carried out through the demonstration of positive personal moral and social qualities. This technique of justification was reflected in various self-presentations, as illustrated by the examples below. In a consumer complaint, it was also important to demonstrate the modesty of the consumer's claims. The text of the following complaint shows how the complainant's claims do not go beyond the established standards:

> The state has established each Soviet family's right to one refrigerator. I am on the waiting list in a store that hasn't been stocked with refrigerators for six months. There are 90 people ahead of me. I would like to know, what are the immediate plans for the delivery of refrigerators to the stores of Vasileostrovskii district?[45]

It is also typical for complaints to be formulated as a manifestation of struggle against small shortcomings against the backdrop of general well-being. The problem is presented as a minor flaw among overall advantages and achievements of the socialist society. Here is an example of how this technique was applied "thanks to the local authorities a lot of standard fences were repaired, and they all were painted; meanwhile, all sorts of swill flow from many courtyards out onto the street ditches, emitting a stench."[46]

Ideal model of the Soviet person

Condemnation is a universal and very common form of argumentation in complaints. While criticism of the Soviet system as a whole was not permissible, it was allowed and even encouraged to criticize specific culprits, especially in the absence of administrative justice. Condemning a wrongdoer—be it a store director, a plumber, or a bus driver—became an almost mandatory element in the late Soviet complaint.

What is peculiar about the methods of condemnation in Soviet appeals is that the culprits are attributed negative characteristics that correlate with the model of an ideal Soviet person. At the same time, the complainant justifies their personal expectations of state care by demonstrating positive aspects of their own social and moral status, also correlated with the ideological model.

Let us compare the ideal Soviet person's characteristics and the way complainants described themselves. It can be argued that there was a common imperative of an "exemplary" Soviet person in the socialist society (Levada 1993:15). According to the Code of the Builder of Communism, Soviet citizens were expected to have certain qualities and meet the following requirements: "conscientious work for the benefit of society," "everyone's concern for the preservation and enhancement of the public domain," "humane relations and mutual respect between people," "honesty and truthfulness," "intransigence to injustice, parasitism, dishonesty, careerism, and possessiveness," and so on (*Moral'nyi kodeks* 1965).

Consumers condemned the wrongdoers by using the categories opposite to those formulated in the Code: "employees of the cafeterias in the department stores Gostinyi Dvor and Passage[47] allow abuse when selling juices and soda."[48]

Or: "The Lenmebel'torg furniture store No. 2 has its delivery service organized in a very strange way … . A group of hacks with state-owned cars offer to drive your purchase to your home."[49]

Here is another example: "salespeople use thick sheets of paper to wrap the purchase. One shouldn't be so negligent about the material and use precious paper in such a wasteful manner."[50] Or:

> I felt very uncomfortable in Chaika [*a store—E.B.*] when I was picking out what I needed. The salespeople answered my questions with indifference, and it was clear that they had no desire to help the customer. The salespeople are neither nice nor helpful. I was deeply saddened by their attitude. So I left without buying anything.[51]

The analysis demonstrates a dichotomy between aspirations and reality: "conscientious work for the benefit of society"—"being negligent"; "everyone's concern for the preservation and enhancement of the public domain"—"using paper in a wasteful manner"; "humane relations and mutual respect between people"—"neither nice nor helpful," "indifferent."

The complainants' self-characteristics, on the contrary, were always positive, as they emphasized their conformity to the expectations of the socialist state. For instance, the complainant's signature may include a socially acceptable status in the late Soviet society: "candidate of economic sciences," "engineer," or "research fellow at the Leningrad University." Certain service to the society may also be mentioned, such as "participant in the Great Patriotic War" or "worker with 35 years of factory job experience."

Condemning the culprit and proving one's own righteousness were extremely important components of the Soviet complaint. Some of the categories used in these components—negligence, for example—were simultaneously part of the ideological discourse and a legal category. It is hard to judge whether the complainants who accused others of negligence knew that it was categorized as a criminal offense. However, it is obvious that their arguments had nothing to do with the legal discourse. It follows from the complaints that the right to protection is not given to any citizen a priori, by birth. This right has to be justified in every single case, wherein not only the culprit's guilt is brought to light, but the complainant's moral and social merits are demonstrated.

Law as justifications

It was not forbidden to appeal to the law in the complaints, but it was not recommended either. There are very few references in the complaints to legislation as a source of norms. Among all Soviet complaints that I have analyzed, authors of only three of them refer to the legislation, appealing rather to the spirit than to the letter of the law; for instance: "According to Stalin's Constitution, everyone has the right to rest." By a stretch of imagination, we can also link typical late Soviet demands that the state take care of things to the law, because the 1977 Constitution stipulates that the state would take care of every citizen. When asking for care, the complainants did not make reference to the Constitution. Due to multiplicity of meanings of the category, originating from the sphere of private and family relations, the request for care in the complaints sounded like a moral justification. However, formally, this is a key code of the late Soviet contract between the state and society, which was fixed in the legislation.

Appealing to the promise of state care was a universally applicable justification of the complaints. Here are some typical phrasings reflecting this type of justifications, found in consumer complaints: "Why won't the state take care of us?";[52] "Where is the promised concern of the state for the interests of consumers?"[53]

Representatives of vulnerable social groups could count on special attention and care on the part of the state. Among the other arguments, the complainants considered it important to add to their last names certain characteristics or statuses that would stress their need for state's care and protection: "old-age pensioner," "disabled person of category II," "mother of three."

The socialist state not only promised the care to everyone. It also prescribed citizens to take care of each other, which is reflected in the complaints. The problem may often be presented in such a manner as if it was observed from the outside, so that the complainant would appear as an empathizer showing concern for others. The example below is a complaint to the newspaper *Izvestiia*, submitted in 1962:

> To the editor of the newspaper Izvestiia of the VtsIK USSR. Mister editor, please publish my note in your respected newspaper. The settlements of Lakhta and Ol'gino in the Sestroretsky district of Leningrad are used to be

> considered as a holiday resort area, but the trouble is that we are very badly prepared to welcome vacationists and children of workers from Leningrad in the summer of 1962. In particular, the stores in Lakhta and Ol'gino are short of bread and buns, especially on weekends, and [they're short of] other groceries, [too;] there is also not enough water, long [and] time-consuming waiting lines, and yet part of the population remains with no bread, no groceries, and no water.[54]

Indirect references to the Soviet legislation were not uncommon. In these cases, offenses were named, but without indication of the corresponding article of the criminal or administrative code: sabotage, negligence, disorderly conduct, or deceit. As each of the above terms was widely popularized in the public discourse, these concepts could denote both offenses and moral misdeeds in the late Soviet discourse. It is still unclear whether the complainants were trying to show their knowledge of the law or merely using categories broadcasted through ideological channels. Did the complainants appeal to official legislation, or did they seek the basis of justice in the area of morality or human values? Here, we should undoubtedly look at the status of law as a regulatory system in the Soviet society. The complainant could choose not to appeal to the legislation not due to a lack of knowledge but because such justifications would most likely be interpreted as a belief in formalism and the soulless bureaucratic machine. In this way, the complainant would be perceived as disregarding the ideologies of a "humane approach" and "attention to the workers' needs." The analysis of complaints and interviews clearly shows that while the complainants may well have been aware of their legally guaranteed rights, legal argumentation was on the sidelines in the text of their complaints.

However, analysis of replies to complaints yields somewhat different results. When composing replies, addressees often translated the narrative description of the problem into legal language. This is evident in the following complaint, delivered to the newspaper *Leningradskaia Pravda*:

> I have to ask you a question that is of concern not only to me but perhaps to almost all the residents of our settlement. We have a department store. Not long ago, I had to deal with the following issue. One day my wife came home for lunch and showed me what she bought. These were shirts, and each of them had a label indicating the size and price. 2 women's shirts for 5.60 rubles and one men's for 9 rubles. In total, all this costs 20.20 rubles. That is, according to the prices on the labels. But my wife was charged 22.90 rubles. There are no other prices on the labels (I'm sending them to you). In fact, we have a village store [*sel'mag—E.B.*], and they charge some extra % for transportation. But it cannot be that knitwear products would have a retail markup of 2.70 rubles per 20.20 rubles. I had to go to that store. When I asked what is the markup for knitwear, the saleswoman answered, up to 8%. I say: "Look, it's more like 13% here." The saleswoman blatantly answers: "We have double markup." I say: "What do you mean, double markup?" The

> answer: "Just like that—the merchandise arrives to the warehouse, there's a markup there, and then it comes to the store, and I do another markup." Later, I went to work. After work, I came there again. This time, there was a more polite saleswoman, who asked me to bring the merchandise, made a recalculation and returned 90 kopecks, i.e. the markup was already 1.80 and not 2.70 rubles. But the saleswoman made that recalculation with great difficulty, just because she doesn't know how much extra to charge. When I asked what their markups were, she openly said: "I don't know for sure. Please show your bills of dispatch, it should be specified there. If you are interested, please welcome to the warehouse, all the bills are over there." Of course, it cannot be that she has no bills of dispatch at hand. Going to the warehouse to find out how much this or that thing is—no one can take it. But to leave the store and contemplate whether you were charged correctly for your purchase is also no good. So judge for yourself—she overcharged me by 90 kopecks. 1.80 rubles the markup—nothing proves that she charged me correctly. What's more, she says: "Go to the warehouse, let them write the interests off my account, I will only thank you." Well, she may thank me, but I cannot thank her for anything but the fact that she put her hand into my wallet in my presence. Dear editors, I ask for your assistance in establishing honest trade practices in the store. 19.03.62.[55]

In the reply below, the addressee refers, albeit indirectly, to Article 156.6 of the Criminal Code, "Violation of State Price Discipline":

> The facts of violation of price discipline were confirmed. The price of men's shirt art. 1063, class II, size 48 is 9 rubles 60 kopecks, plus 1.5% cartage fee of 14 kopecks. Total 9.74 rubles. Women's undershirt art. 1025, class I, size 48 plus 1.5% cartage fee, i.e. 9 kopecks. Total 6 rubles 09 kopecks (you bought two undershirts). Total payable 21 rubles 92 kopecks, and you paid 22.90. The amount overpaid is 98 kopecks. The board of Leningrad Region Consumers' Union [*Lenoblpotrebsoiuz—E.B.*] orders to return the overpayment to Mr. Levchenko. The department store board will consider bringing to justice those responsible for the inflated prices and will issue a decision no later than on 10.04.62.[56]

The addressee found the definition of the problem in the legislation and classified it accordingly. This means that the bureaucratic apparatus responsible for dealing with complaints most likely understood its responsibilities in terms of legislation. In practice, officials working with complaints tried to apply the law in the prescribed manner. In processing the complaint, they examined the problem, checked the facts of violations, classified the problem according to its severity, and determined necessary disciplinary actions. It was not required that the complainant—a citizen—know the law. However, it was required that the official—the addressee of the complaint—have good knowledge of both law and ideology.

Universal justifications: Pre-legal discourse

Much more typical of Soviet complaints were justifications that made no reference to the law but rather represented a request for the protection of basic human rights of freedom and dignity. Among such justifications were claims related to the protection of life and health or the inability to fulfill basic human needs. This is the most common and archaic type of justifications premised on the basic values given to everyone by birth. In the late Soviet system, they did not mature into legal requirements but sounded in the citizens' complaints in their "raw" form, presented as direct experiences and physical suffering perceived by the complainants as an injustice.

One of the Leningrad district executive committees received the following complaint in 1959. The reason for the complaint was incessant noise in the apartment:

> a two-weeks' or a month's stay in such "housing" can lead to a serious nervous disorder … . Some of us, having reached the last limit of patience and exhausted our nervous systems, simply cannot be at home and must go outside so as not to get ill.[57]

Another complaint mentions unacceptable hospital service: "the patients are starving. As a result, there are facts of emaciation and fatigue."[58]

Direct requests for the protection of human and civil honor and dignity were very rare in late Soviet complaints. Here is one example:

> The article "Gears and Morality," published in the newspaper Leningradskaia Pravda, Issue No. 219, tendentiously slanted the facts, which undermined my years-long work and my reputation. I am in danger of civil death. Please help me establish the truth and protect me from my persecutors.[59]

Indirect complaints regarding violations of human dignity were more typical in the late Soviet period. The everyday life, with its long waiting lines, low living standards, and an underdeveloped social safety net could leave citizens with an acute sense of injustice and humiliation. For example, the following expressions are commonly seen in complaints: "I have a very low salary"; "We have to stand in lines for several hours after work"; "I saved money every month and denied myself the basics." These justifications sound particularly bitter when the complainant's status and merits are clearly at odds with the nature of the problem and the role of a supplicant. For example, here is a complaint by a disabled veteran of the Great Patriotic War requesting permission to purchase a refrigerator on a priority basis. The complainant calls attention to his status: "I am ashamed to write to you, but I cannot do otherwise."[60]

Thus, both the formal and spontaneously emerged rules of writing and filing complaints contributed to the preservation of lengthy narratives, personalized and laced with emotion. In the text of complaint to the authorities, the affective and existential components—grievances as the "shorthand" of social ontology (Ries 1997:1)—are not separated from the functional component that conveys the actual message about injustice. Instead, the affective component remained an important functional element of the complaint throughout the Soviet times.

The space of communication between citizens and state bodies developed a system of codes that provided for mutual understanding and enabled the bureaucracy to be remotely effective. Every sustainable form of communication was standardized, and the complaint narratives were highly clichéd. In the complaints' texts, we find certain recurring norms of fairness, as well as particular repetitive techniques of argumentation and justification.

According to Elizabeth Mertz, in the late Soviet years the acts of copying the precise forms of ideological representations became more meaningfully constitutive of everyday life than the adherence to the literal ("semantic") meanings inscribed in those representations. This new "pragmatic model" of language is comparable to how language is viewed in Anglo-American legal practice (Mertz 1996:234). Specific "technical concepts" serve as markers linking the text with a particular context. As soon as these links are established, manifold new interpretations may start developing on top of them. "In the pragmatic model the meaning of texts is neither literal nor final—it profoundly depends on the context and on the reader-interpretation" (Ibid: 234–235).

The codes of complaint are organized into a very complex system, similarly to the way legal language markers operate. The complexity, however, is not due to the fact that the complaint is written in a non-legal language. Rather, the problem is that the language of complaints cannot be associated with a single regulatory system. Predominantly, it is rooted in the system of socialist morality. The most popular justifications refer to the general tenets of Soviet ideology, developed and widely circulated by the 1960s, such as the principles of collectivism, concern of all for the good of each, and the struggle against specific shortcomings. There are also linkages to the specific rules of complaint drafting, such as class approach, substitution of administrative justice, and preference for issues important to the public. However, the language of complaints is not limited by the norms of socialist morality—it also acknowledges legal norms.

It encompasses the rules of contract between citizens and the government. The complaint is a reflection of the whole framework of social relations—both the macro-scale of the paternalistic contract and the micro-scale of interpersonal relationships. To fully understand this common sense, it is not enough to study the basics of law or ideology. One should take into account the ideal Soviet person's internalized qualities, which could be crucial for the effectiveness of a certain complaint. The "concerned," "caring," "humane" attitude of a particular editor or public official to the citizens' complaints was a real force that could influence the outcome of the case. Knowing this fact was part of the common sense. This knowledge, embedded in the text that took the form of appeal to the benevolence of the addressee, could in some cases overcome the ineptitude of the bureaucracy.

Both authors and (most importantly) addressees attempted to classify the violations presented in the complaints to coordinate them with the Soviet law and the norms of socialist morality. However, social, moral, and situational details remain relevant in every case. Over the long history of the Soviet complaint mechanism, there crystallized a complex fusion of legal norms, ideology, and personal qualities of the addressees. Complainants substantiated their cases based on common sense, while addressees separated justice from injustice, identifying and classifying legal problems. Moreover, every complainant presented their problem as unique. The fate of the request for justice—in fact, the legal status of the citizen—depended on justifications and the author's ability to present them correctly in the complaint.

Conclusion

The Soviet mechanism of complaints never was very effective. It never had enough resources to execute the tasks that were prescribed to it. Expectations on the part of the state and case load always exceeded its capacity. Until the very end of the Soviet period the mechanism remained underdeveloped. It showed efficiency only episodically and was dependent to a large degree on the motivation of particular specialists involved in the consideration of complaints. The mechanism compensated for certain gaps in the Soviet judiciary but not all of them. There were large segments of problems that were not covered at all—for example, abuses of office at higher levels of authorities.

On the road to success, the late Soviet complaint met peculiar challenges and barriers. For one, there was a huge number of complaints competing for the right to be considered by the addressee and the whole variety of tricks used by authorities to reduce the number of complaints: losses, non-receipts, runarounds, wrong forwarding, and so on. Also, special assistants could contribute to the effectiveness of the complaint: an acquaintance who was a deputy or a ballet dancer, or a neighbor skilled in writing complaints. As a result, the practice of the late Soviet complaint formed a special idea of efficiency, success, and failure in a search for justice. And the search itself required great persistence and very good knowledge of the formal rules for filing complaints and the informal rules of the functioning of the mechanism.

The border between the formal and informal norms of complaining was flexible and penetrable. These formal and informal norms could not always be clearly separated. It is not always possible to know for sure: if the addressee sent a response on a complaint within 30 days because she was complying with the law or because she was following the socialist moral standards of an attentive and humane attitude to a fellow human being. Still, the research shows that informality was more important than formality in the functioning of the Soviet complaint mechanism. It was the informal rules of addressing the complaints that were the forces that made the mechanism work. Complaints could become more effective if they deviated from formal requirements. Legal validity of a problem underlying a complaint was often neglected. They formed conditions in which legal problems could be solved by non-legal methods and vice versa: complaints with no legal grounds could be supported and granted. Acting as a para-judicial institution and dealing with legal problems, the mechanism of late Soviet complaint formed its own practice of solving problems, without hard procedures, rigid requirements, or the inevitability of punishment. Functioning of the complaint mechanism made formal rules soft and non-binding. They might also have been ignored in cases where they were contrary to the principles of socialist morality or simply complicated the proceedings.

The standardization and bureaucratization of the complaint mechanism took place in the late Soviet years. The mechanism rules became uniform throughout the country, the structure of the bureaucracy that received and processed complaints reached stability, and the rules for its functioning grew more or less predictable. The complaint mechanism clearly stood out as an independent way of solving problems, not overlapping either in structure or in the algorithms of work with the justice system.

We can also say that the professionalization of the actors involved in the functioning of the complaint mechanism, which Parsons deems an important criterion for modernization, also conditionally occurred. Conditionally because the work with complaints was carried out on a voluntary basis until the end of the existence of the Soviet system. Neither educational nor professional standards for handling complaints were designed. Meanwhile, in the late Soviet years, certain features of professional roles developed, which were assumed by both those who worked with complaints and those who wrote them. Both the first and second required the acquisition of competencies, the availability of skills for the implementation of these competencies, and the presence of confidence that the competencies are used in the interests of the entire social system (Parsons 1939).

Acquiring the skills for handling complaints and applying them—in addition to formal instructions and legislative norms—includes a solid layer of informal knowledge about how to handle complaints in a way that shows effectiveness but does not drown the mechanism under their onslaught; how to choose from the mass of complaints those that require a priority response; how to deal with a complaint so as not to incur the wrath of the authorities and not to provoke new complaints, etc. In turn, the preparation of complaints also required sophisticated knowledge of the principles and rules of the bureaucracy. Without this, it was almost impossible to maneuver among the risks of being unheard or punished.

The most paradoxical thing is that such a seemingly shaky mechanism, which was underdeveloped and poorly regulated by formal rules for many Soviet decades, performed an important function supporting the professional contract that exists between the public and the government and making a significant contribution to the stability of the entire Soviet system.

The search for legitimate justifications was carried out in a narrow corridor of possibilities constrained by the norms of socialist morality, Soviet law, and the needs of the complainants. As a result, it developed its own language and its own system of norms of justice, which is broader than legal norms, and its own system of codes that facilitated communication between the complainants and the addressees. The language of the late Soviet complaint is, first of all, the language of ideology (Pecherskaya 2012). Ideology itself is neither rigidly isolated from the norms of law nor contradicts or denies them. It rather translates the law into a proper language when and where it is needed. Often this is not needed since the language of ideology predominates in laws themselves.

Despite the hierarchy of the mechanism and rigidity of the political regime, complaints in the late Soviet period facilitated a dialogue about justice between the complainants and the addressees. This dialogue was incoherent, chaotic, intermittent, intimate, and emotional. It could be interrupted at any moment, or it could unexpectedly bring results in an instant, satisfactory outcome. Within this dialogue, the state promises to protect and care, while the citizens directly or indirectly request the promised care.

The language of appeals is focused on the semantic function of the institution (Boltanski 2011:75), which is appointed by a respected entity able to help in a situation of uncertainty. In the language of late Soviet complaints, the addressee clearly received priority. The addressee was the state represented by executive authorities or the Communist Party, and the complaint mechanism was structurally locked on these institutions. However, we should note that executive power holders and the party were also the main broadcasters of the official ideology, the socialist morality, and the paternalistic contract between the government and the society.

Notes

1 A *torg* was an organizational structure in the Soviet trade system. *Torgs* were agencies of the Ministry of Trade that were in charge of organizing local retail trade. The economic management of *torgs* was carried out by trade departments of executive committees at the city and regional (*oblast'* and *krai*) levels.
2 *Pravda*, April 4, 1981:1.
3 All names, dates, and registration numbers in the quotations are changed unless otherwise noted.
4 *"Khitrov market"* was a real market place in Moscow in pre-Soviet and early Soviet times, known as a shelter for criminals and outcasts.
5 GARF, F. A-410, op. 1, d. 2130, l. 49–49ob.
6 GARF, F. A-410, op. 1, d. 2130, l. 47.
7 Interview with L. R. (see the list of all interviews in Appendix 2).
8 Interview with B. B.
9 RGAE, F. 195, op. 1, ed. khr. 48, ll. 37, 43, 44; RGAE, F. 195, op. 1, ed. khr. 445, ll. 8, 39, 73, 75, 77, 79, 84.
10 RGAE, F. 195, op. 1, ed. khr. 48, ll. 37, 43, 44; RGAE, F. 195, op. 1, ed. khr. 445, ll. 8, 39, 73, 75, 77, 79, 84, 221.
11 Since their very establishment, *ispolkomy* were endowed with directive (*rasporiaditel'nye*) functions, which was formally recognized in the 1984 Code of the RSFSR for Administrative Offenses.
12 In 1962, Moscow was divided into 17 districts. Every year, Moscow *ispolkomy* received about 600,000 letters.
13 Kirishi is a real town in the Leningrad region.
14 Budogoshch is a real industrial settlement in the Kirishi area.
15 Leningrad Regional State Archive in Vyborg (LOGAV), F. R-4514, op. 1, d. 38, ll. 29–29ob.
16 LOGAV, F. R-4514, op. 1, d. 38, ll. 25–26.
17 Interview with P. P.

18 Mery priniaty [Measures taken.] *Vechernii Leningrad*, 1970, February 2:2.
19 Here is a quote from the reply to this complaint: "In order to eliminate public complaints regarding the problem of stale bakery products, the Ispolkom of the Leningrad City Council has adopted a decision of June 25, 1962, No. 751, according to which the delivery of bread and bakery products to the retail network shall be carried out around the clock, wherein 45% of the daily demand for rye bread and 35% of the daily demand for wheat bakery products shall be delivered in the nighttime" (TsGA SPb, F. 7384, op. 42, d. 332, l. 190).
20 *"Krasnyi Treugol'nik"* is the name of a rubber factory in Leningrad/Saint Petersburg.
21 Neudovletvoritelnyi otvet [Unsatisfactory response.] *Vechernii Leningrad*, 1964, November 30:2.
22 Interview with V. D.
23 Interview with V. D.
24 Interviews with V. A. and V. D.
25 Pochemu nuzhny ugrozy? [Why the need for threats?] *Vechernii Leningrad*, 1970, March 13:2.
26 Interview with V. A.
27 Po imeni i otchestvu [By name and patronymic.] *Leningradskaia Pravda*, 1964, December 23:2.
28 Kostiumy bez shvov [Suits with no seams.] *Vechernii Leningrad*, 1970, January 20:2.
29 In order to return to Leningrad after the evacuation during the Second World War, one had to receive a summoning notice from their relatives residing in Leningrad. Meanwhile, many evacuees' relatives died in the blockaded Leningrad of starvation and bombings, so no one could send them such a notice.
30 Interview with B. B.
31 Interview with A. F.
32 Interview with S. V.
33 Interview with J. P.
34 TsGA SPb, F. 7384, op. 42, d. 332, l. 81–89.
35 TsGa SPb, F. 7384, op. 42, d, 332, l. 83.
36 TsGA SPb, F. 7384, op. 42, d. 332, ll. 106–108.
37 Information from an interview conducted for the project *Russian-Mongolian Border: A Prototype of the Eurasioregion*. The project was carried out in conjunction with the Center of Independent Sociological Research in 2003. Data provided by project participant Maria Kudriavtseva.
38 LOGAV, F. R-4514, op. 1, d. 38, l. 16ob.
39 Servis ne terpit ravnodushnykh [The service does not tolerate the indifferent.] *Leningradskaia Pravda*, 1963, March 29:2.
40 Pokupatel' zhdet [The customer is waiting.] *Leningradskaia Pravda*, 1963, March 10:2.
41 Otvetstvennost' i kachestvo [Responsibility and quality.] *Leningradskaia Pravda*, 1964, November 21:2.
42 [Untitled.] *Vechernii Leningrad*, 1963, April 24:2.
43 Lyzhi v kladovke [Skis in the hall closet.] *Leningradskaia Pravda*, 1970, February 26:2.
44 V tesnote i v obide [Squeezed but not pleased.] *Leningradskaia Pravda*, 1964, December 12:2.
45 Pokupatel' vozvraschaetsia [The customer returns.] *Leningradskaia Pravda*, 1970, February 26:2.
46 TsGA SPb, F. 7384, op. 30, d. 53, l. 2.
47 Famous retailers in Leningrad/Saint Petersburg.
48 Mery priniaty [Measures taken.] *Vechernii Leningrad*, 1970, January 8:2.

49 Po sledam nashikh vystuplenii [In the wake of our presentations.] *Vechernii Leningrad*, 1964, December 29:2.
50 Narushiteli pravil torgovli nakazany [Violators of trade rules punished.] *Vechernii Leningrad*, 1964, December 12:2.
51 Kak ia pokupala plat'ie [How I was buying a dress.] *Vechernii Leningrad*, 1964, December 4:2.
52 Ni kupit'…ni sshit' [Cannot buy…And cannot sew.] *Leningradskaia Pravda*, 1964, November 24:2.
53 Pochemu procherk v meniu? [Why the dash on the menu?] *Leningradskaia Pravda*, 1963, April 3:2.
54 TsGA SPb, F. 7384, op. 30, d. 53, l. 2.
55 LOGAV, F. R-3551, op. 7, d. 92, ll. 30–31.
56 LOGAV, F. R-3551, op. 7, d. 92, l. 29.
57 TsGA SPb, F. 7384, op. 30, d. 53, doc. 2633.
58 TsGA SPb, F. 7384, op. 30, d. 53, doc. 1565, l. 101.
59 GARF, F. A-410, op. 1, d. 2130, l. 180.
60 GARF, F. A-410, op. 1, d. 2130, l. 30.

References

Barry, Donald. 1978. "Administrative Justice and Judicial Review in Soviet Administrative Law." Pp. 241–270 in Donald Barry, George Ginsburgs, and Peter Maggs (eds.) *Soviet Law After Stalin: Soviet Institutions and the Administration of Law*. Alphen aan den Rijn: A. W. Sijthoff.

Barry, Donald. 1989. "Administrative Justice: The Role of Soviet Courts in Controlling Administrative Acts." Pp. 63–80 in George Ginsburgs (ed.) *Soviet Administrative Law: Theory and Policy*. Dordrecht: Martinus Sijthoff.

Boltanski, Luc. 2011. *On Critique: A Sociology of Emancipation*. Cambridge: Polity Press.

Chechot, Dmitrii. 1973. *Administrativnaia Iustitsiia. Teoreticheskie problemy*. Leningrad: Izdatel'stvo Leningradskogo Universiteta.

Friedgut, Theodore. 1978. "Citizens and Soviets: Can Ivan Ivanovich Fight City Hall?" *Comparative Politics* 10(4):461–477, 466.

Friedgut, Theodore. 1979. *Political Participation in the USSR*. Princeton: Princeton University Press.

Grekov, Alexander. 1931. *...Kuda, na chto i kak zhalovat'sia*. Leningrad: Tekhnika upravleiia.

Grushin, Boris. 2003. *Chetyre zhizni Rossii v zerkale oprosov obshchestvennogo mneniia: epokha Brezhneva*. Moscow: Progress-Traditsiia.

Kerimov, Dzhangir. 1956. *Obespechenie zakonnosti v SSSR*. Moscow: Gosiurizdat.

Kozlov, Iurii. 1959. *Priem i rassmotrenie zhalob i zaiavlenii trudiashchikhsia v organakh sovetskogo gosudarstvennogo upravleniia*. Moscow: Gosiurizdat.

Kulikov, Vladimir. 2003. *Istoriia gosudarstvennogo upravleniia v Rossii*. Moscow: ACADEMIA.

Lenin, Vladimir.1973. "Nabrosok pravil ob upravlenii sovetskimi uchrezhdeniiami." Pp. 366-367 in *Collected Works* Vol. 37. Moscow: Politizdat.

Levada, Iurii (ed.). 1993. *Sovetskii prostoi chelovek: opyt sotsial'nogo portreta na rubezhe 90-kh*. Moscow: Mirovoi okean.

Mertz, Elizabeth. 1996." Recontextualization as Socialization: Text and Pragmatics in the Law School Classroom." Pp. 229–249 in Michael Silverstein and Greg Urban (eds.) *Natural Histories of Discourse*. Chicago: University of Chicago Press.

Moral'nyi kodeks stroitelia kommunizma, Posobie dlia propagandistov i slushatelei sistemy politicheskogo prosveshcheniia. 1965. Moscow: Politizdat.
Parsons, Talcott. 1939. "The Professions and Social Structure." *Social Forces* 17(4):457–467.
Pecherskaya, Natalia. 2012. "Looking for Justice: The Everyday Meaning of Justice in Late Soviet Russia." *Anthropology of East Europe Review* 30(2):20–38.
Pravda. 1981. April 4:1.
Ries, Nancy. 1997. *Russian Talk: Culture and Conversation during Perestroika.* Ithaca, NY: Cornell University Press.
Solomon, Peter H. 1996. *Soviet Criminal Justice Under Stalin.* Cambridge: Cambridge University Press.
Solomon, Peter H. 2004. "Judicial Power in Russia: Through the Prism of Administrative Justice." *Law and Society Review* 3 (38):549–582.
Spravochnik partiinogo rabotnika. 1981. Vyp. 21. Moscow: Politizdat.
Sungurov, Aleksander. 1998. *Funktsii politicheskoi sistemy: ot zastoia k postperestroike.* Saint Petersburg: Strategiia.
Treushnikov, Mikhail. 1997. *Kommentarii k Grazhdanskomu protsessual'nomu kodeksu RSFSR.* Moscow: Spark.
Utekhin, Il'ia. 2004. "Iz nabliudenii za poetikoi zhaloby." Pp. 274–306 in Albert Baiburin (ed.) *Studia Ethnologica: Trudy fakul'teta etnologii.* Saint Petersburg: Izdatel'stvo Evropeiskogo universiteta v Sankt-Peterburge.
Van den Berg, Gerard. 1985. *The Soviet System of Justice: Figures and Policy.* Dordrecht: Martinus Nijhoff Publishers.
White, Stephen. 1983. "Political Communications in the USSR: Letters to Party, State and Press." *Political Studies* 31(1):43–60.
Zhaloby passazhirov na vagony-restorany. 1934. Moscow.
Zhidkov, Vladimir. 1979. *V otvete za kazhdoe slovo.* Moscow: Mysl'.

Normative documents

Law of the USSR "On the Procedure for Appealing Unlawful Acts of Officials Infringing the Rights of Citizens" [Zakon, SSSR "O poriadke obzhalovaniia v sud nepravomernykh deistvii organov gosudarstvennogo upravleniia i dolzhnostnykh lits, ushchemliaiushchikh prava grazhdan"] from June 30,1987. *Vedomosti Verkhovnogo Soveta SSSR*, 26, st. 388; 42, st. 764.

Newspaper articles

Kak ia pokupala plat'ie [How I was buying a dress.] *Vechernii Leningrad*, 1964, December 4:2.
Kostiumy bez shvov [Suits with no seams.] *Vechernii Leningrad*, 1970, January 20:2.
Lyzhi v kladovke [Skis in the hall closet.] *Leningradskaia Pravda*, 1970, February 26: 2.
Mery priniaty [Measures taken.] *Vechernii Leningrad*, 1970, February 2:2.
Mery priniaty [Measures taken.] *Vechernii Leningrad*, 1970, January 8:2.
Narushiteli pravil torgovli nakazany [Violators of trade rules punished.] *Vechernii Leningrad*, 1964, December 12:2.
Neudovletvoritelnyi otvet [Unsatisfactory response.] *Vechernii Leningrad*, 1964, November 30:2.
Ni kupit'... ni sshit' [Cannot buy... And cannot sew.] *Leningradskaia Pravda*, 1964, November 24:2.

Otvetstvennost' i kachestvo [Responsibility and quality.] *Leningradskaia Pravda*, 1964, November 21:2.
Pochemu nuzhny ugrozy? [Why the need for threats?] *Vechernii Leningrad*, 1970, March 13:2.
Pochemu procherk v meniu? [Why the dash on the menu?] *Leningradskaia Pravda*, 1963, April 3:2.
Po imeni i otchestvu [By name and patronymic.] *Leningradskaia Pravda*, 1964, December 23:2.
Pokupatel' vozvraschaetsia [The customer returns.] *Leningradskaia Pravda*, 1970, February 26:2.
Pokupatel' zhdet [The customer is waiting.] *Leningradskaia Pravda*, 1963, March 10:2.
Po sledam nashikh vystuplenii [In the wake of our presentations.] *Vechernii Leningrad*, 1964, December 29:2.
Servis ne terpit ravnodushnykh [The service does not tolerate the indifferent.] *Leningradskaia Pravda*, 1963, March 29:2.
[Untitled.] *Vechernii Leningrad*, 1963, April 24:2.
V tesnote i v obide [Squeezed but not pleased.] *Leningradskaia Pravda*, 1964, December 12:2.

Archival sources

GARF, F. A-410, op. 1, d. 2130, l. 49-49ob.
GARF, F. A-410, op. 1, d. 2130, l. 47.
GARF, F. A-410, op. 1, d. 2130, l. 180.
GARF, F. A-410, op. 1, d. 2130, l. 30.
RGAE, F. 195, op. 1, ed. Khr. 48, ll. 37, 43, 44.
RGAE, F. 195, op. 1, ed. Khr. 445, ll. 8, 39, 73, 75, 77, 79, 84.
RGAE, F. 195, op. 1, ed. Khr. 48, ll. 37, 43, 44.
RGAE, F. 195, op. 1, ed. Khr. 445, ll. 8, 39, 73, 75, 77, 79, 84, 221.
LOGAV, F. R-4514, op. 1, d. 38, ll. 29–29ob.
LOGAV, F. R-4514, op. 1, d. 38, ll. 25–26.
LOGAV, F. R-4514, op. 1, d. 38, l. 16ob.
LOGAV, F. R-3551, op. 7, d. 92, ll. 30–31.
LOGAV, F. R-3551, op. 7, d. 92, l. 29.
TsGA SPb, F. 7384, op. 30, d. 53, doc. 2633.
TsGA SPb, F. 7384, op. 30, d. 53, doc. 1565, l. 101.
TsGA SPb, F. 7384, op. 30, d. 53, l. 2.
TsGA SPb, F. 7384, op. 30, d. 53, l. 2.
TsGA SPb, F. 7384, op. 42, d. 332, l. 190.
TsGA SPb, F. 7384, op. 42, d. 332, l. 81–89.
TsGA SPb, F. 7384, op. 42, d. 332, ll. 106–108.

5 Post-Soviet transformations of the mechanism of complaints

The coup that took place in Russia in the early 1990s had significant consequences for the mechanism of filing complaints. After decades of state Socialism under the administrative-command system, a liberal turn was declared, with a transition to the market economy and radical restructuring of legal institutions. What happened were a transformation of Russian statehood and an unprecedented decentralization of power.[1] For the first time in 400 years, the central government voluntarily limited its function as the supreme judge in resolving many issues of national importance, including complaints submitted by citizens.

Since 1990, the People's Control, to which the mechanism of complaints had been subordinated, lost its power almost entirely. On May 16, 1991, the fifth session of the Supreme Soviet of the USSR adopted the law "On the Control Chamber of the USSR," which replaced the People's Control. The procession of complaints was excluded from its mandatory functions (Kabashov 2010:144). Shortly thereafter, on August 1, 1991, Boris Yeltsin issued a decree which prohibited the activities of the Communist Party (Decree 1991, para. 4), leading to difficult times for the party newspapers. The most important addressees of citizens' complaints either disappeared or entered a period of crisis. The media, in the conditions of a competitive market and freedom of speech, ceased to be the mouthpiece of the governing structures. The executive authorities survived and continued to work with complaints. However, consideration of complaints was no longer among their obligations.

The Supreme Council of the Russian Federation was terminated in October 1993. Instead of the huge apparatus of the Central Committee of the Communist Party, there was established a small Correspondence and Citizens Reception Department under the Administration of the President. It became the public body dealing with applications in 1992–1994. The regional state structures dealing with citizens' complaints were substantially downsized in a similar way. During the period from 1992 to 1999, the central government maintained the continuity of the legal mechanism for the resolution of complaints based on the normative acts introduced in the USSR. This produced an absurd situation. In Soviet times, there had been a number of institutions that, according to norms, were to serve as the main addressees of complaints. After the collapse many of these institutions were eliminated. The practices of complaining evolved as if there were no corresponding regulations at all.[2] As in the 1920s, internal by-laws assumed the role of binding regulations for dealing with complaints, every organization having its own set of instructions.

Some of the Soviet laws regulating the operation of the complaint mechanism were not abolished; however, the socio-political context changed radically. The judicial reform and strengthening of legal institutions left to the mechanism of complaints the role of a marginal, weakly effective administrative way of solving problems. There are no statistics on the number of complaints sent to the authorities in the early post-socialist period; however, there is a collection of complaint letters addressed to Boris Yeltsin during 1990–1991, numbering about 12,000, in the State Archive of the Russian Federation (GARF).[3] The official practice of complaining faced institutional collapse and people were looking for new legitimate addressees.

Separation of powers as a new priority of the post-Soviet system

The 1993 Constitution proclaimed the independence of each branch of power. According to Article 10 of the Constitution, "the bodies of legislative, executive, and judicial power shall be independent." This means that every branch of power may exercise powers only in its own area of influence, and no branch has the right to substitute or to usurp power from another.

The head of state, the President (Ch. 4, Art. 1), does not belong to any specific branch of power. Instead, the Constitution affords the President ample opportunities to influence every branch. With respect to legislative power, the President can introduce legislative initiatives; with respect to executive power, the President can appoint key public officials. The independence of the judiciary is separately emphasized in the Constitution (Ch. 7, Art. 120). However, it is unclear how exactly the President may intervene in protecting the rights and freedoms of persons and citizens.

The administration of justice is defined in the Constitution as a unique function of the judiciary. Yet in order for this function to be truly unique, it is necessary to make a precise distinction between the judiciary and the restoration of civil rights and freedoms. In actual practice, it is not so simple to draw a clear line between them. In accordance with the spirit of the Constitution, the rights and freedoms of persons and citizens determine the meaning, content, and application of laws; these rights and freedoms also determine the activities of all state institutions and bodies of local self-government. In a broad sense, the efforts of all branches of power, including the President, should be directed to the observance, protection, and full guarantee of civil rights. The President is the guarantor of civil rights and freedoms. The presidential oath mentions the President's duty to respect and protect the rights and freedoms of persons and citizens as well as to faithfully serve the people of Russia. While protecting the rights and freedoms of persons and citizens, the President relies upon the entire system of state government bodies. Functioning as a guarantor of the rights and freedoms of persons and citizens, the President must be constantly concerned with the effectiveness of the executive, legislative, and judicial powers. Formally, the President's powers in this area are limited by the principle of non-intervention in the sphere of competence related to each branch of power.

In the Russian language, such expressions as "protection of the rights" (*zashchita prav*), "restoration of violated rights" (*vosstanovlenie narushennykh prav*), and "safeguarding the rights" (*okhrana prav*) are similar in spirit and letter of the law. Currently there is no consensus among either legal scholars or lawmakers about the distinction between these related but non-identical concepts (Smirnov 2010:123). Besides, the expression "restoration of violated rights" practically coincides in meaning with the concept of "justice." It is not easy for a non-professional to differentiate these concepts or to understand the semantics behind each phrasing. The safeguarding and protection of rights that have not yet been violated are the concern of various legal, governmental, and social institutions. On the contrary, if there has been a violation of rights and freedoms, it is a question of their restoration, not protection. The restoration of rights and freedoms can be carried out in court (through due process of law) or out of court (administratively, by filing a complaint with the appropriate public authority).

However, some researchers interpret the phrasing "protection of the rights" in a broad sense, as identical to "safeguarding the rights" (Stoiakin 1973:30–35) or "restoration of the rights" (Alekseev 1981:280). This confusion has made a direct impact on the accountability of legal institutions and the administrative instruments of problem solving. As there is no obvious distinction between the concepts, it is impossible to restrict the application of the corresponding legal tools. More generally, due to the semantic proximity of concepts and a lack of a clear procedure for their application, the principle of separation of powers cannot be fully exercised. The unique function of justice, namely the restoration of legitimate rights and freedoms of citizens, is compromised. If no one doubts that justice is the unique function of the judiciary branch, then the restoration of violated rights and the activities related thereto become a task shared by the judiciary and the administrative apparatus processing complaints and representing the executive branch.

Reform of the judiciary

The post-socialist judicial reforms were launched to strengthen juridical instruments and to restructure the entire Soviet judiciary on the model of European justice (Mironov 2001:34). The initial plan of the post-socialist legal reform involved strengthening the judicial institutions. In the opinion of Peter Solomon and Todd Foglesong (2000), the reform achieved significant results in its first ten years.

The Federal Constitutional Law No. 1-FKZ "On the Judicial System of the Russian Federation" (dated December 31, 1996) established a uniform court procedure and a universal judiciary, which reproduced a five-part judicial system similar to the pre-revolutionary one. The federal level includes the Supreme Court of the Russian Federation and federal judicial boards. The Constitutional Court of the Russian Federation also belongs to the federal level, but sits apart as a special type of court. On the regional level are regional (*oblastnye*, *kraevye*) courts. The local level is represented by city courts and the Justices of the Peace. Four areas of court proceedings were identified: constitutional, civil, administrative, and criminal.

The Constitution of 1993 defined law as a unique base determining the rules and norms of justice as well as the justiciary as a unique function of the Court: "The judiciary shall be independent and operate independently of the executive and legislative branches of the government" (Art. 1.2). The principle of autonomy and independence of the judiciary was enshrined in the law "On the Judicial System of the Russian Federation." A complex system of appeals and supervisory reviews was established within the judiciary system involving the Presidium of the Supreme Court of the Russian Federation—the highest judicial authority.

The concepts of "complaint" and "appeal" (*obzhalovanie*) are mentioned in the 1993 Constitution, albeit only as judicial instruments (Art. 46, Art. 125.4). The complaint is never mentioned as a form of communication with the authorities. Instead, the generic term "application" is used: "Citizens of the Russian Federation shall have the right to address personally, as well as to submit individual and collective applications to state organs and local self-government bodies" (Art. 33).

In 1990–1992, civil law was substantially reinforced. In particular, those legal spheres that had had no clear legal basis in Soviet times were transformed. In 1992, the following acts were adopted: the law "On Protection of Consumer Rights," the law "On Enterprises and Entrepreneurial Activity," and the Presidential Decree on Free Trade. Article 35 of the 1993 Constitution enshrined the right to private property. In 1994, the Civil Code of the Russian Federation came into force, and in 1995 the Family Code of the Russian Federation. In effect, these were full-fledged instruments created to regulate civil, business, and property relations. According to judicial statistics, the annual number of civil, criminal, and administrative cases tried in courts quadrupled from 1995 to 2017. Notably, the number of criminal cases slightly decreased. At the same time, the number of administrative and civil cases rose 250% from 1995 to 2006. By 2017, the number of administrative cases tried in Russian courts increased more than threefold, while the number of civil cases increased by 450% (see Appendix 1).

The Constitutional Court of the Russian Federation assumed a special role in ensuring a uniform legal framework. In 1991–1993, this judicial body was empowered to decide cases on the constitutionality of law enforcement based on individual complaints of citizens and legal entities. After the enactment of the Constitution, in July 1994, in accordance with Article 125 of the Constitution, the Federal Constitutional Law "On the Constitutional Court of the Russian Federation" was introduced. One of the important areas of judicial protection became citizens' complaints to the Constitutional Court of the Russian Federation regarding violations of their constitutional rights by government agencies (Golik 2007:64; Shurgina 2004:133).

Thus, the conditions for solving problems through legal instruments began to be formed in the early post-Soviet years. Over the course of time, citizens' attitudes towards the judiciary changed significantly, as did their recognition of the court as an instrument to resolve civil and administrative conflicts. The judicial system, judicial legislation, and the system of appeals against unsatisfactory decisions of the court saw substantial reforms.

Administrative justice in the post-Soviet period

As post-Soviet Russia took measures to build a system of administrative justice, so the concepts of "complaint" and "complaint procedure" resumed their special position in legislation. There was no system of administrative courts established in post-socialist Russia. Instead, as in the late socialist period, the bet was made on a "judicial procedure for the settlement of administrative disputes in the jurisdictional bodies" (Zelentsov 2009:82–83).

The legislative instruments for judging the offenses of officials were improved across all segments of the judiciary: criminal, civil, arbitration, and administrative. After a serious revision of Soviet legislation, two primary articles on the relevant crimes were included in *the Criminal Code* (1996): Article 285 "Abuse of Official Authority" (*Zloupotreblenie dolzhnostnymi polnomochiiami*) and Article 286 "Excess of Official Authority" (*Prevyshenie dolzhnostnykh polnomochii*). These articles prescribe punishments such as fines, forced labor, or imprisonment up to 10 years (Bannikov 2016). In the sector of *civil* justice, elements of abuse of office are covered by a large number of legal acts related to labor law, electoral rights, and environmental pollution, as well as laws related to administrative justice.

In April 1993, the Law of the Russian Federation "On Appealing to the Court Actions and Decisions Violating the Rights and Freedoms of Citizens" was adopted, replacing two earlier laws on administrative justice of 1987 and 1989. The new law dramatically extended the right of citizens to bring claims to courts regarding illegal actions of officials, even when taken in the name of a collective body, covering virtually any action by any official, whether normative or non-normative, that violated the rights and freedoms of citizens. On April 28, 1993, the Supreme Council of the Russian Federation adopted the law "On Amendments and Additions to the Code of Civil Procedure of the RSFSR." Here, Chapter 24-1 was revised and newly entitled "Complaints About the Actions of State Bodies, Public Organizations, and Officials Violating Citizens' Rights and Freedoms." The preceding Chapter 24 of the Code of Civil Procedure had been formulated in an era when citizens' rights to appeal to the court against the actions (or inaction) of administrative bodies and officials was under limitations (1964). At that time, the priority was to seek administrative solutions to such issues. In fact, Chapter 24-1 put complaints on cases arising from administrative offenses under the jurisdiction of judicial bodies, assigning the courts a dominant role in solving such cases. Nevertheless, legislators retained the opportunity for citizens to file complaints to higher state bodies, public organizations, or officials (Code of Civil Procedure, Art. 239-4). Meanwhile, Chapter 24-1 reinforced the dominant role of the judiciary in considering complaints. In particular, the court was to forward complaints to the administrative structures only in certain cases stipulated by the legislation. Legislative norms were recognized as the main ground for consideration of any complaints, and poor decisions made by administrative structures were to be appealed against in court. The legal procedure for the execution of decisions on complaints was also determined in Chapter 24-1.

After this Chapter was introduced into the Code of Civil Procedure (Articles 239-1 to 239-8), the Constitution of the Russian Federation came into force in 1993. The Constitution consolidated the trend towards the expansion of the court's jurisdiction and the removal of any restrictions regarding the subject of appeal. The right to bring appeals before the court received full constitutional recognition in Article 46, Part 2. Later, in 1995, the target of potential complaints was expanded from "officials," or persons in responsible positions, to any and all government employees (*sluzhashchie*) (Khamaneva 1997:100–115; Federal Law "On Amending the Law On Appealing to the Court of Wrongful Acts," 1995). These laws established full-fledged administrative justice and gave the courts a significant role in handling citizens' claims against officials.

The number of lawsuits against officials grew rapidly from the very beginning of the 1990s. Russians found much to complain about, and the number of lawsuits against officials rose steadily—from 4,944 in 1990, to 20,326 in 1994, to 56,659 in 1997, to approximately 160,000 in 2000 (Solomon and Foglesong 2000:68–71; Verkhovnyi Sud RF 2000:54–57). The success rate of citizens' lawsuits was high. The overall rate of redress for these lawsuits, according to official statistics from 1999, was 82.8%. The figures for 1996 and for 1997 were similar: 74.4% and 83.4% respectively (Khamaneva and Salishcheva 2001:36; Verkhovnyi Sud RF 1998:55–58; Verkhovnyi Sud RF 1999:51–53).

In the field of administrative proceedings, one major event occurred, namely the adoption of the Code of Russian Federation for Administrative Offenses (CRFAO). The work on the Code began in 2001, and on July 1, 2002, the Code was put into effect, abolishing the then-existing Code of the RSFSR for Administrative Offenses. The legislative base of the administrative judiciary now is still in the process of formation. The CRFAO went through a long period of revisions. The Code of Administrative Court Proceedings was enacted on September 15, 2015. Among other things, it has put administrative cases under the jurisdiction of courts and administrative bodies (Articles 17–27). The most recent amendments to the CRFAO were introduced in 2018. The Code covers a great variety of offenses committed by officials. Although these offenses have no criminal component, they are serious enough to be considered in court (at the level of justices of the peace as well as in lower-level ordinary courts) or by executive power bodies. Among them are Article 14.24 Violating Legislation on Commodity Exchanges and Exchange Trade, Article 7.32 Violation of the Terms and Conditions of a Contract, Article 14.7 Deception of Consumers, and Article 14.51 Violating Legislation on Tourist Activities. In general, the Code contains about 50 articles regulating crimes committed by officials, assuming lesser forms of punishment such as warnings, fines, and forced labor. The Code of Administrative Court Proceedings (2015) also includes procedures for administrative justice cases (Chapters 21 and 22).

Despite the fact that administrative courts were never created institutionally, post-Soviet Russia has made significant efforts to create administrative judiciary instruments. In particular, legislation was developed to address administrative offenses in court. In the Russian understanding, administrative offenses encompassed a wide scope of violations, including offenses related to abuse of office, traffic violations, and non-payment for utility services. Clearly, we see a lack of distinction between abuse of office and other administrative offenses; in fact, abuse of office is dissolved among lesser administrative violations, which has become a significant obstacle to building full-fledged administrative justice. This represents, in a sense, a legacy of the Soviet approach to understanding and addressing administrative offenses. In the late Soviet period, a whole set of offenses, of varying degrees of severity, were merged under the umbrella term "abuse of office": from grand bribes to insulting language (Lampert 1985). Terminological confusion also persisted, as the term "administrative complaint" was still applied both to a complaint filed to a state body (i.e. out of court, administratively) and to a complaint filed to the court regarding administrative violations.

The first post-Soviet innovations in the field of administrative justice showed definite signs of legal modernization. The development of legal norms for regulating both groups of offenses was a significant step forward. Most of the violations that used to be under the jurisdiction of the complaint mechanism in Soviet years were now subject to the new instruments of administrative justice. Thanks to legislative innovations, the classification of problems, as well as the translation of the facts presented by the citizens into legal language, became the work of professional lawyers. Throughout the segment of administrative offenses, the priority obviously shifted from para-legal instruments towards judicial institutions. The field of administrative justice saw unprecedented developments. The citizen's right to challenge wrongdoings committed by officials was enshrined in law and, quite shortly, gained a significant precedent of positive judicial decisions (Solomon 2004; Trochev 2012).

Ombudsman versus procuracy: The post-socialist signs of legal modernization and the first steps back

Complaints to the procuracy and complaints to the Ombudsman are to be distinguished from complaints to state authorities. Neither the procuracy nor the Ombudsman's office are involved in the administrative complaint mechanism in the sense in which it is addressed in this book. However, the boundaries of this mechanism are permeable for both these institutions. In some cases, the state authorities, the procuracy, and the Ombudsman represent equally suitable options for submitting a complaint. Therefore, we cannot look into the mechanism of complaints without addressing the two latter bodies.

The procuracy has existed in Russia since Peter the Great. The Ombudsman's office, by contrast, was established in the early 1990s. However different, these two bodies have much in common: they do not belong to any branch of power, they have similar missions, and they are involved in working with complaints in similar ways. Thus, it is worthwhile to consider them alongside one another, in the same section, in order to compare their influence, their popularity as recipients of complaints, and their cooperation-related trends.

The Ombudsman and other "democratic" addressees of complaints in post-Soviet Russia

It would be naïve to think that, under post-Soviet reforms, the centuries-old practice of complaining to authorities instantly transformed into lawsuits following the reinforcement of judicial institutions. In the 1990s, the vast majority of Russia's population experienced a severe socio-economic crisis—massive lay-offs, unemployment, wage payment delays, and shortages of basic commodities. The decade saw a mass creation of the first cooperatives, and there were the first attempts at commercial activity, which did not always result in success stories. This created disputes and various problematic situations that had to be addressed. While the citizens' habit of seeking help from the authorities produced new waves of complaints, the bureaucracy that used to process them was almost completely destroyed. People continued to routinely complain to deputies of all levels and to various executive power bodies. The executive branch did not lose its decision-making powers with regard to complaints. Therefore, they continued to be highly popular as complaint recipients. However, work with complaints ceased to be the responsibility of executive committees, which affected the frequency and quality of responses.

In response, the government decided to strengthen and revamp the channels for appeals. The improvements assumed the shape of democratic legal instruments. The Presidential Decree "On Some Measures of State Support for the Civil Rights Movement in the Russian Federation" was issued on June 13, 1996. In accordance with the Decree, commissions on human rights were established under the executive branch (Shishkina 2004:47). These commissions were intended to work with citizens and, in most cases, played a certain role in the protection of their rights. In the regions, public organizations that specialized in the protection of civil rights gained support. Let us look at an example. The Consumer Rights Protection Society (*Obshchestvo zashchity prav potrebitelei*) was established in Leningrad as early as 1988. The number of consumer complaints to the Society grew dramatically since the mid-1990s (see Table 5.1).[4] From 1996 to 2000, the number of the Society's clients increased almost tenfold:

Table 5.1 Growth of clients of the Consumer Rights Protection Society (1996–2000)

Year	*1996*	*1997*	*1998*	*1999*	*2000*
Number of Applicants to the CRPS	1,250	2,950	3,550	5,100	12,000

Source: Statistics of the Consumer Rights Protection Society. Quoted from: Bogdanova 2003:175

The post of human rights Ombudsman was introduced in Russia in 1993 by the Constitution (Article 103.1e) and was first filled by Sergei A. Kovalyov, a prominent dissident who had been held in a Soviet prison camp for his political views. The appointment of Kovalyov was no doubt meant to reinforce Yeltsin's democratic credentials. In many respects, it imbued the newly established institution with a reflection of the intellectual ideals of many within the dissident culture of the 1970s, the goal of which was "to provide some justice to those suffering under a fragile state and to facilitate an exit from authoritarianism through rational problem-solving and moral persuasion" (Gilligan 2010:578).

The Federal Constitutional Law "On the Human Rights Ombudsman in the Russian Federation" caused heated debate in the Duma and was presented six times in the Parliament (Duma Endorses Bill 1996). On February 26, 1997, it was finally approved by the Federal Assembly and signed by the President. Similar laws on regional commissioners for human rights were subsequently adopted by the constituent entities of the Russian Federation (Mironov 2004:72.)

The Ombudsman's office was created as an auxiliary function supplementing the state bodies' competence. The Ombudsman's activity was focused on monitoring human rights in all spheres of society. The Ombudsman was given a separate sphere of authority which greatly enhanced not only the legal but also the humanitarian, legislative, and outreach-related aspects of human rights protection. The commissioner for human rights had free access to government authorities, had the right to request any documents from state structures and officials, to conduct inspections, and to look into case files. The Ombudsman was also endowed with certain regulatory functions that concerned effective enforcement of respect for human rights by the aforementioned bodies. However, the Ombudsman had no general control over the activities of these bodies.

The human rights commissioner did not receive the authority to take punitive measures against violators. As Gilligan wrote, the establishment of the Ombudsman's office was a gesture that sought to compensate for the absence of criminal punishment, lustration, or a truth and reconciliation commission in post-Soviet Russia … . This is not to suggest that the office of the human rights ombudsman was a replacement for punishment, "but it was a gesture aimed exclusively and optimistically toward the future through democratic institution building" (Gilligan 2010:578).

In cases where the information about violations of the law or human rights was confirmed, the Ombudsman was obliged to transmit the complaint to the procuracy or court.

Generally, the function entrusted to the Ombudsman overlapped with the function of the Soviet complaint mechanism; however, there were also some differences between the two. The Ombudsman was empowered to consider citizens' complaints concerning decisions and actions (or inaction) of state bodies, bodies of local self-government, and officials in cases where the complainant alleged a violation of their human rights (Federal Constitutional Law "On Human Rights," Art. 16.1).

The rules for submission of complaints to the Ombudsman are fairly simple. A complaint to the Ombudsman is not subject to any state fee (Ibid. Art. 18) so there

Table 5.2 Individual and collective complaints and applications of citizens to the Office of the Human Rights Ombudsman in 2011–2017

Year	*2011*	*2012*	*2013*	*2014*	*2015*	*2017*
Number of complaints to the Human Rights Ombudsman's office	26,197	24,930	22,997	32,382[5]	38,093[6]	41,840[7]

Sources: *Doklady Upolnomochennogo po pravam cheloveka* 2015, 2016, 2018

is no barrier of financial affordability. However, a complaint to the Ombudsman requires legal justification (Ibid. Art. 17.2), or, more precisely, substantiation of the alleged violation of human rights. If the complaint is incompetent, it may not be accepted. After receiving a complaint, the Ombudsman can take it into consideration, explain to the applicant different ways of resolving the problem, forward the complaint to the authorities, or refuse to consider the complaint altogether. One cannot appeal against the Ombudsman's refusal to consider a complaint (Ibid. Art. 20.3).

The Ombudsman can only consider a complaint if the complainant has already appealed against the action in question (in court or administratively) but did not agree with the decision taken with regard to the appeal (Ibid. Art. 16.1) (Korniushenkov 2004:39). This represents a significant accessibility barrier to the Ombudsman's help. Although this rule emphasizes the priority of human rights and international norms of justice as instruments of the Ombudsman's work, it also greatly reduces the number of potential complainants—not every person facing a certain problem tries to resolve it in court. Moreover, not all the people who still go to court or try to address the problem administratively will eventually receive a decision that can then be brought before the Ombudsman.

By the beginning of the 2000s, certain practices had developed regarding complaints to the Ombudsman. In 2004 and 2005, the Ombudsman's office received 30,392 and 33,425 citizen complaints respectively. By the beginning of the 2010s, the number of complaints slightly decreased; however, by 2017 it increased again, exceeding the figures from the beginning of 2000s (see Table 5.2).

Certain thematic niches have been formed where the Ombudsman's competence is justified. Among these are:

- high-profile cases;
- cases concerning prisoners' rights;
- political rights and freedoms (journalists' rights, voting rights, the right to freedom of assembly and association, undesirable organizations (since 2016), religious organizations);
- civil rights (indigenous people's rights, migration processes and migrants' rights, the right to freedom of information and information security, issues of invasion of privacy and inviolability, alimony);

- economic and labor rights (extortion, economic rights, labor rights, housing rights, rights of persons in military service and their family members, orphans' housing rights);
- social rights and the right to healthcare (housing rights—46% of all social rights; labor rights—14%; issues regarding pension provision and benefit payments—13%; social protection for certain citizen categories—11%; access to quality healthcare—5%);
- cultural and educational rights (the right to education, the rights of future generations).

The main categories of complaints received by the Ombudsman's office in 2015 are the following:

- criminal proceedings (30%);
- penal proceedings (14%);
- housing rights and utility services (16%);
- social security and welfare (5%);
- defense matters (4%);
- migration and citizenship (4%);
- respect for or restoration of other rights (27%).

The Ombudsman has limited ability to influence the solution of problems or to participate in the legislative process. The human rights commissioner's main means of influence are annual recommendations on improving the protection of human rights, which are addressed to supreme state governing bodies. The latter include the State Duma of the RF, the Government of the RF, bodies of state power of the constituent entities of the RF, the Ministry of Justice of the RF, the Ministry of Foreign Affairs of the RF, the Central Bank of the RF, and the Supreme Court of the RF.

In sum, the Ombudsman's office was conceived as a fairly influential institution. Over the years of its existence, this institution has occupied a special niche among the citizens' options to protect their rights and interests. However, at the beginning, the activities of the Ombudsman's office primarily compensated for the shortcomings of the independent judiciary—in particular, for the weak segment of administrative justice. Since the very beginning, working with complaints was the top priority of the Ombudsman's office, while the correction of legislation and the promotion of human rights remained secondary tasks. In other words, the Ombudsman's office, with its high mission, became more popular as the new addressee of citizens' complaints and was legitimate in the context of a democratizing society.

The procuracy in post-socialist Russia and its role in work with complaints

According to the new political and legal logic, the procuracy was not supposed to play a key role in dealing with complaints. The dominant task of the procuracy had always been the protection of the interests of the state. However, in the context of a state that declared itself democratized, protecting the interests of the citizens was to become the primary task.

At the time of the drafting of the 1993 Constitution, there was considerable discussion over limiting the role of the procuracy to the prosecution of criminal cases and coordination of the fight against crime (Savitskii 1994). The proponents of this position wanted to strip the procuracy of its traditional wide-ranging powers of supervision. In particular, some felt that the procuracy needed to be weakened in order to permit the court and the Ministry of Justice to assume dominance in the evolving legal system; that "as long as the procuracy retained the powers it enjoyed during the communist era, the courts will never gain supremacy" (Smith 2007:2). Rather than tackle these contentious issues, it was decided to leave out of the Constitution any delineation of the procuracy's powers or functions. The Federal Law "On the Procuracy of the Russian Federation" was adopted on January 17, 1992. A bit later it was brought in line with the Constitution—by introducing the 1995 Federal Law "On Amending the Law of the RF On the Procuracy of the Russian Federation." According to the law, the procuracy retained most of the powers and functions it enjoyed throughout the Soviet era. The only major function for which it was no longer responsible was supervision of the courts, which was vested in the Ministry of Justice.

According to the updated legislation, the main tasks of the procuracy were the following: supervising compliance with the Constitution, implementing the laws in force in the territory of the RF (Art. 1.1), and supervising human rights. The Russian procuracy, as well as the Soviet one, was entrusted with receiving written communications, complaints, and other appeals (Art. 10). In order for the procuracy to accept a complaint, it must contain information that the law has been violated. The procuracy has the same procedure and deadlines for the consideration of complaints as the other addressees. The prosecutors also have powers enabling them to take measures to hold accountable for the persons who committed offenses (Art. 10.4). In cases where the procuracy lacks resources and powers to solve the problem, its function is limited to commenting on the validity of the problem and the further recourse to the court.

Besides the fact that the procuracy retained almost all its functions and powers from the Soviet years, it also quickly formed a strong bond with the government. Since the breakup of the USSR, the procuracy has been engaged in a series of politically motivated criminal investigations—the murder of the TV journalist Vlad Listiev, the dismissal of Moscow police chief Ponomariov, and the suspension of Vice President Aleksandr Rutskoi (Smith 1996:366–368). The effect of these political involvements was to undermine much of the legitimacy that the procuracy possessed. It appears that President Yeltsin used the procuracy to further his political interests in several instances, strengthening its rapprochement with the authorities.

Under Putin, the procuracy began to get involved in the investigation of high-profile cases and accidents and contributed to the criminal prosecution of oligarchs such as Mikhail Khodorkovskii, Vladimir Gusinskii, and Boris

Berezovskii. The involvement of the procuracy in these cases reinforced its image as a heavily politicized institution—"the eyes of the tsar"—that has been utilized by Putin to further his own agenda (Smith 2007:6–7). Officially, the procuracy does not belong to any of the branches of power. In most legal settings, this institution functions in all three arenas: executive, legislative, and judicial (Ibid). In fact, Putin has created the prerequisites for a new strengthening of the procuracy and its supervising function in order to involve it in criminal proceedings and to improve his own ability to influence the work of the procuracy.

For now, the procuracy is realizing two main tasks. The first one, related to combating crime, reflects the recognition by judicial reformers of the need for some prosecutorial supervision. The second one is processing complaints of citizens. Of these two parts, the first is undoubtedly dominant; however, it is exactly this part that duplicates the unique function of the court.

Meanwhile, prosecutorial supervision of citizen's complaints has some attractive features. It is free and faster than judicial review (unlike use of the courts). Since many citizens in the early post-Soviet years did not know how to lodge a complaint in court, the availability of procuracy review made sense, even if it recognized their real status as subjects rather than citizens (Smith 1996:353). To lodge a complaint with the procuracy, one must know the legislation; the complaint must contain the legal reasoning underpinning the problem. Finally, unlike many other addressees of complaints, the procuracy is empowered to independently resolve a range of issues in accordance with the law. Taken together, these conditions have made the procuracy a very popular recipient of complaints. The number of complaints addressed to the procuracy has always been high (see Table 5.3).

At the same time, turning to the procuracy was much less likely to produce success in comparison with going to court. According to statistics, from 2011 to 2017, the procuracy annually considered 70–72% of the total number of submitted complaints and applications. By contrast, the performance of courts approaches 100% (Rassmotrenie sudami 2018). The percentage of success in applications filed to the procuracy does not exceed 10–11%, while courts redress the demands of the claimants in more than 90% of civil and administrative cases and in approximately 70% of cases in criminal proceedings (Dannye sudebnoi statistiki 2011–2017).

The jurisdiction of the procuracy encompasses issues mostly related to criminal offenses of varying gravity. However, the functions of the procuracy also include "prosecution of administrative offenses and conducting administrative investigations in accordance with the powers established by the Code of the Russian Federation on Administrative Offenses and by other federal statutes" (Federal Law On the Procuracy 1992, Art. 1.2). This pertains to crimes "involving corruption" and offenses related to abuse of office (Articles 285 and 286 of the Criminal Code). Among the applications filed to the procuracy there are also claims regarding violations of social rights.

Obviously, the function of the procuracy intersects with the activities of the courts. However, there also exists a segment of problems where it is equally legitimate to appeal to the procuracy and the Ombudsman's office. Indeed,

Table 5.3 Main indicators of activities of the procuracy in 2011–2017 years

	2011	*2012*	*2013*	*2014*	*2015*	*2016*	*2017*
Complaints submitted during the reporting period (no duplicates)	3,500,304	3,637,314	3 983 604	4,020,380	4,412,370	4,739,071	4,813,043
Total complaints considered	2,540,474	2,616,509	2,833,328	2,872,208	3,142,387	3,330,582	3,393,266
Complaints resolved (no duplicates)	1,992,295	1,987,435	2,050,869	1,988,412	2,103,001	2,108,247	2,078,182
Complaints redressed (no duplicates)	403,527	399,087	412,415	396,620	416,965	404,751	391,213

Sources: *Statisticheskie dannye ob osnovnykh pokazateliakh deiatel'nosti prokuratury RF za ianvar'–dekabr' 2011–2012, 2013, 2015, 2017 gg*. Available at: https://genproc.gov.ru/stat/data

human rights protection and monitoring, which are the main objectives of the Ombudsman, are also assigned to the procuracy in accordance with the law "On the Procuracy of the Russian Federation."

Traditionally, joint human rights activities, wherein both the procuracy and the Ombudsman exercise their authority, are directed at cases regarding the rights and freedoms of persons on military service, persons dismissed from military service, and members of their families. It is important to note that the procuracy interacts with the Ombudsman in cases related to compliance with the law by the administrative authorities and institutions that enforce penalties and apply measures of a coercive nature handed down by the courts. The procuracy also works with the human rights commissioner's office when it comes to violations committed by administrations of places of detention and remand centers.

With regard to civil affairs, the procuracy and the Ombudsman work in sync to resolve problems related to violations of labor law, of the Housing Code, in the sector of utility services, breaches of law pertaining to the rights of legal entities and self-employed entrepreneurs, and violations of the rights and interests of minors.

The proportion of complaints to the procuracy on violations in the course of criminal and penal proceedings is 2.5 times smaller than that of the same type of complaints addressed to the Ombudsman: 44% and 17% respectively (data from 2016). However, the actual number of complaints on these issues submitted to the procuracy is almost 50 times higher. According to data from 2015, the proportion of complaints to the Ombudsman regarding housing rights is almost six times higher than that of the complaints filed with the procuracy: 16% and 2.6% respectively. In this case, the number of complaints to the procuracy also exceeds that of the complaints addressed to the Ombudsman by a factor of 19.

The relationship between the procuracy and the Ombudsman is regulated by law. However, since the late 1990s there has been a tendency that strengthens the role of the procuracy in this cooperation. For example, on July 24, 1998, an Agreement was concluded "On the Forms of Interaction between the Prosecutor's General Office of the Russian Federation and the Commissioner for Human Rights to Ensure Guarantees of State Protection of Civil Rights and Freedoms." This document, as well as the Order that organized its implementation (1998),[8] proclaimed that the two sides cooperate on almost equal terms with equal authority. However, on May 3, 2007, another Agreement entered into effect between the Ombudsman and the Prosecutor General—"On Cooperation in Protection of the Rights and Freedoms of Persons and Citizens." This document emphasized that the procuracy is the main institution responsible for the protection of human rights. According to the Order of the General Prosecutor of the Russian Federation of February 9, 2009, No. 33/7R "On the Organization of Execution of the Agreement between the Human Rights Ombudsman in the Russian Federation and the General Prosecutor of the Russian Federation on Cooperation in Matters of Protection of the Human and Civil Rights and Freedoms," the procuracy was actually designated as the main human rights authority whereas the Ombudsman performed a supporting function acting as a liaison between the procuracy and the general public (4). The same Order abolished the former Order of 1999.

The Ombudsman's office, as the independent, non-systemic structure cross-referencing all the activities of government agencies with international human rights values has weakened. In particular, this is reflected in the appointment of the new human rights commissioner in 2016. The new Ombudsman, Tatiana Moskal'kova, worked her way through the ranks of the Soviet and Russian police for more than two decades, rising to become Major-General of the Ministry of the Interior. Ms. Moskal'kova retired in 2007 and won a seat in the parliament, or Duma, as a member of "The Just Russia," a left-leaning pro-government party. Unlike most of her predecessors in the post, Ms. Moskal'kova lacks experience as a human rights activist (Nechepurenko 2016).

The procuracy and the Ombudsman, along with government authorities, represent important institutions where citizens can submit their complaints. Clearly, the Ombudsman's office represents a component and instrument of democratization and legal modernization. On the contrary, the procuracy is a traditional Russian instrument of state supervision mostly associated with the periods of monarchy and Stalin's rule.

During the formation of the aforementioned institutions in post-Soviet Russia, the procuracy initially received much more power and many more capabilities compared to the Ombudsman's office. The procuracy's equipment, personnel, and legislative support highly surpasses that of the Ombudsman's office. Besides, in comparison with the Ombudsman, the procuracy is much closer to the authorities as well as the court; it performs the function of public prosecution in court. It is also authorized to institute criminal proceedings and to take measures to prosecute perpetrators of various offenses on par with the court. The procuracy also looks more attractive in the eyes of the citizens as the addressee of complaints—the number of complaints filed with the procuracy is a hundred times higher than the number of complaints submitted to the Ombudsman's office.

The transformations of recent years clearly reveal a progression towards a strengthening of the procuracy and deliberate weakening of the Ombudsman's position. The procuracy is slowly but steadily taking over the status of the main human rights organization from the Ombudsman's office. The Ombudsman's procedure for the consideration of complaints, rather than directly responding to every problem, involves systematically enhancing the status of the human rights—the cornerstone of any democracy—both within society and throughout the system of state administration. This approach fundamentally stands out because of its democratic character. However, it is the procuracy that has received a development boost at the behest of the authorities in recent years—which also prioritized it as an addressee of complaints. Given that the procuracy is a traditional, government-supervised institute, this tendency distorts the very idea of human rights activity.

(Re-)establishing the complaint mechanism

During the entire period of Yeltsin's rule, the complaint mechanism existed as a marginal, secondary problem-solving option. While legal instruments were undergoing evolution, the mechanism was mostly relevant at the lower levels, in the context of local government, representing a feedback channel. The complaint mechanism never stopped working and sometimes it helped promote complaints to the highest state level—for example, in cases when a complaint concerned officials. Citizens were complaining about regional and local executive officials to the Administration of the President; since 1994, when the corresponding institution was introduced, they have also been filing appeals regarding these issues to the President's representatives in the constituent entities of the Russian Federation.

Evidently, the trend of increasing presidential authority emerged almost immediately after Putin came to power; a prominent role here was played by the mechanism of complaints. The revamped mechanism demonstrated an obvious connection with the centuries-old tradition; however, it also acquired specific features which are discussed in this section.

Hotlines and the formation of a new model of communication between citizens and the authorities

Annual hotlines (*Priamaia Liniia*) with the president are indirectly related to the complaint mechanism as a bureaucratic apparatus. At the same time, they reflect an important background that is the shift of the general political discourse; the main model of communication between the citizens and the government has been redefined.

From the very beginning of Putin's leadership, multiple forms of direct communication with him were declared available to the people. One of the first events acquainting people with Putin presented the possibility of direct interaction with the new leader of Russia. This was the hotline of the president with citizens, held for the first time in 2001. It was broadcast live, with Putin answering questions from people calling in to the studio. Since 2001, hotlines with president Putin have been occurring annually, broadcast by two national TV channels—*ORT* and *RTR*. In addition, the number of questions answered by the president during these hotlines increased with each year, as did the number of callers. From 2001 to 2013, the length of the hotlines gradually increased from 2 hours 20 minutes to 4 hours 47 minutes. During the entire period from 2001 to 2018, there were only two years when hotlines did not take place: in 2004 and in 2012. In both cases, the hotlines were canceled after presidential elections returned Putin to power. In 2018, also after presidential elections, the hotline with the citizens was replaced by a hotline with ministers, regional mayors, and other officials. In 2019, the year of Putin's rating drop, the hotline with the people was arranged again.

As with any form of direct communication, hotlines bring emotionalization into interactions between citizens and the president and support the popularity of the latter (Frajman 2014:502). Hotlines made a significant contribution to the personalization of the president's influence. They demonstrated that the amount of Putin's power, his authority, and people's trust in him were actually independent of the position he occupied at any moment. As is well known, in the period from 2008 to 2012, the function of the president was executed by Dmitrii Medvedev.

Despite this fact, the format of the annual hotlines did not change. They were held by Vladimir Putin before, during, and after Medvedev's presidency.

Based on the testimonies of people who addressed Putin live, it appears that citizens' questions for the hotlines go through a careful screening process. According to participants, they had sent some complaints to one of the offices receiving and processing applications beforehand. Prior to the hotline, they were contacted and invited to ask their questions live.

As a rule, the topics that have attracted public attention during the year are discussed during the hotlines. It is important to note that the debates usually included questions, the investigation of which involved certain members of the United Russia party or Putin himself. Thus, in 2009 and 2010, problems surrounding mining and monocities were actively discussed. In May 2010, a serious accident took place at Raspadskaia, one of Russia's largest mines. At that time, Putin visited Mezhdurechensk—the town where the crash occurred—right after the accident.

The other topics of discussion are usually questions about people's permanent concern. The problems of interethnic relations, political protests, corruption, low salaries and pensions, communal services and ramshackle housing, landfills, and healthcare are typically discussed in every hotline. Alongside significant, state-level problems, Putin's live broadcasts also cover local issues and even personal topics—for example, specific problems of economic enterprises or the difficulty of innovation in production. Callers inquire about where to buy a Christmas tree, when winter will come, or how Putin's dog is doing. Certain techniques are used to represent the interactions during the hotlines as real: "uncomfortable," "sharp" questions, failures of communication, and thanks are also included in the live broadcast.

Now, a direct application to the president can be submitted by any means of communication—mail, telephone, Internet, or mobile connection. In 2017, reportedly two million applications were registered before and during the hotline, and only 70 of them (0.0035%) were answered by the president. The rate is extremely low, although the questions discussed on live broadcast typically receive an immediate response from the president. Success stories are widely presented in the national media, and, as a result of this wonderful turn, citizens usually undertake multiple efforts to solve their problems in the ways discussed.

The set of problems solved with Putin's assistance is very diverse and has no clearly defined boundaries. Some questions are always welcome for discussion and some others tabooed (Wengle and Evans 2018:396–398). The media regularly reports that certain housing problems were solved with Putin's assistance. Almost every week the media delivers a piece of news saying that President Putin helped a disabled person to receive a long-awaited wheelchair or that a new medical care center opened after an application to Putin was filed, or that a ramshackle house, where a single old woman lives, was reconstructed on his orders.

During one of the hotlines (2008), a little girl named Daria Varfolomeeva (*real name—E.B.*) called Putin and asked him for "a Cinderella dress." As a result, Putin—then prime minister—invited the girl to the Kremlin, gave her the dress, a laptop, and other gifts. Sometime later, all the social infrastructure buildings in the girl's native village underwent reconstruction. The girl's portrait was hung in pride of place at the school's entrance (*RIA Novosti* 2011).

The list of popularized success stories is long. With the help of these stories, the media creates an idea that the mechanism of appeals is a super-efficient way of solving particular problems. This method of dispute resolution, in many senses, stands in opposition to all other methods which are recognized as less efficient, less humanistic, and less familiar. The mechanism of complaints is customized as familiar, clear, credible, helpful, and just. The central figure of this mechanism is President Putin, who gets the questions moving.

Meanwhile, not all complaints entail successful resolutions of problems. Moreover, not all attempts to declare a problem are secure for the complainants. Along with success stories, there are also some well-known cases of repression. As in all other eras of Russian history, complaints are now used by citizens as a way to deliver information on offenses committed by officials from below. As usual, local officials make efforts to resist such complaints and their consequences. In April 2015, Anton Tiurishev (*real name—E.B.*), a worker at the Pacific Bridge Construction Company (*Tikhookeanskaia Mostostroitel'naia Kompaniia*), who was engaged in the construction of the spaceport *Vostochnyi*, complained of unpaid wages at the direct line with the president. After that, local authorities took measures: the current and former chief executive officers of the company were arrested. In late December 2015, workers sent a repeated appeal to Putin, where they reported that the problem with wages had not been resolved. In April 2016, right before the next direct line with the president, Anton Tiurishev was arrested for five days. According to his colleagues, he was intending to reraise the issue of wages (Gavrilko et al. 2017).

Moreover, some talks on live broadcast have an undesirable or even opposite effect on the image of the president, showing his irresponsiveness and inability to change the system. In 2017 Daria Starikova (*real name—E.B.*), a 24-year-old cancer patient, a resident of the northern city Apatity, had a talk with the president during the hotline. She complained about the dramatic degradation of medical infrastructure in her city and false diagnostics, because of which she was unable to start her treatment in time. She asked Putin to change the situation with access to medical care and support the medical infrastructure in her region. In response, the president told Daria about his father, who also suffered from cancer, and promised to help her personally. After this talk medical centers in Apatity received some equipment and several vehicles, although no political decisions that would change the situation with medical care in the country, or even in the region, were made. Daria was moved to one of the Moscow cancer centers, where she died about six months later (Bystritskaia 2018).

Complaints addressed to the president do have effect. However, this effect is not always predictable. In some cases, it may be an immediate solution to the problem. Here we can mention an important feature; in the vast majority of cases the president helps a particular complainant to solve a specific problem. Systemic changes or policy decisions provoked by the complaints are rarely reported on in public. This is true even for collective complaints. However, it does not mean that complaints, in fact, did not entail such effects. Thus, the value of direct personal communication with the president—and the futility of any struggle for the common good—is publicly emphasized.

Almost from the beginning, hotlines with the president were not just an act of communication, i.e. an opportunity to ask questions directly, but largely a tool to shape the symbolic face of the state and of the presidency (Wengle and Evans 2018). Most of the appeals made during the hotline involve issues of fairness and are essentially complaints. The format of the hotlines translates this complaint communication between citizens and the president into a symbolic dimension. Simultaneously, it opens up symbolic dimensions in the restoration of justice in the ritual of communication between citizens and the president, and, finally, in the social contract.

It orients more towards to the monarchical absolutist pattern than the Soviet one. During the Soviet period, direct applications to the head of the state were not forbidden, but complaining to Joseph Stalin or Leonid Brezhnev was never a mass phenomenon. Nérard (2004), who conducted scrupulous analysis of archival materials including applications and responses of the 1930s, emphasized the role of institutions as addressers of complaints already in that early Soviet period.[9] The personal responsibility of the head of the state to respond to complaints was never proclaimed during Stalin's rule. In all other periods of the Soviet epoch, people wrote letters to the heads of the state but this practice was never mass or broadly advertised. Arguing about the conditions of the Soviet social contract, supported by the complaint mechanism, researchers agree that it was concluded between society and the state (Zavisca 2012:165; Cook and Dimitrov 2017). At any rate, the Soviet-era social contract made the state responsible for guaranteeing standards of living. Hotlines construct—at least in a symbolic dimension—a contract between society and the president—not just with the president as a functionary, but personally with Putin.

Legislative innovations: The Law No. 59–FZ

The adoption of the 2006 Law No. 59-FZ "On the Order of Considering of Citizens' Applications in the Russian Federation" provided a new impetus for improving the work with citizens' appeals at all levels of executive authority. According to this law, every citizen of the Russian Federation has the right to submit suggestions, statements, and complaints to a state authority or a local government representative, and the range of issues that may be raised in the applications has no restrictions. Having entered into force, the law superseded all the normative documents regulating the work with complaints as well as those in force since Soviet times. Article 17 of the Law abolished the *Decree of Presidium of the Supreme Council* of 1968, the amendment of 1980, and all other laws and decrees that had not been abolished after the collapse of the Soviet system but formally remained in force until 2006. In fact, Law No. 59, despite having created new mechanisms, displayed considerable continuity with its Soviet predecessor.

While Law No. 59 made complaints a formal element of the modern national legal system, the bureaucracy that processed these complaints remained outside of the judiciary. First and foremost, Law No. 59 is an instrument of executive power. However, it generally determines the rules for handling all kinds of complaints, including the ones submitted to the procuracy and to the Ombudsman. Despite abolishing the Soviet normative documents, Law No. 59 has preserved many features of the Soviet complaint mechanism. The deadline for consideration of complaints remained unchanged—30 days from the date of registration (Art. 12.1). As with the Decree of Presidium (1968), the law prohibits the prosecution of complainants (Art. 6.1). Moreover, as in Soviet times, the law prohibits directing the complaint to any addressees, the actions/inaction of which are subject to appeal (Art. 8.6). However, instead of the Soviet rule that a complaint is to be directed to the guilty person's supervisors, a new rule has been established—a complaint can be submitted "to the state body, local government body, or official that has jurisdiction in the issues presented in the application" (Art. 8.1).

Like the 1968 Decree, the 2006 law included the concept of "complaint" under the umbrella term "applications"—along with other terms such as "statement" and "proposal." The new definition has preserved the meaning of the complaint as a para-judicial instrument. The law defines a complaint as "a citizen's request for the restoration or protection of her violated rights, freedoms, or legitimate interests, or rights, freedoms, or legitimate interests of others" (Art. 4.4). It has much in common with the definition of a lawsuit. The difference between them is that the grounds for filing a lawsuit are limited to violations of the law, while the grounds for a complaint may be found in a large variety of arguments that are subjectively felt by the addresser to be unjust. The tasks that the addressees of complaints are entrusted with are also defined through the function of rights protection. Indeed, the exact formulation includes both "protection" and "restoration" of the "violated rights and freedoms and lawful interests of citizens" (Art. 10.3). Thus, the addressees' tasks include not just preventing violations but also working directly with the violations committed.

In fact, by introducing Law No. 59, the state usurped the right to receive and address complaints. The addressees of complaints are defined by the law as "bodies of state power, bodies of local self-government, and officials" (Art. 1.1). Note that public and human rights organizations, which usually have non-profit status, have been excluded from the list of addressees, whereas leaders of non-governmental organizations (NGOs) are problematic to be categorized as "officials" due to ambiguities in the legislation. Based on the interpretation provided by Law No. 59, the circle of addressees of complaints is confined to official state representatives and municipal authorities (Art. 4.5). Thus, the law reproduces the historical model of the complaint mechanism that existed in Russia before and after the Revolution of 1917.

According to the aforementioned law, the activities of the complaint mechanism are, in fact, insulated within the administrative apparatus of the executive power. The problem described in the complaint is considered within the administrative system. The authorities that are the recipients of complaints cannot turn to the court or to bodies conducting investigations and initial inquiries even in order to request additional information on the issue (Art. 10.2). However, they can forward the complaint to, or request information from, law enforcement agencies or bodies of control and supervision—particularly regarding violations of migration legislation (Art. 8.3.1). In relation to the complaint mechanism, the court performs a function that is defined as "supervisory" within the judicial system. One can appeal, administratively or judicially, against a decision taken with regard to their complaint, or against a violation of the procedure for handling complaints, as it is defined in Law No. 59 (Art. 5.4). However, the law does not permit appeals against a court decision by way of administrative complaint (Art. 11.2).

Apart from court appeals against decisions on complaints, the law does not imply virtually any external oversight. According to Article 14, the monitoring of the procedure of handling complaints performed by state bodies, local self-government bodies, and officials is entrusted to those same "state bodies, local self-government bodies, and officials." At the same time, the lines of authority and subordination between the controlling and the controlled have not been specified.

Currently, the complaint mechanism remains the most accessible and convenient channel for filing complaints and solving problems. There is no fee for filing administrative complaints as they are taken into consideration free of charge. This form of appeals does not require legal justification either. The complainant only needs to "describe the problem." The mechanism in question implies that a system of internal navigation is in place, i.e. the complainant does not need to specify the exact addressee for the solution of their problems (Art. 8.3). Here are the reasons for appeal as defined in the law: violation of or disrespect for rights and interests, misconduct by government representatives and bodies, and "improvement of the socio-economic and other areas of activity of the state and society" (Art. 4.2). The latter formulation expands the possible topics of address to infinity. Importantly, the mechanism allows complaints from third parties. This means that relatives, neighbors, or sympathetic parties can submit a complaint in place of the wronged individual. The same opportunity is available in cases of complaints to the Ombudsman; however, it is not possible to do so without having a special power of attorney when resorting to the help of the procuracy or the court.

Thus, Law No. 59 outlined the general procedure for handling citizens' complaints and created a normative base within the executive branch which would contribute to the reconstruction of the complaint-handling bureaucracy. The legislative innovations of the following years have contributed to the expansion and strengthening of the mechanism.

At the Ninth Congress in 2008, Vladimir Putin was elected Chairman of the United Russia party, known in Russia today as the "ruling party." At the same Congress, there were adopted regulations on the establishment of a network of reception offices of the party United Russia in all 83 regions of Russia. The ruling party's active involvement in the work with complaints obviously connoted the activities of the Central Committee of the Communist Party.

The next steps expressly aimed to construct a vertical bureaucracy of complaints as well as to strengthen the role of the president as the main addressee.

In 2009, the Regulation on the Reception Office of the President of the Russian Federation in the Federal District came into force. The Regulation implied that another network of public reception offices be created which would establish a direct link with the president in federal districts through the office of the president's plenipotentiary representative. Three main functions of the reception offices are enshrined in the Regulation: 1) operational accumulation and delivery of all received complaints to the president's office, which provides a direct link between the federal district and the president's office; 2) regular and detailed statistical and analytical processing of complaints; 3) monitoring and supervision of complaint handling by state bodies, local self-government bodies, and officials within the federal district. The List of Reception Offices of the President of the Russian Federation was approved by the Regulation on the Reception Office (2009). As a result, reception offices opened in the Central, Northwest, South, Volga, Ural, and Siberian federal districts.

The Administrative Office of the President of the RF on Work with Applications of Citizens and Organizations was established in 2010 by special decree of the president to centralize the management of the mechanism. This institution can be contacted directly (orally or in writing), by telephone, by mail, or through a special website. The Administrative Office accumulates all data regarding appeals to the president which are received through public reception offices in the federal districts. The Administrative Office carries out activities to address the issues identified in the appeals. This is the highest level of complaint handling: the apparatus is endowed with wide powers to request documents and data that allow for the disentangling of problems at various levels of state and municipal power. Also, in all seven plenipotentiary offices of the president in the regions there are public receptions that receive applications from citizens. On the basis of plenipotentiary offices, 56 reception rooms were also organized in the regions, territories, and republics of Russia.

Apart from actually handling complaints, the Administrative Office regularly prepares proposals on improvement of legislation and other normative legal acts based on an analysis of citizens' applications (Decree of the President 2010:5). The Administrative Office of the President also supervises reception offices in federal districts (Ibid P. 5z), controls the effectiveness of work with complaints, and oversees the implementation status of the decisions taken at all levels of the mechanism. The latter means that the reconstructed complaint mechanism is ultimately short-circuited within the executive branch of power: the apparatus of the president, while being situated within the mechanism itself, is designated as the main supervisory authority to control complaint handling at all levels.

The Traveling Reception Office of the President was introduced in 2011 and tasked with combating malfeasance. The Traveling Reception Office is supposed to immediately come over to regions in response to citizens' complaints about the actions (or inaction) of officials. The operations of the Traveling Reception Office are regulated by Law No. 59. The establishment of the Traveling Reception Office clearly outlined the function of administrative justice within the framework of the complaint mechanism. In the Soviet years, the latter was largely used to compensate for the underdeveloped administrative justice segment of the legal and judicial system. However, in the USSR, this function had never been performed under the patronage of a particular office, let alone a political figure.

By the time Putin returned to the presidency in 2012, a powerful, multilevel, hierarchical bureaucracy had been constructed to handle complaints from the population, and the pinnacle of this pyramid was the president of the Russian Federation. He represented the terminal point, controlling all transmission belts of the mechanism. The president has been both explicitly and indirectly defined as the main recipient of all complaints submitted at different levels of the mechanism in different parts of the country. The specially designed reception offices network, the hotlines, and the live broadcasts from all over the country are all intended to create an illusion of direct contact with the president, readily available at any given moment. The modern means of communication and mobile parts of the mechanism are to maintain the illusion that the president himself is involved in solving citizens' problems and that he personally oversees both high-level and local officials.

The legal basis for whistleblowing in contemporary Russia

A number of legislative initiatives, implemented in recent years, create favorable conditions for whistleblowing. The adoption of the so-called Law on Foreign Agents[10] has not only introduced the concept, direct connotations with the Stalinist laws against espionage, but also created a label applicable to any independent initiative. The law also spawned a series of trials involving the judiciary, and at the same time, a wave of publications, denouncing the vices of the respective—mainly non-governmental—organizations. The law and its consequences had a significant impact on the work of the Russian third sector, provoked multiple cases of forced emigration of citizens, and the closure and reorganization of non-profit initiatives and independent media.

Adoption of the so-called "Iarovaia's Package" (*Paket Iarovoi*)[11] unambiguously strengthened the prerequisites for the emergence of whistleblowing. Similarly to the Soviet Article 58 Paragraph 12 of the Criminal Code in 1927 redaction, which designated failure to signal as a crime, in July 6, 2016, Article 205.6. of the Criminal Code of the RF "Failure to report a crime" (*Nesoobshchenie o prestuplenii*) was introduced. It provides liability for: "Failure to report to authorities, authorized to consider reports of a crime; about a person(s) who, according to reliable information, prepares, commits, or has committed at least one of the crimes," including terrorism and aiding terrorism, the organization of illegal military formations and participation in them, encroachment on the life of a statesman and public figure (277), violent seizure and enforced retention of power (278), armed rebellion (279), attack on representatives of other states (360), and international terrorism (361). The penalty for non-reporting varies from a fine of up to 100,000 rubles to imprisonment for up to a year.

The first sentence under the article "Failure to report a crime" was passed by the Kirovsky District Court of Astrakhan on December 6, 2017. The jury found local resident Ulukbek Gafurov (*real name—E.B.*) guilty and sentenced him to a fine of 70,000 rubles. The court found that Gafurov knew that his friend Ravshan Akbarov (*real name—E.B.*), a citizen of Kyrgyzstan, had been trained in a militant camp and fought on the side of the terrorists, but he did not report this to the police.

The receipt of anonymous or non-anonymous signals is often used by law enforcement and regulatory agencies to justify unscheduled inspections and searches and to initiate legal proceedings. Among the significant cases are numerous inspections and litigations of the European University at Saint Petersburg, lasting from mid-2016 until 2018; an audit of the human rights organization "Citizen's Watch" in 2016; searches at the offices of the Alexey Navalny Anti-Corruption Foundation on March 26, 2017: and "Open Russia" on April 27, 2017. In the latter two cases, the searches were procedurally disguised as "inspection of the scene of the incident by an anonymous signal."

Conclusion

The necessary legal institutions to solve problems and disputes were created anew, or at least seriously revamped, in the first post-Soviet decade. The civil and administrative legislation was substantially reformed and modified. These segments were largely undeveloped in the Soviet period, while their function, as a rule, was performed by para-judicial problem-solving mechanisms. Meanwhile, according to judicial statistics, the renewed legal instruments quickly found themselves in high demand.

Against this backdrop, the restoration of the complaint mechanism in the mid-2000s looks strange and redundant from the legal point of view. However, it fits into the general conservative turn, both as a means to centralize and personalize power and as a very effective tool to draw up a certain contract between the government and society. In the introduction, it was shown that the complaint is a very flexible tool with a large range of capabilities—it can be applied both in a democratic manner and as an instrument of totalitarian governance. Clearly, the post-Soviet complaint mechanism has been configured towards the authoritarian option. Virtually all opportunities to use a complaint as an instrument of deliberative democracy—as a tool to protect the common good—are either mitigated or not used openly. The study shows a consistent strengthening of the authoritarian components of the complaint mechanism (such as the procuracy) and a consistent weakening of its democratic forms (such as the institution of Ombudsman). This demonstrates the priorities of functions expected from the complaint mechanism.

The post-Soviet design of the complaint mechanism combines both Soviet and Tsarist features. The post-Soviet complaint mechanism has a Soviet-type structure involving multilevel bureaucracy at all government levels. The major addressees of complaints include the political party, the government, state and local bodies, and officials at all levels. Just as in the Soviet period, officials are required to respond to complaints. On the one hand, this provides citizens with an easy and inexpensive way to solve their problems outside of the courts; on the other hand, it reinforces the legitimacy of state power and the authoritarian contract between the state and society. At the same time, the mechanism in question is no less (or, perhaps, even more) centralized and personalized than its pre-revolutionary, Tsarist analog. The president, being the main addressee of complaints, occasionally involves himself personally in the consideration and resolution of complaints, which supports the legitimacy of growing authoritarianism.

This artificial reincarnation of an institution of the past has automatically reanimated its corresponding practices, rules, and specificities. The complaint mechanism of today is effectively similar to its late Soviet antecedent as it still represents an alternative method for restoring justice where a conflict can be resolved with or without legal underpinnings. Thus, a gray zone of informality is being developed within the sphere of justice restoration. The boundary between a simple request for help and a legal issue is not clearly defined, as well as the extent to which the executive can intervene in the protection of citizens' rights. These developments shape conditions wherein the unique function of the court may be easily violated.

Officially, the complaint mechanism has been instrumental in shaping the contemporary image of the state authority as a hierarchical structure with a clearly defined pinnacle. It is part of the language of power in which today's citizens are invited to communicate with the authorities. However, this image must be distinguished from the actual functioning of the complaint mechanism in practice. State-run media are making efforts to broadcast complaints to the president as an ultra-effective way of solving problems. However, the most superficial analysis of the implications of complaints shows that presidential directives are not enforced in each and every instance; moreover, they can be misconstrued in the process of execution. The information on successful complaints is distributed through all media outlets; nevertheless, the general public also finds out about the failures later.

Notes

1 After the events of August 1991, Boris Yeltsin issued the Decree of the President of the RSFSR "On Some Issues of Activity of the Executive Authorities in the RSFSR" [Ukaz Prezidenta RSFSR "O nekotorykh voprosakh deiatel'nosti organov ispolnitel'noi vlasti v RSFSR] from August 22, 1991, No. 75. *KonsultantPlus*. Retrieved on July 19, 2019 (www.consultant.ru/cons/CGI/online.cgi?req=doc&base=EXP&n=221425#014741655544208032). The Decree introduced a vertical hierarchical structure for the executive authorities, which increased the powers of local authorities and lasted until 1996. "The Head of the Administration…within the limits of his or her competence, issues decisions and orders which shall be binding within the territory concerned" (Decree 1991, p. 4).

2 Formally, the Decree of Presidium of the Supreme Soviet of the USSR of April 12, 1968, No. 2534-VII "On the Order for Considering Citizens' Suggestions, Statements, and Complaints" was not cancelled until 2006.

3 Kollektsiia pisem B.N. Yeltsinu, 1991.GARF. F.A.-664, op. 1, doc. 48.

4 See the list of all tables in Appendix 3.

5 Doklad Upolnomochennogo po pravam cheloveka za 2014 god. 2015. Moscow. *Apparat Upolnomochennogo po pravam cheloveka*. Retrieved on July 19, 2019 (http://ombudsmanrf.org/upload/files/docs/appeals/doklad2014.pdf).

6 Doklad Upolnomochennogo po pravam cheloveka za 2015 god. 2016. Moscow. *Apparat Upolnomochennogo po pravam cheloveka*. Retrieved on July 19, 2019 (http://ombudsmanrf.org/www/upload/files/docs/appeals/doclad2015web.pdf).

7 Doklad Upolnomochennogo po pravam cheloveka za 2017 god. 2018. Moscow. *Apparat Upolnomochennogo po pravam cheloveka*. Retrieved on July 19, 2019 (http://ombudsmanrf.org/upload/files/docs/lib/lite2-doclad_20.04.18.pdf).

8 See also: Order of the General Prosecutor of the Russian Federation "On the Organization of the Execution of the Agreement 'On Forms of Interaction Between the General Prosecutor's Office of the Russian Federation and the Commissioner for Human Rights to Ensure Guarantees of State Protection of Civil Rights and Freedoms'" [Rasporiazhenie "Ob organizatsii ispolneniia soglasheniia 'O formakh vsaimodeistviia general'noi prokuratury RF i Upolnomochennogo po pravam cheloveka v tseliakh obespecheniia garantii gosudarstvennoi zashchity prav i svobod grazhdan'"] from January 14, 1999, No. 6/7R. *KonsultantPlus*. Retrieved on July 19, 2019 (www.consultant.ru/cons/cgi/online.cgi?req=doc&ts=1300887630060610483396979 74&cacheid=2BA1BE299E5DFF23513149907022C90B&mode=splus&base=EXP&n=369350&rnd=0.48660531387225947#035078449096176856).

9 The addressees were the Workers and Peasants' Inspectorate (RKI), All-Union Communist Party Bolsheviks (VKP(b)) and the mass media. A large number of personal applications were sent to Mikhail Kalinin, who held the position of the head of the Central Executive Committee in the 1930s (Nérard 2004).

10 See: Federal Law "On amending certain federal laws regarding regulation of activities of non-profit organizations performing functions of foreign agents" ["O vnesenii izmenenii v otdel'nye zakonodatel'nye akty Rossiiskoi Federatsii v chasti regulirovaniia deiatel'nosti nekommercheskikh organizatsii, vypolniaiushchikh funktsii inostrannogo agenta"] from June 20, 2012. *Garant*. Retrieved on July 19, 2019 (http://base.garant.ru/70204242).

11 Federal Law "On Amendments to the Criminal Code of the Russian Federation and the Code of Criminal Procedure of the Russian Federation regarding the establishment of additional counter-terrorism measures and ensuring public safety" [Federal'nyi zakon "O vnesenii izmenenii v Ugolovnyi kodeks RF i Ugolovno-protsessual'nyi kodeks RF v chasti ustanovleniia dopolnitel'nykh mer protivodeistviia terrorizmu i obespecheniia obshchestvennoi bezopasnosti"] from July 6, 2016, No. 375-FZ. *KonsultantPlus*. Retrieved on July 19, 2019 (www.consultant.ru/document/cons_doc_LAW_201087/).

References

Alekseev, Sergei. 1981. *Obshchaia teoriia prava*. Vol. 1. Moscow: Iuridicheskaia literatura.

Bannikov, Gennadii. 2016. "Praktika rassmotreniia ugolovnykh del o prestupleniiakh so zloupotrebleniem i prevysheniem dolzhnostnymi polnomochiiami (stat'i 285 i 286 UK RF.)" *Penzenskii oblastnoi sud*. Retrieved on July 19, 2019 (http://www.oblsud.penza.ru/item/a/1170/).

Bogdanova, Elena. 2003. "Konstruirovanie problemy zashchity prav potrebitelei. Retrospektivnyi analiz." *Rubezh. Al'manakh sotsial'nykh issledovanii* 18:80–94.

Bystritskaia, Tatiana. 2018. "V Murmanskoi oblasti ot zapushchennogo raka umiraiut vsio chashche. Sluchai Dar'i Starikovoi nichego ne izmenil." *Novaia Gazeta* No. 54, May 25. Retrieved on July 3, 2019 (https://www.novayagazeta.ru/articles/2018/05/25/76597-meditsine-stavyat-diagnoz).

Cook, Linda and Martin Dimitrov. 2017. "The Social Contract Revisited: Evidence from Communist and State Capitalist Economies." *Europe-Asia Studies, Special Section: Authoritarian Powers: Russia and China Compared* 69(1):8–26.

Dannye sudebnoi statistiki. 2011–2017. *Ofitsial'nyi sait Sudebnogo departamenta pri Verkhovnom Sude RF*. Retrieved on July 19, 2019 (http://www.cdep.ru/index.php?id=79).

Doklad Upolnomochennogo po pravam cheloveka za 2014 god. 2015. *Apparat Upolnomochennogo po pravam cheloveka*. Moscow. Retrieved on July 19, 2019 (http://ombudsmanrf.org/upload/files/docs/appeals/doklad2014.pdf).

Doklad Upolnomochennogo po pravam cheloveka za 2015 god. 2016. *Apparat Upolnomochennogo po pravam cheloveka*. Moscow. Retrieved on July 19, 2019 (http://ombudsmanrf.org/www/upload/files/docs/appeals/doclad2015web.pdf).

Doklad Upolnomochennogo po pravam cheloveka za 2017 god. 2018. *Apparat Upolnomochennogo po pravam cheloveka*. Moscow. Retrieved on July 19, 2019 (http://ombudsmanrf.org/upload/files/docs/lib/lite2-doclad_20.04.18.pdf).

Frajman, Eduardo. 2014. "Broadcasting Populist Leadership: Hugo Chávez and Aló Presidente." *Journal of Latin American Studies* 46(3):501–526.

Gavrilko, Aleksei, Alekseenko, Filipp and Iuliia Sapronova. 2017. "Lineinaia funktsiia: k chemu privodili zhaloby Putinu vo vremia priamoi linii." *RBC*. Retrieved on July 19, 2019 (https://www.rbc.ru/photoreport/27/06/2017/59523ff49a7947d7f047ad1d).

Gilligan, Emma. 2010. "The Human Rights Ombudsman in Russia: The Evolution of Horizontal Accountability." *Human Rights Quarterly* 32(3):575–600.

Golik, Nina 2007. "Kharakteristika obrashchenii grazhdan v Konstitutsionnyi sud RF." *Rossiiskaia iustitsiia* 10:64.

Khamaneva, Nataliia. 1997. *Zashchita prav grazhdan v sphere ispolnitel'noi vlasti*. Moscow: IGPRAN.

Khamaneva, Nataliia and Nadezhda Salishcheva. 2001. *Administrativnaia iustitsiia i administrativnoe sudoproizvodstvo v Rossiiskoi Federatsii*. Moscow: IGPRAN.

Korniushenkov, Gennadii. 2004. "Dopustimost' obrashchenii grazhdan v konstitutsionnye (ustavnye) sudy sub"ektov Rossiiskoi Federatsii." *Rossiiskii sud'ia* 11:36–41.

Lampert, Nicholas. 1985. *Whistle-Blowing in the Soviet Union Complaints and Abuses under State Socialism*. London: Palgrave McMillan.

Mironov, Mikhail. 2001. *Obrashcheniia grazhdan kak element sistemy zashchity prav cheloveka i osnovnykh svobod: pravo i praktika*. Moscow: Iuridicheskaia literatura.

Mironov, Oleg (ed.). 2004. *Teoriia i praktika zashchity prav cheloveka*. Moscow: Iurisprudentsiia.

Nechepurenko, Ivan. 2016. "Russia's New Human Rights Ombudsman is Former Police General." *The New York Times*. April 22. Retrieved on July 19, 2019 (https://www.nytimes.com/2016/04/23/world/europe/russias-new-human-rights-ombudsman-is-former-police-general.html).

Nérard, François-Xavier. 2004. *Cinq pour cent de vérité: La dénonciation dans l'URSS de Staline (1928–1941)*. Paris: Editions Tallandier.

Rassmotrenie sudami obshchei iurisdiktsii del i materialov za 2010–2017 gg. 2018. *Ofitsial'nyi sait Sudebnogo departamenta pri Verkhovnom Sude RF*. Retrieved on July 19, 2019 (http://www.cdep.ru/index.php?id=79).

RIA Novosti. 2011. "Putin navestil devochku, kotoroi 3 gda nazad podaril 'plat'e Zolushki'." July 1. Retrieved on February 18, 2013 (http://ria.ru/society/20110701/396082180.html#ixzz2MU5lA05L).

Savitskii, Valerii. 1994. "Sterzhnevaia funktsiia prokuratury – osushchestvlenie ugolovnogo presledovaniia." *Rossiiskaia iustitsiia* 10:39–42.
Shishkina, Natalia. 2004. "Organizatsiia i deiatel'nost' komissii po pravam cheloveka v sub"ektakh Rossiiskoi Federatsii i perspektivy ikh razvitiia." *Sibirskii iuridicheskii vestnik* 2:47.
Shugrina, Ekaterina. 2004. "Praktika obrashcheniia v Konstitutsionnyi sud RF: aktual'nye problemy." *Pravo i politika* 3:133–135.
Smirnov, Alexander. 2010. "Sootnoshenie poniatii 'Okhrana prav' i 'Zashchita prav'." *Vestnik Tomskogo gosudarstvennogo universiteta* 331:123–125.
Smith, Gordon. 1996. "The Struggle over the Procuracy." Pp. 349–373 in Peter Solomon (ed.) *Reforming Justice in Russia, 1864–1994: Power, Culture and the Limits of Legal Order. Power, Culture and the Limits of Legal Order*. New York: Routledge.
Smith, Gordon. 2007. "The Procuracy, Putin, and the Rule of Law in Russia." Pp. 1–14 in Ferdinand Feldbrugge (ed.) *Russia, Europe, and the Rule of Law*. Leiden: Brill.
Solomon, Peter. 2004. "Judicial power in Russia: through the prism of administrative justice." *Law and Society Review* 3(38):549–582.
Solomon, Peter and Todd Foglesong. 2000. *Courts and Transition in Russia: the Challenge of Judicial Reform*. Oxford and New York: Routledge.
Statisticheskie dannye ob osnovnykh pokazateliakh deiatel'nosti prokuratury RF za ianvar'–dekabr' 2011–2012, 2013, 2015, 2017 gg. *Ofitsial'nyi sait General'noi Prokuratury RF*. Retrieved on July 19, 2019 (https://genproc.gov.ru/stat/data).
Stoiakin, Gennadii. 1973. "Poniatie 'zashchita grazhdanskikh prav'." Pp. 30–35 in Vladimir Semenov (ed.) *Problemy grazhdansko-pravovoi otvetstvennosti zashchity grazhdanskikh prav*. Sverdlovsk: Izdatel'stvo UrGIuU.
Trochev, Alexei. 2012. "Suing Russia at Home." *Problems of Post-Communism* 59(5):18–34.
Verkhovnyi Sud, R.F. 1998. "Rabota raionnykh sudov obshchei iurisdiktsii v. 1997 g." *Rossiiskaia iustitsiia* 7:55–58.
Verkhovnyi Sud, R.F. 1999. "Rabota raionnykh sudov obshchei iurisdiktsii v. 1998 g." *Rossiiskaia iustitsiia* 9:51–53.
Verkhovnyi Sud, R.F. 2000. "Rabota raionnykh sudov obshchei iurisdiktsii v pervom polugodii 2000 g." *Rossiiskaia iustitsiia* 12:54–57.
Wengle, Susanne and Christine Evans. 2018. "Symbolic state-building in contemporary Russia." *Post-Soviet Affairs* 34(6):384–411.
Zavisca, Jane. 2012. *Housing the New Russia*. Ithaca, NY: Cornell University Press.
Zelentsov, Alexander. 2009. *Administrativnaia iustitsiia*. Moscow: RUDN.

Normative documents

Agreement "On the Forms of Interaction between the Prosecutor's General Office of the Russian Federation and the Commissioner for Human Rights to Ensure Guarantees of State Protection of Civil Rights and Freedoms" [Soglashenie "O formakh vzaimodeistviia general'noi prokuratury RF i Upolnomochennogo po pravam cheloveka v tseliakh obespecheniia garantii gosudarstvennoi zashchity prav i svobod grazhdan.' "] from July 24, 1998. *KonsultantPlus*. Retrieved on July 19, 2019 (http://www.consultant.ru/cons/cgi/online.cgi?req=doc&base=EXP&n=271303#08362388273711405).

Civil Code of the Russian Federation [Grazhdanskii kodeks RF] from November 30, 1994, No. 51-FZ. *KonsultantPlus*. Retrieved on July 19, 2019 (http://www.consultant.ru/document/cons_doc_LAW_5142/).

Code of Civil Procedure of the RSFSR [Grazhdanskii protsessual'nyi kodeks RSFSR] from October 1, 1964). *KonsultantPlus*. Retrieved on July 29, 2019 (http://www.consultant.ru/document/cons_doc_LAW_2237/).

Code of the RSFSR for Administrative Offenses [Kodeks RSFSR ob administrativnykh pravonarusheniiakh] from June 20, 1984. *KonsultantPlus*. Retrieved on July 19,2019 (http://www.consultant.ru/document/cons_doc_LAW_2318/).

Code of Russian Federation for Administrative Offenses [Kodeks Rossiiskoi Federatsii ob administrativnykh pravonurusheniiakh] from December 30, 2001, No. 195-FZ. *KonsultantPlus*. Retrieved on July 19, 2019 (http://www.consultant.ru/document/cons_doc_LAW_34661/).

Constitution of the RF [Konstitutsiia (osnovnoi zakon) RF] from December 12, 1993. *KonsultantPlus*. Retrieved on July 19, 2019 (http://www.consultant.ru/document/cons_doc_LAW_28399/).

Criminal Code of Russian Federation [Ugolovnyi kodeks Rossiiskoi Federatsii] from June 13, 1996, No. 63-FZ. *KonsultantPlus*. Retrieved on July 19, 2019 (http://www.consultant.ru/document/cons_doc_LAW_10699/).

Decree of the President of the RSFSR "On Some Issues of Activity of the Executive Authorities in the RSFSR" [Ukaz Prezidenta RSFSR "O nekotorykh voprosakh deiatel'nosti organov ispolnitel'noi vlasti v RSFSR] from August 22, 1991, No. 75. *KonsultantPlus*. Retrieved on July 19,2019 (http://www.consultant.ru/cons/CGI/online.cgi?req=doc&base=EXP&n=221425#014741655544208032).

Decree of the President of the Russian Federation "On Free Trade" [Ukaz Presidenta RF "O svobodnoi torgovle"] from January 29, 1992, No. 65. *KonsultantPlus*. Retrieved on July 19, 2019 ((http://www.consultant.ru/document/cons_doc_LAW_288/).

Decree of the President of the Russian Federation "On Administrative Office of the President of the RF on Work with Applications of Citizens and Organizations" [Ukaz Prezidenta RF "Ob Upravlenii Prezidenta Rossisskoi Federatsii po rabote s obrashcheniiami grazhdan i organizatsii"] from February 17, 2010 No. 201 (as amended by Decrees of the President of the Russian Federation of January 14, 2011 No. 38, of November 3, 2012 No. 1474, and of July 25, 2014 No. 529). *Ofitsial'nyi sait Upravleniia Prezidenta po rabote s obrashcheniiami grazhdan i organizatsii*. Retrieved on July 19, 2019 (http://letters.kremlin.ru/info-service/acts/12).

Duma Endorses Bill on Human Rights Representative. 1996. TASS, March.

Family Code of the Russian Federation [Semeinyi kodeks RF] from December 29, 1995, No. 223-FZ. *KonsultantPlus*. Retrieved on July 19, 2019 (http://www.consultant.ru/document/cons_doc_LAW_8982/).

Federal Constitutional Law "On the Constitutional Court of the Russian Federation" [O Konstitutsionnom sude RF] from July 27, 1994, No. 1-FKZ. 1994. *Collected Legislation of the Russian Federation* (*SZ RF*), No. 13. Art. 1447.

Federal Constitutional Law "On the Human Rights Ombudsman in the Russian Federation" [Federal'nyi Konstitutsionnyi zakon "Ob upolnomochennom po pravam cheloveka v RF"] from February 26, 1997, No. 1-FKZ. *KonsultantPlus*. Retrieved on July 19, 2019 (http://www.consultant.ru/document/cons_doc_LAW_13440/).

Federal Constitutional Law "On the Judicial System of the Russian Federation" [Federal'nyi Konstitutsionnyi zakon "O sudebnoi sisteme RF"] from December 31, 1996, No. 1-FKZ. *KonsiltantPlus*. Retrieved on July 19,2019 (http://www.consultant.ru/document/cons_doc_LAW_12834/).

Federal Law of the RF "On the Procuracy of the Russian Federation" [Federal'nyi zakon "O prokurature RF"] from January 17, 1992. *KonsiltantPlus*. Retrieved on July 19, 2019 (http://www.consultant.ru/document/cons_doc_LAW_262/).

Federal Law "On Amending the Law of the RF On the Procuracy of the Russian Federation" [O vnesenii izmenenii i dopolnenii v Zakon RF "O prokurature RF"] from November 17, 1995, No. 168-FZ. *Garant*. Retrieved on July 19, 2019 (https://base.garant.ru/10105477/).

Federal Law "On Amending the Law 'On appealing to the court of wrongful acts and decisions violating the rights and freedoms of citizens' [Zakon RF "O vnesenii izmenenii i dopolnenii v zakon Rossiiskoi Federatsii 'Ob obzhalovanii v sud deistvii i reshenii, narushaiushchikh prava i svobody grazhdan'"] from December 14, 1995, No. 193-FZ. *KonsultantPlus*. Retrieved on July 19, 2019 (http://www.consultant.ru/document/cons_doc_LAW_8595/).

Federal Law "On Amending Certain Federal Laws Regarding Regulation of Activities of Non-profit Organisations Performing Functions of Foreign Agents" ["O vnesenii izmenenii v otdel'nye zakonodatel'nye akty Rossiiskoi Federatsii v chasti regulirovaniia deiatel'nosti nekommercheskikh organizatsii, vypolniaiushchikh funktsii inostrannogo agenta"] from June 20, 2012. *Garant*. Retrieved on July 19, 2019 (http://base.garant.ru/70204242).

Federal Law "On Amendments to the Criminal Code of the Russian Federation and the Code of Criminal Procedure of the Russian Federation, regarding the establishment of additional counter-terrorism measures and ensuring public safety" [Federal'nyi zakon "O vnesenii izmenenii v Ugolovnyi kodeks RF i Ugolovno-protsessual'nyi kodeks RF v chasti ustanovleniia dopolnitel'nykh mer protivodeistviia terrorizmu i obespecheniia obshchestvennoi bezopasnosti"] from July 6, 2016, No. 375-FZ. *KonsultantPlus*. Retrieved on July 19, 2019 (http://www.consultant.ru/document/cons_doc_LAW_201087/).

Law "On Protection of Consumer Rights" [Zakon "O zashchite prav potrebitelei"] from February 7, 1992, No. 2300-1. *KonsultantPlus*. Retrieved on July 19, 2019 (http://www.consultant.ru/document/cons_doc_LAW_305/).

Law of the RSFSR "On Enterprises and Entrepreneurial Activity" [Zakon RSFSR "O predpriiatiiakh i predprinimatel'skoi deiatel'nosti"] from December 25, 1990, No. 445-1. *KonsultantPlus*. Retrieved on July 19, 2019 (http://www.consultant.ru/cons/cgi/online.cgi?req=doc&base=LAW&n=29304&fld=134).

Law of the Russian Federation "On Appealing to the Court Actions and Decisions Violating the Rights and Freedoms of Citizens" [Zakon RF "Ob obzhalovanii v sud deistvii i reshenii, narushaiushchikh prava i svobody grazhdan"] from April 1993. VSND VS RF No. 19, Art. 685. *KonsultantPlus*. Retrieved on July 19, 2019 (http://www.consultant.ru/document/cons_doc_LAW_1889/).

Law of the Russian Federation "On Amendments and Additions to the Code of Civil Procedure of the RSFSR" [Zakon RF "O vnesenii izmenenii i dopolnenii v Grazhdanskii protsessual'nyi kodeks RSFSR"] from April 28, 1993, No. 4882-1. *KonsultantPlus*. Retrieved on July 19, 2019 (http://www.consultant.ru/document/cons_doc_LAW_8497/).

Order of the General Prosecutor of the Russian Federation "On the Organization of the Execution of the Agreement 'On Forms of Interaction Between the General Prosecutor's Office of the Russian Federation and the Commissioner for Human Rights to Ensure Guarantees of State Protection of Civil Rights and Freedoms ' " [Rasporiazhenie General'nogo prokurora RF "Ob organizatsii ispolneniia soglasheniia 'O formakh vzaimodeistviia general'noi prokuratury RF i Upolnomochennogo po pravam cheloveka v tseliakh obespecheniia garantii gosudarstvennoi zashchity prav i svobod grazhdan' "] from January 14, 1999, No. 6/7R. *KonsultantPlus*. Retrieved on July 19, 2019 (http://www.consultant.ru/cons/cgi/online.cgi?req=doc&ts=130088763006061048339697974&cacheid=2BA1BE299E5DFF23513149907022C90B&mode=splus&base=EXP&n=369350&rnd=0.4866053138722594 7#035078449096176856).

Order of the General Prosecutor of the Russian Federation "On the Organization of Execution of the Agreement between the Human Rights Ombudsman in the Russian Federation and the General Prosecutor of the Russian Federation on Cooperation in Matters of Protection of the Human and Civil Rights and Freedoms" [Rasporiazhenie General'nogo prokurora RF "Ob organizatsii ispolneniia Soglasheniia Upolnomochennogo po pravam cheloveka v Rossiiskoi Federatsii i General'nogo prokurora Rossiiskoi Federatsii o vzaimodeistvii v voprosakh zashchity prav i svobod cheloveka i grazhdanina"] from February 09, 2009, No. 33/7r. 2007. *TEXTARCHIVE.RU*. Retrieved on July 19, 2019 (https://textarchive.ru/c-1145242-p7.html).

Order of the Administration of the President of the Russian Federation "On the Traveling Reception Office of the President of the Russian Federation" [Rasporiazhenie Administratsii Presidenta Rossiiskoi Federatsii "O mobil'noi priiomnoi Presidenta Rossiiskoi Federatsii"] from May 10, 2011 No. 631. *Ofitsial'nyi sait Upravleniia Prezidenta po rabote s obrashcheniiami grazhdan i organizatsii*. Retrieved on July 19,2019 (http://letters.kremlin.ru/info-service/acts/32).

Regulation on the Network of Public Reception Offices of the All-Russian Political Party "United Russia" [Polozhenie o seti obshchestvennykh priiomnykh Vserossiiskoi politicheskoi partii "Edinaia Rossiia"] from January 30, 2008. *Official website of the party "Edinaia Rossiia."* Retrieved on January 19, 2019 (https://er.ru/news/182572/userdata/files/2019/06/24/polozhenie_ITIHpsj.pdf).

Regulation on the Reception Office of the President of the Russian Federation in the Federal District [Polozhenie o priiomnoi Prezidenta RF v federal'nom okruge] from October 2, 2009, No. 1441. *Ofitsial'nyi sait Upravleniia Prezidenta po rabote s obrashcheniiami grazhdan i organizatsii*. Retrieved on July 19, 2019 (http://letters.kremlin.ru/info-service/acts/26).

The Presidential Decree "On Some Measures of State Support for the Civil Rights Movement in the Russian Federation" [Ukaz Presidenta "O nekotorykh merakh gosudarstvennoi podderzhki pravozashchitnogo dvizheniia v RF"] from June 13, 1996. *Garant*. Retrieved on July 19, 2019 (https://base.garant.ru/135151/).

6 New mechanism of complaints in action

What's changed?

Contemporary bureaucracy of the complaint mechanism: Challenges of formality

In spite of all the shortcomings of the present-day judiciary, Russian legal institutions have never been as well developed as in the post-Soviet period. The stage has also been set for complaint-based problem solving. A large network of addressees reviewing and handling complaints has been reconstructed in post-Soviet Russia. Every level of executive power has a feedback channel connecting it with citizens, implemented through applications that mostly comprise complaints. Complainants have wider technical capabilities compared to the late Soviet period; yet all the former methods of complaint delivery have also been preserved. Today, complaints can be lodged orally in person, in writing by mail, or presented in a form of digital collective petition (see, for example: http://change.org). In my analysis I focus on complaints, addressed directly to the state authorities—similar to the complaints of the Soviet period.

Obviously, the post-Soviet complaint mechanism could not be an exact copy of its Soviet predecessor. The new structure of government bodies differs from that of the late Soviet era. Some addressees, such as the official media, lost almost all of their power; others were segregated from the general executive power structure, acquiring special functionality and place in the complaint mechanism. Despite these transformations, the post-Soviet addressees I have selected to analyze in this chapter more or less correspond to their Soviet-era counterparts.

Executive bodies: Local and regional levels

An important continuity with the Soviet past is the crucial role that local and regional executive bodies play in the work with citizens' complaints. The local and regional executive authorities, which during the Soviet period consisted of a centralized and hierarchical system of executive committees (*ispolkomy*) of different levels, are now represented by an assortment of more diffuse administrations, committees, inspections, and services. As for the rules of the complaint mechanism, they are currently being reformed, which would make them much more standardized than in the Soviet era. Law No. 59 "On the Order of Consideration of Citizens' Applications in the Russian Federation" defines the general rules and norms of working with complaints that apply to all addressees—not only the executive bodies, but also all supervisory bodies, such as the procuracy and so on. Besides, every problem complained about is assigned a number according to a classification code, which lists more than 2,000 violations and is used by all levels of authorities working with complaints.[1]

In 2017, citizens filed 349,490 complaints to the executive bodies of Saint Petersburg at the district and city levels (Report on handling citizens' complaints 2017). Traditionally, the number one concern is housing and public utilities, with 39.3% of complaints falling into this category. Next come questions regarding various compensations and benefits. Classified under "economy," these complaints comprise 30.2%. The third place (18.4%) is predictably taken by social issues, such as places in kindergartens, pensions, and such. The rest of the grievances concern issues of public management, politics, legality, security, and so forth (see Table 6.1).

The data from Saint Petersburg shows that the complainants have slim chances to solve their problems by appealing to local executive authorities (see Table 6.2). In Saint Petersburg in 2017, 14.6% of all the received complaints were redressed at the local level, and during the first three quarters of 2018 the number of redressed complaints was 8.8%.

Table 6.1 Subjects of complaints to the executive bodies of Saint Petersburg at the district and city levels in 2017–2018

	2017 (%)	*2018 (%)*
Housing and public utilities	39.3	32.3
Economy	30.2	31.6
Social issues	18.4	20.5
Public management, politics, legality, security	12.1	15.6

Source: Report on handling citizens' complaints by the executive authorities of Saint Petersburg in 2017 and 2018

Table 6.2 Results of local complaint handling according to Saint Petersburg administration in 2017–2018[2]

	2017	*First three quarters of 2018*
Total received	349,490	281,439
Reviewed	76.4%	81.8%
Clarifying responses	50.1%	53.3%
Redressed	14.6%	8.8%
including the reply "measures taken"	7.9%	4.6%
Dismissed	1.8%	0.5%

Source: Report on handling citizens' complaints by the executive authorities of Saint Petersburg in 2017 and 2018

However, these figures require a clarification based on the study of the established practice of complaint handling. The lowest-level executive bodies in Russia are plagued by resource scarcity. Administrations, services, and inspections distribute the resources available to them depending on the demands of the citizens. In this way, planned service delivery is turned into reactive emergency relief or a band-aid approach. The limited set of sanctions that local executives can impose on offenders is much narrower than that of the Soviet executive authorities of the same level. Nowadays, the sanctions include administrative action, such as formal warning or administrative fines.

The demands are usually expressed in complaints concerning such issues as a leaking roof, water in the basement, lack of available places in kindergartens, or problems with neighbors in a communal apartment. When the complaint reaches some as executive bodies, it gets registered, which means that it becomes part of the grievances statistics. Usually, local officials cannot address the issue within one month, as required by law. They have no resources to do that, and they already have a queue of previous complaints. But at the same time they cannot ignore the complaint even for the time being, because by doing so they would break the law. As a result, the addressee usually composes a reply within a month explaining their capacities and efforts. This answer is also registered, falling into the category of "clarifying responses." As for the problem in the complaint itself, it may be put in the queue of similar pending problems. Thus, the issue can be resolved in one, two, or more years. During the time between the first response to the complaint and its final resolution, the executing agency may regularly inform the complainant about the ongoing work. All these information letters are also registered as "clarifying responses."

Below is an example of a correspondence in connection with a complaint about repairs of an attic in an apartment building in Saint Petersburg. This example illustrates the work of the mechanism at the lower levels of authority, partially explaining low numbers of redressed complaints. This is a typical communication reproduced in thousands of complaint cases and mostly determined by structural conditions. Here, the initial complaint was filed with the district Housing and Public Utilities Service (*Zhilkomservis*) on December 5, 2011. The issue was that the roofing was about to collapse into the top floor apartment. For this reason, the part of the attic with the damaged roof was not winterized—this would overburden the weak roofing and exacerbate the problem.

The *Zhilkomservis* did not reply. Then, repeat complaints were lodged to the procuracy and the Saint Petersburg State Housing Inspection, a regional executive body, a year after the original complaint to *Zhilkomservis* on December 12, 2012. The reply from the procuracy, dated January 18, 2013, stated that a preliminary inspection had revealed multiple violations of housing regulations by the *Zhilkomservis*: "In view of the audit findings, the legal representative of the *Zhilkomservis* in [name of the] district has been summoned to the inspection to record [the problem as] an administrative offense under Art. 7.22 of the Code of Administrative Offenses."[3] A special examination of the roofing was also scheduled.

The executing agency—the *Zhilkomservis*—came to the attention of the procuracy and the supervisory housing agency. After that, the complainant received a series of letters, which are excerpted below.

April 26, 2013 Clarifying response to the complainant from the Administration of district N[4] of Saint Petersburg:

> an examination of the beams in the building's attic has been conducted by a specialized organization. After an engineering opinion is received, dates and workload for the necessary repairs will be established. Results will be reported before August 8, 2013.

August 1, 2013 Clarifying response to the complainant from the Administration of district N of Saint Petersburg:

> an examination of the beams in the building's attic has been conducted by a specialized organization. An engineering opinion will be solicited before September 2, 2013. After the engineering opinion is received, dates and workload for the necessary repairs will be established.

August 8, 2013 Clarifying response to the complainant from the Administration of district N of Saint Petersburg:

> the [report on the] technical examination of the beams in the building's attic has been prepared in electronic form. The engineering opinion will be sent to the management company after an inspection. Results will be reported before November 20, 2013.

December 10, 2013 Clarifying response to the complainant from the Administration of district N of Saint Petersburg:

> an examination of the construction structures has been conducted by a specialized organization. To ensure save living conditions for the residents, the management company took measures to address the risk of a beam collapsing into the apartment (temporary roofing was set up).

January 29, 2014 Clarifying response to the complainant from the Administration of district N of Saint Petersburg:

> the engineering opinion following the examination of the construction structures, carried out by a specialized organization, has not yet been received. The management company has sent a letter to the specialized organization requesting to expedite the production of the engineering opinion. Results will be reported before April 1, 2014.

March 27, 2014 Clarifying response to the complainant from the Administration of district N of Saint Petersburg:

> earlier, a letter was sent to the specialized organization requesting to expedite the production of the engineering opinion following the examination of the construction structures of the house. Currently, according to

> the letter of guarantee from the specialized organization, the engineering opinion will be provided to the management company no later than May 13, 2014.

May 5, 2014 Clarifying response to the complainant from the Administration of district N of Saint Petersburg:

> Due to new paperwork regulations received from the superior bodies, the engineering opinion following the examination of the construction structures of the building has been sent for review. Results will be reported before September 10, 2014.

August 7, 2014 Clarifying response to the complainant from the Administration of district N of Saint Petersburg:

> The examination has shown that the roofing in the attic above apartment Z is sloping towards the external wall.

September 10, 2014 Clarifying response to the complainant from the Administration of district N of Saint Petersburg:

> The engineering opinion following the examination of the roofing above apartment Z has been solicited. Currently, a document package is being put together for review by the district interdepartmental commission. Results will be reported before November 11, 2014.

October 7, 2014 Clarifying response to the complainant from the Administration of district N of Saint Petersburg:

> The housing agency of district N has put together and sent the document package to the interdepartmental commission under the Administration of district N to make a decision to include the house in the 2015 regional program upon its realization.

The roofing was finally repaired in June 2016, and the attic was winterized only in autumn 2018.

The problem was solved administratively without the involvement of the court and it took seven years. The immediate executing agency—the district housing and utilities service—stepped up its efforts, after the superior bodies, such as the procuracy and the Saint Petersburg State Housing Agency, became aware of the problem.

During 2013 and 2014, the executing agency sent nine explanatory letters to the complainant. This suggests that the lower level of the complaint mechanism is under a lot of pressure from the higher levels of authority which control the work with the complaints. If a problem has not been solved at the lower level, the complainant acquires the right to complain to a superior body. Therefore, the primary addressee has incentives to keep communication with the complainant at the primary level. This is the exact purpose of all the explanatory letters. These "precautionary" clarifying responses comprise a large proportion of the total complaint correspondence; if they are removed from the statistics, the share of positive decisions will be more significant.

Control and pressure from above force the lowest level of the mechanism not only to work with the complaints but to effectively solve the problems brought up by complaints. The consistent decline in negative decisions on complaints attests to this. The data from Saint Petersburg (see Table 6.3) demonstrate that complaint dismissals are minimal, which contributes to the image of the mechanism as a responsive and efficient tool.

Official reviews of complaint handling results indicate that local executive authorities are indeed addressing a large scope of problems brought forward by citizens. They repair residential and non-residential spaces (like a municipal swimming pool), provide places in kindergartens, evict people with socially dangerous diseases (like tuberculosis), dismantle unauthorized retail kiosks, probe residential wastewaters, resolve conflicts between different housing management companies, monitor heating, maintain peace and quiet, and so on.

Thus, the existence of complaints at the local level is functionally justified. The complaint is an important conduit for public demands. When the resources are scarce, these demands are what largely define the activity of local executive bodies, namely the order of distributing efforts to create satisfactory living conditions. Despite its limited capacity to redress complaints, the local level is under much pressure from the superior levels of the mechanism. The efficiency of working with complaints is assessed, among other criteria, by the number of complaints redressed. This means that the mechanism has another task besides direct work with complaints, which is maintaining the image of an efficient problem-solving method.

Just like in the Soviet years, in order to increase chances for success, a complainant has to know the informal rules to accelerate the work of the complaint mechanism. These rules include perseverance, good familiarity with bureaucratic standards, and seeking assistance from influential actors. Addressees, in turn, also apply informal strategies of complaint handling, which allows them to keep the complaint at the primary level and minimize the pressure from the superior levels. However, citizens now seek assistance from different sources than in the Soviet era: supervisory bodies and the procuracy.

Table 6.3 Dismissals of complaints by the executive authorities of Saint Petersburg in 2017–2018

	2nd quarter of 2017	*3rd quarter of 2017*	*4th quarter of 2017*	*1st quarter of 2018*	*2nd quarter of 2018*	*3rd quarter of 2018*
Dismissed	3%	1.5%	1%	0.6%	0.57%	0.33%

Source: Report on handling citizens' complaints by the executive authorities of Saint Petersburg in 2017 and 2018

Political parties and the government of the Russian Federation

The role of political parties and the government in handling complaints is quite ambiguous now in Russia. Officially Russia has a multiparty system where every party elected to the Duma works with applications from the citizens accepting and handling complaints. Parties like United Russia and the Liberal Democratic Party (LDPR) are particularly active in this regard. Political parties are not government bodies and party members are not government officials, although the number of complaints addressed to the parties elected to the Russian parliament, the Duma, is constantly growing, having almost tripled over the past four years (see Table 6.4). The number of complaints actually reviewed, however, has shrunk from 15.1% to 3.1%.

The government of the Russian Federation is superior to the local and regional levels of the executive hierarchy. According to the number of complaints, the government is not a very popular addressee in comparison, for example, with local executive authorities. In 2017, it received 204,550 complaints from across the entire country (Data 2017).[5]

In addition to the State Duma and the government, the chairman of United Russia is highlighted in law and in the structure of the complaint mechanism as a separate addressee in the complaint mechanism. The United Russia reception offices in every region present themselves as a structure that enables direct contact with the party chairman. However, between 2008 and 2020 the same person served as both the chairman of United Russia and the head of government.[6] Many more complaints are lodged with the United Russia local offices than with any other political party or even the federal government. According to my interviews,[7] over a million of complaints are registered every year at all the United Russia's local offices. The offices have a shared digital database and can collaborate on resolving similar cases.

The reception offices of the United Russia are an easily accessible addressee. The network of regional public offices of the party is not limited to the chairman's office in the regional center; the party has multiple offices throughout each region, all of which accept complaints from the public.

The public reception offices are not legal entities. Party members and reception office employees are not state officials; therefore, their work is not directly regulated by Law No. 59. For them, this law works rather as a general framework for managing applications—for instance, they are obliged to reply to the complainant within one month as specified in the law. An additional regulatory framework was

Table 6.4 Work with complaints in the State Duma in 2015–2018

	2015	*2016*	*2017*	*2018*
Received	63,513	115,811	169,422	176,842
Reviewed	9,610 (15.1%)	16,462 (14.2%)	16,994 (10%)	5,547 (3.1%)

Source: Statistika obrashchenii v Gosudarstvennuiu Dumu 2017–2019

created to regulate the activity of the reception offices. In 2008, when the network of United Russia chairman's reception offices was created, the instruction "On the Organization and Order of Working with Citizens' Applications" was issued by the Presidium of the General Council of the party United Russia (Instruction of the Presidium 2008). The instruction grants the reception office employees the authority to review citizens' applications and involve a large circle of the United Russia deputies in solving the reported issues. Reception offices can involve deputies of all levels, from those working in municipal representative bodies up to the members of the State Duma. In 2012, the instruction was amended to include the "Methodological Recommendations," which clearly determine the order of working with people's complaints and explicitly point out issues that reception offices should and should not react to. In particular, the "Recommendations" prohibit replying to any applications containing legal issues. These complaints should be redirected to the procuracy or other supervisory organs; otherwise, the United Russia office employee should explain to the complainant the grounds for and rules of legal action. Therefore, it is recommended to hire people with legal education to work in the reception offices (Methodological Recommendations 2012:2.4). In practice, reception offices often cooperate with legal clinics of local universities.[8]

From time to time, heads of reception offices get special instructions approved by the Presidium of the General Council of the party United Russia correcting or directing their focus of attention. For instance, according to these instructions, reception office employees work not only with complaints coming directly from the citizens but also with various expressions of discontent, including reports in the media and videos posted on YouTube:

> when the utilities fees were raised in the middle of the summer, all of them … we had an instruction what to regard as an appeal, including media reports about those fees, specific remarks on a specific district, specific house, etc., and also what turns up on social networks. That's why we are tasked with this.[9]

Complaints to the reception offices concern issues similar to those dealt with by local executive bodies. About a third of the total number of complaints comprises questions of housing maintenance and upkeep and public utilities. The second largest issue is various social problems (compensations, benefits, pensions, large families, disabled persons). The third place is taken by requests to improve living conditions. Sometimes, this composition of issues changes but insignificantly, depending on the period or the situation. Sometimes, financial problems will surface—issues related to salary payment, employment, or enterprise bankruptcy. At other times, forest wildfires and their consequences (housing reconstruction, financial assistance, property losses, etc.) come to the foreground. In winter, snow and ice removal become an acute problem, as do the injuries and damage sustained from the weather.

According to an interview, complaints to the United Russia reception offices yield positive results more often than do complaints to local executive bodies, an average of 22–25% annually.[10] If a United Russia deputy is involved in the work with a complaint, the chances of a positive outcome increase dramatically. As deputies are state officials by status, they are entitled to send queries, put forward claims against the culprit, and create special commissions composed of deputies with regard to certain issues. Forty to fifty percent of complaints forwarded to deputies are resolved positively.[11]

As reception offices cooperate with the United Russia deputies in regional legislatures, complaints are sometimes used as grounds to initiate and pass bills. Based on citizens' appeals, deputies submit to the party proposals that often lead to legislative changes. Every year, legislators in each of Russia's 85 regions introduce up to six or seven legal initiatives regarding urgent social problems: housing for large families, the rights of defrauded shareholders, peace and quiet, park amenities, and urban beautification.

However, it is difficult to trace direct connections between a certain complaint and legislative changes. The legislature drafting process is not accompanied by public debates, and the authors of complaints are not informed that their appeals drew attention of the lawmakers. Besides, changes in the law are usually deferred, happening long after the complaint that might have caused them is filed. Thus, without corroboration by experts, we cannot contend that complaints cause significant systemic transformations. The link between these events remains complicated and hard to prove.

A complainant can lodge the same grievance to a public reception office and several other addressees. According to the markings on complaint forms, complaints are most often filed simultaneously to the United Russia reception offices and the presidential administration. Complaints can also be lodged to local executive bodies, human rights organizations, or the procuracy. Meanwhile, people most often complain to the United Russia party reception offices when they have already exhausted the capacities of local executive bodies. According to the management of reception offices, complainants often perceive them as a supervisory body overseeing both the local executives and the courts:

> especially in the first year, when [Vladimir] Putin's reception offices, the [United Russia] party chairman's reception offices, were formed, citizens somehow decided that we're like the almighty enforcers [*oprichniki—E.B.*], whom you can approach with a complaint, and they will correct all the court decisions. They were bringing us piles of court decisions.[12]

"The Methodological Recommendations" forbids reception offices not to accept complaints. However, they also have no right to interfere with legal issues. The only help they do provide in this regard is navigating the complaint within the mechanism and giving consultations. In this event, a reception office can explain to the complainant what agencies to appeal to if they want to challenge a court's decision or tell them how to file a lawsuit (Methodological Recommendations 2012:1.4–1.5).

Sometimes people come to the reception office not after the court but instead of it. Complaints indicating overt violations of the law are usually forwarded to the procuracy:

> We ask them to review [the complaint], make an inquiry, and, if necessary, intervene and give us a reply that they are doing their job well and promptly. They write us an extensive, clear, and detailed reply.[13]

It is very important to give a comprehensible reply to the complainant. According to our interviews, about 60% of people complaining to the reception offices are senior citizens who have already received an answer from the primary agency—usually the local executive body—but did not understand the message. A reception office can describe the steps the complainant can take to resolve the problem or explain the rejection they received (some complainants perceive adversely even fully substantiated dismissals). Reception offices are expected to help unconditionally:

> Here they come with their letters, saying it's a runaround. We say, you know, it's not a runaround, it's a rejection, it's much worse than a runaround. If it was a runaround, we would still be able to fight, but it's a rejection based on the law—and here we explain why. Sometimes people walk away, and sometimes they say: "You're exactly like them!"[14]

The United Russia reception offices of the United Russia have limited capacities to settle complaints. These agencies have no supervisory functions, cannot interfere with decisions made by executive authorities, challenging or objecting to them, and so forth. Unlike the executive bodies, public reception offices cannot impose even the simplest administrative sanctions. According to the employees, the reception offices have a single resource that allows resolving issues not addressed at the local executive level. This resource is expert knowledge of the way the executive power system is designed and the way the state works, as well as knowledge of the rules to draft an effective appeal. The opportunity to involve United Russia deputies in the process is seen as a particularly valuable resource:

> knowing how to properly pose a question to an executive body, for example [...] Here, we take over the work with these appeals, I mean, in terms of legal analysis, in terms of state officials' involvement, and in terms of assistance from deputies. I'm going to put it bluntly: our objective—and it seems to me, it's not exactly formulated anywhere—is to attach deputies' legs to citizens' complaints. This is what results in a settlement.[15]

Thus, the United Russia's public reception offices are quite an ambiguous addressee in the structure of the complaint mechanism. This ambiguity is partially explained by the dual status of the key person on whose behalf the reception offices essentially act. He represents, on the one hand, the most influential party, and on the other, the highest level of the executive power. However, in both cases, the complaint addressee is personified.

United Russia public reception offices are a decorative but very significant element of the currently existing complaint mechanism. In today's conditions, the reception offices network, which does not fit in the structure of government bodies, is artificially inserted in their ranks. The ambiguous nature of reception offices requires special regulations, and therefore additional regulatory instruments have been created. The network of public reception offices is supported by the government, which indicates its important place in the complaint mechanism. The party structure in the complaint mechanism resembles the Soviet tradition of complaining to party organs and—more generally—recreates connections to the Soviet past.

Despite its limited capacities, this addressee is quite effective. Due to their special interdepartmental position, reception offices can involve both executive and party authorities in problem solving. Besides, they can recourse to legal advisers, human rights advocates, and supervisory bodies. The main resource of the reception offices, however, is knowledge of the formal and informal rules of the bureaucratic and administrative systems. The relatively high efficiency of the reception offices indicates that it is not easy to make the mechanism work despite the apparent simplicity of its rules. Just like in the Soviet years, besides knowing the official standards, one should be well versed in the hidden or informal rules of the mechanism. These rules are not always available to the citizens. However, experts like reception office employees and United Russia deputies are familiar with them.

The reception offices are accessible and in high demand. However, their power and capacities are not fully understood by the citizens. The ambiguous logic of the reception offices contributes to this frustration. On the one hand, they have professional lawyers on staff and are closely engaged with the procuracy and judicial structures. On the other hand, their work is mostly based on the traditional personalized-narrative complaint model; in particular, they give personalized replies. The "democratic" opportunity for introducing solutions from below, which is embedded into any complaint mechanism, is not ignored by the addressee: complaints may be used by the deputies of the United Russia as a basis for legislative initiatives. However, the connection between complaints and systemic changes in the law is kept deliberately out of sight.

President of the Russian Federation

The Administrative Office of the President regularly publishes the aggregate analytical reports on the number of appeals received and their outcomes. These reports combine all of the data regarding complaints addressed to the president throughout the country. The Administrative Office of the President registers all the complaints addressed to the president (see Table 6.5). According to the figures kept by the office for the last decade, it receives close to a million complaints annually.

Table 6.5 Number of complaints registered by the Administrative Office of the President of the Russian Federation Working with Applications from Citizens and Organizations, 2009–2018

2009	*2010*	*2011*	*2012*	*2013*	*2014*	*2015*	*2016*	*2017*	*2018*
683,841	832,734	960,326	835,941	970,605	987,775	1,103,605	930,683	889,714	935,926[16]

Source: Website of the Administrative Office of the President of the Russian Federation Working with Applications from Citizens and Organizations (www.letters.kremlin.ru)

Table 6.6 Subjects matter of complaints, addressed to the president in 2017

Segment	*Content*	*Proportion*
Defense, security, legality	National defense, security and law enforcement, criminal law, enforcement of penalties, justice, procuracy, judiciary, trial attorneys, notaries	22.5%
State, society, politics	Constitutional order, basic public management, international relations and international law, legal acts of personal origin related to human resources, awards, pardons, citizenship, and honorary titles	20%
Social issues	Family, employment, social benefits and social security, education, science, culture, healthcare, physical fitness and sports, tourism	21%
Economy	Financial issues, business activities, international trade, customs, natural resources and environment, information and computerization	19.2%
Housing and public utilities	Housing legislation and its usage, residential and non-residential properties, securing the right to housing, residential property upkeep and public utilities	17.4%

Source: Informatsionno-statisticheskii obzor 2017 (www.letters.kremlin.ru)

According to the Constitution, "Citizens of the Russian Federation shall have the right to address personally and to submit individual and collective appeals to state organs and local self-government bodies" (Art. 33). The president has the right to intervene in the decision on a complaint in two cases: when there has been an infringement on constitutional rights or when human rights have been violated "until the issue is solved by the appropriate court" (Art. 85.2 of the Constitution). Despite the fact that the president can react to a very limited set of problems, the Administrative Office and/or Reception Offices of the President of the Russian Federation in the Federal Districts accept all complaints addressed to the president. Further, the complaints are sorted by jurisdiction and importance and redirected to the local, regional, or federal executive level depending on the problem described.

A large portion of complaints addressed to the president concerns the usual social and housing problems. However, as compared to other levels of the complaint mechanism, there are more complaints regarding national defense, legality, and public management (see Table 6.6).

Most issues associated with *State, society, politics* and *Defense, security, legality* are handled at the federal level. In 2017, these two topics comprised 63.5% of all federally reviewed complaints. At the same time, only 3.7% of housing-related complaints were handled at the federal level. We see that local and regional levels are mainly involved in solving problems associated with housing and public utilities (83.4%), the economy (48.1%), and social problems (41.4% of all related issues considered in the complaint mechanism). At the same time, issues of defense, security, and legality are nearly always handled at the federal level.

Every year, the statistics lists the 30 most popular complaint topics, where the number of related complaints increased during the previous year. In the last few years, these top 30 issues include an increasing number of questions about the operations of various government and executive bodies. In 2017, 9 of the 30 issues were related to the work of the procuracy, bailiffs, law enforcement agencies, executive bodies of the country's federal subjects, tax services, and so on. Eleven more topics were associated with housing problems—upkeep and management of residential premises, purchase of homes, housing repairs, and residential construction. The remaining ten topics dealt with issues like new legislation, roads and transportation, the environment, and social infrastructure (Informatsionno-statisticheskii obzor 2017).

According to the statistics, complaints to the president are distributed across various levels and agencies of the complaint mechanism (see Table 6.7). In 2017, 19% of issues were considered by the Administrative Office of the President itself. Thirty-seven percent of all the received complaints were forwarded to the federal-level bodies, including federal ministries and federal government bodies; 33.6% of complaints got redirected to the regional level and 10.1% to the local level; 8.8% of all redirected complaints were forwarded to supervisory bodies, mostly the procuracy, while 1.2% were rerouted to be considered elsewhere, as prescribed by federal constitutional laws and other federal laws (Informatsionno-statisticheskii obzor 2017).

Among applications sent to the president, complaints against officials of various levels are especially prominent. No other addressee in the complaint mechanism receives so many complaints of this kind. Detailed statistics, available on the website of the Administrative Office of the President, indicate that a significant proportion of complaints addressed to the president are devoted to the

Table 6.7 Redistribution of complaints received by the Administrative Office of the President of the Russian Federation Working with Applications from Citizens and Organizations in 2017

Total received	889,714
Considered at the federal level	56%
• including those considered promptly by the office of the resident	19%
• forwarded to federal-level executive agencies	37%
Forwarded to regional-level executive agencies	33.6%
Forwarded to local-level executive agencies	10.1%

Source: Informatsionno-statisticheskii obzor 2017 (www.letters.kremlin.ru)

Table 6.8 Number of complaints against officials addressed to the president in 2015–2017

	2015	*2016*	*2017*
Operations of the procuracy	19,764	21,491	34,819
Activities of bailiffs	16,267	19,286	21,044
Activities of bodies of internal affairs	10,649	12,692	13,668
Activities of local government bodies and their leaders	4,208	5,212	5,593
Operations of the executive bodies of the subjects of the Russian Federation	3,675	4,126	5,434
Activities of government bodies and local self-government bodies in the field of land relations	1,526	2,708	3,753
Operations of ministries and other federal executive bodies	1,872	2,366	3,711
State traffic police of the Russian Federation (GIBDD)	2,700	3,341	3,416
Local government officials	1,465	1,488	1,657
Execution of official duties by state civil servants of subjects of the Russian Federation	251	167	1,172
Activities of deputies, committees, and the State Duma apparatus	525	669	1,119
Activities of the government of the Russian Federation	463	853	1,054
Activities of the Investigative Committee of the Russian Federation	527	598	808
Penitentiary authorities	288	349	565
Activities of social welfare bodies and their officials	330	497	559
Execution of official powers and duties	199	501	509
Unlawful behavior of employees of the Federal Bailiff Service of Russia	102	68	204
Activities of members of the Federation Council	23	35	112
Activities of the judiciary	50	97	100
Administration of the President of the Russian Federation	91	84	98
Supreme Court of the Russian Federation	20	21	49
…	…	…	…
Total complaints against officials	**64,995 (5.9%)**	**76,649 (8.2%)**	**99,444 (11.2%)**
Total complaints addressed to the president	**1,103,605**	**930,683**	**889,714**

Source: Informatsionno-statisticheskii obzor 2015, 2016, 2017 (www.letters.kremlin.ru)

abuse of office. In this respect, complaints addressed to the president duplicate the function of administrative justice as they discipline the actions or inaction of officials and local governments. An overview of the data gives the following figures: (see Table 6.8).

An example of a typical complaint to the president is provided below. The addressee is presented as someone able to influence the actions or inaction of the highest judicial and supervisory bodies, as the chief referee and protector of citizens in the face of any iniquity. Note that the president is not represented as an alternative to any legal attempts to solve the problem. He is rather defined as an aide, an additional resource to provide the right impetus to the legal institutions:

> Request to President of the Russian Federation V. V. Putin to provide assistance in the enforcement of a court order. Complainer Zakharov Aleksander.[17] Dear Vladimir Vladimirovich! I, Aleksander Zakharov, have appealed to YOU on 16.02.2016, requesting assistance in the enforcement of a court order regarding the provision of another residence (instead of the emergency [*residence—E.B.*] about to collapse). On 23.03.2016 I received the reply No. 111 that my appeal was forwarded for consideration by the Federal Bailiff Service. On 14.04.2016 I received an answer from the FSSP [Federal Bailiff Service] No. 222 that my appeal was redirected to the Russian Directorate of the Federal Bailiff Service in Moscow. I haven't received any further reply. I also appealed to the Investigative Committee of the Russian Federation, providing materials of enforcement proceedings of 10.07.2014 to reach a decision in accordance with the law. A reply was received: "It is forwarded to the General Procuracy of the Russian Federation. The results will be reported to YOU" … . No measures have been taken, the answer has not been received to date. Dear Vladimir Vladimirovich, please give me a substantive response: why aren't court decisions carried out with regard to me, a person disabled from childhood, and my minor grandchildren left in danger. The court decision is attached [Date and signature].[18]

Complaints about abuse of office perpetrated by a wide variety of officials are usually listed as a separate item in statistical reports on complaints. Of all the complaints addressed to the president, the number of complaints caused by abuse of office is not so high; however, their number—both absolute and relative—has been steadily growing over the past three years.

Officially, the president cannot interfere in such cases. The Administrative Office of the President usually sorts complaints by jurisdiction and forwards them to the higher levels of the agency mentioned in the complaint. For example, complaints about bailiffs are sent to the Federal Bailiff Service, complaints about internal affairs bodies to the Ministry of Internal Affairs, and complaints about the procuracy to the General Procuracy. This happens in 100% of the cases.

Meanwhile, the media publicize success stories in which complaints addressed to the president have immediate effect and problems are solved fast. However, if the president personally intervenes in an issue described in a complaint, there may be informal elements which are sometimes contrary to the law. For instance, during a recent hotline (2017) with President Putin, several families from Izhevsk called in to complain about poor living conditions. The president promised to visit them later. After that, a house in Izhevsk, the capital city of the Udmurt Republic, became the subject of close attention by local officials, the procuracy, and the investigative committee. It was lightly renovated, and the courtyard around the house was paved. At the end of June of 2017, the president visited the house and spoke with the acting head of Udmurtia right in front of it:

President Putin (P): How many families have to be resettled? How many families need new housing?
Mayor (M): Eleven.
P: They must be resettled within this neighborhood.
M: We have a new apartment building in this area. It is not ready yet, but we plan to complete it in a year.
P: Do you have enough available apartments there?
M: At the moment we have one or two apartments available in the building.
P: So, by the end of this year all eleven families must be resettled in the new building.
M: I'm not sure. We will do our best to make the right decision.
P: Try to do that.
M: Yes. We will do our best. We will discuss each and every situation individually.

The president receives millions of complaints from citizens during his hotlines. Some problems articulated in the complaints, like the one mentioned above, have no clear legal solution. It is a challenging task to provide 11 apartments in a new building, when only one or two are available while all the others are sold out. It is currently unclear if the local official's promise was fulfilled in the end, but it is obvious that this order of the president can hardly be executed without bending legal rules or procedures—which is a form of abuse of office.

Despite the fact that complaints to the president are very common, their efficiency is quite modest. According to statistics, not all complaints received by the Office of the President are considered at all, ending up in a judgment like "redressed," "dismissed," or "clarified." The higher the level of the mechanism considering the complaint, the higher the percent of complaints reviewed. The following proportions of all lodged complaints were handled at various levels:

In 2018:

Federal level 37.8%
Regional level 28.9%
Local level 8.8% (Informatsionno-statisticheskii obzor 2018)

In 2017:

Federal level 27.8%
Regional level 23.4%
Local level 6.7% (Informatsionno-statisticheskii obzor 2017)

Positive resolutions of the complaints received by the Administrative Office of the President, however, are more often achieved at the lower levels (see Table 6.9). In 2018, federal-level executive authorities approved only 4.9% complaints,[19] and the federal government bodies[20] supported only 1.2% of complaints (Informatsionno-statisticheskii obzor 2018).[21] Meanwhile, at the regional and local levels these numbers were 5.9% and 7.6%, respectively.

In 2017, the highest proportion of complaints officially satisfied by the federal executive bodies amounted to 7.8% and by the federal government bodies of Russia amounted to 1.5% (Informatsionno-statisticheskii obzor 2017). The average percent of positive outcomes at the regional level was 8.1% and at the local level 13.1%.

Complaints to the president are very prevalent in Russia today. The million complainers registered by the president's Administrative Office are only a fraction of this very widespread practice. At the nationwide hotline (see details in Chapter 5), the president receives several million every year (e.g. 3.25 million in 2015, 2.3 million in 2018). Most of these phone calls are demands for justice. Complaints addressed to the president are even featured in popular television talk shows. In this context, the numbers of complaints addressed to the president that are favorably resolved seem unexpectedly low. According to the statistics, lawsuits brought to the courts for issues related to abuse of office have much better chances for positive resolution than complaints sent to the president. For instance, in 2015 judges handled 105,966 civil lawsuits on abuse of office, of which 31.5% were found in the plaintiff's favor. In 2017, the proportion of redressed complaints was higher—50.9%—and criminal statistics demonstrates an even higher win rate in cases of abuse (Otchet o rabote sudov 2015a, 2015b, 2016a, 2016b). At the same time, the share of positively resolved complaints from those received by the president's Administrative Office, considered immediately in the Office or readdressed to the other levels of authorities, was 4.6% in 2017 and did not exceed 4% in 2018 (Informatsionno-statisticheskii obzor 2017, 2018).

My analysis shows that the mechanism of complaints at the level of the president has limited abilities to solve problems, similar to the lower levels of the executive branch. Nevertheless, we can identify several special functional aspects of the presidential level. First, it accepts all types of complaints. The input filters

Table 6.9 Positive resolution of complaints reviewed by the Administrative Office of the President of the RF, including those readdressed to the federal, regional, and local levels in 2017–2018

	Federal level		*Regional level*	*Local level*
	Federal government bodies	*Executive bodies of federal level*		
2017	1.5%	7.8%	8.1%	13.1%
2018	1.2%	4.9%	5.9%	7.6%

Source: Informatsionno-statisticheskii obzor 2017, 2018 (www.letters.kremlin.ru)

work in the same way as at the other levels. However, after the complaints are redistributed to the local and regional levels, the presidential office is left with an array of special issues related to defense, security, public management, legality, law enforcement, and abuse of office.

When the complaint mechanism functions according to the law, it does not work very effectively. Meanwhile, the president occasionally happens to personally involve himself in solving some of the complaints' problems, and such cases are usually broadly reported by the media. Based on these cases—which are usually success stories—it is possible to argue that formal rules are bypassed at the level of selection of problems to be considered by the president and also at the level of presidential orders. Even more important is that this bending of formal rules has become a part of the presidential image and discourse.

Coexistence of the contemporary mechanism of complaints with the judiciary

Nowadays the judiciary and the complaint mechanism in Russia function in spheres adjacent to each other. The jurisdiction of legal problems is now specified much more precisely than it was in the late Soviet era. However, the diversity of issues in complaints to authorities is extremely broad, and it is not always obvious whether or not a certain complaint contains a legal component.

At the same time, the principle of separation of powers strictly prohibits the executive authorities from interfering with justice. In this respect, specific restrictions have been introduced with regard to the highest levels of the complaint mechanism. Two examples of such regulatory documents are the Constitution of the Russian Federation and the Provision "On the Administration of the President of the Russian Federation" (2004). These documents do not allow the president, any official, or the presidential administration to resolve on the merits any questions posed in citizens' appeals that might be associated with procedural activities of the courts, the procuracy, investigative agencies, and so on.

Available data shows that the Administrative Office of the President makes efforts to comply with these rules. Here is a typical reply from the office to a complaint about a judicial decision:

> The Administrative Office of the President of the RF Working with Applications from Citizens and Organizations. April 25, 2017.
>
> To Borisova E. L.
>
> As follows from the application, the issues you described were a subject of judicial consideration.
>
> We inform [you] that, according to Article 10 of the Constitution, state power in the Russian Federation is exercised on the basis of separation into legislative, executive, and judicial [branches]. The bodies of legislative, executive, and judicial power are independent from each other. Courts exercise judicial power independently of anyone's will [and] are subject solely to the law (Art. 120 of the Constitution, Articles 1 and 5 of the Federal

> Constitutional Law of December 31, 1996, "On the Judicial System of the Russian Federation," Articles 9 and 10 of the Law of the Russian Federation of June 26, 1992, No. 3132-1 "On the Status of Judges in the Russian Federation," Federal Law of March 14, 2002, No. 30-FZ "On Organs of the Judicial Community in the Russian Federation").
>
> The current legislation does not provide for subordination and submission of the courts to other government bodies or persons in government positions in the Russian Federation. We clarify that the legality and validity of judicial acts may be verified solely through the processes of appeal, cassation, or judicial review; any other reconsideration of judicial acts shall not be allowed (resolution of the Constitutional Court of the Russian Federation of January 25, 2001, No. 1-P).[22]

However, the executive apparatus tries to manage the flow of complaints whenever possible. Complaints to the government bodies containing a legal problem are usually returned to the author with advice to take legal action. The law does not provide for direct forwarding of complaints to the courts (Law No. 59-FZ, Art. 11.2). Interference with legal issues is banned at all levels of the mechanism. The local and regional levels of the complaint mechanism have no actual practice of redirecting appeals to the judiciary. Nevertheless, these lower levels have direct functional continuity with the judicial system, compensating for weak and underdeveloped instruments of pre-trial problem solving. As for the higher levels of the mechanism, they duplicate the courts in many ways, accepting complaints about officials or law enforcement.

There is also a federal practice of forwarding complaints to the courts. In 2017, 0.2% complaints to the presidential office were forwarded to the federal and regional courts (Informatsionno-statisticheskii obzor 2017). These cases are marked as "extraordinary" in the statistics. More frequently, complaints are redirected from executive bodies to supervisory organs, mainly the procuracy. These redirections occur not only at the federal but also at the lower levels of the mechanism. As a result, the procuracy's twofold role is reinforced. As a government body, it can handle complaints. As a supervisory body, it has the authority to carry out inspections and impose administrative sanctions. The executive bodies have no such authority. However, this ambiguity of position is exactly what allows the procuracy to deal with the problem described in a citizen's complaint.

In practice, citizens frequently regard the complaint mechanism and the judiciary either as interchangeable instruments or as different links of the same chain. People often use the complaint mechanism along with judicial institutions, bringing their problem simultaneously to the court and to the government. Complainants have particularly high expectations of the federal and presidential levels of the mechanism, which are often perceived as a powerful tool that can bypass the courts and legal considerations or even influence court decisions. Among the appeals addressed to the president, many concern the imperfections of the judicial system. This includes dissatisfaction with court decisions, reports of non-enforcement of judgments, or complaints about illegal actions of the judicial community.

Below is an example. A single mother of two children, who has been trying to solve a housing problem for ten years with no result, appeals to the president:

> In early 2016, I went to court. I won. I was one of the first in line for the long-sought new-build housing. I was assured that I would receive an apartment in late 2016 or early 2017. It's been a year already, 2017. I've had my second child. I am calling them, and they are telling me [it will be ready] next year, again. It turns out that neither the court nor the procuracy nor the civil servants can help me. Meanwhile, I'm bumming around rented apartments with two children, one of whom is disabled and the other is a newborn. Now I see that I'm powerless and I'm being played. Still I can do nothing. EVEN THROUGH THE COURT.[23]

Another example is a complaint by a defrauded shareholder regarding what looks like biased justice shattering human faith in a fair trial:

> 18.08.2017
>
> The company "Breath" took our money, 1 million 500 thousand [rubles], considering that we have to pay them two years' penalties, as we haven't paid our share contribution since 2015. Judge Poroshina simply turned a blind eye to it. I wonder where the justice is and how one seeks justice from the court, if the court does the bidding of such disreputable companies. We looked at the website where Judge Poroshina led trials against the company "Breath," all these people lost the trial. Help us restore justice. Where else would a poor peasant turn (signature).[24]

Formally, the complaint mechanism and the courts are independent entities, and the normal practice of the complaint mechanism observes this separation. Meanwhile, the courts and the complaint mechanism can overlap in jurisdictional terms with regard to some issues, duplicating each other's function. Breaches in formality have appeared in the functioning of the complaint mechanism—more or less systematic deviations from the formal rules. The highest levels of the mechanism practice direct forwarding of complaints to judicial structures. The presidential level allows for interfering with issues subject to judicial consideration. These breaches are created both by the authorities and the practical functioning of the complaint mechanism. Citizens also invent their own strategies to restore justice, which include judicial instruments and complaints as complexly intertwined and interconnected equivalent forces.

Thus, it is impossible to give unambiguous universal characteristics to the contemporary mechanism of complaints. It apparently serves two purposes: functional and symbolic. The functional purpose is mostly implemented at the lower levels of the complaint mechanism. They serve as a feedback channel for the lower structures of the executive power, which are responsible for creating satisfactory living conditions for the people. Besides, when the lower levels of the mechanism handle complaints, they compensate for weak and underdeveloped institutions of pre-trial settlement, taking on an additional institutional burden.

At the higher levels, in fact, the complaint mechanism is functionally redundant. Most questions selected for consideration at those levels fall under the jurisdiction of the courts and supervisory bodies. The highest complaint mechanism levels usually implement the image-related objective associated with maintaining the chain of command and supporting the current president. However, the symbolic dimension has extra functionality. The contemporary mechanism is strictly hierarchical, involving features of both Soviet and pre-Soviet counterparts. When the mechanism levels differ in terms of capacities and competences over issues complained about, the president stands out from the general structure of the addressees. If the lower levels of the complaint mechanism are mainly responsible for solving housing and social problems, the presidential level has assumed responsibility for the spheres of national security, public management, legality, citizenship, and pardon. Most of the filed complaints are against the activities of the procuracy, the Ministry of Internal Affairs, judicial and security bodies, and high-ranking officials. This speaks, first of all, to the specifics of judicial practice, which may be influenced by excessive presidential treatment of the abuse of office committed by representatives of these departments. Another interpretation, which does not contradict the first one, is that the president usurps an exclusive oversight function, which enables him to correct the operations of all the institutions in the country out of court.

Despite the complaint mechanism and the judiciary being strictly separated at the institutional level, they overlap in the practice of the handling of complaints, either directly or as mediated by the supervisory authorities. In comparison with the Soviet period, the law and the courts play a significantly more important role today. Human rights activists and lawyers are involved by citizens as assistants and intermediaries in complaint handling. When filing complaints to the authorities, citizens take into account various legal norms and capacities of the judicial system. Therefore, the complaint mechanism can be perceived as an alternative to the judiciary or as a supervisory resource.

In regular practice, the mechanism works in accordance with the law, which requires solving problems through the executive apparatus, preventing interference with legal issues. Adherence to these rules entails that only a tiny fraction of complaints is generally subject to consideration by the executive or state authorities of any level. In this sense, the capacities of the mechanism are much more limited than in the Soviet years. Formally, the complaint mechanism has to review complaints that have no legal underpinnings, that is complaints caused by an inefficiency of executive bodies or bureaucratic blunders.

Working in line with legal norms, the mechanism cannot be highly effective. Given the immense number of complaints, the proportion of settled issues is not very high in comparison with the courts. Bureaucratic inaccuracy and errors, the deputies' administrative resources that help avoid punishment for inefficiency, and deviation from formal legal rules become important components in the productivity of the mechanism. The mechanism becomes more effective whenever any deviation from formal rules is possible. Unlike judicial instruments, the complaint mechanism allows for informality. The attractiveness of the present-day complaint mechanism is due exactly to the opportunity to depart from formal regulations. The higher-level addressees demonstrate ample opportunities to deviate from formalities, including in public. Apart from maintaining the generally familiar pattern of interaction with the authorities, the complaint mechanism continues to be a lottery for the citizens where one can lose or win. The low chances of winning only increase its value, especially if all other opportunities to restore justice are unavailable or have been exhausted. Meanwhile, the government, being the designer of the post-Soviet mechanism, is still well equipped to control this lottery.

Justifications of contemporary complaints

In this analysis I want to maintain the possibility of comparing modern complaints with their Soviet-era counterparts. Therefore, the complaints selected for analysis were the ones addressed to different levels of executive power, the Russian president, and the United Russia party. What differs from the Soviet era is that some modern complaints make use of modern technology to increase effectiveness. For example, people publish video addresses on YouTube to quickly spread the information on the problem in the public sphere. Activist groups use the internet and computer software to create applications for mass mailing complaints to the authorities, which delivers shocking blows to the bureaucracy, turns the complaint into an instrument of civil resistance, and effectively brings the problem to the attention of the government.[25] These peculiar methods of using the complaint mechanism are outside of the scope of my analysis.

The requirement for comparability also suggested preserving thematic similarity between the complaints. The most persistent subjects of complaints to the authorities are actions of officials, housing problems, and social welfare. These topics remain as significant in today's complaints as they were in the Soviet times. A small number of complaints regarding consumer issues analogous to their Soviet counterparts were also considered. Compared to the Soviet era, the complaints about consumer issues are not common today. In the early post-Soviet years, the new government adopted the Law "On Protection of Consumer Rights" (1992), and the whole subject moved to the courts, human rights organizations, and supervisory bodies like *Rospotrebnadzor*. One cannot say, however, that consumers do not lodge any complaints with the executive bodies. They do so but much less often than they did in the Soviet period. However, concerns about housing problems, public utilities, and social security issues, ubiquitous in the Soviet-era complaints, still remain common today.

Formal requirements for letters of complaint in contemporary Russia

There is no standardized form for the post-Soviet complaint. Like in the pre-revolutionary era and the Soviet period, citizens filing a complaint to the authorities have to lay out their grievances in the form of a free narrative. Also like previously, normative documents suggest only the most basic rules for composing the text: to indicate the addressee's and the complainant's contact information, to specify if the appeal is being concurrently filed with any other agency, and to use plain language with no profanities (Law No. 59-FZ). In other respects, complainants and their assistants are free to determine the arguments that would emphasize the problem's importance in the eyes of the addressees.

The variety of sources providing citizens with the rules and samples for complaint writing is more limited than in the late Soviet years. This is due to the fact that the mechanisms of feedback from the authorities, which had never been completely transparent, are now almost entirely opaque. In the late Soviet years, citizens' public complaint-related interactions with the authorities resembled two-way communication much more than they do today. Responses to complaints were much more visible in the Soviet period. Local and central newspapers and magazines usually had feedback sections, titled “In the Wake of Your Letters” (*Po sledam vashikh pisem*) or “You Wrote Us” (*Vy nam pisali*). These sections published complaints by citizens and responses compiled by the editors. The texts of complaints could be edited and responses from the authorities could be retold indirectly. Nevertheless, at least some reactions to citizens' complaints were publicly available, which made the connection between the citizens and the depersonalized authorities visible. In contemporary Russia, thousands of complaints are accessible in the archives of local administrations, public reception offices, or online;[26] however, only random examples of replies are available to the general public.

Meanwhile, if a complaint comes to the attention of the highest authorities and gets replied to personally by the president, the answer is distributed widely and aggressively. These success stories publicize the model of problem solving through complaints. However, these success stories are just a tiny proportion among all submitted grievances.

Law and other formal regulations

The first fact that stands out to attention upon analyzing the texts is almost total absence of the Soviet rhetoric in the contemporary complaints to the authorities. Having disappeared from the political discourse, the language of Soviet ideology also vanished from the complaints. The most prominent feature of contemporary complaints is normalized argumentation directly or indirectly based on, or related to, the law.

Within the complaint mechanism, many complaints filed can be classified as “legally valid.” They are compiled in a legally correct manner. Every part of these texts is verified: the sphere of the addressee's responsibilities, the position of the addressee, the problem statement (containing references to legislation), the signature, and the contact information for the complainant. Such complaints are likely to be drafted by lawyers. As a rule, this type of complaint is filed concurrently with the complainant's attempt to solve their problem in court. Complaints like this are usually addressed to the higher levels of the mechanism—the federal authorities or the United Russia party's public reception offices. In complicated cases, when the complainant is unable to obtain justice in any place including the court, a complaint might travel a long way. In this case, the author gains a wealth of experience communicating with the courts and they know everything about the official procedures and protocols. They go through dozens of litigations or file dozens of applications to various judicial bodies. As a result, the citizen learns to utilize the formally correct language of complaint and submits another complaint to the alternative mechanism. Often, the latter complaint sounds like the last hope for justice.

Another type of justification involves references to official normative regulations. Specific laws may be directly mentioned:

> Article 16 of the Law on Privatization and the Decision of the Supreme Court of April 11, 2007, regarding this article are not observed. [...] The Minister of Housing and Town Planning L. H. Burt, reporting to the president, claimed that his ministry is very seriously engaged in repairing dilapidated housing. I wrote a letter to the ministry, complaining that the house is not under repairs, not on the list of the approved program, and not recognized as dilapidated. I received a reply No. 45 of December 4, 2016—a boilerplate letter recommending to appeal to the city administration (they drive me in a circle).[27]

Law can be mentioned indirectly, when the name of the offense is indicated without an explicit reference to the relevant act (here, the anti-monopoly law):

> I am a client of these gas companies. Due to the universal introduction of gas meters, our life has turned into a nightmare. [...] Organization that collects money from us is a monopolist.[28]

Besides legal references, complaint authors also base their argumentation on sanitary norms, "rules of providing public utilities to the citizens," and the president's May decrees:[29]

> Appeal by citizen O.F. Liubinskaia, raising a 3.9-year-old child—on the violation of Government Decision No. 442 and the violation of May Decrees of the President on Mother and Child Welfare. O. F. Liubinskaia explained that on June 30, 2016, at 12:00, her apartment was illegally entirely cut off from the power supply by Mosenergosbyt employees, without any written warning.[30]

Other popular official regulations may be also invoked:

> The café's dumpster enclosure is also located at the rear wall of the house, under the owners' windows, which is a violation of the norms (Sanitary

> Regulations 2.3.6.1079-01 Item 2.6). The café systematically violates its established opening hours till 10 p.m., we have called the police multiple times, the district police officer came and had a conversation with the café management, all in vain. [...] We live in the constant noise from the café, which is working seven days a week, almost round the clock. We ask you to look into the situation.[31]

In justifying their requests and claims, complainants may demonstrate good knowledge of their civil rights without any direct references to the legislation. The complaint below states a violation of rights—a failure to respect the norms of living space per person given the complainants' right to improve their living conditions—without mentioning any additional legal grounds:

> We ask you to help us in obtaining a home. Our family is on the waiting list for improved housing, but there is no advancement whatsoever. We have been on the waiting list since 2000, there are 5 of us living in a 10.8-square-meter room. We wrote to the city programs for improvement, but they are not offering us anything. We ask you to look into this issue. We are waiting for your help!!![32]

Universal pre-legal justifications: A threat to life and health

Modern complaints also rely on the justifications that in the previous chapters I defined as "pre-legal." Trying to communicate acute emotional distress associated with the violation of basic justice and thus bolster their complaint, authors cite the threat to life and health. This type of justification has persisted since the Soviet era, and the discourse of human rights subtly concealed behind them in the Soviet complaints also remains disguised in their contemporary successors:

> No matter how many times we tried going places, writing letters, all for nothing. Our administration committee does not recognize our house as dilapidated. If only they tried living in these conditions themselves. We are wasting our health and our nerves. Since November 2015, my 6-year-old child has been diagnosed with arthritis, we had a serious inflammation of foot joints; the child has a disability. How do you live with a child who has such a condition, who is not supposed get his feet cold? It's very hard in our house, with amenities like that.[33]

The theme of suffering children and older persons is especially conspicuous in contemporary complaints. The protection of children and the elderly is a universal justification, also used in the late Soviet complaints to stress the importance of the problem. However, in the contemporary context, the justifications associated with various suffering experiences of these two categories of citizens have become very popular and diverse. This resonates with the demographic agenda in the public discourse. Since the early 2010s, the public attention has been consistently drawn to the issues of childhood—especially orphanhood—and the problems of the elderly.

Justifications associated with the safety and well-being of children and older people are used to bolster complaints addressed to any level of power. Below is a complaint to a public reception office of United Russia. This text, based on the victims' statements, was compiled by someone well-versed in the rules of composing complaints, namely by the adviser of the Department of Civilian Review of the International Human Rights Advocates' Alliance:

> Two small children (3.9 and 4 years old), two single mothers, and an elderly woman with a severe chronic illness are staying home at night without electricity. Due to the power cutoff, milk products for the children and all food products for the adults were spoilt.[34]

Here is another example—a complaint filed to the housing and utilities services of a district in Saint Petersburg in 2014. The text of the complaint, concerning inadequate apartment heating, was dictated by the head of the house management, the lowest level of the housing and utilities services. Soon, the problem was solved:

> When it is −10 C outside, the air temperature in our apartment is +15 C, which is below the norm. We have a small child, and this is unacceptable. Please winterize the attic's flooring.[35]

What is obvious in the last two examples is that the justifications were prompted by the mediators well versed in the workings of the bureaucracy.[36] They found it important to emphasize the suffering and the damages done to the lives and health of the most vulnerable citizens. Indeed, these justifications get the attention of the addressees, leading to a positive outcome.

Complaints in opposition to legal grounds

The contemporary complaint mechanism is mostly used as an addition to the legal ways of problem solving. Complaints are filed concurrently with lawsuits, prior to them, or after a bad experience with the courts. However, the modern complaint mechanism has preserved a unique function not found in the judiciary—it may solve problems where no legal grounds exist or even where the complainant consciously rejects the existing regulations. In such cases, all kinds of moral and other justifications are put into action to stress the importance of the problem and the need for help. For example, the following situation can be associated with the incoherence of the bureaucracy creating an impasse situation for the citizens:

> In order to get housing, we have to be put on the waiting list, but in order to be put on the waiting list, we need to be registered [*at a place of residence—E.B.*]. Please help me and my children to get housing without the registration.[37]

Legally, one cannot receive housing without such registration. Besides, allocation of social housing usually takes years from the moment of application. Meanwhile, a complaint to the highest level of power brings hope for a positive and quick outcome.

Complaints are also filed when the problem may be resolved through legal channels, but that would involve a lot of trouble and—above all—would not guarantee a favorable outcome. In such cases, the complaint is a method to solve the issue in circumvention of the bureaucracy with its complicated documents, long lines, and rejections by various agencies. In the following example, the complainant is aware that the problem is unlikely to be solved and formulates her request in terms of a miracle:

> Call for help. Hello Vladimir Vladimirovich! I am a mother of three, and as New Year is coming, one wants to believe in miracles. So I decided you might help us, although I understand that my letter is just one of thousands. Our family of five persons lives in a two-room 46-square-meter apartment. Me and my husband had earned enough to buy it without any help (thanks for the maternity capital). All our earnings have been covering the mortgage, we've been denying ourselves and our children everything. Due to the present economic situation, we have acquired the status of the poor. But our biggest and only dream [sic] is to move to a spacious apartment, so that the children have their own rooms. And we only need about a million rubles. But we cannot pay the mortgage anymore. Be our Santa Claus [*Ded Moroz—E.B.*], help us receive an interest-free subsidy.[38]

Legal references can be also used in a quite different manner when the author demonstrates their knowledge of the law and experience in interacting with the judiciary but does not recognize the law, the actions, or the court's decision as just. In this case, the complainant assumes a position that I would call "by law but not by conscience" [*po zakonu, no ne po sovesti—E.B.*]. In the example below, an elderly woman did not receive a supplement to her pension given to most old-age pensioners. This development had legal grounds: the woman has a job while only unemployed pensioners are entitled to the supplement. However, the citizen believes this decision is unjust:

> I am the village head, and in order for me not to spend my hard-earned pennies for the headwoman's work (phone calls, transportation), they were paying me a whole thousand [rubles], deducting the income tax. Therefore, when the pensioners received supplements to their dole [that's what the author calls the pension] in August and then in February, I was denied it, because it turned out I am not a community worker but an employed citizen. [...] How dares our government rob the pensioners who have worked all their lives, sacrificed their health but haven't earned for a decent old age. I have hope that my letter might end up in the hands of an honest, decent person. Maybe there are people around you for whom honor is not an empty word. They would help return these handouts at least. It seems nothing good is going to happen anymore. June 12, 2016.[39]

While denying the rightfulness of the legal grounds, the author supports her claim with a rich collection of alternative arguments, including the following pre-legal justifications: a threat to health, a feeling of unfair resource distribution, moral appeals to the conscience and honor, references to government promises, and, finally, a targeted, direct plea to the addressee reading the complaint. In this wholly different reality, moral grounds and honor seem more just to the complaint's author than the legal grounds.

Another case is a complaint about unduly uncomfortable living conditions which do not meet official norms of minimum living space per person. A family of four is cooped up in a 13-square-meter dormitory room. The complainant mentions their previous attempt to solve the problem officially and legally, also suggesting an alternative solution based on their subjective idea of justice:

> Now, we had our second child in 2016, and it's impossible to live in a space of 12.9 [*square meters—E.B.*]. The elder child has no place to do homework, while the younger is five months old, and she has nowhere to play and develop.[…] The city administration rejected our application for living conditions improvement and living space extension. We have also been registered as needing better housing since 2010, number 2015 on the waiting list. Help us find a solution. Also, a lot of families with infants live in the dormitory, five or four persons in rooms under 18 meters. However, there are families with a single child, or even single people, who live in the dormitory in one-room and two-room apartments, not sharing them with anyone [*bez podseleniia—E.B.*]. Please consider this issue. Can the dormitory residents be rehoused so that young families can live and raise children in comfortable conditions? People got settled into apartments in a strange way. Please help us resolve these issues.[40]

Thus, argumentation based on legal norms and other official regulations seems to play a leading role in contemporary complaints addressed to various levels of authority. Legal justifications are provided in the form of direct references to the legislation and other normative documents. They may also take the form of the complainant demonstrating good knowledge of their rights and the duties of the executing agents—or implicitly referring to the official legal bases. In today's communications about injustice, legal language provides common codes that enable mutual understanding between citizens and government representatives. This is an important development of the post-Soviet complaint mechanism that reflects the modernization of legal consciousness and the increased role of the law as a regulating system. The fact that legal argumentation has found its way into the language of complaints is a sign that the addressees in positions of power are ready to engage in a dialogue with the citizens on justice in legal terms.

However, some complaints also involve alternative justifications based on subjective ideas of justice, morality, and even miracles. Although the alternative justifications are implicitly or explicitly related to legal grounds, they also help construct the bodies of authority as the source of "other" justice.

Appealing to promises by the authorities: Probing for the terms of a new contract between the state and the society

Like in the late Soviet period, citizens look for possible justifications among the government's promises. A legal equivalent would be appealing to the guarantor of the Constitution and the rights of the citizens; however, this formula is only applicable in a complaint to the president and occurs only a few times among the complaints analyzed. In the following example, government promises are invoked in a different version of the legal equivalent—namely, a reference to the rights of taxpayers, which the complainant finds violated:

> The city is covered with snow. People clear away [*the snow—E.B.*] on their own, as far as they can. Some snow banks reach 3–4 meters [*in height—E.B.*]. [...] They say that an amount of 14 billion [*rubles—E.B.*] was allocated for these purposes [*of clearing the snow—E.B.*]. This is money from our pockets (taxes). I petition not for myself but for all of us, many people are ready to sign on to it. We cannot bear this indifference on the part of the officials. But we also don't know who to go to. Best regards.[41]

Far more often, however, justifications take the form of a reference to government's promises expressed in the form of political programs, announcements, or statements personally delivered by the local head of administration during an office appointment with the complainant. The complaint below, addressed to the chairman of United Russia, mentions another attempt to resolve a housing problem in the presence of legal grounds (violation of living space norms for large families):

> We filed an application with the Administration of the Oktiabr'skii okrug of our city and the governor of our region, and we were put on the list as those needing better housing, but the line is so long that we would have to wait for the apartment for about 15 (fifteen) years. We may not live for this long. [...] Where is the state's support for Russian citizens' birthrate? Based on the laws of the Russian Federation, public statements and special programs of the Russian Federation, and announcements by president V. V. Putin regarding state support and facilitation in solving demographic problems, especially for the birth of the fourth and the following children, I ask you: Please provide our family with a bonus of 7,000,000.00 (seven million) rubles, on the maximum concessionary terms, for the construction of a house or for a purchase of an adequate residence.[42]

There is no special formula for the present-day contract between the society and the state, in contrast to the late Soviet one. Every individual case requires searching for appropriate justifications—policies regarding maternity and childhood, defrauded shareholders, large families, security, old-age pensions, and so on. As certain social groups become targets of the state's policy of social welfare and support, complainants find it important to mention their status as members of these groups.

Since the terms of the current social contract are very vague, complainants sometimes manage to base their argumentation on their subjective feeling of imbalance between their social contributions and the expected recompenses from the state. Like in the late Soviet complaints, demonstration of a socially vulnerable status has an important place among their arguments. The following complaint uses the suffering of socially vulnerable groups to bolster the argument:

> I asked the deputies and the administration for help, but they said there's nothing they can do—it's against the rules. While they were giving me the runaround with these papers, the time was passing. I had a child. (Who could never fully learn to talk. He is registered as disabled now.)[43]

Another example:

> My husband Daniil is an orphan. [...] We live in a two-room apartment, 7 people, 3 of us children. Me and my family have nowhere to live. Help us.[44]

However, complaints can also come from socially privileged people who found themselves in trouble. They also search for justifications to support their claims, expecting help from the government in response to their own social contributions. This can be an honored teacher, helpless in the face of a housing problem:

> This is a cry for help. I have never thought I would write you one day, but life made me do it. I am E. Petrova, a geography teacher [...] I have worked in education for 36 years of my life, I am a winner of the Russia's Best Teacher contest, a labor veteran, member of the United Russia party, deputy of the village council.[45]

Or a former military officer who could not pay his mortgage on time:

> Now the bank is suing me, and if I do not pay the full debt to the bank, I will lose the apartment. I have a family, a wife and two children, we would have nowhere to go. Please help.[46]

Or a former criminal investigator who worked dutifully until retirement but ended up with no apartment:

> People who served their homeland most of their lives, fighting crime rather than searching for material benefits, are ultimately forced to beg the state for that what is guaranteed.[47]

Testing the balance between their own civil status and the government's promises, complainants base their argumentation on their subjective ideas about the contract between the state and society. In the eyes of the complainants, the contract exists merely because there is a government that suggests filing complaints. This contract is not mediated by the law but is constructed in the primitive "pre-legal" form as a contract between the society and the power holders. When the argumentation has anything other than the law at its basis, the author has trouble generalizing it by referring to an established source or commonly accepted concept. In such cases, the contract presupposed the immediate representative of the government or the executive power in general as the source and provider of social policies.

Indeed, complaints can involve legal justifications that appeal to state guarantees inscribed in the Constitution. This type of argumentation is used mainly in the complaints addressed to the president as the guarantor of the citizens' rights and freedoms. Exactly his promise to safeguard the rights and freedoms of citizens, given in the presidential oath, is cited in the complaints. However, these justifications alone are not enough—they are usually supplemented by some others.

The ideal model of a contemporary Russian citizen

Similar to late Soviet complaints, important elements of the modern complaint are the author's positive self-presentation, on the one hand, and condemnation of the guilty party, on the other. A "legal" complaint would involve a clear law-based substantiation: "citizen X violated the law N." Less concrete reasoning—accusations of corruption, illegal actions, or lack of responsiveness to complaints—claims that there has been a violation but requires additional clarification. Most diverse justifications, characterizing both the perpetrator and the victim in a specific way, may be used in parallel. These characteristics are difficult to put together in a system similar to the model of the late Soviet ideal citizen. Quite popular are positive self-characteristics based on general morals—"honor," "honesty," and "integrity." Similarly, the actions (or inaction) of the guilty party are explained by various general moral characteristics like deceit, dishonesty, bad management, irresponsibility, and indifference: "The employee of the state service did not want to put himself in my shoes, talked to me in a disrespectful manner, arrogantly calling me a deliberate non-payer, etc."[48]

Another example:

> Considering all of the above, please point out to [*the manufacturer—E.B.*] the defects in the snowmobiles they produce as well as the recklessness and complacency of the employees of this enterprise.[49]

Justifying their aspiration to get help from the state, one needs to demonstrate that they diligently perform their civic duties. This usually follows three rules of self-characterization: First, abidance by the law, or stating that the complainant has not violated any laws: "I dutifully pay all my bills," "I submitted all the documents on time," "I returned the item to the store within the established time limit," and so on. Second, demonstrative loyalty, as in the complaint below, which, while being very critical of the utility services and infrastructure still expresses loyalty to the ruling party:

> We are happy that Moscow is becoming more beautiful and has clean water supply. [...] Yet we understand that Russia is unfortunately not united. That people can live like us only 200 km away from Moscow. As we do not recognize any other parties but United Russia, we simply won't go to the polls.[50]

Third, a description of prior efforts that had been undertaken to solve the problem but did not produce the desired result.

The three characteristics of the ideal citizen, which modern complainants use to demonstrate that they are worthy of help from the authorities, speak for themselves. A new development since the Soviet times is the demonstration of law abidance: relating one's own actions to the norms of law and recognizing the law as an important, commonly accepted foundation of justice. However, the demonstration of loyalty and the emphasis on playing by the rules attest to the persistence of the archaic complaint ritual. The third characteristic reflects the place and role of the complaint mechanism in the system of problem-solving tools available to the citizens. The mechanism appears as the final authority with the power to correct the actions of other authorities, influence them, and punish them for wrong decisions.

Hierarchy as a justification

The structure of the modern complaint mechanism embodies the paternalistic, patriarchal, personalized model of hierarchy. The very use of the complaint mechanism as a problem-solving tool is a passive recognition of the hierarchical relationship between the complainant and the addressee. The use of the complaint mechanism implies loyalty; however, there is a difference from the late Soviet complaints. If the latter emphasized the hierarchical relationship between the author and the addressee at any power level, be it the *raiispolkom*, the *partkom*, or the Kremlin, the modern complaint addressed to the local level rarely involves justifications based on hierarchy. In this sense, the president obviously stands out from other addressees, receiving more hierarchy-related justifications—when appealing to the president, complainants most often place emphasis on his status and power.

Complaints addressed to the highest level of state authority stress the unique capacities of the president that stand apart from all other capacities to restore justice: "We cannot turn to anyone but you."[51] "We have all the papers, but we cannot get that rock to move. Help us. You're our only help."[52]

Duplicate complaints are a widespread phenomenon at any level of the mechanism. Complaints to the presidential level, which is at the top of the hierarchy, are often repeated multiple times—in some cases, dozens of times. This is a sign of serious problems within the institutions designed to resolve issues under their respective jurisdictions. It also demonstrates the complainants' belief in the president's capacity to tackle any problem:

> Dear Vladimir Vladimirovich! I am writing to you for the fifth time. [...] Me, my husband, and our small child are renting an apartment and paying mortgage on a non-existent apartment [...] I am writing not to a random someone but to the President of the Russian Federation, I hope that this time you will sort out the situation at hand and restore order.[53]

Complaints to the president bookend the long path to justice through the lower levels of the mechanism and often also through judicial proceedings. Frequently, these complaints represent the final steps in a long series of attempts to solve the problem, so they are assigned the mission of "the last hope":

> Having depleted the resources of influence, I consider this complaint as the last step. Now everything depends on your decision! Thank you.[54]
>
> Dear Vladimir Vladimirovich, I am asking you for help, because our bailiffs cannot do it.[55]

Dear President of Russia! We love you and believe in you. You are our one and only.[56]

The lodging of a complaint usually represents loyal recognition of the hierarchical relationship between the complainant and the addressee. Both modern and Soviet-era complaints construct hierarchical relations; however, complainants apparently differentiate between various authorities. Hierarchy is clearly established and acknowledged when addressing the president, but not necessarily when addressing local state bodies. Thus, hierarchical relations between the citizens and the authorities are recognized as common sense; however, this hierarchy is not continuous but intermittent—with an emphasis on the relationship between the complainant and the highest level of state authority.

Public good as a justification

The Soviet complainants had shared values that allowed them to generalize their problems, making them look common and involving interests of large groups or even society as a whole. However, it is very difficult to identify similar generalizations in contemporary complaints. Soviet ideology that served as the main basis for the "public good" generalizations has lost its meaning. The Russian Constitution prohibits any official ideology; however, since early 2006, some officials associated with Putin, including Vladislav Surkov, have been calling for articulation of the ideology of the ruling party, United Russia (Evan 2008). While some researchers insist that it is impossible to identify specific norms and values comprising present-day Russian ideology in the classical sense, as defined by Karl Marx or Karl Mannheim, others agree that elite groups are attempting to articulate key national values.

Researching government documents and statements, Galina Zvereva found that the key elements of the Russian ideology are crystallized in the formula pronounced by Deputy Prime Minister Sergei Ivanov: "[Our] society must unite around the new triad of national values. These are sovereign democracy, strong economy, and military power" (Zvereva 2007). Igor Panarin, a reputed researcher of Putin's regime, distinguishes three other pillars upholding the new state ideology—spirituality, greatness, and dignity (Panarin 2012). Political scientist Maria Lipman identified the following main ideological tenets of Putin's third term (2012–2018) after the annexation of Crimea: state nationalism based on Russia's greatness and "special path," aggressive anti-Western and anti-liberal stance, quasi-traditionalism, infallibility of the state and Putin as the only leader, and intolerance towards autonomous activism, whether civic or political (Lipman 2015).

Of all the values attributed to contemporary Russian ideology, only two are reflected in contemporary complaints. The first one is intolerance towards autonomous activism and any collective initiative. Usually formulated as a personal request, complainants generally do not involve any discussion based on the concept of the "public good." The second "ideological" principle permeating the complaints is Putin as the only leader. Other values of the new ideology are not reflected in the complaints. All power levels, except the president, are subject to criticism, and the president stands out as the main addressee among the many.

One argument that takes the place of the public good in the complaints, even though it is not included in any ideological projects, is the fight against officials' excesses. Over and over, citizens refer to the reluctance of state representatives to perform their duties or to their malignant abuse of office. This is cited as the main cause of problems and of the impossibility to resolve them. Wordings like "abuse of office," "corruption," or "failure to perform" are codes that do not require any explanation or proof:

> There are periods in the development of society when theft and immorality are punished by lawful actions of the superiors and supervisory bodies, and also periods of the bureaucracy's impunity and the supervisory bodies using the moment for personal gain.[57]

Another argument that aspires to replace the public good rationale is the search for justice—mainly legal justice. Abidance by the law—forcing the administration to carry out its duties, forcing the bailiffs to implement judicial decisions, stopping the corruption, ensuring the admission of a lawsuit, and so on—is seen as public good:

> all the child's rights were violated by officials of the city Lipetsk, especially by the police and the procuracy. What is the child's fault? That he was born? I think that these misters and ladies tarnished his childhood, excluded him from the world, he has no one to trust, is there any good in this world? That is called Russia![58]

Allegations of disobedience to the law are extended to all levels of power and sometimes aimed at the addressees themselves, even if they belong to a higher level, like the government of the Russian Federation:

> Dear Dmitrii Anatol'evich, the results of audits, i.e. letters from officials, indicate that you and your government's cabinet violate the Constitution and the Criminal Code of the Russian Federation (Art. 165).[59]

Post-Soviet Russia has not established any new ideology. On the one hand, the democratic Constitution prohibits it, proclaiming the indisputable value of law. On the other hand, the attempts to improve any of the informal ideological projects in circumvention of official limitations have been unsuccessful. The public good generalizations in modern complaints are directly or indirectly related to the norms and values of the law. The only rationale acting simultaneously as a national idea, as part of the public discourse, and as a complaint justification is the trust in the president—in fact, the belief in him: "We want to believe in you!"[60]

Thus, the modern complaint maintains its narrative form. This means that there remains a variable set of codes to formulate the request for justice. The main sign of legal modernization in the post-Soviet society is the language of law finding its way into the complaints addressed to the authorities. The rationale for justice, social statuses of complainants, which they articulate in the texts, and the hopes for help, expressed in the complaints, are directly or indirectly connected with the norms of law. Among all arguments, legal ones are the most frequent and persuasive. Besides the fact that complainants strive to describe their problems in legal terms, this indicates several other important changes. First, the public discourse, which always acts as a source of complaint justifications, recognizes and reproduces the priority of law. Second, the law has become a legitimate code that enables the communication between the citizens and the authorities. Finally, Soviet ideology was not succeeded by any other strong, stable ideology that would be able to compete with the law.

Meanwhile, complaint argumentation in contemporary Russia encompasses much more than mere legal reasons. The set of commonly known codes, which the authorities are ready to accept, consider, and discuss, is much wider than the legal basis. As the modern complaint maintains a space for moral and ethical justifications, ethical and legal arguments are found side by side in people's appeals. Rhetorically, legal justifications prevail; however, it is hard to determine which ones attract more attention from the addressees and which are more efficient. Nevertheless, it is important to note that the authorities are perceived by complainants as a source of both legal justice and alternative justice—the one sensitive to personal factors and feelings, allowing for mistakes and omissions, and giving hope for a miracle that is more flexible and humane justice. Thus, complaints provide hope to solve problems that are impossible to tackle within the bounds of legal institutions.

The format of the complaint guides the search for justifications in the direction of the social contract within which the state should generally protect the citizens.

The current contract between the state and society originates from the Constitution that defines the president as the main guarantor of the rights of citizens. The president's figure is the most stable element of the new social contract reproduced in complaints. However, as regards to the capacities and authority of the president, the new contract has rather loose interpretations and a great range of expectations. As a result, the modern complaint presents elements of an absolutist contract, where everything depends on the monarch's favor.

Conclusion

The post-Soviet complaint mechanism is popular but less effective than justice. Similarly to the Soviet years, the complaint mechanism experiences a shortage of resources. However, its inefficiency is due not so much to the lack of resources as to the limitations imposed by the principles of the rule of law. The complaint mechanism has no right to consider complaints wherein legal problems are described. Thus, only part of the complaints entering the mechanism is to be resolved by the mechanism alone.

Does the separation of powers really work in Russia? My research clearly demonstrates that the principle of separation of powers influences the operation of the complaint mechanism—which is a sign of legal modernization. The breach of this principle is highly undesirable at all levels of the complaint mechanism. However, the more appropriate answer to the question would be ambivalent: yes and no. The lower the level of power, the more strictly the principle is observed; the higher the level of power, the more opportunities there are to ignore the principle.

The design of the complaint mechanism, involving different branches of power, allows circumventing their separation. The agencies involved in the work with complaints form a complex web with many diverse addressees enmeshed in it. The executive bodies, the United Russia party and human rights organizations, the supervisory bodies, and the judiciary—all of them are brought together by the complex routing system. Every addressee is obligated to review citizens' complaints. At the same time, the addressees' jurisdictions remain blurred, and an *ad hoc* trajectory is developed for every complaint. In such a trajectory, the efforts made by a United Russia deputy can be consolidated by an audit of the supervisory body or a judicial decision. Most free to transgress the separation of powers is the highest level of the mechanism. It is only the presidential level that readdresses complaints directly to the court. Besides, the success stories publicly demonstrate the president's involvement in the matters of justice.

The functionality of the modern complaint mechanism can be divided into two purposes, which is reflected in its structure. The lower levels of the mechanism carry out the purpose of informing, helping the executive bodies to allocate scarce resources and address local issues. The lower levels compensate for the lack of institutions of pre-trial problem solving and the general weakness of executive bodies in contemporary Russia. The higher levels of the mechanism intervene in the administration of justice, thus duplicating the judiciary. From a functional point of view, they are redundant. Their existence is justified by a different, symbolic purpose: supporting the image of the current government, and particularly the figure of acting president, and increasing the influence of the executive power relative to other branches of power.

Since the Soviet era, the language of appeals for justice has gone through considerable changes. Looking for justice, people apply to the mechanism of complaints, but they still use the language and form of official law. Importantly, legal argumentation has become legitimate in the context of the complaint mechanism. Legally valid complaints are a concise and effective way of lodging an application without violating the rules of political loyalty. The rule of law is legitimate in the modern mechanism of complaints, and law abidance is an important characteristic of a person requesting the state's assistance.

However, despite its frequent use, legal argumentation of complaints remains optional. In present-day complaints, moral justifications are found side by side with legal ones. The separation of powers forces the mechanism to consider moral claims along legal arguments. It is the complaints without obvious legal underpinnings that can ensure that the complaint mechanism looks most effective in the eyes of the complainants and supervisory bodies alike.

According to Luc Boltanski (2011), the use of legal justifications in complaints must indicate the priority of legal institutions. If a complaint, written in the language of law, is addressed to the executive bodies, this means that the latter are constructed as legislators and law enforcers, or that distinction between the executive and legislative powers is unmanifest. The complaint's capacity to reproduce legal language shows some signs of legal modernization in the sense that now the law is accepted as grounds for mutual understanding between complainants and addressees of complaints. However, it cannot confirm the process of legal modernization as itself. While the request for justice is translated into the language of law, there are no guarantees that it will not disappear from complaints if an alternative communication language emerges—for example, if an official ideology makes a comeback.

Notes

1 "Tipovoi obshcherossiiskii tematicheskii klassifikator obrashchenii grazhdan, organizatsii i obshchestvennykh ob"edinenii" from June 28, 2013, No. A1-3695v. *KonsultantPlus*. Retrieved on July 19, 2019 (www.consultant.ru/cons/CGI/online.cgi?req=doc&base=EXP&n=567595&dst=100240#06144359062871974).
2 The percentages represent proportions of the total number of complaints lodged.
3 Complaints from the author's personal archive.
4 The district administration oversees the work of several *Zhilkomservises* in the district, i.e. is directly responsible for the actions of the *Zhilkomservis* that received the initial complaint.
5 Among them, 58.6% were considered by the federal government itself, 18.5% were forwarded to the federal-level executive authorities (ministries, services and agencies, representing executive branch on the federal level), 11.4% to the executive authorities at the local and regional level, and 9.3% to other organizations.

Data on the Number of Written and Oral Complaints by the Citizens between December 1, 2017 and December 31, 2017 [Svedeniia o kolichestve postupivshikh pis'mennykh i ustnykh obrashchenii grazhdan s 01.12.2017 g. po 31.12.2017 g.

Pravitel'stvo Rossii. Retrieved on July 19, 2019. (http://static.government.ru/media/files/NNb7RkGpdlvuiI89tECtAn6cQ1MRiPxa.pdf).

6 On January 15, 2020, Dmitrii Medvedev resigned as prime minister but retained office of the chairman of the United Russia party.
7 Interviews with V. V. and A. V.
8 Interview with V. V.
9 Interview with G. N.
10 Interview with G. N.
11 Interviews with G. N. and V. V.
12 Interview with G. N.
13 Interview with A. V.
14 Interview with G. N.
15 Interview with G. N.
16 In different years, complaints to the president comprised from 25% to 75% of all applications. Other written communications included requests for information and suggestions. The total yearly correspondence addressed to the president amounts to 3–4 million letters. Henceforth only numbers of complaints are taken into account in the analysis.
17 All names, dates, and registration numbers are changed.
18 Pros'ba okazat' sodeistvie v voprose ispolneniia resheniia suda [Request for assistance in the execution of the court decision.] A complaint addressed to the president of the RF from December 2017. *Pis'ma prezidentu*. Retrieved on July 19, 2019 (http://xn--80aicbidd2apldmjyp6k.xn--p1ai/zhile/prosba-okazat-sodejstvie-v-voprose-ispolneniya-resheniya-suda.html).
19 According to the official statistical reports of the Administrative Office of the President, the "Federal-level executive bodies" are defined as a system of ministries, services, and agencies, representing executive power on the federal level.
20 According to the official statistical reports of the Administrative Office of the President, the "Federal government bodies" are Russian authorities at the federal level. This set of authorities includes the Apparatuses of the State Duma, Federal Assembly, and Government; the Accounts Chamber, the General Prosecutor's Office, the Investigative Committee, the Central Bank, the Pension Fund, the Federal Compulsory Medical Insurance Fund, the Social Insurance Fund, and the Central Election Commission.
21 A proportion of the total number of decisions made.
22 A response to a complaint, given by the Administrative Office of the President (2017)
23 Ia sirota. Mne ne daiut zhil'e [I'm an orphan. They deprive me from housing.] A complaint addressed to the president of the RF from 2017. *Pis'ma prezidentu*. Retrieved on July 19, 2019 (http://xn--80aicbidd2apldmjyp6k.xn--p1ai/zhile/ya-sirota-mne-ne-dayut-zhile.html).
24 Ob obespechenii dosuga i otdykha gorozhan [Providing leisure and recreation for townspeople.] A complaint addressed to the public reception office to the United Russia party from July 2017.
25 See, for example, the civil initiative Beautiful Petersburg *(Krasivyi Peterburg)*. Retrieved on July 15, 2019 (http://красивыйпетербург.рф/about).
26 See description of websites, containing original texts of complaints in open access in Chapter 1.
27 Vetkhoe zhil'e [Dilapidated housing.] A complaint addressed to the public reception office to the United Russia party from May 23, 2016.
28 Proshu navesti poriadok v gazovoi kompanii [I ask you to put things in order in gas companies.] A complaint addressed to the public reception office to the United Russia party from December 2, 2016.
29 A series of 11 decrees signed by Vladimir Putin on May 7, 2012, the day he (re)assumed the office of the President of the Russian Federation, that contain 218 instructions to the

Government of the Russian Federation to be executed in 2012–2020. They set targets for public sector salaries, improvement of social and medical public services, development of the demographic policy, and other areas.

30 Deti Ostalis' Bez Sveta [Children Left With No Light.] A complaint addressed to the public reception office to the United Russia party from May 19, 2016.

31 Kafe meshaet zhit' [A café prevents to live.] A complaint addressed to the president of the RF from April 2017. *Pis'ma prezidentu*. Retrieved on July 19, 2019 (http://xn--80aicbidd2apldmjyp6k.xn--p1ai/zhile/kafe-meshaet-zhit.html).

32 Zhilishchnyi vopros [A housing question.] A complaint addressed to the president of the RF from February 2017. *Pis'ma prezidentu*. Retrieved on July 19, 2019 (http://xn--80aicbidd2apldmjyp6k.xn--p1ai/zhile/zhilishhnyj-vopros-5.html).

33 Proshu pomoshchi [I ask you for help.] A complaint addressed to the president of the RF from June 2017. *Pis'ma prezidentu*. Retrieved on July 19, 2019 (http://xn--80aicbidd2apldmjyp6k.xn--p1ai/zhile/vetxoe-zhilyo.html).

34 Deti Ostalis' Bez Sveta [Children Left With No Light.] A complaint addressed to the public reception office to the United Russia party from May 19, 2016.

35 A complaint to the local housing and utilities service from the author's personal archive.

36 Interview with K. M.

37 Zhil'e [A housing.] A complaint addressed to the president of the RF from January 2017. *Pis'ma prezidentu*. Retrieved on July 19, 2019 (http://xn--80aicbidd2apldmjyp6k.xn--p1ai/zhile/zhile-6.html).

38 Pros'ba o pomoshchi [A request for help.] A complaint addressed to the president of the RF from December 2016. *Pis'ma prezidentu*. Retrieved on July 19, 2019 (http://xn--80aicbidd2apldmjyp6k.xn--p1ai/zhile/prosba-o-pomoshhi-12.html).

39 Pensiia ili podachka? [A pension or a dole?] A complaint addressed to the president of the RF from February 20, 2017. *Pis'ma prezidentu*. Retrieved on July 19, 2019 (http://xn--80aicbidd2apldmjyp6k.xn--p1ai/zhaloba/pensiya-ili-podachka.html).

40 Zhilishchnyi vopros dlia molodoi sem'i [A housing problem of the young family.] A complaint addressed to the president of the RF from September 2016. *Pis'ma prezidentu*. Retrieved on July 19, 2019 (http://xn--80aicbidd2apldmjyp6k.xn--p1ai/zhile/zhilishhnyj-vopros-dlya-molodoj-semi.html).

41 Ne vyvoziat sneg iz goroda [They do not take snow out of the city.] A complaint addressed to the president of the RF from March 2018. *Pis'ma prezidentu*. Retrieved on July 19, 2019 (http://xn--80aicbidd2apldmjyp6k.xn--p1ai/zhaloba/ne-vyvozyat-sneg-iz-goroda.html).

42 Mnogodetnaia sem'ia [A family with many children.] A complaint addressed to the president of the RF from February 6, 2017. *Pis'ma prezidentu*. Retrieved on July 19, 2019 (http://xn--80aicbidd2apldmjyp6k.xn--p1ai/zhile/mnogodetnaya-semya-4.html).

43 Ia sirota. Mne ne daiut zhil'e [I'm an orphan. They deprive me from housing.] A complaint addressed to the president of the RF from 2017. *Pis'ma prezidentu*. Retrieved on July 19, 2019 (http://xn--80aicbidd2apldmjyp6k.xn--p1ai/zhile/ya-sirota-mne-ne-dayut-zhile.html).

44 Pomoshch' v postanovke na ochered'po zhil'iu [Need help in being put on the housing waiting list.] A complaint addressed to the president of the RF from January 2016. *Pis'ma prezidentu*. Retrieved on July 19, 2019 (http://xn--80aicbidd2apldmjyp6k.xn--p1ai/zhile/pomoshh-v-postavke-na-ochered-po-zhilyu.html).

45 Krik o pomoshchi [A cry for help.] A complaint addressed to the president of the RF from January 2018. *Pis'ma prezidentu*. Retrieved on July 19, 2019 (http://xn--80aicbidd2apldmjyp6k.xn--p1ai/zhile/krik-o-pomoshhi-7.html).

46 Voennaia ipoteka [Mortgage for the military.] A complaint addressed to the president of the RF from February 2017. *Pis'ma prezidentu*. Retrieved on July 19, 2019 (http://xn--80aicbidd2apldmjyp6k.xn--p1ai/zhile/voennaya-ipoteka.html).

47 Usmotrenie vozmozhnosti ispol'zovaniia edinovremennoi sotsial'noi vyplaty dlia pogasheniia kredita poluchennogo dlia priobreteniia nedvizhimosti [Repayment of a housing loan.] A complaint addressed to the president of the RF from January 2017. *Pis'ma prezidentu.* Retrieved on July 19, 2019 (http://xn--80aicbidd2apldmjyp6k.xn--p1ai/zhile/usmotrenie-vozmozhnosti-ispolzovaniya-edinovremennoj-socialnoj-vyplaty-dlya-pogasheniya-kredita-poluchennogo-dlya-priobreteniya-nedvizhimosti.html).

48 A complaint from a family, who were victims of a fire, addressed to the local housing and utilities service from October 23, 2017.

49 Zhaloba na kompaniiu [A complaint to a company.] A complaint addressed to the president of the RF from November 2017. *Pis'ma prezidentu.* Retrieved on July 19, 2019 (https://xn--80aicbidd2apldmjyp6k.xn--p1ai/potrebiteli/ZHaloba-na-OAO-Russkaya-mekhanika.html).

50 My Ne Poidiom Golosovat'—My Ne Verim V Edinstvo Rossii [We Won't Go To The Polls—We Don't Believe In Russia's Unity.] A complaint addressed to the public reception office to the United Russia party from August 31, 2016.

51 Proshu navesti poriadok v gazovoi kompanii [I ask you to put things in order in gas companies.] A complaint addressed to the public reception office to the United Russia party from December 2, 2016.

52 Detskoe posobie [A child allowance.] A complaint addressed to the president of the RF from July 2018. *Pis'ma prezidentu.* Retrieved on July 19, 2019 (http://xn--80aicbidd2apldmjyp6k.xn--p1ai/semya/detskie-posobie.html).

53 Obmanutyi dol'shchik [A defrauded shareholder.] A complaint addressed to the president of the RF from January 2018. *Pis'ma prezidentu.* Retrieved on July 19, 2019 (http://xn--80aicbidd2apldmjyp6k.xn--p1ai/zhile/obmanutyj-dolshhik-2.html).

54 Ravnodushie i ego posledstviia [Indifference and its consequences.] A complaint addressed to the president of the RF from February 2017. *Pis'ma prezidentu.* Retrieved on July 19, 2019 (http://xn--80aicbidd2apldmjyp6k.xn--p1ai/potrebiteli/ravnodushie-i-ego-posledstviya.html).

55 Privlech Vinovnogo K Otvetstvennosti [Bring The Perpetrator To Justice. The complaint was found in the archive of the public reception office from November 15, 2017. It was addressed simultaneously to the president and the public reception office of the United Russia party.

56 Pravookhranitel'nye organy narushili prava rebionka [Law enforcement authorities violated the rights of the child.] A complaint addressed to the president of the RF from September 2017. *Pis'ma prezidentu.* Retrieved on July 19, 2019 (https://xn--80aicbidd2apldmjyp6k.xn--p1ai/potrebiteli/Pravookhranitelnye-organy-narushili-prava-rebjonka.html).

57 Vetkhoe zhil'e [Dilapidated housing.] A complaint addressed to the public reception office to the United Russia party from May 23, 2016.

58 Pravookhranitel'nye organy narushili prava rebionka [Law enforcement authorities violated the rights of the child.] A complaint addressed to the president of the RF from September 2017. *Pis'ma prezidentu.* Retrieved on July 19, 2019 (https://xn--80aicbidd2apldmjyp6k.xn--p1ai/potrebiteli/Pravookhranitelnye-organy-narushili-prava-rebjonka.html).

59 Kto VY? [Who are YOU?] A complaint addressed to the public reception office to the United Russia party from November 12, 2016.

60 Pravookhranitel'nye organy narushili prava rebionka [Law enforcement authorities violated the rights of the child.] A complaint addressed to the president of the RF from September 2017. *Pis'ma prezidentu.* Retrieved on July 19, 2019 (https://xn--80aicbidd2apldmjyp6k.xn--p1ai/potrebiteli/Pravookhranitelnye-organy-narushili-prava-rebjonka.html).

References

Data on the Number of Written and Oral Complaints by the Citizens between December 1, 2017 and December 31, 2017 [Svedeniia o kolichestve postupivshikh pis'mennykh i ustnykh obrashchenii grazhdan s 1 dekabriz 2017 g. po 31 dekabria 2017 g. *Pravitel'stvo Rossii.* Retrieved on July 19, 2019 (http://static.government.ru/media/files/NNb7RkGpdlvuiI89tECtAn6cQ1MRiPxa.pdf).

Evan, Alfred B. Jr. 2008. *Power and Ideology: Vladimir Putin and the Russian Political System.* William Chase Bob Donnorummo and Ronald H. Linden (eds.) The Carl Beck Papers. No. 1902, January.

Informatsionno-statisticheskii obzor rassmotrennykh v 2015 godu obrashchenii grazhdan, organizatsii i obshchestvennykh ob'edinenii, adresovannykh Presidentu RF, a takzhe rezul'tatov rassmotreniia i priniatykh mer. 2015. *Ofitsial'nyi sait Upravleniia Presidenta po rabote s obrashcheniiami grazhdan i organizatsyi.* Retrieved on July 19, 2019 (http://static.kremlin.ru/media/letters/digests//e3CBXTdHrNoeAcHpNAsRVlIgvCpOGyub.pdf).

Informatsionno-statisticheskii obzor rassmotrennykh v 2016 godu obrashchenii grazhdan, organizatsii i obshchestvennykh ob'edinenii, adresovannykh Presidentu RF, a takzhe rezul'tatov rassmotreniia i priniatykh mer. 2016. *Ofitsial'nyi sait Upravleniia Presidenta po rabote s obrashcheniiami grazhdan i organizatsyi.* Retrieved on July 19, 2019 (http://static.kremlin.ru/media/letters/digests//tH3Miwovxt39aWMgvUb6rfc8zx79yySv.pdf).

Informatsionno-statisticheskii obzor rassmotrennykh v 2017 godu obrashchenii grazhdan, organizatsii i obshchestvennykh ob'edinenii, adresovannykh Presidentu RF, a takzhe rezul'tatov rassmotreniia i priniatykh mer. 2017. *Ofitsial'nyi sait Upravleniia Presidenta po rabote s obrashcheniiami grazhdan i organizatsyi.* Retrieved on July 19, 2019 (http://static.kremlin.ru/media/letters/digests//UBHnFDfwnQmlPQvOknupXuVfe7eCMs7c.pdf).

Informatsionno-statisticheskii obzor rassmotrennykh v 2018 godu obrashchenii grazhdan, organizatsii i obshchestvennykh ob'edinenii, adresovannykh Presidentu RF, a takzhe rezul'tatov rassmotreniia i priniatykh mer. 2018. *Ofitsial'nyi sait Upravleniia Presidenta po rabote s obrashcheniiami grazhdan i organizatsyi.* Retrieved on July 19, 2019 (http://static.kremlin.ru/media/letters/digests//76kvGYZr1ErA2dpiIAHLozITaTXnjhrY.pdf)

Lipman, Maria. 2015. "Putin's 'Besieged Fortress' and Its Ideological Arms." Pp. 110–136 in: Maria Lipman and Nikolai Petrov (eds.) *The State of Russia: What Comes Next?* London: Palgrave Pivot.

Otchet o rabote sudov obshchei iurisdiktsii po rassmotreniiu ugolovnykh del po pervoi instantsii za 2015 g. 2015a. *Ofitsial'nyi sait Sudebnogo Departamenta pri Verkhovnom Sude RF.* Retrieved on July 19, 2019 (http://www.cdep.ru/index.php?id=79&item=3417).

Otchet o rabote sudov obshchei iurisdiktsii po rassmotreniiu grazhdanskikh, administrativnykh del po pervoi instantsii za 2015 g. 2015b. *Ofitsial'nyi sait Sudebnogo Departamenta pri Verkhovnom Sude RF.* Retrieved on July 19, 2019 (http://www.cdep.ru/index.php?id=79&item=3417).

Otchet o rabote sudov obshchei iurisdiktsii po rassmotreniiu grazhdanskikh, administrativnykh del po pervoi instantsii za 2016 g. 2016a. *Ofitsial'nyi sait Sudebnogo Departamenta pri Verkhovnom Sude RF.* Retrieved on July 19, 2019 (http://www.cdep.ru/index.php?id=79&item=3832).

Otchet o rabote sudov obshchei iurisdiktsii po rassmotreniiu grazhdanskikh, administrativnykh del po pervoi instantsii za 2016 g. 2016b. *Ofitsial'nyi sait Sudebnogo*

Departamenta pri Verkhovnom Sude RF. Retrieved on July 19, 2019 (http://www.cdep.ru/index.php?id=79&item=3832).

Panarin, Igor. 2012. "Post-election Russia: Putin's new ideology." *RT*. April 20. Retrieved on February 20, 2013 (http://rt.com/politics/russia-putin-ideology-panarin-535/).

Report on handling citizens' complaints by the executive authorities of Saint Petersburg in 2017 [Otchiot o rabote s obrashcheniiami grazhdan v ispolnitel'nykh organakh gosudarstvennoi vlasti Sankt-Peterburga za 2017g.]. 2017. *Ofitsial'nyi sait administratsii Sankt-Peterburga*. Retrieved on July 19, 2019 (https://www.gov.spb.ru/gov/obrasheniya-grazhdan/otchet-obrasheniya/9125/).

Report on handling citizens' complaints by the executive authorities of Saint Petersburg in 2018 [Otchiot o rabote s obrashcheniiami grazhdan v ispolnitel'nykh organakh gosudarstvennoi vlasti Sankt-Peterburga za 2018 g.]. 2018. *Ofitsial'nyi sait administratsii Sankt-Peterburga*. Retrieved on July 19, 2019 (https://www.gov.spb.ru/gov/obrasheniya-grazhdan/otchet-obrasheniya/13984/).

Statistika obrashchenii v Gosudarstvennuiu Dumu. 2017–2019. *Priiomnaia Gosudarstvennoi Dumy*. Retrieved on July 19, 2019 (https://priemnaya.duma.gov.ru/ru/stat_page/all/).

"Tipovoi obshcherossiiskii tematicheskii klassifikator obrashchenii grazhdan, organizatsii i obshchestvennykh ob"edinenii" from June 28, 2013, No. A1-3695v. *KonsultantPlus*. Retrieved on July 19, 2019 (http://www.consultant.ru/cons/CGI/online.cgi?req=doc&base=EXP&n=567595&dst=100240#06144359062871974).

Zvereva, Galina. 2007. "Postroit' Matritsu: diskurs rossiiskoi vlasti v usloviiah setevoi kul'tury." *Polit.ru*. April 11. Retrieved on February 18, 2013 (http://www.polit.ru/article/2007/04/11/zvereva/).

Normative documents

Constitution of the RF [Konstitutsiia (osnovnoi zakon) RF] from December 12, 1993. *KonsultantPlus*. Retrieved on July 19, 2019 (http://www.consultant.ru/document/cons_doc_LAW_28399/).

Instruction of the Presidium of the General Council of the All-Russian Political Party United Russia "On the Organization and Order of Working with Citizens' Applications" [Instruktsiia Presidiuma General'nogo Soveta Vserossiiskoi Partii Edinaia Rossiia "Ob organizatsii i poriadke raboty s obrashcheniiami grazhdan"] from September 8, 2008, Record No. 18. *Ofitsial'nyi sait partii Edinaia Rossiia*. Retrieved on July 19, 2019 (https://er.ru/news/182574/userdata/files/2019/06/24/instruktsiya.pdf).

Law "On Protection of Consumer Rights" [Zakon "O zashchite prav potrebitelei"] from February 7, 1992, No. 2300-1. *KonsultantPlus*. Retrieved on July 19, 2019 (http://www.consultant.ru/document/cons_doc_LAW_305/).

Methodological Recommendations on the Organization of Operations of the Regional Offices of the All-Russian Political Party "United Russia" [Metodichestie rekomendatsii po voprosam organizatsii raboty obshchestvennykh priiomnykh Vserossiiskoi politicheskoi partii "Edinaia Rossiia"] from November 14, 2012. *Ofitsial'nyi sait partii Edinaia Rossiia v Murmanske*. Retrieved on July 19, 2019 (murmansk.er.ru).

Provision "On the Administration of the President of the Russian Federation" [Polozhenie Prezidenta "Ob administratsii Prezidenta RF"] from April 6, 2004, No. 490. *KonsultantPlus*. Retrieved on July 19, 2019 (http://www.consultant.ru/document/cons_doc_LAW_47272/9375930629345c3f977dbbf1bf3730404b9afbd2/).

Empirical sources

A complaint of a family, suffered from fire, addressed to the local housing and utility service from October 23, 2017.

Deti Ostalis' Bez Sveta [Children Left With No Light.] A complaint, addressed to the public reception office to the party "United Russia" from May 19, 2016.

Detskoe posobie [A child allowance.] A complaint, addressed to the president of the RF from July 2018 . *Pis'ma presidentu.* Retrieved on July 19, 2019 (http://xn--80aicbidd2apldmjyp6k.xn--p1ai/semya/detskie-posobie.html).

Kafe meshaet zhit' [A café prevents to live.] A complaint, addressed to the president of the RF from April 2017. *Pis'ma presidentu.* Retrieved on July 19, 2019 (http://xn--80aicbidd2apldmjyp6k.xn--p1ai/zhile/kafe-meshaet-zhit.html).

Krik o pomoshchi [A cry for help.] A complaint, addressed to the president of the RF from January 2018. *Pis'ma presidentu.* Retrieved on July 19, 2019 (http://xn--80aicbidd2apldmjyp6k.xn--p1ai/zhile/krik-o-pomoshhi-7.html).

Kto VY? [Who are YOU?] A complaint, addressed to the public reception office to the party United Russia from November 12, 2016.

Ia sirota. Mne ne daiut zhil'e [I'm an orphan. They deprive me from housing.] A complaint, addressed to the president of the RF from 2017. *Pis'ma presidentu.* Retrieved on July 19, 2019 (http://xn--80aicbidd2apldmjyp6k.xn--p1ai/zhile/ya-sirota-mne-ne-dayut-zhile.html).

Mnogodetnaia semia [A family with many children.] A complaint, addressed to the president of the RF from February 6, 2017. *Pis'ma presidentu.* Retrieved on July 19, 2019 (http://xn—80aicbidd2apldmjyp6k.xn—p1ai/zhile/mnogodetnaya-semya-4.html).

My Ne Poidiom Golosovat'—My Ne Verim V Edinstvo Rossii [We Won't Go To The Polls—We Don't Believe In Russia's Unity.] A complaint, addressed to the public reception office to the party United Russia from August 31, 2016.

Ne vyvoziat sneg iz goroda [They do not take snow out of the city.] A complaint, addressed to the president of the RF from March 2018. *Pis'ma presidentu.* Retrieved on July 19, 2019 (http://xn--80aicbidd2apldmjyp6k.xn--p1ai/zhaloba/ne-vyvozyat-sneg-iz-goroda.html).

Obmanutyi dol'shchik [A defrauded shareholder.] A complaint, addressed to the president of the RF from January 2018. *Pis'ma presidentu.* Retrieved on July 19, 2019 (http://xn--80aicbidd2apldmjyp6k.xn--p1ai/zhile/obmanutyj-dolshhik-2.html).

Ob obespechenii dosuga i otdykha gorozhan [Providing leisure and recreation for townspeople.] A complaint, addressed to the public reception office to the party United Russia from July 2017.

Pensiia ili podachka? [A pension or a dole?] A complaint, addressed to the president of the RF from February 20, 2017. *Pis'ma presidentu.* Retrieved on July 19, 2019 (http://xn--80aicbidd2apldmjyp6k.xn--p1ai/zhaloba/pensiya-ili-podachka.html).

Pomoshch' v postavke na ochered' po zhil'iu [Need help in being put on the housing waiting list.] A complaint, addressed to the president of the RF from January 2016. *Pis'ma presidentu.* Retrieved on July 19, 2019 (http://xn--80aicbidd2apldmjyp6k.xn--p1ai/zhile/pomoshh-v-postavke-na-ochered-po-zhilyu.html).

Pravookhranitel'nye organy narushili prava rebionka [Law enforcement authorities violated the rights of the child.] A complaint, addressed to the president of the RF from September 2017. *Pis'ma presidentu.* Retrieved on July 19, 2019 (https://xn--80aicbidd2apldmjyp6k.xn--p1ai/potrebiteli/Pravookhranitelnye-organy-narushili-prava-rebjonka.html).

Privlech Vinovnogo K Otvetstvennosti [Bring The Perpetrator To Justice,]—the complaint was found in the archive of the public reception office from November 15, 2017. It was addressed simultaneously to the president and the public reception office the party United Russia.

Pros'ba okazat' sodeistvie v voprose ispolneniia resheniia suda [Request for assistance in the execution of the court decision.] A complaint, addressed to the president of the RF from December 2017. *Pis'ma presidentu.* Retrieved on July 19, 2019 (http://xn--80aicbidd2apldmjyp6k.xn--p1ai/zhile/prosba-okazat-sodejstvie-v-voprose-ispolneniya-resheniya-suda.html).

Pros'ba o pomoshchi [A request for help.] A complaint, addressed to the president of the RF from December 2016. *Pis'ma presidentu.* Retrieved on July 19, 2019 (http://xn--80aicbidd2apldmjyp6k.xn--p1ai/zhile/prosba-o-pomoshhi-12.html).

Proshu navesti poriadok v gazovoi kompanii [I ask you to put things in order in gas companies.] A complaint, addressed to the public reception office to the party United Russia from December 2, 2016.

Proshu pomoshchi [I ask you for help.] A complaint, addressed to the president of the RF from June 2017. *Pis'ma presidentu.* Retrieved on July 19, 2019 (http://xn--80aicbidd2apldmjyp6k.xn--p1ai/zhile/vetxoe-zhilyo.html).

Ravnodushie i ego posledstviia [Indifference and its consequences.] A complaint, addressed to the president of the RF from February 2017. *Pis'ma presidentu.* Retrieved on July 19, 2019 (http://xn--80aicbidd2apldmjyp6k.xn--p1ai/potrebiteli/ravnodushie-i-ego-posledstviya.html).

Usmotrenie vozmozhnosti ispol'zovaniia edinovremennoi sotsial'noi vyplaty dlia pogasheniia kredita poluchennogo dlia priobreteniia nedvizhimosti [Repayment of a housing loan.] A complaint, addressed to the president of the RF from January 2017. *Pis'ma presidentu.* Retrieved on July 19, 2019 (http://xn--80aicbidd2apldmjyp6k.xn--p1ai/zhile/usmotrenie-vozmozhnosti-ispolzovaniya-edinovremennoj-socialnoj-vyplaty-dlya-pogasheniya-kredita-poluchennogo-dlya-priobreteniya-nedvizhimosti.html).

Vetkhoe zhil'e [Dilapidated housing.] A complaint, addressed to the public reception office to the party United Russia from May 23, 2016.

Voennaia ipoteka [Mortgage for the military.] A complaint, addressed to the president of the RF from February 2017. *Pis'ma presidentu.* Retrieved on July 19, 2019 (http://xn--80aicbidd2apldmjyp6k.xn--p1ai/zhile/voennaya-ipoteka.html).

Zhaloba na kompaniiu [A complaint to a company.] A complaint, addressed to the president of the RF from November 2017. *Pis'ma presidentu.* Retrieved on July 19, 2019 (https://xn--80aicbidd2apldmjyp6k.xn--p1ai/potrebiteli/ZHaloba-na-OAO-Russkaya-mekhanika.html).

Zhil'e [A housing.] A complaint, addressed to the president of the RF from January 2017. *Pis'ma presidentu.* Retrieved on July 19, 2019 (http://xn--80aicbidd2apldmjyp6k.xn--p1ai/zhile/zhile-6.html).

Zhilishchnyi vopros dlia molodoi sem'i [A housing problem of the young family.] A complaint, addressed to the president of the RF from September 2016. *Pis'ma presidentu.* Retrieved on July 19, 2019 (http://xn--80aicbidd2apldmjyp6k.xn--p1ai/zhile/zhilishhnyj-vopros-dlya-molodoj-semi.html).

Zhilishchnyi vopros [A housing question.] A complaint, addressed to the president of the RF from February 2017. *Pis'ma presidentu.* Retrieved on July 19, 2019 (http://xn--80aicbidd2apldmjyp6k.xn--p1ai/zhile/zhilishhnyj-vopros-5.html).

7 Conclusion

Whether one wants it or not, a book on Russian law turns into a book on Russian politics. In contemporary Russia, we are witnessing the latest historical cycle of existence of the mechanism of complaints addressed to the authorities. In the history of Russian society, the complaint mechanism has declined and recovered again at least six times. Each of the versions of the mechanism had its own peculiarities; each, in its own way, came into conflict with the emerging demands for legal modernization. None of the versions could survive without the support of the authorities.

A complaint is a very special phenomenon in Russian society. No other genre of communication between citizens and the authorities has endured this long in Russian history. In its centuries-long development, the mechanism has never overcome the ambiguity of the concept of the complaint and the ability of this concept to denote a request for justice in a variety of circumstances: from a private solicitation to an official trial. In the Russian tradition, it has always existed as a tool to support authoritarianism and the paternalistic patriarchal contract, in its various forms, between the authorities and society. The capacity for flexibility and transformability inherent in the mechanism made it possible to weaken or, conversely, to strengthen the conditions for an authoritarian contract without changing the contract's fundamentals.

In Russia, the complaint mechanism has always been a project of power, a tool to strengthen the current government (the executive), maintain its primacy, and stay in power. Throughout its development, the mechanism never shed its archaic features. It always combined the functions of governance and justice, exercising great influence in both areas. The mechanism always had its own bureaucracy, which was closely intertwined with the bodies of the executive power. However, the obligation to work with complaints, at least in the Soviet and post-Soviet versions of the mechanism, extended to departmental structures supervisory bodies and the judiciary. It is difficult to find another mechanism in the entire system of public administration that would bind together such an assortment of power institutions. By creating additional reasons for interaction, the mechanism contributed to the strengthening of connections within the entire public administration system long before the principles of the separation of powers and the rule of law began to penetrate the Russian reality.

The mechanism has always occupied an important place among the easily accessible opportunities to restore justice, creating a powerful alternative to judicial institutions, covering whole segments of problems that are legal in nature, regulating relations, and setting off decades and centuries of para-judicial practices. At the same time, in a certain sense, the mechanism has always had its advantages compared to the courts. Until relatively recently, this was the only option for solving problems that was available to most citizens. Even when there was a choice between the complaint mechanism and the trial, filing a complaint was cheaper and faster. The claimants have not needed to spend extra resources at each level of justice or to have special knowledge in the field of law. At the institutional level the late-Soviet mechanism of complaints has been autonomous from the judiciary. Simultaneously, it has never been completely isolated, which forced the general judicial practice to take into account the principles of functioning of the para-judicial mechanism. In different historical periods the complaint mechanism could move closer to the judicial system or move away from it. In any case, it normalized the ability of the executive power to interfere in matters of justice.

Mechanism of complaints has always accepted a wide range of arguments which extend far beyond the formal legal norms. Against the background of a formalized, impersonal, and "soulless" justice system, the complaint mechanism has always retained the advantages of a direct personal request, which gives a chance (even if a small one) to find empathy and sympathy besides justice. Argumentation used in complaints is never accidental. It correlates with the power discourse, it develops its own codes and formulas, forms its own field of justice, which is legitimate in the space of the complaint communication, and at the same time it can diverge from, or even contradict, the legal norms. Orientation to its own justice norms emphasizes the distinction of the mechanism from the judiciary and simultaneously the peculiarity of the function of restoring justice performed outside of the judiciary.

In Russia, a complaint to the authorities has always been associated with informality, challenging certainty, accuracy, and rationality that are necessary for successful modernization of the Western type. Mechanism of complaints, at least in the last hundred years, has always had a regulatory framework designed to govern its activities. Meanwhile, informal rules and practices are the force that put it into action and made it effective. Historically, the Russian complaint to the authorities is a mediator between formality and informality, not only connecting formal and informal rules, but also blurring the boundaries between them. This mediator is very deeply rooted in and tightly connected with the cultural and historical foundations of society. Therefore, it is very strong and effective, having survived two revolutions over the past hundred years.

While a number of the mechanism's features remain unchanged over the centuries, each era brings its own characteristics and determines the role of the mechanism in legal modernization in different ways. The complaint mechanism underwent significant changes over 70 Soviet years, which included modernization of the possibilities of protecting the rights and interests of citizens. The most momentous change is that for the first time in Russian history authorities were mandated to respond to citizens' complaints. Coupled with citizens' significantly increased literacy, this drastically enhanced most people's access to the protection of their rights and interests.

The Soviet project was neither legal nor monarchical. In a sense, it was anti-monarchist and never adhered to the principles of the rule of law. As part of the Soviet project, the Soviet version of the complaint mechanism was designed to supplant the *Tsarist* version, and this intention contributed to the modernization of the social contract between the authorities and society. From a monarchical, personalized form of interaction, provided by the Tsarist complaint bureaucracy, the Soviet mechanism moved on to interaction of citizens with institutions. The practice of complaining to the country's leaders never stopped in the Soviet epoch; however, the main request of the Soviet, and especially of the late Soviet complaint, was addressed to the relevant institution. The late-Soviet mechanism preserved an authoritarian paternalistic contract but the contract itself changed. Instead of archaic models of royal mercy, it was now based on the exchange of citizens' political loyalty and obedience for the care and protection provided by the Soviet state.

The existence of the Soviet mechanism was functionally justified. Under the Soviet approach to law, it became an important supplement to both the judiciary and the Soviet command-administrative system. With limited, always inadequate resources allocated for maintenance of the mechanism, it always performed unique functions that were not duplicated by either the judiciary or the public administration. The efficiency of the Soviet mechanism of complaints was directly related to the efficiency and stability of the system: economic, political, and social.

Since the Soviet system officially denied the principle of the separation of powers and the primacy of law, the functioning of the mechanism never entered into an overt conflict or direct dependence with the judiciary. Attempts during the late Soviet period to make the mechanism effectively contributed to its formalization. By the end of the Soviet period, the mechanism turned into a para-judicial institute. The complaint, both in how it was defined in the legislation and as it was practiced, came closer and closer to the concept of a lawsuit. The language of the Soviet complaint was never legalistic but the persistence of stock phrases used by the complainants made the form of the complaints' arguments similar to that of legal cases. So, in the late Soviet years, the complaint mechanism was showing signs of formalization and modernization.

However, one should not forget that this modernization occurred under the conditions of the Soviet system, which never pursued the tasks of legal modernization of the Western type. For the complaint mechanism, informality has always been more important than formality. However, with respect to the late Soviet complaint mechanism, one other peculiarity is true: efficiency is more important than informality, formality, or the distinction between them. The late Soviet complaint mechanism was separated from the judiciary; it was served by a complex self-sufficient bureaucratic apparatus. Communication between the authors of the complaints and the addressees was carried out through a special code system based primarily on the norms of socialist morality. However, the mechanism does not preclude legal practice and legal justifications. This is true also because the socialist morality deeply penetrated the Soviet law, and separating one from the other is not always possible. In attempts to be effective, the complaint mechanism accepted legitimate arguments based on ideological justifications, references to legal norms, and court decisions.

The late-Soviet complaint mechanism also successfully performed the function of supporting the authorities. The request for justice was formulated in the language of Soviet ideology and directed, first of all, to the institutions that generated this ideology: the organs of the Soviet government and the authority of the Communist Party. It allowed to minimize uncertainty in search of appropriate arguments and to confirm legitimacy of the acting power in each complaint.

The contemporary complaint mechanism combines features of the Soviet and the pre-revolutionary, monarchical mechanisms. Structurally the contemporary mechanism is very similar to the Soviet one, and this similarity is deliberately constructed. Some of its structural elements, such as the United Russia party, are pulled into the mechanism artificially, giving the illusion of a direct reproduction of the Soviet version. Meanwhile, the main task of the contemporary mechanism of complaints is to legitimize a sole-leader model of state ruling, which was supported by the pre-revolutionary version of the mechanism. The Soviet pattern acts as the main historical refrain (Gel'man et al. 2014), the main source of the legitimacy of the mechanism's existence in today's Russia. Because of its roots in history, the complaint mechanism legitimizes the past in general. It does not bridge the gaps between the eras, but simply offers to forget about the dramatic conflict between the post-socialist and the Soviet and between the Soviet and the monarchist. It allows bringing back features of the Soviet and monarchical rule without reviving wholesale the Soviet system or the monarchy.

The modernization of the complaint mechanism is associated with overcoming its pre-modern features. On the contrary, the modern design of the mechanism is aimed at their preservation and maintenance. The mechanism was reestablished precisely because of its archaic nature and the ability to reconstruct features of the past—both in the public administration and in the field of justice. In particular, the ability of the mechanism of complaints to legitimize informality and to define and build an authoritarian contract between the state and society on the state's terms is in demand. At the same time, the democratic possibilities of the mechanism to offer grassroots initiatives are used by the authorities from time to time, but never publicly advertised.

The contemporary complaint mechanism was not established to assist the judiciary. However, having arisen, it clearly revealed considerable achievements in the legal modernization of the first post-Soviet decades. Among them are strengthening of the institutions of law and justice, development of the practice of judicial resolution of civil and administrative issues, promotion of the principle of the separation of powers, translation of a request for justice into the language of law, and so on. Traces of all these achievements are present in the texts of complaints and in the practice of working with complaints. Meanwhile, the popularity of the complaint mechanism today also shows that post-Soviet legal reforms targeted the institutional level without significant attempts to modify the authoritarian contract between the state and society.

There is no doubt that the modern complaint mechanism is a project that supports the interests of ruling elites. The complaint mechanism exemplifies a historical institution that is successfully used to reach certain political goals in Russia today. According to Vladimir Gel'man, an appeal to the legacy is "for the most part, a social construct created and supported by ruling groups in order to maximize their own power" (Gel'man 2016: 99–100). The complaint mechanism is used purposefully to build a certain form of government. Today it is used not as a passive conductor of a dialogue between citizens and the authorities, but as an active tool influencing the format and genre of this dialogue, as a sophisticated political technology.

The contemporary mechanism is divided into two parts: functional, acting mainly at the lower levels of the executive power, and symbolic, operating at the highest levels. The symbolic is the main one, but it can hardly operate successfully without the functional part. The large functional part of the mechanism provides an important regular connection between the people and executive bodies, such as between the consumers and those responsible for providing satisfactory living conditions. It explains the existence of the complaint mechanism in contemporary Russia, supports the practice of complaining to the authorities at all the levels, and veils the tasks of the symbolic part.

The general design of the contemporary mechanism is centralized and personalized. The main addressee of complaints is not just the president as the highest official, but personally Vladimir Putin. The presidential level is assigned a special segment of complaints (security, legality, abuse of office at the highest levels of government) and special opportunities to influence their resolution. Thus, the symbolic part of the complaint mechanism supports the autocratic features of government.

The request of a contemporary complaint addressed to the authorities is formulated primarily in the language of law. The absence of a specific system of codes that provides communication between the complainants and the addressees—and which existed in the Soviet times—prevents complaints from becoming a serious alternative to the judiciary. A complaint addressed to authorities and formulated in the language of law demonstrates high uncertainty in which the authors of complaints are forced to select their arguments (Boltanski 2011:70–75). The contemporary addressees of the complaints, who are primarily the executive authorities, speak the language of law. So far, the complaint reproduces the language of law, which further confirms the legitimacy of law. As long as the complaint mechanism has no language of its own, it has no autonomy from the legal institutions and is forced to correlate its decisions with the norms of law. To strengthen the ability of intervention into justice issues, the executive branch needs weak legal institutions, or the establishment of an alternative normative system like official ideology or religious doctrine.

Obviously, the complaint mechanism cannot function in today's context in the same manner as it did in the past. Such an important foundation of autocracy as faith in the divine origin of power does not exist in contemporary Russia. Moreover, no new ideology has been successfully established that could explain the terms of the new authoritarian contract. The most stable element in the contemporary monarchical project is the figure of the president on whom both the complaint mechanism and the new authoritarian contract rely. It is noteworthy, however, that the terms of this contract have a legal dimension, including not only the political loyalty of citizens, but also their compliance with the law and respect for the rule of law, and the president's duty to guarantee citizens' rights and freedoms.

After the post-socialist reform of legal institutions the existence of a monarchical complaint mechanism gives rise to an acute conflict with the principle of the rule of law, which is established by the Russian Constitution. Historical experience shows that autocracy and legality, guaranteed by a judicial institution that protects the primacy of subjective rights, are incompatible (Pravilova 2000:141). It creates a hybrid, which requires a constant compromise between the rule of law and the power of the first person in the state.

The practice of dealing with complaints at this stage of the complaint mechanism development demonstrates attempts to ease this conflict. The complaint mechanism today is structured in such a way that its interventions in the sphere of justice and the sphere of governance can potentially be very significant. However, how the complaint mechanism functions shows that the authorities hold back its possibilities. They take the principle of the separation of powers seriously and try not to allow overt violation of it. They also, especially at the lower levels of the mechanism, make efforts to comply with this principle. The law does not permit to complain to the authorities against a court decision (Law No. 59 2006, Art. 11.2), and the authorities try to comply with this norm also. Such appeals are often found among complaints addressed to the chairman of the United Russia party or to the president; however, the addressees avoid interfering in such complaints publicly. The practice of working with complaints at different levels of the mechanism shows that today the authorities are not trying to replace the legal system with para-judicial instruments like the mechanism of complaints. All these things suggest that Russia does not abandon legal modernization in general. However, the successful parallel development in both directions is hardly possible. It means that some compromise between the rule of law and the turn towards autocracy must be achieved. This compromise determines the new Russian legal modernization project, which includes both legality and informality.

With notable efforts to smooth out the conflict, a devastating impact on law still occurs. The authorities must be able to control something that is not controlled by the law in order to demonstrate their indispensability and omnipotence in the conditions of the declared rule of law. After the legal modernization of the 1990s, the scope of issues not regulated by law significantly diminished. The authorities have two ways of strengthening their position, both of which are harmful to legal modernization and to the legal system as a whole. The first is the weakening of legal institutions and their ability to restore justice. The second is the expansion of the space of uncertainty, blurring the boundaries between the formal and the informal, the legal and the illegal. Under such conditions, the complaint mechanism can work efficiently but the judiciary cannot. To strengthen the position of the authorities, it is beneficial to recognize informality, admit it, normalize and usurp the function of control over it. Complaints are the traditional tools of informal governance (Ledeneva 2012:23), and strengthening of the complaint mechanism means strengthening of informal governance itself—and of the informal part of the modernization project.

References

Boltanski, Luc. 2011. *On Critique: A Sociology of Emancipation.* Cambridge: Polity Press.

Federal Law "On the Order of Consideration of Citizens' Applications in the Russian Federation" [Federal'nyi zakon "O poriadke rassmotreniia obrashchenii grazhdan Rossiiskoi Federatsii"] from 2 May 2006 No. 59-FZ. *KonsultantPlus.* Retrieved on July 19, 2019 (http://www.consultant.ru/cons/cgi/online.cgi?req¼doc&ts¼56845078202006210516992326&caheid¼6341A834A0DF5BBDFF43BE44B12D34E5&mode¼splus&base¼LAW&n¼283578&rn¼E1CB8E44A90433FE7135F1A230170A07#09858153796272937).

Gel'man, Vladimir. 2016. "Politicheskie osnovaniia 'nedostoinogo pravleniia' v postsovetskoi Evrazii. Pereosmyslivaia issledovatel'skuiu povestku dnia." *Politiia* 3(82):90–115.

Gel'man, Vladimir, Marganiya, Otar and Dmitrii Travin. 2014. *Reexamining Economic and Political Reforms in Russia, 1985—2000: Generations, Ideas, and Changes.* Lanham, MD: Carlisle.

Ledeneva, Alena. 2012. "Sistema—Russia's informal system of power." Pp. 17–27 in: Katynka Barysch (ed.) *Three views on modernization and the rule of law in Russia.* Published by Centre for European Reform. Retrieved on July 19, 2019 (http://www.cer.org.uk/sites/default/files/publications/attachments/pdf/2012/e_3views_russia_23jan12-4553.pdf).

Pravilova, Ekaterina. 2000. *Zakonnost' i prava lichnosti: administrativnaia iustitsiia v Rossii (vtoraia polovina XIX v.- oktiabr' 1927 g.)* Saint Petersburg: Institut Rossiiskoi Istorii RAN.

Appendices

Appendix 1

Number of court appeals in civil, criminal cases and to courts of general jurisdiction and to The Justices of The Peace (without military courts) 1995–2018.[1]

	Civil cases	*Criminal cases*	*Administrative offenses*	*Total*
1995	2,806,600	1,074,900	1,927,300	5,808,800
1996	3,057,900	1,198,700	1,923,000	6,179,900
1997	3,881,600	1,056,400	1,879,500	6,817,500
1998	4,751,900	1,137,200	1,813,400	7,702,500
1999	5,012,000	1,271,200	1,824,800	8,108,000
2000	5,057,400	1,330,500	1,464,300	7,852,200
2001	4,923,900	1,364,000	1,498,700	7,786,600
2002	4,987,500	1,048,000	1,934,700	7,970,200
2003	5,194,800	970,000	3,272,100	9,436,900
2004	5,831,500	1,042,800	4,205,600	11,079,900
2005	6,741,200	1,148,200	4,287,600	12,177,000
2006	7,563,900	1,224,900	5,004,800	13,793,600
2007	9,019,839	1,170,546	5,553,466	15,743,851
2008	10,621,941	1,124,006	5,414,819	17,160,766
2009	13,375,770	1,102,269	5,650,949	20,128,988
2010	14,122,200	1,064,538	5,326,878	20,513,616
2011	12,686,552	989,231	5,321,537	18,997,320
2012	10,306,700	947,647	5,742,442	16,996,789
2013	12,903,316	946,474	5,820,950	19,670,740
2014	13,935,450	936,771	6,460,861	21,333,082
2015	15,928,860	966,416	6,617,317	23,512,593
2016	12,778,069	954,255	6,419,802	20,152,126
2017	14,517,997	915,716	6,540,003	21,973,716
2018	17,270,149	883,993	7,055,780	25,209,922

Data of the Judicial Department at the Supreme Court of the Russian Federation www.cdep.ru/index .php?id=79&pg=1

Appendix 2

Details about Informants

	Code	*Gender*	*Year of birth*	*Period of treatment with the mechanism of complaints/work in the bureaucracy of the mechanism of complaints*	*Cases/Positions*
1.	S.V.	M.	1945	1965–1975	Regular complaints to different authorities
2.	B.B.	F.	1953	1959	Personal experience of complaining and description of the mother's experience.
3.	A.F.	F.	1951	1979	Complaining on housing issues
4.	P.P.	F.	1949	1969	Multiple complaints on public transport issues
5.	L.R.	F.	1950	1970s	Complaints to different authorities on consumption issues
6.	V.A.	F.	1955	1977–1990	Merchandise specialist in a department store
7.	T.M.	F.	1948	1972–1978	An employee of the complaints department at 'Household appliances repair' *(Rembyttekhnika)*
8.	V.D.	F.	1946	1968–2006	Editor of the letters department at the newspaper *Leningradskaia Pravda/Saint Petersburg Vedomosti*
9.	J.P.	M.	1919	1957–1973	People's deputy
10.	G.N.	M.	1949	2010–present	Head of regional public reception offices of the party United Russia
11.	A.V.	M.	1957	2015–present	Head of regional public reception offices of the party United Russia
12.	V.V.	M.	1965	2013–present	Head of regional public reception offices of the party United Russia
13.	K.M.		1956	2005–2015	Employee of local house management service
14.	U.N.	F.	1986	2014–present	Employee of the complaints department at local Housing and Public Utility Service
15.	I.M.	F	1954	2012	Personal experience of complaining
16.	O.L.	F	1978	2010–2018	Personal experience of complaining
17.	D.B.	M.	1969	2015	Personal experience of complaining

Bibliography

Alekseev, Sergei. 1981. *Obshchaia teoriia prava*. Vol.1. Moscow: Iuridicheskaia literatura.

Almbjär, Martin. 2019. "The Problem with Early-Modern Petitions: Safety Valve or Powder Keg?" *European Review of History* 26(6):1013–1039.

Arnason, Johann. 2002. "Communism and Modernity." Pp. 61–90 in Shnuel Eisenstadt (ed.) *Multiple Modernities*. London: Transaction Publishing.

Bannikov, Gennadii. 2016. "Praktika rassmotreniia ugolovnykh del o prestupleniiakh so zloupotrebleniem i prevysheniem dolzhnostnymi polnomochiiami (stat'i 285 i 286 UK RF)." *Penzenskii oblastnoi sud*. Retrieved on July 19, 2019 (http://www.oblsud.penza.ru/item/a/1170/).

Barry, Donald. 1978. "Administrative Justice and Judicial Review in Soviet Administrative Law." Pp. 241–270 in Donald Barry, George Ginsburgs and Peter Maggs (eds.) *Soviet Law After Stalin: Soviet Institutions and the Administration of Law*. Alphen aan den Rijn: A. W. Sijthoff.

Barry, Donald. 1989. "Administrative Justice: The Role of Soviet Courts in Controlling Administrative Acts." Pp. 63–80 in George Ginsburgs (ed.) *Soviet Administrative Law: Theory and Policy*. Dordrecht: Martinus Sijthoff.

Baum, Richard. 1986. "Modernization and Legal Reform in Post-Mao China: The Rebirth of Socialist Legality." *Studies in Comparative Communism* 19(2):69–103.

Blankenburg, Erhard. 1980. "Möbilisierung von Recht." *Zeitschrift für Rechtssoziologie* 1(1):33–64.

Blankenburg, Erhard, Schönholz, Siegfried and Ralf Rogowski. 1979. *Zur Soziologie des Arbeitsgerichtsverfahrens*. Darmstadt: Luchterhand.

Bogdanova, Elena. 2003."Konstruirovanie Problemy Zashchity prav potrebitelei. Retrospektivnyi analiz." *Rubezh. Al'manakh sotsial'nykh issledovanii* 18:80-94.

Bogdanova, Elena. 2006. "Traditziia pravovoi zashchity ili 'v ozhidanii zaboty'." *Zhurnal sotsiologii i sotsial'noi antropologii* 9(1):77–90.

Bogdanova, Elena. 2014. "Religious Justifications of Complaints, Addressed to the President in Contemporary Russia." *Laboratorium: Russian Review of Social Research* 3:55–79.

Bogdanova, Elena. 2015. "The Soviet Consumer – More Than Just a Soviet Man." Pp. 113–138 in Timo Vihavainen and Elena Bogdanova (eds.) *Communism and Consumerism. The Soviet Alternative to the Affluent Society*. Leiden and Boston: Brill.

Boim, Leon. 1974. "Ombudsmanship in the Soviet Union." *American Journal of Comparative Law* XXII:509–540.

Boim, Leon. 1978. "Introduction." Pp. vii–xvi in Leon Boim and Glenn Morgan (eds.) *The Soviet Procuracy Protests, 1937–1973 : A Collection of Translations*. Leiden: Alphen aan den Rijn: Sijthoff & Noordhoff.

Boltanski, Luc. 2011. *On Critique: A Sociology of Emancipation*. Cambridge: Polity Press.

Boltanski, Luc and Laurent Thévenot. 2000. "The Reality of Moral Expectations: A Sociology of Situated Judgement." *Philosophical Explorations* 3:208–231.

Bowen, Glenn. 2009. "Document Analysis as a Qualitative Research Method." *Qualitative Research Journal* 9(2):27–40.

Buliulina, Elena. 2010. "'Zhalobshchiki' i 'udruchionnye': o rabote s zaiavleniiami grazhdan v raboche-krestianskoi inspektsii v 1919–1920-e gg." *Istoriia Rossii* 2:98–105.

Burbank, Jane. 2004. *Russian Peasants Go to Court: Legal Culture in the Countryside, 1905–1917*. Bloomington: Indiana University Press.

Burg, Elliot. 1977. "Law and Development: A Review of the Literature and Critique of 'Scholars in Self- Estrangement'." *American Journal of Comparative Law* 25:492–530.

Bystritskaia, Tatiana. 2018. "V Murmanskoi oblasti ot zapushchennogo raka umiraiut vsio chashche. Sluchai Dar'i Starikovoi nichego ne izmenil." *Novaia Gazeta No. 54*, May 25. Retrieved on July 3, 2019 (https://www.novayagazeta.ru/articles/2018/05/25/76597-meditsine-stavyat-diagnoz).

Cambridge Dictionary. Petition. Retrieved on June 30, 2019 (https://dictionary.cambridge.org/ru/словарь/английский/petition).

Chechot, Dmitrii. 1973. *Administrativnaia Iustitsiia. Teoreticheskie problemy*. Leningrad: Izdatel'stvo Leningradskogo Universiteta.

Christiansen, Thomas and Christine Neuhold. 2012. *International Handbook on Informal Governance*. Cheltenham Glos: Edward Elgar.

Cieślewska, Anna. 2014. "From Shuttle Trade to Businesswomen: The Informal Bazaar Economy in Kyrgyzstan." Pp. 120–134 in Jeremy Morris and Abel Polese (eds.) *The Informal Post-Socialist Economy. Embedded Practices and Livelihoods*. London: Routledge.

Cook, Linda and Martin Dimitrov. 2017. "The Social Contract Revisited: Evidence from Communist and State Capitalist Economies." *Europe-Asia Studies*, Special Section: Authoritarian Powers: Russia and China Compared 69(1):8–26.

Creutzfeldt-Banda, Naomi. 2013. "The Origins and Evolution of Consumer Dispute Resolution Systems in Europe." Pp 228–252 in Christopher Hodges and Astrid Stadler (eds.) *Resolving Mass Disputes*. Northampton: Edward Elgar.

Dal', Vladimir. 1996[1863]. *Tolkovyi slovar' zhivogo velikorusskogo iazyka v 4 tomakh. Tom 1*. Zhaloba. SPb: Diamant.

Dannye sudebnoi statistiki. 2011–2017. *Ofitsial'nyi sait Sudebnogo departamenta pri Verkhovnom Sude RF*. Retrieved on July 19, 2019 (http://www.cdep.ru/index.php?id=79).

Data on the Number of Written and Oral Complaints by the Citizens between December 1, 2017 and December 31, 2017 [Svedeniia o kolichestve postupivshikh pis'mennykh i ustnykh obrashchenii grazhdan s 1 dekabria 2017 g. po 31 dekabria 2017 g. *Pravitel'stvo Rossii*. Retrieved on July 19, 2019 (http://static.government.ru/media/files/NNb7RkGpdlvuiI89tECtAn6cQ1MRiPxa.pdf).

De Bruijn, Hans and Hans Hufen. 1998. "The Traditional Approach to Policy Instruments." Pp. 11–33 in Guy Peters and Frans van Nispen (eds.) *Public Policy Instruments: Evaluating the Tools of Public Administration*. Cheltemham: Edward Elgar.

Dimitrov, Martin. 2013. "Vertical Accountability in Communist Regimes: The Role of Citizens Complaints in Bulgaria and China." Pp. 276–303 in Martin Dimitrov (ed.) *Why*

Communism Did Not Collapse: Understanding Authoritarian Regime Resilience in Asia and Europe. Cambridge: Cambridge University Press.
Dimitrov, Martin, Gandhi, Jennifer and Adam Przeworski. 2007. "Authoritarian Institutions and the Survival of Autocrats." *Comparative Political Studies* 40(11):1279–1301.
Doklad Upolnomochennogo po pravam cheloveka za 2014 god. 2015. *Apparat Upolnomochennogo po pravam cheloveka*. Moscow. Retrieved on July 19, 2019 (http://ombudsmanrf.org/upload/files/docs/appeals/doklad2014.pdf).
Doklad Upolnomochennogo po pravam cheloveka za 2015 god. 2016. *Apparat Upolnomochennogo po pravam cheloveka*. Moscow. Retrieved on July 19, 2019 (http://ombudsmanrf.org/www/upload/files/docs/appeals/doclad2015web.pdf).
Doklad Upolnomochennogo po pravam cheloveka za 2017 god. 2018. *Apparat Upolnomochennogo po pravam cheloveka*. Moscow. Retrieved on July 19, 2019 (http://ombudsmanrf.org/upload/files/docs/lib/lite2-doclad_20.04.18.pdf).
Drew, Paul and Elizabeth Holt. 1988. "Complainable Matters: The Use of Idiomatic Expressions in Making Complaints." *Social Problems* 35(4):398–417.
Ellis, Frank. 1998. "The Media as Social Engineer." Pp. 192–223 in Catriona Kelly and David Shepherd (eds.) *Russian Cultural Studies. An Introduction*. Oxford: Oxford University Press.
European Consumer Law Group. 2001. *Soft Law and the Consumer Interest*. ECLG/071/2001 – March. Retrieved on September 20, 2013 (http://ec.europa.eu/consumers/policy/eclg/rep03_en.pdf).
Evan, Alfred B. Jr. 2008. *Power and Ideology: Vladimir Putin and the Russian Political System*. William Chase Bob Donnorummo and Ronald H. Linden (eds.) The Carl Beck Papers. No. 1902, January.
Fair Trading Act. 1986. *Consumer New Zealand*. Retrieved on September 19, 2019 (https://www.consumer.org.nz/articles/fair-trading-act).
Fel'dman, David. 2006. *Terminologiia vlasti. Sovetskie politicheskie terminy v istoriko-kul'turnom kontekste*. Moscow: RGGU.
Fitzpatrick, Sheila. 1996a. "Signals from Below: Soviet Letters of Denunciation of the 1930s." *Journal of Modern History* 68(4):831–866.
Fitzpatrick, Sheila. 1996b. *Stalin's Peasants: Resistance and Survival in the Russian Village after Collectivization*. Oxford: Oxford University Press.
Flick, Uwe. 2010. *An Introduction to Qualitative Research*. London: SAGE.
Frajman, Eduardo. 2014. "Broadcasting Populist Leadership: Hugo Chávez and Aló Presidente." *Journal of Latin American Studies* 46(03):501–526.
Friedgut, Theodore. 1978. "Citizens and Soviets: Can Ivan Ivanovich Fight City Hall?" *Comparative Politics* 10(4):461–477, 466.
Friedgut, Theodore. 1979. *Political Participation in the USSR*. Princeton: Princeton University Press.
Galanter, Marc. 1983. "Reading the Landscape of Disputes: What We Know and Don't Know (And Think We Know) About Our Allegedly Contentious and Litigious Society." *UCLA Law Review* 31(4):5–72.
Gavrilko, Aleksei, Alekseenko, Filipp and Iuliia Sapronova. 2017. "Lineinaia funktsiia: k chemu privodili zhaloby Putinu vo vremia priamoi linii." *RBC*. Retrieved on July 19, 2019 (https://www.rbc.ru/photoreport/27/06/2017/59523ff49a7947d7f047ad1d).
Gel'man, Vladimir. 2016. "Politicheskie osnovaniia 'nedostoinogo pravleniia' v postsovetskoi Evrazii. Pereosmyslivaia issledovatel'skuiu povestku dnia." *Politiia* 3(82):90–115.

Gel'man, Vladimir, Marganiya, Otar and Dmitrii Travin. 2014. *Reexamining Economic and Political Reforms in Russia, 1985—2000: Generations, Ideas, and Changes*. Lanham, MD: Carlisle.

Giddens, Anthony. 1984. *The Constitution of Society. Outline of the Theory of Structuration*. Cambridge: Camgridge University Press.

Gilligan, Emma. 2010. "The Human Rights Ombudsman in Russia: The Evolution of Horizontal Accountability." *Human Rights Quarterly* 32(3):575–600.

Gitelman, Zvi and Wayne DiFrancesco. 1984. "Soviet Political Culture and Covert Political Participation." *American Political Science Review* 78:603–621.

Golik, Nina 2007. "Kharakteristika obrashchenii grazhdan v Konstitutsionnyi sud RF." *Rossiiskaia iustitsiia* 10:64.

Gorlizki, Yoram. 1998. "Delegalization in Russia: Soviet Comrades' Courts in Retrospect." *The American Journal of Comparative Law* 46(3):403–425.

Grekov, Alexander. 1931. *...Kuda, na chto i kak zhalovat'sia*. Leningrad: Tekhnika upravleiia.

Grushin, Boris. 2003. *Chetyre zhizni Rossii v zerkale oprosov obshchestvennogo mneniia: epokha Brezhneva*. Moscow: Progress-Traditsiia.

Halfin, Igal and, Jochen Hellbeck 2002. "Interview." *Ab Imperio* 3:217–260.

Hendley, Kathryn. 1997. "Legal Development in Post-Soviet Russia." *Post-Soviet Affairs* 13(3):228–251.

Hendley, Kathryn. 2017. *Everyday Law in Russia*. Ithaca: Cornell University Press.

Henry, Laura. 2012. "Complaint-Making as Political Participation in Contemporary Russia." *Communist and Post-Communist Studies* 3–4(45):243–254.

Informatsionno-statisticheskii obzor rassmotrennykh v 2015 godu obrashchenii grazhdan, organizatsii i obshchestvennykh ob'edinenii, adresovannykh Presidentu RF, a takzhe rezul'tatov rassmotreniia i priniatykh mer. 2015. *Ofitsial'nyi sait Upravleniia Presidenta po rabote s obrashcheniiami grazhdan i organizatsyi*. Retrieved on July 19, 2019 (http://static.kremlin.ru/media/letters/digests//e3CBXTdHrNoeAcHpNAsRVlIgvCpOGyub.pdf).

Informatsionno-statisticheskii obzor rassmotrennykh v 2016 godu obrashchenii grazhdan, organizatsii i obshchestvennykh ob'edinenii, adresovannykh Presidentu RF, a takzhe rezul'tatov rassmotreniia i priniatykh mer. 2016. *Ofitsial'nyi sait Upravleniia Presidenta po rabote s obrashcheniiami grazhdan i organizatsyi*. Retrieved on July 19, 2019 (http://static.kremlin.ru/media/letters/digests//tH3Miwovxt39aWMgvUb6rfc8zx79yySv.pdf).

Informatsionno-statisticheskii obzor rassmotrennykh v 2017 godu obrashchenii grazhdan, organizatsii i obshchestvennykh ob'edinenii, adresovannykh Presidentu RF, a takzhe rezul'tatov rassmotreniia i priniatykh mer. 2017. *Ofitsial'nyi sait Upravleniia Presidenta po rabote s obrashcheniiami grazhdan i organizatsyi*. Retrieved on July 19, 2019 (http://static.kremlin.ru/media/letters/digests//UBHnFDfwnQmlPQvOknupXuVfe7eCMs7c.pdf).

Informatsionno-statisticheskii obzor rassmotrennykh v 2018 godu obrashchenii grazhdan, organizatsii i obshchestvennykh ob'edinenii, adresovannykh Presidentu RF, a takzhe rezul'tatov rassmotreniia i priniatykh mer. 2018. *Ofitsial'nyi sait Upravleniia Presidenta po rabote s obrashcheniiami grazhdan i organizatsyi*. Retrieved on July 19, 2019 (http://static.kremlin.ru/media/letters/digests//76kvGYZr1ErA2dpiIAHLozITaTXnjhrY.pdf).

Ingulov, Sergei. 1928. *Samokritika i praktika eio provedeniia*. Moscow: Gosizdatel'stvo.

Iz Saratova cherez Penzu. Peshii pokhod k prezidentu Rossii. 2016. *Argumenty i fakty*, 26, June 29. Retrieved on July 15, 2019 (http://www.penza.aif.ru/society/iz_saratova_cherez_penzu_peshiy_pohod_k_prezidentu_rossii).

Izvestiia. 1988. June 29, 2, col. 1.

Jacobsson, Kerstin. 2001. "Employment and Social Policy Coordination. A New System of EU Governance." Paper for the Scancor workshop on *"Transnational regulation and the transformation of states."* June 22–23. Stanford.

Jacobsson, Kerstin. 2002. *Soft Regulation and the Subtle Transformation of States: The Case of EU Employment Policy*. Retrieved on 19 July 2019 (https://www.score.su.se/polopoly_fs/1.26588.1320939800!/20024.pdf).

Kabashov, Sergei. 2010. *Organizatsiia raboty s obrashcheniiami grazhdan v istorii Rossii*. Moscow: Flinta.

Kerimov, Dzhangir. 1956. *Obespechenie zakonnosti v SSSR*. Moscow: Gosiurizdat.

Khamaneva, Nataliia. 1997. *Zashchita prav grazhdan v sphere ispolnitel'noi vlasti*. Moscow: IGPRAN.

Khamaneva, Nataliia and Nadezhda Salishcheva. 2001. *Administrativnaia iustitsiia i administrativnoe sudoproizvodstvo v Rossiiskoi Federatsii*. Moscow: IGPRAN.

Kivinen, Markku. 2006. "Classes in the Making? Russian Social Structure in Transition." Pp. 247–294 in Goran Therborn (ed.) *Inequalities of the World. New Theoretical Frameworks, Multiple Empirical Approaches*. London: Verso.

Kivinen, Markku. 2009. "Russian Societal Development: Challenges Open." Pp. 112–144 in Hiski Haukkala and Sari Sinikukka (eds.) *Russia, Lost or Found*. Helsinki: Edita: Ministry of Foreign Affairs in Finland.

Kivinen, Markku. 2013. "Interdisciplinary Approach to Russian Modernization." *Zhurnal sotsiologii i sotsial'noi antropologii* 4:12–28.

Knudsen, Ida Harboe. 2014. "The Story of Šarūnas: An Invisible Citizen of Lithuania." Pp. 35–51 in Jeremy Morris and Abel Polese (eds.) *The Informal Post-Socialist Economy. Embedded Practices and Livelihoods*. London: Routledge.

Korniushenkov, Gennadii. 2004. "Dopustimost' obrashchenii grazhdan v konstitutsionnye (ustavnye) sudy sub"ektov Rossiiskoi Federatsii." *Rossiiskii sud'ia* 11:36–41.

Kotkin, Stephen. 1995. *Magnetic Mountain: Stalinism as a Civilization*. Berkeley: University of California Press.

Koveneva, Olga. 2007. "Grani opyta v svete amerikanskogo pragmatizma." *Chelovek, Soobshchestvo. Upravlenie* 4:39–63.

Kozlov, Iurii. 1959. *Priem i rassmotrenie zhalob i zaiavlenii trudiashchikhsia v organakh sovetskogo gosudarstvennogo upravleniia*. Moscow: Gosiurizdat.

Kozlova, Natal'ia and Irina Sandomirskaia. 1996. *Ia tak khochu nazvat' kino: "Naivnoe pis'mo": Opyt lingvo-sotsiologicheskogo chteniia*. Moscow: Gnozis.

Kudriavtsev, Petr (ed.). 1956. *Iuridicheskii slovar'*. T.2. Pravovoe gosudarstvo. Moskow: Gosiurizdat.

Kulikov, Vladimir. 2003. *Istoriia gosudarstvennogo upravleniia v Rossii*. Moscow: ACADEMIA.

Lampert, Nicholas. 1985. *Whistle-Blowing in the Soviet Union Complaints and Abuses under State Socialism*. London: Palgrave McMillan.

Lebow, Katherine. 2014. "Autobiography as Complaint: Polish Social Memoir between the World Wars." *Laboratorium: Russian Review of Social Research* 6(3):13–26.

Ledeneva, Alena. 1997. "Lichnye sviazi i neformal'nye soobshchestva: Transformatsiia blata v postsovetskom obshchestve." *Mir Rossii* 2:89–106.

Ledeneva, Alena. 1998. *Russia's Economy of Favours*. Cambridge: Cambridge University Press.

Ledeneva, Alena. 2008. "Telephone Justice in Russia." *Post-Soviet Affairs* 24(4):324–350.

Ledeneva, Alena. 2012. "*Sistema*—Russia's Informal System of Power." Pp. 17–27 in Katynka Barysch (ed.) *Three Views on Modernisation and the Rule of Law in Russia*.

Published by Centre for European Reform. Retrieved on July 19, 2019 (http://www.cer.org.uk/sites/default/files/publications/attachments/pdf/2012/e_3views_russia_23jan12-4553.pdf).
Lenin, Vladimir. 1969a[1918]. "Ocherednye zadachi sovetskoi vlasti." Pp. 127–166 in *Polnoe sobranie sochinenii. T. 36*. Moscow: Izdatel'stvo politicheskoi literatury.
Lenin, Vladimir. 1969b[1918]. "Nabrosok tezisov o tochnom sobliudenii zakonov ot 2 noiabria 1918." Pp. 129–131 in *Polnoe sobranie sochinenii. T. 47*. Moscow: Izdatel'stvo politicheskoi literatury.
Lenin, Vladimir. 1970[1922]. "O 'dvoinom' podchinenii i zakonnosti." Pp. 197–202 in *Polnoe sobranie sochinenii. T. 45*. Moscow: Izdatel'stvo politicheskoi literatury.
Lenin, Vladimir. 1973. "Nabrosok pravil ob upravlenii sovetskimi uchrezhdeniiami." Pp. 366–367 in *Collected Works* Vol. 37. Moscow: Politizdat.
Levada, Iurii (ed.). 1993. *Sovetskii prostoi chelovek: opyt sotsial'nogo portreta na rubezhe 90-kh*. Moscow: Mirovoi okean.
Levitsky, Serge. 1990. "The Restructuring of Perestroika: Pragmatism and Ideology (The Preamble to the Soviet Constitution of 1977 Revisited)." *Cornell International Law Journal* 23:227–230.
Lipman, Maria. 2015. "Putin's 'Besieged Fortress' and Its Ideological Arms." Pp. 110–136 in Maria Lipman and Nikolai Petrov (eds.) *The State of Russia: What Comes Next?* London: Palgrave Pivot.
Lobacheva, Galina. 1999. *Samoderzhets i Rossiia: obraz tsaria v massovom soznanii rossiian (konets XIX- nachalo XX vv.)*. Saratov: Saratovskii gosudarstvennyi technicheskii universitet.
Lozansky, Tanya. 1989. "The Role of the Dissident in the Soviet Union Since 1953." *The Concord Review Inc.* 2/1:7–8.
Lukach, Georg. 2004. "Rol' morali v kommunisticheskom proizvodstve." Pp. 449–455 in *Moral' v politike. Khrestomatiia*. Moscow: Izdatel'stvo Moskovskogo Universiteta.
Magnette, Paul. 2003. "Between parliamentary control and the rule of law: The political role of the Ombudsman in the European Union." *Journal of European Public Policy* 5(10):677–694.
Manov, Grigorii. 1989. "Sotsialisticheskoe pravovoe gosudarstvo: Problemy i perspektivy." *Sovetskoe Gosudarstvo i parvo* 3:3–10.
Markevich, Andrei. 2002. *Soldatskie pis'ma v tsentral'nye sovety kak istochnik dlia izucheniia obshchestvennykh nastroenii v armii 1917 g*. Moscow: Avtoreferat na soiskanie stepeni kandidata istoricheskikh nauk.
Markovits, Inga. 1986. "Pursuing One's Rights under Socialism." *Stanford Law Review* 38(3):689–761.
Markovits, Inga. 2007. "The Death of Socialist Law?" *Annual Review of Law and Social Science* 3, December:465–511.
Marx, Karl. 1970[1875]. "Critique of the Goths program." Pp. 13–30 in Marx Karl and Engels Friedrich. *Selected Works*, Vol. 3. Moscow: Progress Publishers.
Merl, Stephan. 2012. *Politische Kommunikation in der Diktatur: Deutschland und die Sowjetunion im Vergleich*. Göttingen, Germany: Wallstein.
Mertz, Elizabeth. 1996." Recontextualization as Socialization: Text and Pragmatics in the Law School Classroom." Pp. 229–249 in Michael Silverstein and Greg Urban (eds.) *Natural Histories of Discourse*. Chicago: University of Chicago Press.
Minzner, Carl F. 2006. "Xinfang: An Alternative to Formal Chinese Legal Institutions." *Stanford Journal of International Law* 42:103–180.

Mironov, Boris. 2003. *Sotsial'naia istoriia Rossii perioda imperii (XVIII – nachalo XX v.): v 2-kh tomakh.* T.2. Saint Petersburg: Dmitrii Bulanin.

Mironov, Mikhail. 2001. *"Obrashcheniia grazhdan kak element sistemy zashchity prav cheloveka i osnovnykh svobod: pravo i praktika.* Moscow: Iuridicheskaia literatura.

Mistelis, Loukas. 2006. "ADR in England and Wales: A successful case of public private partnership." Pp. 139–180 in Nadja Alexander (ed.) *Global Trends in Mediation* (2nd edition). Alphen aan den Rijn: Kluwer Law International.

Mommsen, Margareta. 1987. *Hilf mir, mein Recht zu finden. Russische Bittschriften von Iwan dem Schrecklichen bis Gorbatschow.* Frankfurt am Main: Ullstein.

Moral'nyi kodeks stroitelia kommunizma. Posobie dlia propagandistov i slushatelei sistemy politicheskogo prosveshcheniia. 1965. Moscow: Politizdat.

Morgan, Glenn. 1966. "The Protests and Representations Lodged by the Soviet Procuracy against the Legality of Governmental Enactments: 1937–1964." Pp. 103–289 in Leon Boim, Glenn Morgan, and Alexander Rudzinski (eds.) *Legal Control in the Soviet Union.* Alphen aan Den Rijn: Sijthoff and Noordhoff.

Morris, Jeremy, and Abel Polese. 2014. "Introduction: Informality—Enduring Practices, Entwined Livelihood." Pp. 1–18 in Jeremy Morris and Abel Polese (eds.) *The Informal Post-Socialist Economy. Embedded Practices and Livelihoods.* London: Routledge.

Nechepurenko, Ivan. 2016. "Russia's New Human Rights Ombudsman is Former Police General." *The New York Times.* April 22. Retrieved on July 19, 2019 (https://www.nytimes.com/2016/04/23/world/europe/russias-new-human-rights-ombudsman-is-former-police-general.html).

Nérard, François-Xavier. 2004. *Cinq pour cent de vérité: La dénonciation dans l'URSS de Staline (1928–1941).* Paris: Editions Tallandier.

Nikolaeva, Liubov'. 1960. "Zadachi i metody deiatel'nosti Komissii sovetskogo kontrolia Soveta Ministrov SSSR." *Pravovedenie* 3:15–24.

North, Douglass. 1990. *Institutions, Institutional Change and Economic Performance.* New York: Cambridge University Press.

Oda, Hiroshi. 1984. "Judicial Review of the Administration in the Countries of Eastern Europe." *Public Law* 29:112–34.

Online Etymology Dictionary. Complaint. Retrieved on June 30, 2019 (http://www.etymonline.com/index.php?allowed_in_frame=0&search=complaint).

Orlova, Galina. 2004. "Rossiiskii donos i ego metamorfozy: Zametki o poetike politicheskoi kommunikatsii." *Polis* 2:133–145.

Otchet o rabote sudov obshchei iurisdiktsii po rassmotreniiu ugolovnykh del po pervoi instantsii za 2015g. 2015a. *Ofitsial'nyi sait Sudebnogo Departamenta pri Verkhovnom Sude RF.* Retrieved on July 19, 2019 (http://www.cdep.ru/index.php?id=79&item=3417).

Otchet o rabote sudov obshchei iurisdiktsii po rassmotreniiu grazhdanskikh, administrativnykh del po pervoi instantsii za 2015g. 2015b. *Ofitsial'nyi sait Sudebnogo Departamenta pri Verkhovnom Sude RF.* Retrieved on July 19, 2019 (http://www.cdep.ru/index.php?id=79&item=3417).

Otchet o rabote sudov obshchei iurisdiktsii po rassmotreniiu grazhdanskikh, administrativnykh del po pervoi instantsii za 2016g. 2016a. *Ofitsial'nyi sait Sudebnogo Departamenta pri Verkhovnom Sude RF.* Retrieved on July 19, 2019 (http://www.cdep.ru/index.php?id=79&item=3832).

Oxford Dictionary. Complaint. Retrieved on June 30, 2019 (https://en.oxforddictionaries.com/definition/complaint).

Oxford Dictionary. Petition. Retrieved on June 30, 2019 (https://en.oxforddictionaries.com/definition/petition).
Panarin, Igor. 2012. "Post-Election Russia: Putin's New Ideology." *RT*. April 20. Retrieved on February 20, 2013 (http://rt.com/politics/russia-putin-ideology-panarin-535/).
Parsons, Talcott. 1939. "The Professions and Social Structure." *Social Forces* 17(4):457–467.
Parsons, Talcott. 1964. "Evolutionary Universals in Society." *American Sociological Review* 29(3):339–357.
Parsons, Talcott. 1971. *The System of Modern Societies*. Englewood Cliffs: Prentice-Hall.
Pecherskaya, Natalia. 2012. "Looking for Justice: The Everyday Meaning of Justice in Late Soviet Russia." *Anthropology of East Europe Review* 30(2):20–38.
Pipes, Richard. 1977. *Russia under the Old Regime*. Harmondsworth: Penguin.
Polese, Abel, Morris, Jeremy and Borbála Kovács. 2016. "'State' of Informality in Post-Socialist Europe (and beyond)." *Journal of Contemporary Central and Eastern Europe* 24(3):181–190.
Pravda. 1981. April 4:1.
Pravilova, Ekaterina. 2000. *Zakonnost' i prava lichnosti: Administrativnaia iustitsiia v Rossii (vtoraia polovina XIX v.- oktiabr' 1927 g.)* Saint Petersburg: Institut Rossiiskoi Istorii RAN.
Pyzhikov, Aleksandr. 2001. "Vnutripartiinaia bor'ba i evoliutsiia sistemy vlasti (1953–1957)." *Vestnik Rossiiskoi Akademii Nauk* 71(3):246–251.
Quigley, John. 1990. "The Soviet Union as a State under the Rule of Law: An Overview." *Cornell International Law Journal* 23(2):205-225.
Quigley, John. 2007. *Soviet Legal Innovation and the Law of the Western World*. New York: Cambridge University Press.
Rassmotrenie sudami obshchei iurisdiktsii del i materialov za 2010–2017 gg. 2018. *Ofitsial'nyi sait Sudebnogo departamenta pri Verkhovnom Sude RF*. Retrieved on July 19, 2019 (http://www.cdep.ru/index.php?id=79).
Remnev, Anatolii. 1997. *Kantseliariia proshenii v samoderzhavnoi sisteme pravleniia kontsa XIX stoletiia. Istoricheskii ezhegodnik*. Omsk: Omskii Universitet.
Report on handling citizens' complaints by the executive authorities of Saint Petersburg in 2017 [Otchiot o rabote s obrashcheniiami grazhdan v ispolnitel'nykh organakh gosudarstvennoi vlasti Sankt-Peterburga za 2017g.]. 2017. *Ofitsial'nyi sait administratsii Sankt-Peterburga*. Retrieved on July 19, 2019 (https://www.gov.spb.ru/gov/obrasheniya-grazhdan/otchet-obrasheniya/9125/).
Report on handling citizens' complaints by the executive authorities of Saint Petersburg in 2018 [Otchiot o rabote s obrashcheniiami grazhdan v ispolnitel'nykh organakh gosudarstvennoi vlasti Sankt-Peterburga za 2018 g.]. 2018. *Ofitsial'nyi sait administratsii Sankt-Peterburga*. Retrieved on July 19, 2019 (https://www.gov.spb.ru/gov/obrasheniya-grazhdan/otchet-obrasheniya/13984/).
Rhode, Deborah. 2003. "Access to Justice: Connecting Principles and Justice." *Georgetown Journal of Legal Ethics* 17:372–373.
RIA Novosti. 2011. "Putin navestil devochku, kotoroi 3 gda nazad podaril 'plat'e Zolushki'." July 1. Retrieved on February 18, 2013 (http://ria.ru/society/20110701/396082180.html#ixzz2MU5lA05L).
Ries, Nancy. 1997. *Russian Talk: Culture and Conversation during Perestroika*. Ithaca, NY: Cornell University Press.
Rose, Richard. 1998. "Getting Things Done in an Anti-Modern Society: Social Capital Networks in Russia." Social Capital Initiative Working Paper No. 6. World Bank.

Retrieved on December 12, 2019 (http://siteresources.worldbank.org/INTSOCIALCAPITAL/Resources/Social-Capital-Initiative-Working-Paper-Series/SCI-WPS-06.pdf).

Rose, Richard. 2001. "Living in Anti-Modern Society." Pp. 293–303 in Archie Brown (ed.), *Contemporary Russian Politics: A Reader*. Oxford: Oxford University Press.

Ross, Laurence and Neil Littlefield 1978. "Complaint as a Problem-Solving Mechanism." *Law and Society Review* 12(2):199–216.

Salishcheva, Nadezhda. 2003. "Administrativnoe sudoproizvodstvo trebuet kodifikatsii." *EZh-Iurist* 12:1–2.

Savitskii, Valerii. 1994. "Sterzhnevaia funktsiia prokuratury – osushchestvlenie ugolovnogo presledovaniia." *Rossiiskaia iustitsiia* 10:39–42.

Semionov, Anton. 2003. *Etimologicheskii slovar' russkogo iazyka*. Moscow: IUNVES. Retrieved on June 30, 2019 (http://evartist.narod.ru/text15/011.htm).

Shabalina, Evgeniia. 2007. Istoriko-pravovoe issledovanie mesta i roli organov prokuratury v mekhanizme Sovetskogo gosudarstva: 1920–1930 gg. XX veka. Dissertatsiia na soiskanie stepeni kandidata iuridicheskikh nauk (unpublished). *Elektronnaia biblioteka dissertatsii*. Retrieved on July 15, 2019 (https://www.dissercat.com/content/istoriko-pravovoe-issledovanie-mesta-i-roli-organov-prokuratury-v-mekhanizme-sovetskogo-gosu).

Shatkovskaia, Tat'iana. 2000. "Zakon i obychai v pravovom bytu krest'ian vtoroi poloviny XIX veka." *Voprosy istorii* 11–12:47.

Shelton, Dinah. 2000. *Commitment and Compliance. The Role of Non-binding Norms in the International Legal System*. Introduction. Oxford: Oxford University Press.

Shishkina, Natalia. 2004. "Organizatsiia i deiatel'nost' komissii po pravam cheloveka v sub"ektakh Rossiiskoi Federatsii i perspektivy ikh razvitiia." In Natalia Shishkina and Valentina Chuksina (eds.) *Sibirskii iuridicheskii vestnik* 2:47.

Shugrina, Ekaterina. 2004. "Praktika obrashcheniia v Konstitutsionnyi sud RF: aktual'nye problemy." In Ekaterina Shugrina (ed.) *Pravo i politika* 3:133–135.

Smirnov, Alexander. 2010. "Sootnoshenie poniatii 'Okhrana prav' i 'Zashchita prav'." *Vestnik Tomskogo gosudarstvennogo universiteta* 331:123–125.

Smith, Gordon. 1978. *The Soviet Procuracy and the Supervision of Administration*. Alphen aan Den Rijn: Sijthoff and Noordhoff.

Smith, Gordon. 1988. *Soviet Politics*. London: Palgrave.

Smith, Gordon. 1996. "The Struggle over the Procuracy." Pp. 349–373 in Peter Solomon (ed.) *Reforming Justice in Russia, 1864–1994: Power, Culture and the Limits of Legal Order. Power, Culture and the Limits of Legal Order*. New York: Routledge.

Smith, Gordon. 2007. "The Procuracy, Putin, and the Rule of Law in Russia." Pp. 1–14 in Ferdinand Feldbrugge (ed.) *Russia, Europe, and the Rule of Law*. Leiden: Brill.

Sokolov, Andrei. 1999. *Kurs sovetskoi istorii 1917-1940*. Moscow: Vysshaia shkola.

Solomon, Peter H. 1995. "The Limits of Legal Order in Post-Soviet Russia." *Post-Soviet Affairs* 11(2):89–114.

Solomon, Peter H. 1996. *Soviet Criminal Justice Under Stalin*. Cambridge: Cambridge University Press.

Solomon, Peter H.. 2004. "Judicial Power in Russia: Through the Prism of Administrative Justice." *Law and Society Review* 3(38):549–582.

Solomon, Peter H. and Todd Foglesong. 2000. *Courts and Transition in Russia: The Challenge of Judicial Reform*. Oxford and New York: Routledge.

Spanbauer, Julie. 1993. "The First Amendment Right to Petition Government for a Redress of Grievances: Cut from a Different Cloth." *Hastings Constitutional Law Quarterly* 21:15–69.

Spencer, David and Michael Brogan. 2006. *Mediation Law and Practice*. Cambridge: Cambridge University Press.

Spravochnik partiinogo rabotnika. 1981. vyp. 21. Moscow: Politizdat.

Statisticheskie dannye ob osnovnykh pokazateliakh deiatel'nosti prokuratury RF za ianvar'–dekabr' 2011–2012, 2013, 2015, 2017 gg. *Ofitsial'nyi sait General'noi Prokuratury RF*. Retrieved on July 19, 2019 (https://genproc.gov.ru/stat/data).

Statistika obrashchenii v Gosudarstvennuiu Dumu. 2017–2019. *Priiomnaia Gosudarstvennoi Dumy*. Retrieved on July 19, 2019 (https://priemnaya.duma.gov.ru/ru/stat_page/all/).

Stoiakin, Gennadii. 1973. "Poniatie 'zashchita grazhdanskikh prav'." Pp. 30–35 in Vladimir Semenov (ed.) *Problemy grazhdansko-pravovoi otvetstvennosti zashchity grazhdanskikh prav*. Sverdlovsk: Izdatel'stvo UrGIuU.

Sukharev, Alexander (ed.) 2007. *Bol'shoi iuridicheskii slovar.'* Isk. Moscow: INFRA-M.

Sungurov, Aleksander. 1998. *Funktsii politicheskoi sistemy: ot zastoia k postperestroike*. Saint Petersburg: Strategiia.

Mironov, Oleg (ed.). 2004. *Teoriia i praktika zashchity prav cheloveka*. Moscow: Iurisprudentsiia.

Thelen, Tatjana. 2011. "Shortage, Fuzzy Property and other Dead Ends in the Anthropological Analysis of (Post)socialism." *Critique of Anthropology* 31(1):43–61.

"Tipovoi obshcherossiiskii tematicheskii klassifikator obrashchenii grazhdan, organizatsii i obshchestvennykh ob"edinenii" from June 28, 2013, No. A1-3695v. *KonsultantPlus*. Retrieved on July 19, 2019 (http://www.consultant.ru/cons/CGI/online.cgi?req=doc&base=EXP&n=567595&dst=100240#06144359062871974).

Treushnikov, Mikhail. 1997. *Kommentarii k Grazhdanskomu protsessual'nomu kodeksu RSFSR*. Moscow: Spark.

Trochev, Alexei. 2012. "Suing Russia at Home." *Problems of Post-Communism* 59(5):18–34.

Trubek, David and Marc Galanter. 1974. "Scholars in Self-Estrangement: Some Reflections on the Crises in Law and Development Studies." *Wisconsin Law Review*: 1:1061–1101.

Utekhin, Il'ia. 2004. "Iz nabliudenii za poetikoi zhaloby." Pp. 274–306 in Albert Baiburin (ed.) *Studia Ethnologica: Trudy fakul'teta etnologii*. Saint Petersburg: Izdatel'stvo Evropeiskogo universiteta v Sankt-Peterburge.

Vail', Peter and Alexander Genis. 1996. *60-e: Mir sovetskogo cheloveka*. Moscow: NLO.

Van den Berg, Gerard. 1985. *The Soviet System of Justice: Figures and Policy*. Dordrecht: Martinus Nijhoff Publishers.

Vasmer, Max. 1967. *Etimologicheskii slovar' russkogo iasyka*. T.2. Zhalovan'e. Moscow: Progress.

Verkhovnyi Sud, R.F. 1998. "Rabota raionnykh sudov obshchei iurisdiktsii v. 1997 g." *Rossiiskaia iustitsiia* 7:55–58;

Verkhovnyi Sud, R.F. 1999. "Rabota raionnykh sudov obshchei iurisdiktsii v. 1998 g." *Rossiiskaia iustitsiia* 9:51–53.

Verkhovnyi Sud, R.F. 2000. "Rabota raionnykh sudov obshchei iurisdiktsii v pervom polugodii 2000 g." *Rossiiskaia iustitsiia* 12:54–57.

Vihavainen, Timo. 2004. *Vnutrennii vrag. Bor'ba s meshchanstvom kak moral'naia missiia russkoi intelligentsii*. Saint Petersburg: Izdatel'skii dom "Kolo".

Volkov, Sviatoslav. 1974. *Leksika russkikh chelobitnykh XVII veka: Formuliar, traditsionnye etiketnye i stilevye sredstva*. Leningrad: Izdatel'stvo Leningradskogo universiteta.

Vyshinksii, Andrei. 1934. *Revoliutsionnaia zakonnost' i zadachi sovetskoi zashchity*. Moscow: Redaktsionno-izdatel'skii sector mosoblispolkoma.

Wagner, Peter. 2008. *Modernity as Experience and Interpretation*. Cambridge: Polity.

Weber, Max. 1968. *Economy and Society*. Berkeley: University of California Press.

Wengle, Susanne and Christine Evans. 2018. "Symbolic State-Building in Contemporary Russia." *Post-Soviet Affairs* 34(6):384–411.

White, Stephen. 1983. "Political Communications in the USSR: Letters to Party, State and Press." *Political Studies* 31(1):43–60.

Zagriatskov, Matvei. 1924. *Administrativnaia iustitsiia i parvo zhaloby*. Moscow: Kooperativnoe izdatel'stvo.

Zavisca, Jane. 2012. *Housing the New Russia*. Ithaca, NY: Cornell University Press.

Zelentsov, Alexander. 2009. *Administrativnaia iustitsiia*. Moscow: RUDN.

Zhaloby passazhirov na vagony-restorany. 1934. Moscow: Steklograf.

Zhidkov, Vladimir. 1979. *V otvete za kazhdoe slovo*. Moscow: Mysl'.

Zvereva, Galina. 2007. "Postroit' Matritsu: diskurs rossiiskoi vlasti v usloviiah setevoi kul'tury." *Polit.ru*. April 11. Retrieved on February 18, 2013 (http://www.polit.ru/article/2007/04/11/zvereva/).

Normative documents

Agreement "On the Forms of Interaction between the Prosecutor's General Office of the Russian Federation and the Commissioner for Human Rights to Ensure Guarantees of State Protection of Civil Rights and Freedoms" [Soglashenie "O formakh vzaimodeistviia general'noi prokuratury RF i Upolnomochennogo po pravam cheloveka v tseliakh obespecheniia garantii gosudarstvennoi zashchity prav i svobod grazhdan.' "] from July 24, 1998. *KonsultantPlus*. Retrieved on July 19, 2019 (http://www.consultant.ru/cons/cgi/online.cgi?req=doc&base=EXP&n=271303#08362388273711405).

Circular Decree of Presidium of the VTsIK "On measures for consideration of peasants' complaints" [Tsirkuliarnoe Postanovlenie Presidiuma VTsIK "O meropriiatiiakh po rassmotreniiu krest'ianskikh zhalob. 1930] from April 20, 1930, No. 130. 1930. *Izvestiia TsIK* No. 118.

Circular Directive of the VTsIK "On the Order of Submitting Complaints and Statements" [Tsirkuliarnoe postanovlenie VTsIK "O poriadke podachi zhalob i zaiavlenii"] from June 30, 1921. 1944. *Sobranie uzakonenii i raskoriazhenii pravitel'stva za 1921 g*. No. 49, st. 254. Moscow.

Civil Code of the RSFSR [Grazhdanskii Kodeks RSFSR] from October 1, 1964. *KonsultantPlus*. Retrieved on July 29, 2019 (http://www.consultant.ru/document/cons_doc_LAW_1838/).

Civil Code of the Russian Federation [Grazhdanskii kodeks RF] from November 30, 1994, No. 51-FZ. *KonsultantPlus*. Retrieved on July 19, 2019 (http://www.consultant.ru/document/cons_doc_LAW_5142/).

Code of Administrative Court Proceedings [Kodeks administrativnogo sudoproizvodstva Rossiiskoi Federatsii] from March 8, 2015 No. 21-FZ. *KonsultantPlus*. Retrieved on July 19, 2019 (http://www.consultant.ru/document/cons_doc_LAW_176147/).

Code of Civil Procedure of the RSFSR [Grazhdanskii protsessual'nyi kodeks RSFSR] from October 1, 1964). *KonsultantPlus*. Retrieved on July 29, 2019 (http://www.consultant.ru/document/cons_doc_LAW_2237/).

Code of Russian Federation for Administrative Offenses [Kodeks Rossiiskoi Federatsii ob administrativnykh pravonurusheniiakh] from December 30, 2001, No. 195-FZ. *KonsultantPlus*. Retrieved on July 19, 2019 (http://www.consultant.ru/document/cons_doc_LAW_34661/).

Code of the RSFSR for Administrative Offenses [Kodeks RSFSR ob administrativnykh pravonarusheniiakh] form June 20, 1984. *KonsultantPlus*. Retrieved on July 29, 2019 (http://www.consultant.ru/document/cons_doc_LAW_2318/).

Constitution of the RF [Konstitutsiia (osnovnoi zakon) RF] from December 12, 1993. *KonsultantPlus*. Retrieved on July 19, 2019 (http://www.consultant.ru/document/cons_doc_LAW_28399/).

Constitution of the RSFSR [Konstitutsiia (osnovnoi zakon) RSFSR] from July 10, 1918. *KonsultantPlus*. Retrieved on July 15, 2019 (http://www.consultant.ru/cons/cgi/online.cgi?req=doc&base=ESU&n=2929#07830313927410344).

Constitution of the USSR [Konstitutsiia (osnovnoi zakon) SSSR], 1977. *Garant*. Retrieved on July 19, 2019 (http://www.constitution.garant.ru/DOC_1449448.htm.)

Constitutional court of the RF in the Decree "In the case of the constitutionality of the second part of Article 266 and paragraph 3 of the first part of Article 267 of the RSFSR Code of Administrative Offenses in connection with complaints of citizens" [Konstitutsionnyi Sud RF v Postanovlenii "Po delu o proverke konstitutsionnosti chasti vtoroi stat'i 266.3 i chasti pervoi stat'i 267 Kodeksa RSFSR ob administrativnykh pravonarusheniiakh v sviazi s zhalobami grazhdan"] from of May 28, 1999, No. 9-P. 1999. *SZ RF* No. 23. Art. 2890.

County Heads Law [Zakon o zemskikh nachal'nikakh] from July 12, 1889. 1891. *Polnoe sobranie zakonov Rossiiskoi Imperii (PSZ RI)*. Vol. IX, No. 6196.

Criminal Code of the RSFSR [Ugolovnyi kodeks RSFSR]. 1922. *KonsultantPlus*. Retrieved on July 15, 2019 (http://www.consultant.ru/cons/cgi/online.cgi?req¼doc&base¼ESU&n¼3006#02329189944766851).

Criminal Code of the RSFSR [Ugolovnyi kodeks RSFSR]. 1926. *KonsultantPlus*. Retrieved on July 15, 2019 (http://www.consultant.ru/cons/cgi/online.cgi?req¼doc&ts¼39327870578912835746757 7&cacheid¼DFCA20D6D70CF9C518315827B660D1C0&mode¼splus&base¼ESU&n¼44458&rnd¼0.7541976983375034#06237323093016762).

Criminal Code of the RSFSR [Ugolovnyi kodeks RGFSR] with corrections by July 1, 1937. 1937. Moscow: Iuridicheskoe izdatel'stvo NKIu SSSR.

Criminal Code of Russian Federation [Ugolovnyi kodeks Rossiiskoi Federatsii] from June 13, 1996, No. 63-FZ. *KonsultantPlus*. Retrieved on July 19, 2019 (http://www.consultant.ru/document/cons_doc_LAW_10699/).

Decree of Presidium of the Supreme Council "On the Approval of Regulations on Comrade Courts and Regulations on Public Councils for the Work of Comrade Courts" [Ukaz Prezidiuma Verkhovnogo Soveta "Ob utverzhdenii polozheniia o tovarishcheskikh sudakh i polozheniia ob obshchestvennykh sovetakh po rabote tovarishcheskikh sudov"] from March 11, 1977. *KonsultantPlus*. Retrieved on July 15, 2019 (http://www.consultant.ru/cons/cgi/online.cgi?req=doc&base=ESU&n=1788#04989597648942343).

Decree of Presidium of the Supreme Council of the USSR on Establishment of Commission of Soviet Control [Postanovelenie Prezidiuma Verkhovnogo Soveta SSSR ob organizarsii Komissii Sovetskogo kontrlia] from August 23, 1957.1957. *Vedomosti Verkhovnogo Soveta SSSR No. 18, Art. 474*. Moscow: Verkhovnyi Sovet SSSR.

Decree of Presidium of the Supreme Soviet of the USSR "On the Order for Considering Citizens' Suggestions, Statements, and Complaints" [Ukaz Presidiuma Verkhovnogo Soveta SSSR "O poriadke rassmotreniia predlozhenii, zaiavlenii i zhalob grazhdan"] from 12 April 1968. No. 2534-VII. *KonsultantPlus*. Retrieved on July 19, 2019 (http://www.consultant.ru/document/cons_doc_LAW_1929/).

Decree of SNK RSFSR "On Courts" [Dekret SNK RSFSR "O sude"] from November 22, 1917. *KonsultantPlus*. Retrieved on June 30, 2019 (http://www.consultant.ru/cons/cgi/online.cgi?req=doc&base=ESU&n=4029#04957375764177958).

Decree of SNK RSFSR "On the Abolition of Chancellery for Receiving Applications under the Provisional Government" [Postanovlenie ob uprazdnenii "Kantseliarii dlia priniatiia proshenii pri Vremennom pravitel'stve"] from December 6, 1917. 1956. *Dekrety Sovetskoi vlasti*. Vol. 25. Moscow: Politizdat.
Decree of SNK RSFSR "On the Elimination of Red Tape" [Dekret SNK RSFSR "Ob ustranenii volokity "] from December 30, 1919. 1974. *Dekrety Sovetskoi vlasti*. Vol. VII, December 10, 1919 – March 31, 1920. Moscow: Politizdat.
Decree of the NKGK "Guidelines for Local Branches of the Central Bureau for Complaints and Statement" [Postanovlenie NKGK "O mestnykh otdeleniiakh Tsentral'nogo Biuro Zhalob i Zaiavlenii" (Prilozhenie)] from May 24, 1919. 1943. *Sobranie uzakonenii i rasporiazhenii pravitel'stva za 1919 g*. Moscow: Upravlenie delami Sovnarkoma SSSR.
Decree of the President of the RSFSR "On Some Issues of Activity of the Executive Authorities in the RSFSR" [Ukaz Prezidenta RSFSR "O nekotorykh voprosakh deiatel'nosti organov ispolnitel'noi vlasti v RSFSR] from August 22, 1991, No. 75. *KonsultantPlus*. Retrieved on July 19, 2019 (http://www.consultant.ru/cons/CGI/online.cgi?req=doc&base=EXP&n=221425#014741655544208032).
Decree of the President of the Russian Federation "On Administrative Office of the President of the RF on Work with Applications of Citizens and Organizations" [Ukaz Prezidenta RF "Ob Upravlenii Prezidenta Rossisskoi Federatsii po rabote s obrashcheniiami grazhdan i organizatsii"] from February 17, 2010 No. 201 (as amended by Decrees of the President of the Russian Federation of January 14, 2011 No. 38, of November 3, 2012 No. 1474, and of July 25, 2014 No. 529). *Ofitsial'nyi sait Upravleniia Prezidenta po rabote s obrashcheniiami grazhdan i organizatsii*. Retrieved on July 19, 2019 (http://letters.kremlin.ru/info-service/acts/12).
Decree of the President of the Russian Federation "On Free Trade" [Ukaz Presidenta RF "O svobodnoi torgovle"] from January 29, 1992, No. 65. *KonsultantPlus*. Retrieved on July 19, 2019 ((http://www.consultant.ru/document/cons_doc_LAW_288/).
Decree of VTsIK "On Ordering of Consideration and Resolution of Complaints" [Postanovlenie VTsIK "Ob uporiadochenii dela rassmotreniia i razresheniia zhalob"] from July 1, 1934. *KonsultantPlus*. Retrieved on July 15, 2019 (http://www.consultant.ru/cons/cgi/online.cgi?req=doc&base=ESU&n=24417#09754120112081706).
Decree of VTsIK and the SNK of the RSFSR "On State Control" [Dekret VtsIK i SNK "O gosudarstvennom kontrole"] from April 12, 1919. 1943. *Sobranie uzakonenii i rasporiazhenii pravitel'stva za 1919 g*. Moscow.
Desiatyi s"ezd RKP(b). *Stenographicheskii otchiot*. Mart 1921g. 1963. Moscow.
Duma Endorses Bill on Human Rights Representative. 1996. TASS, March.
Family Code of the Russian Federation [Semeinyi kodeks RF] from December 29, 1995, No. 223-FZ. *KonsultantPlus*. Retrieved on July 19, 2019 (http://www.consultant.ru/document/cons_doc_LAW_8982/).
Federal Constitutional Law "On the Constitutional Court of the Russian Federation" [O Konstitutsionnom sude RF] from July 27, 1994, No. 1-FKZ. 1994. *Collected Legislation of the Russian Federation* (*SZ RF*), No. 13. Art. 1447.
Federal Constitutional Law "On the Human Rights Ombudsman in the Russian Federation" [Federal'nyi Konstitutsionnyi zakon "Ob upolnomochennom po pravam cheloveka v RF"] from February 26, 1997, No. 1-FKZ. *KonsultantPlus*. Retrieved on July 19, 2019 (http://www.consultant.ru/document/cons_doc_LAW_13440/).
Federal Constitutional Law "On the Judicial System of the Russian Federation" [Federal'nyi Konstitutsionnyi zakon "O sudebnoi sisteme RF"] from December 31, 1996, No. 1-FKZ.

KonsiltantPlus. Retrieved on July 19, 2019 (http://www.consultant.ru/document/cons_doc_LAW_12834/).

Federal Law "On Amending the law 'On appealing to the court of wrongful acts and decisions violating the rights and freedoms of citizens' [Zakon RF "O vnesenii izmenenii i dopolnenii v zakon Rossiiskoi Federatsii 'Ob obzhalovanii v sud deistvii i reshenii, narushaiushchikh prava i svobody grazhdan' "] from December 14, 1995, No. 193-FZ. *KonsultantPlus*. Retrieved on July 19, 2019 (http://www.consultant.ru/document/cons_doc_LAW_8595/).

Federal Law "On Amendments to the Criminal Code of the Russian Federation and the Code of Criminal Procedure of the Russian Federation, regarding the establishment of additional counter-terrorism measures and ensuring public safety" [Federal'nyi zakon "O vnesenii izmenenii v Ugolovnyi kodeks RF i Ugolovno-protsessual'nyi kodeks RF v chasti ustanovleniia dopolnitel'nykh mer protivodeistviia terrorizmu i obespecheniia obshchestvennoi bezopasnosti"] from July 6, 2016, No. 375-FZ. *KonsultantPlus*. Retrieved on July 19, 2019 (http://www.consultant.ru/document/cons_doc_LAW_201087/).

Federal Law "On Appealing to the Court Actions and Decisions Violating the Rights and Freedoms of Citizens" [Zakon of RF "Ob obzhalovanii v sud deistvii i reshenii, narushaiushchikh prava i svobody grazhdan"] from 27 April 1993 N 4866–1. *KonsultantPlus*. Retrieved on July 19, 2019 (http://www.consultant.ru/document/cons_doc_LAW_1889/).

Federal Law "On Amending Certain Federal Laws Regarding Regulation of Activities of Non-profit Organisations Performing Functions of Foreign Agents" ["O vnesenii izmenenii v otdel'nye zakonodatel'nye akty Rossiiskoi Federatsii v chasti regulirovaniia deiatel'nosti nekommercheskikh organizatsii, vypolniaiushchikh funktsii inostrannogo agenta"] from June 20, 2012. *Garant*. Retrieved on July 19, 2019 (http://base.garant.ru/70204242).

Federal Law "On Amending the Law of the RF On the Procuracy of the Russian Federation" [O vnesenii izmenenii i dopolnenii v Zakon RF "O prokurature RF"] from November 17, 1995, No. 168-FZ. *Garant*. Retrieved on July 19, 2019 (https://base.garant.ru/10105477/).

Federal Law "On the Order of Consideration of Citizens' Applications in the Russian Federation" [Federal'nyi zakon "O poriadke rassmotreniia obrashchenii grazhdan Rossiiskoi Federatsii"] from 2 May 2006 No. 59-FZ. *KonsultantPlus*. Retrieved on July 19, 2019 (http://www.consultant.ru/cons/cgi/online.cgi?req¼doc&ts¼56845078202006210516992326&caheid¼6341A834A0DF5BBDFF43BE44B12D34E5&mode¼splus&base¼LAW&n¼283578&rn¼E1CB8E44A90433FE7135F1A230170A07#09858153796272937).

Federal Law of the RF "On the Procuracy of the Russian Federation" [Federal'nyi zakon "O prokurature RF"] from January 17, 1992. *KonsiltantPlus*. Retrieved on July 19, 2019 (http://www.consultant.ru/document/cons_doc_LAW_262/).

Instruction of the Presidium of the General Council of the All-Russian Political Party United Russia "On the Organization and Order of Working with Citizens' Applications" [Instruktsiia Presidiuma General'nogo Soveta Vserossiiskoi Partii Edinaia Rossiia "Ob organizatsii i poriadke raboty s obrashcheniiami grazhdan"] from September 8, 2008, Record No. 18. *Ofitsial'nyi sait partii Edinaia Rossiia*. Retrieved on July 19, 2019 (https://er.ru/news/182574/userdata/files/2019/06/24/instruktsiya.pdf).

Law "On Protection of Consumer Rights" [Zakon "O zashchite prav potrebitelei"] from February 7, 1992, 2300–1. *KonsultantPlus*. Retrieved on July 19, 2019 (http://www.consultant.ru/document/cons_doc_LAW_305/).

Law "On the Control Chamber of the USSR [Zakon "O kontrol'noi palate SSSR"] from May 16, 1991. *Garant*. Retrieved on July 19, 2019. (https://base.garant.ru/6335024/).

Law "On the Procuracy in the USSR" [Zakon "O prokurature SSSR"] from November 30, 1979 No. 1162-X. *KonsultantPlus*. Retrieved on July 15, 2019 (http://www.consultant.ru/cons/cgi/online.cgi?req=doc&base=ESU&n=44512#05763704096986295).

Law of the RSFSR "On Enterprises and Entrepreneurial Activity" [Zakon RSFSR "O predpriiatiiakh i predprinimatel'skoi deiatel'nosti"] from December 25, 1990, No.s 445–1. *KonsultantPlus*. Retrieved on July 19, 2019 (http://www.consultant.ru/cons/cgi/online.cgi?req=doc&base=LAW&n=29304&fld=134).

Law of the RSFSR "On the Judicial System of the RSFSR" [Zakon RSFSR "O sudoustroistve RSFSR"] from July 8, 1981. *KonsultantPlus*. Retrieved on July 19, 2019 (http://www.consultant.ru/document/cons_doc_LAW_913/b45d333b1ef0087c643cdd1c12ca68f3062f1dbb/).

Law of the Russian Federation "On Amendments and Additions to the Code of Civil Procedure of the RSFSR" [Zakon RF "O vnesenii izmenenii i dopolnenii v Grazhdanskii protsessual'nyi kodeks RSFSR"] from April 28, 1993, 4882–1. *KonsultantPlus*. Retrieved on July 19, 2019 (http://www.consultant.ru/document/cons_doc_LAW_8497/).

Law of the Russian Federation "On Appealing to the Court Actions and Decisions Violating the Rights and Freedoms of Citizens" [Zakon RF "Ob obzhalovanii v sud deistvii i reshenii, narushaiushchikh prava i svobody grazhdan"] from April 1993. VSND VS RF No. 19, Art. 685. *KonsultantPlus*. Retrieved on July 19, 2019 (http://www.consultant.ru/document/cons_doc_LAW_1889/).

Law of the USSR "On the Procedure for Appealing Unlawful Acts of Officials Infringing the Rights of Citizens" [Zakon, SSSR "O poriadke obzhalovaniia v sud nepravomernykh deistvii organov gosudarstvennogo upravleniia i dolzhnostnykh lits, ushchemliaiushchikh prava grazhdan"] from June 30,1987. *Vedomosti Verkhovnogo Soveta SSSR*, 26, st. 388; 42, st. 764.

Law of the USSR "On the Procedure for Appealing Unlawful Acts of Officials Infringing the Rights of Citizens" [Zakon, SSSR "O poriadke obzhalovaniia v sud nepravomernykh deistvii organov gosudarstvennogo upravleniia i dolzhnostnykh lits, ushchemliaiushchikh prava grazhdan"] from 1989. *Vedomosti Verkhovnogo Soveta SSSR*, 22, st. 416.

Law of the USSR "On People's Control in the USSR" [Zakon "O narodnom kontrole v SSSR"] from November 30, 1979. No. 1159-H. *KonsultantPlus*. Retrieved on July 15, 2019 (http://www.consultant.ru/cons/cgi/online.cgi?req=doc&base=ESU&n=44514#0005390165657626067).

Letter of the General Prosecutor "On Improving the Work of Considering Citizens' Letters, Complaints, and Statements" from October 29, 1958.

Methodological Recommendations on the Organization of Operations of the Regional Offices of the All-Russian Political Party "United Russia" [Metodichestie rekomendatsii po voprosam organizatsii raboty obshchestvennykh priiomnykh Vserossiiskoi politicheskoi partii "Edinaia Rossiia"] from November 14, 2012. *Ofitsial'nyi sait partii Edinaia Rossiia v Murmanske*. Retrieved on July 19, 2019 (murmansk.er.ru).

Model Provision (Polozhenie) on Record Keeping as Regards Citizens' Suggestions, Statements, and Complaints [Tipovoe polozhenie o vedenii deloproizvodstva po predlozheniiam, zaiavleniiam i zhalobam grazhdan v gosudarstvennykh organakh, na predrpiiatiiakh, v uchrezhdeniiakh i organizatsiiakh] from November 30, 1981. No/ 463/162/298. *Garant*. Retrieved on July 19, 2019 (https://base.garant.ru/70417292/#friends).

Order of the Administration of the President of the Russian Federation "On the Traveling Reception Office of the President of the Russian Federation" [Rasporiazhenie Administratsii Presidenta Rossiiskoi Federatsii "O mobil'noi priiomnoi Presidenta Rossiiskoi Federatsii"] from May 10, 2011 No. 631. *Ofitsial'nyi sait Upravleniia Prezidenta po rabote s obrashcheniiami grazhdan i organizatsii*. Retrieved on July 19,2019 (http://letters.kremlin.ru/info-service/acts/32).

Order of the General Prosecutor "On the Procedure for Resolving Citizens' Complaints and Applications by Organs of Prosecution" from December14, 1957.

Order of the General Prosecutor of the Russian Federation "On the Organization of the Execution of the Agreement 'On Forms of Interaction Between the General Prosecutor's Office of the Russian Federation and the Commissioner for Human Rights to Ensure Guarantees of State Protection of Civil Rights and Freedoms'" [Rasporiazhenie General'nogo prokurora RF "Ob organizatsii ispolneniia soglasheniia 'O formakh vsaimodeistviia general'noi prokuratury RF i Upolnomochennogo po pravam cheloveka v tseliakh obespecheniia garantii gosudarstvennoi zashchity prav i svobod grazhdan' "] from January 14, 1999, No. 6/7R. *KonsultantPlus*. Retrieved on July 19, 2019 (http://www.consultant.ru/cons/cgi/online.cgi?req=doc&ts=130088763006061048339697974&cacheid=2BA1BE299E5DFF23513149907022C90B&mode=splus&base=EXP&n=369350&rnd=0.48660531387225947#035078449096176856).

Order of the General Prosecutor of the Russian Federation "On the Organization of Execution of the Agreement between the Human Rights Ombudsman in the Russian Federation and the General Prosecutor of the Russian Federation on Cooperation in Matters of Protection of the Human and Civil Rights and Freedoms" [Rasporiazhenie General'nogo prokurora RF "Ob organizatsii ispolneniia Soglasheniia Upolnomochennogo po pravam cheloveka v Rossiiskoi Federatsii i General'nogo prokurora Rossiiskoi Federatsii o vzaimodeistvii v voprosakh zashchity prav i svobod cheloveka i grazhdanina"] from February 09, 2009, No. 33/7r. 2007. *TEXTARCHIVE.RU*. Retrieved on July 19, 2019 (https://textarchive.ru/c-1145242-p7.html).

Provision "On the Administration of the President of the Russian Federation" [Polozhenie Prezidenta "Ob administratsii Prezidenta RF"] from April 6, 2004, No. 490. *KonsultantPlus*. Retrieved on July 19, 2019 (http://www.consultant.ru/document/cons_doc_LAW_47272/9375930629345c3f977dbbf1bf3730404b9afbd2/).

Regulation on the Network of Public Reception Offices of the All-Russian Political Party "United Russia" [Polozhenie o seti obshchestvennykh priiomnykh Vserossiiskoi politicheskoi partii "Edinaia Rossiia"] from January 30, 2008. *Official website of the party "Edinaia Rossiia."* Retrieved on January 19, 2019 (https://er.ru/news/182572/userdata/files/2019/06/24/polozhenie_ITIHpsj.pdf).

Regulation on the Reception Office of the President of the Russian Federation in the Federal District [Polozhenie o priiomnoi Prezidenta RF v federal'nom okruge] from October 2, 2009, No. 1441. *Ofitsial'nyi sait Upravleniia Prezidenta po rabote s obrashcheniiami grazhdan i organizatsii*. Retrieved on July 19, 2019 (http://letters.kremlin.ru/info-service/acts/26).

Resolution of Disciplinary Responsibility VTsIK "On Disciplinary Action for Violation of Official Discipline in Soviet Organizations [Postanovlenie o distsiplinarnoi otvetstvennosti VTsIK "O distsiplinarnykh vzyskaniiakh za narushenie sluzhebnoi distsipliny v sovetskikh uchrezhdeniiakh"] from January 27, 1921. 1986. *Dekrety sovetskoi vlasti v 14 tomakh*, Vol. 12. Moscow: Politizdat, pp 224–225.

Resolution of Government of the Russian Federation "On the recognition of certain acts and provisions of the RSFSR and the Russian Federation, as invalid" [Postanovlenie

Pravitel'stva RF "O priznaniin utrativshimi silu nekotorykh aktov RSFSR i Rossiiskoi Federatsii i ikh otdel'nykh polozhenii"] from January 13, 2020. *KonsultantPlus*. Retrieved on February 10, 2020 (http://www.consultant.ru/cons/cgi/online.cgi?rnd=5B32A9ADB43291D701C374D9FE92E11D&req=doc&base=LAW&n=342928&dst=100086&fld=134&stat=refcode%3D16876%3Bdstident%3D100086%3Bindex%3D0#b6gc5d300pk).

Resolution of NKGK "On Local Branches of the Central Bureau for Complaints and Statements" [Prilozhenie k § 13 Postanovleniia NKGK "O mestnykh otdeleniiakh Tsentral'nogo Biuro Zhalob i Zaiavlenii"] from May 24, 1919. 1943. *Sobranie uzakonenii i rasporiazhenii pravitel'stva za 1919 g.* Moscow: Upravlenie delami Sovnarkoma SSSR, pp. 392–394.

Resolution of Presidium of the Supreme Council of the RSFSR "On Citizens' Suggestions, Statements, and Complaints Addressed to the Session of the Supreme Council" [Postanovlenie Presidiuma Verkhovnogo Soveta RSFSR "O predlozheniiakh, zaiavleniiakh i zhalobakh grazhdan, postupaiushchikh v adres Verkhovnogo Soveta RSFSR"] from July 15, 1968. *Pravovaia Rossiia*. Retrieved on July 19, 2019 (https://www.lawru.info/dok/1968/07/15/n1190104.htm).

Resolution of Presidium of the TsIK SSSR "On Considering Workers' Complaints and Taking Required Measures" [O rassmotrenii zhalob trudiashchikhsia i priniatii po nim neobkhodimykh mer] from April 13, 1933. *Sobranie zakonov i rasporiazhenii Raboche-Krest'ianskogo Pravitel'stva SSSR za 1933 g. No. 26*. Retrieved on January 19, 2019 (http://istmat.info/node/36152).

Resolution of the People's Control Commission at SNK SSSR "On Consideration of Worker's Complaints" [Postanovlenie Komissii Sovetskogo Kontrolia pri SNK SSSR "O rassmotrenii zhalob trudiashchikhsia"] from May 30, 1936. 1946. *Sobranie zakonov i rasporiazhenii Raboche-Krest'ianskogo Pravitel'stva SSSR za 1936 g.* No. 31, Art. 276.

Resolution of the Plenum of the Supreme Court of the RSFSR [Postanovlnie Plenuma Verkhovnogo Suda RSFSR] from January 28, 1970, No. 53. *Garant*. Retrieved on July 19, 2019 (https://www.garant.ru/products/ipo/prime/doc/1682130/).

Resolution of the Sixth Extraordinary All-Russian Congress of Soviets "On the Exact Observance of Laws" [Postanovlenie VI Vserossiiskogo Chrezvychainogo S″ezda Sovetov "O tochnom sobliudenii zakonov"] from 8 November 1918 g. 1935. *S″ezdy Sovetov Vserossiiskie i Soiuza SSR v postanovleniiakh i rezoliutsiiakh*. Moscow. pp. 103–104.

Resolution of the TsIK of SSSR "On the Situation with the Consideration of Workers' Complaints," [Postanovlenie TsIK SSSR "O polozhenii del s razborom zhalob trudiashchikhsia] from December 14, 1935. 1942. *Spravochnik raionnogo prokurora*. Moscow: Iuridicheskoe izdatel'stvo NKIu SSSR.

Resolution of the TsK KPSS "On Measures to Further Improve the Consideration of Letters and the Reception of Workers" [Ob uluchshenii raboty po rassmotreniiu pisem i organizatsii priioma trudiashchikhsia] from August 29, 1967. 1972. *Osnovnye zakonodatel'nye akty po sovetskomu gosudarstvennomu stroitel'stvu i pravu*. Vol. 1. Moscow: Mysl'.

Resolution of TsIK SSSR, SNK SSSR "On Extension of Rights of Working-Peasant Inspection" [Postanovlenie TsIK SSSR, SNK SSSR "O raschirenii prav raboche-krest'ianskoi inspektsii"] from May 4, 1927. *Pravovaia Rossiia*. Retrieved on July 25, 2019 (https://www.lawru.info/dok/1927/05/04/n1202100.htm).

Resolution of TsIK, SNK RSFSR "On Discilinary Responsibility in Order of Subordination" [Postanovlenie TsIK i SNK RSFSR "O distsiplinarnoi otvetstvennosti v poriadke podchinionnosti"] from March 20, 1932. *SU RSFSR*. No. 32, art. 152.

Resolution of VTsIK and SNK RSFSR "On Approval of the Regulations on Disciplinary Responsibility in the Order of Subordination" [Postanovlenie VTsIK i SNK RSFSR "Ob utverzhdenii Polozheniia o distsiplinarnoi otvetstvennosti v poriadke podchinionnosti"] from July 4, 1927. *KonsultantPlus*. Retrieved on July 19, 2019 (http://www.consultant.ru/cons/cgi/online.cgi?base=ESU&n=20689&req=doc#00213578280886883358).
Resolutions of the Plenum of the Supreme Court of the RSFSR "On Improving the Work of Courts of the RSFSR on Fighting against Deceit of Consumers" [Postanovlenie Plenuma Verkhovnogo Suda RSFSR "Ob uluchshenii raboty sudov RSFSR po bor'be s obmanom pokupatelei"] from December 11, 1968, No. 43. *Garant*. Retrieved on July 19, 2019 (https://base.garant.ru/10164481/).
Resolutions of the Plenum of the Supreme Court of the RSFSR "On Judicial Practices in Cases of Deceit of Consumers" [Postanovlenie Plenuma Verkhovnogo Suda RSFSR "O sudebnoi praktike po delam ob obmane pokupatelei"] from December 12, 1964, No. 24. 1965. *Biulleten' Verkhovnogo Suda RSFSR*. No. 2. Moscow.
Rezoliutsii XVII s"ezda VKP(b). 1934. Moscow: Partizdat.
Statute on the Organs of People's Control in the USSR [Polozhenie ob organakh narodnogo kontrolia v SSSR] from December 19, 1968. *KonsultantPlus*. Retrived February 12, 2020 (shttp://www.consultant.ru/cons/cgi/online.cgi?req=doc&base=ESU&n=17477#04274782552555565).
Statutes for the Provincial and County Institutions [Polozhenie o gubernskikh i uezdnykh zemskikh uchrezhdeniiakh ot 1 ianvaria 1884 goda]. 1864. Pp. 1–10 in *Polnoe sobranie zakonov Rossiiskoi Imperii. Part I*, Vol. 39, No. 40457.
The Basic Principles of Civil Law of the USSR and federal republics [Osnovy grazhdanskogo zakonodatel'stva SSSR i soiuznykh respublik] from May 1, 1962. *StudFiles*. Retrieved on July 29, 2019 (https://studfiles.net/preview/1956207/page:71/).
The Basic Principles of Civil Procedure of the USSR and federal republics [Osnovy grazhdanskogo sudoproizvodstva SSSR i soiuznykh respublik] from May 1, 1962. *StudFiles*. Retrieved on July 29, 2019 (https://studfiles.net/preview/1956207/page:87/).
The Presidential Decree "On Some Measures of State Support for the Civil Rights Movement in the Russian Federation" [Ukaz Presidenta "O nekotorykh merakh gosudarstvennoi podderzhki pravozashchitnogo dvizheniia v RF] from June 13, 1996. *Garant*. Retrieved on July 19, 2019 (https://base.garant.ru/135151/).
The Rules on the Order of Accepting and Redirecting Applications and Complaints Submitted to His Majesty [Pravila o poriadke priniatiia i napravleniia proshenii i zhalob, na vysochaishee imia prinosimikh]. 1906. *Polnoe sobranie zakonov Rossiiskoi Imperii (PSZ RI)*. Vol. XXVI. No. 27808.
The Statute on the Judiciary of the RSFSR" [Polozhenie o sudoustroistve RSFSR] from November 11, 1922. *KonsultantPlus*. Retrieved on July 15, 2019 (http://www.consultant.ru/cons/CGI/online.cgi?req=doc&base=ESU&n=8322#09004516584234421).

Archival sources

GARF, F. A-410, op. 1, d. 2130, l. 47.
GARF, F. A-410, op. 1, d. 2130, l. 49–49ob.
GARF, F. A-410, op. 1, d. 2130, l. 30.
GARF, F. A-410, op. 1, d. 2130, l. 180.
RGAE, F. 195, op. 1, ed. Khr. 48, ll. 37, 43, 44.

RGAE, F. 195, op. 1, ed. Khr. 445, ll. 8, 39, 73, 75, 77, 79, 84.
RGAE, F. 195, op. 1, ed. Khr. 445, ll. 8, 39, 73, 75, 77, 79, 84, 221.
LOGAV, F. R-3551, op. 7, d. 92, l. 29.
LOGAV, F. R-3551, op. 7, d. 92, ll. 30–31.
LOGAV, F. R-4514, op.1, d. 38, l. 16ob.
LOGAV, F. R-4514, op.1, d. 38, ll. 25–26.
LOGAV, F. R-4514, op.1, d. 38, ll. 29–29ob.
TsGA SPb, F. 7384, op. 30, d. 53, doc. 2633.
TsGA SPb, F. 7384, op. 30, d. 53, doc. 1565, l. 101.
TsGA SPb, F. 7384, op. 30, d. 53, l. 2.
TsGA SPb, F. 7384, op. 30, d. 53, l. 2.
TsGA SPb, F. 7384, op. 42, d. 332, l. 190.
TsGA SPb, F. 7384, op. 42, d. 332, l. 81–89.
TsGA SPb, F. 7384, op. 42, d. 332, ll. 106–108.

Soviet newspaper articles

Kak ia pokupala plat'ie [How I was buying a dress.] *Vechernii Leningrad*, 1964, December 4:2.
Kostiumy bez shvov [Suits with no seams.] *Vechernii Leningrad*, 1970, January 20:2.
Lyzhi v kladovke [Skis in the hall closet.] *Leningradskaia Pravda*, 1970, February 26:2.
Mery priniaty [Measures taken.] *Vechernii Leningrad*, 1970, February 2: 2.
Mery priniaty [Measures taken.] *Vechernii Leningrad*, 1970, January 8: 2.
Narushiteli pravil torgovli nakazany [Violators of trade rules punished.] *Vechernii Leningrad*, 1964, December 12:2.
Neudovletvoritelnyi otvet [Unsatisfactory response.] *Vechernii Leningrad*, 1964, November 30:2.
Ni kupit'... ni sshit' [Cannot buy... And cannot sew.] *Leningradskaia Pravda*, 1964, November 24:2.
Otvetstvennost' i kachestvo [Responsibility and quality.] *Leningradskaia Pravda*, 1964, November 21:2.
Pochemu nuzhny ugrozy? [Why the need for threats?] *Vechernii Leningrad*, 1970, March 13:2.
Pochemu procherk v meniu? [Why the dash on the menu?] *Leningradskaia Pravda*, 1963, April 3:2.
Po imeni i otchestvu [By name and patronymic.] *Leningradskaia Pravda*, 1964, December 23:2.
Pokupatel' vozvraschaetsia [The customer returns.] *Leningradskaia Pravda*, 1970, February 26:2.
Pokupatel' zhdet [The customer is waiting.] *Leningradskaia Pravda*, 1963, March 10:2.
Po sledam nashikh vystuplenii [In the wake of our presentations.] *Vechernii Leningrad*, 1964, December 29:2.
Servis ne terpit ravnodushnykh [The service does not tolerate the indifferent.] *Leningradskaia Pravda*, 1963, March 29:2.
[Untitled.] *Vechernii Leningrad*, 1963, April 24:2.
V tesnote i v obide [Squeezed but not pleased.] *Leningradskaia Pravda*, 1964, December 12:2.

Contemporary complaints

A complaint of a family, suffered from fire, addressed to the local housing and utility service from October 23, 2017.

Deti Ostalis' Bez Sveta [Children Left With No Light.] A complaint, addressed to the public reception office to the party United Russia from May 19, 2016.

Detskoe posobie [A child allowance.] A complaint, addressed to the president of the RF from July 2018. *Pis'ma presidentu.* Retrieved on July 19, 2019 (http://xn--80aicbidd2apldmjyp6k.xn--p1ai/semya/detskie-posobie.html).

Ia sirota. Mne ne daiut zhil'e [I'm an orphan. They deprive me from housing.] A complaint, addressed to the president of the RF from 2017. *Pis'ma president.* Retrieved on July 19, 2019 (http://xn--80aicbidd2apldmjyp6k.xn--p1ai/zhile/ya-sirota-mne-ne-dayut-zhile.html).

Kafe meshaet zhit' [A café prevents live.] A complaint, addressed to the president of the RF from April 2017. *Pis'ma president.* Retrieved on July 19, 2019 (http://xn--80aicbidd2apldmjyp6k.xn--p1ai/zhile/kafe-meshaet-zhit.html).

Krik o pomoshchi [A cry for help.] A complaint, addressed to the president of the RF from January 2018. *Pis'ma president.* Retrieved on July 19, 2019 (http://xn--80aicbidd2apldmjyp6k.xn--p1ai/zhile/krik-o-pomoshhi-7.html).

Kto VY? [Who are YOU?] A complaint, addressed to the public reception office to the party United Russia from November 12, 2016.

Mnogodetnaia semia [A family with many children.] A complaint, addressed to the president of the RF from February 6, 2017. *Pis'ma president.* Retrieved on July 19, 2019 (http://xn--80aicbidd2apldmjyp6k.xn--p1ai/zhile/mnogodetnaya-semya-4.html).

My Ne Poidiom Golosovat'—My Ne Verim V Edinstvo Rossii [We Won't Go To The Polls—We Don't Believe In Russia's Unity.] A complaint, addressed to the public reception office to the party United Russia from August 31, 2016.

Ne vyvoziat sneg iz goroda [They do not take snow out of the city.] A complaint, addressed to the president of the RF from March 2018. *Pis'ma president.* Retrieved on July 19, 2019 (http://xn--80aicbidd2apldmjyp6k.xn--p1ai/zhaloba/ne-vyvozyat-sneg-iz-goroda.html).

Obmanutyi dol'shchik [A defrauded shareholder.] A complaint, addressed to the president of the RF from January 2018. *Pis'ma president.* Retrieved on July 19, 2019 (http://xn--80aicbidd2apldmjyp6k.xn--p1ai/zhile/obmanutyj-dolshhik-2.html).

Ob obespechenii dosuga i otdykha gorozhan [Providing leisure and recreation for townspeople.] A complaint, addressed to the public reception office to the party United Russia from July 2017.

Pensiia ili podachka? [A pension or a dole?] A complaint, addressed to the president of the RF from February 20, 2017. *Pis'ma president.* Retrieved on July 19, 2019 (http://xn--80aicbidd2apldmjyp6k.xn--p1ai/zhaloba/pensiya-ili-podachka.html).

Pomoshch' v postavke na ochered' po zhil'iu [Need help in being put on the housing waiting list.] A complaint, addressed to the president of the RF from January 2016. *Pis'ma president.* Retrieved on July 19, 2019 (http://xn--80aicbidd2apldmjyp6k.xn--p1ai/zhile/pomoshh-v-postavke-na-ochered-po-zhilyu.html).

Pravookhranitel'nye organy narushili prava rebionka [Law enforcement authorities violated the rights of the child.] A complaint, addressed to the president of the RF from September 2017. *Pis'ma president.* Retrieved on July 19, 2019 (https://xn--80aicbidd2apldmjyp6k.xn--p1ai/potrebiteli/Pravookhranitelnye-organy-narushili-prava-rebjonka.html).

Privlech Vinovnogo K Otvetstvennosti [Bring The Perpetrator To Justice,]—the complaint was found in the archive of the public reception office from November 15, 2017. It was addressed simultaneously to the president and the public reception office the party United Russia.

Pros'ba okazat' sodeistvie v voprose ispolneniia resheniia suda [Request for assistance in the execution of the court decision.] A complaint, addressed to the president of the RF from December 2017. *Pis'ma presidentu*. Retrieved on July 19, 2019 (http://xn--80aicbidd2apldmjyp6k.xn--p1ai/zhile/prosba-okazat-sodejstvie-v-voprose-ispolneniya-resheniya-suda.html).

Pros'ba o pomoshchi [A request for help.] A complaint, addressed to the president of the RF from December 2016. *Pis'ma presidentu*. Retrieved on July 19, 2019 (http://xn--80aicbidd2apldmjyp6k.xn--p1ai/zhile/prosba-o-pomoshhi-12.html).

Proshu navesti poriadok v gazovoi kompanii [I ask you to put things in order in gas companies.] A complaint, addressed to the public reception office to the party United Russia from December 2, 2016.

Proshu pomoshchi [I ask you for help.] A complaint, addressed to the president of the RF from June 2017. *Pis'ma presidentu*. Retrieved on July 19, 2019 (http://xn—80aicbidd2apldmjyp6k.xn—p1ai/zhile/vetxoe-zhilyo.html).

Ravnodushie i ego posledstviia [Indifference and its consequences.] A complaint, addressed to the president of the RF from February 2017. *Pis'ma presidentu*. Retrieved on July 19, 2019 (http://xn--80aicbidd2apldmjyp6k.xn--p1ai/potrebiteli/ravnodushie-i-ego-posledstviya.html).

Usmotrenie vozmozhnosti ispol'zovaniia edinovremennoi sotsial'noi vyplaty dlia pogasheniia kredita poluchennogo dlia priobreteniia nedvizhimosti [Repayment of a housing loan.] A complaint, addressed to the president of the RF from January 2017. *Pis'ma presidentu*. Retrieved on July 19, 2019 (http://xn--80aicbidd2apldmjyp6k.xn--p1ai/zhile/usmotrenie-vozmozhnosti-ispolzovaniya-edinovremennoj-socialnoj-vyplaty-dlya-pogasheniya-kredita-poluchennogo-dlya-priobreteniya-nedvizhimosti.html).

Vetkhoe zhil'e [Dilapidated housing.] A complaint, addressed to the public reception office to the party United Russia from May 23, 2016.

Voennaia ipoteka [Mortgage for the military.] A complaint, addressed to the president of the RF from February 2017. *Pis'ma presidentu*. Retrieved on July 19, 2019 (http://xn--80aicbidd2apldmjyp6k.xn--p1ai/zhile/voennaya-ipoteka.html).

Zhaloba na kompaniiu [A complaint to a company.]A complaint, addressed to the president of the RF from November 2017. *Pis'ma presidentu*. Retrieved on July 19, 2019 (https://xn--80aicbidd2apldmjyp6k.xn--p1ai/potrebiteli/ZHaloba-na-OAO-Russkaya-mekhanika.html).

Zhil'e [A housing.] A complaint, addressed to the president of the RF from January 2017. *Pis'ma presidentu*. Retrieved on July 19, 2019 (http://xn--80aicbidd2apldmjyp6k.xn--p1ai/zhile/zhile-6.html).

Zhilishchnyi vopros [A housing question.] A complaint, addressed to the president of the RF from February 2017. *Pis'ma presidentu*. Retrieved on July 19, 2019 (http://xn--80aicbidd2apldmjyp6k.xn--p1ai/zhile/zhilishhnyj-vopros-5.html).

Zhilishchnyi vopros dlia molodoi sem'i [A housing problem of the young family.] A complaint, addressed to the president of the RF from September 2016. *Pis'ma presidentu*. Retrieved on July 19, 2019 (http://xn--80aicbidd2apldmjyp6k.xn--p1ai/zhile/zhilishhnyj-vopros-dlya-molodoj-semi.html).

Index

Page numbers in **bold reference tables.

For Product Safety Concerns and Information please contact our EU
representative GPSR@taylorandfrancis.com
Taylor & Francis Verlag GmbH, Kaufingerstraße 24, 80331 München, Germany

www.ingramcontent.com/pod-product-compliance
Ingram Content Group UK Ltd.
Pitfield, Milton Keynes, MK11 3LW, UK
UKHW020010200926
475702UK00015B/2569
9781032003078